ECONOMIC
AND SOCIAL
HISTORY
OF THE
MIDDLE AGES

ECONOMIC
AND SOCIAL
HISTORY
OF THE
MIDDLE AGES
(300-1300)

JAMES WESTFALL THOMPSON

VOLUME II

FREDERICK UNGAR PUBLISHING CO.
NEW YORK

First published 1928

Republished 1959

Printed in the United States of America

Library of Congress Catalog Card No. 59-10886

CONTENTS

Volume II

MAPS

CHAPTER XIX

HOHENSTAUFEN GERMANY (1125–1273)

FLANDERS AND THE LOW COUNTRIES

IN common with the rest of western Europe during the epoch of the Crusades, Germany under the Hohenstaufen (1125–1250) greatly advanced in material civilization. Part of this advancement was due to the stimulation of trade owing to the eastern movement, but much of the progress was organic and potent within Germany itself and independent of the influence of the Crusades.

The chief evidences of it are: (1) the increase of population; (2) the growth of the older towns in Rhenish and Danubian Germany, and the multiplication of new towns; (3) the multiplication of markets, fairs, and tolls; (4) the growth of a money economy beyond anything known before; (5) the development of industry and the spread of gild organization; (6) a great increase of German trade relations with Italy; (7) the establishment of permanent trade connections abroad with the Champagne Fairs, with Flanders, England, Scandinavia, and Livonia; (8) the rise in the value of land in the older provinces of Germany; (9) the steady reduction of the area of forest and swamp lands; (10) the aggressive expansion on the eastern frontier and the occupation and colonization of the "new east" by the reduction or expulsion of the native Slavonic peoples found there.

All these things are indicative of the enormous physical activity and tireless application of the German people.

The chief evidences of the increase of population are found in the growing activity of urban life and the constant drift of the surplus population in old, western Germany into the new lands in the east without apparent impairment of the productivity of the older provinces. The population of Germany probably increased from between five and six millions in the eleventh century to between seven and eight millions in the twelfth century.

Cologne passed Mainz in the twelfth century and became the largest city in Germany. In the south, Regensburg was the greatest town, although rivaled by Augsburg and Nuremberg. Nearly everywhere in old Germany the ancient town walls which had been built in the Saxon or Salian epochs became too confining for the population, were torn down, and new walls of wider circuit were erected. Almost every

499

city in the Rhine-Danube provinces was thus twice enlarged, once in the twelfth century, and again in the thirteenth. In 1281 Cologne's wall had sixty-five towers and thirteen gates. This expansion was one of urban agglomeration; that is to say, the towns incorporated the faubourgs which had grown up around the earlier wall and then the villages in the environs around them. Even yet street names and local terminology in many German cities preserve traces of this medieval expansion in the "ring" formation of certain inner streets (for example, in Vienna and Munich) which have been laid out upon the site of former walls, and in the preservation of ancient names like Wallstrasse, Thurmstrasse, Alte Markt. Now and then even the remains of an old medieval tower have been spared from demolition and still stand as mute witnesses to the old order of things. Another evidence of the growth of the towns is the general movement toward parish reorganization manifest in these two centuries. Not only were new parishes incorporated into the cities by the process of urban expansion and enclosure, but within the old town the growth of the population often necessitated partition of old parishes and the erection of new churches. Indeed, the number of churches in the towns whose foundations go back to the twelfth and thirteenth centuries is of itself a striking historical evidence of the growth of the German cities at this time.

No corporate body of citizens appears in the German cities before the thirteenth century. Indeed, the words *cives* and *burgenses* only came into usage in the twelfth century. The distinction was between the inhabitants of the *civitas* and the walled *burg*. All the inhabitants who were merchants, artisans, or *ministeriales* were included in the names *cives* or *burgenses*. When the city walls were enlarged the difference between *cives* and *burgenses* was obliterated.

The multiplication of market dues within the towns and an increase of tolls along road and river routes naturally attended this economic growth. The former were more legitimate assessments than the latter. Theoretically the emperor was the suzerain of rivers and the lord of the roads, and was supposed to be the supreme protector of merchants and travelers. But in practice the imperial prerogative was universally usurped by the great feudalized bishops and the high nobles. As a result a widespread feud was engendered between the towns and the feudal princes of every degree and status, which was detrimental to trade and often culminated in local warfare. The emperor Lothar II is the last German ruler who made a serious endeavor to suppress these usurpations. In 1132 he restored the ancient tariff on the lower Rhine in favor of Utrecht; in 1136 he lowered the tolls on the Elbe. But he was not always able to protect commerce from feudal extortion. The revenues of the Rhenish bishops were largely derived from the river and towpath tolls they imposed. The same is true of the arch-bishop of Trèves, to whom pertained the tolls exacted at Coblenz; on the Elbe the archbishop of Magdeburg possessed three toll stations. Again, the increased use of money (*Geldwirtschaft*) attests this prosperity. We find local taxes and rents more and more defrayed with money instead of with produce or service, and larger and more frequent employment of the cash nexus in trade. The town archives abound with evidences of a growing money economy. Even the chronicles reflect the change, notably that of Otto of St. Blasien, which is rich in mention of gold and silver and currency.

In industrial history the formation and rapid spread of gild organization (*confederationes sive juramenta*) demonstrates a similar change. The oldest example is the weavers' gild in Cologne, which appears in 1112 and by 1149 had become a compact association. A gild of cobblers appears at Halle in 1157. By the thirteenth century practically the whole world of industry in the German cities had become organized upon the gild basis. The development is indicative of the breakdown of industry in the manors, of the drift of the working population from country to town, of the potency of the new industrialism. It is significant that, from their earliest appearance, the German gilds were intimately associated with the new sense of burgher liberty abroad in the towns. The gild of Cologne in 1112 is described by the annalist as "formed for liberty" (*facta est pro libertate*). Weaving of linen was the most important industry of Augsburg and Ulm, weaving of woolen cloth the most essential occupation of Nuremberg. Workmen of the same or allied industries lived in certain sections of the city devoted to that trade. Industrial differentiation makes its appearance in the twelfth century. Thus the weavers' gild was subdivided into wool-combers, cloth-shearers, fullers, cloth-binders, cloth-stretchers, dyers, etc.

If now we turn from the internal economic development of Germany under the Hohenstaufen to its external economic history, there, too, we find the same energy. The expansion of German commerce beyond the national borders of the country was very great. The beginnings of this expansion, except in the case of contact with the Champagne Fairs, may be found in the Salian and even in the Saxon period, but during the Hohenstaufen age this commerce acquired a magnitude, not known before, in Lombardy, Flanders, England, the Baltic and the Slavonic borderlands.

Not long after the Crusades began the Venetians obtained commercial privileges from the German emperors, notably Lothar II (1125–37). But these privileges related to the kingdom of Italy and not to Germany. Not until the commercial effect of the Crusades was fully felt did the cities of Italy begin to reach actively beyond the Alps. When that began the German cities like Augsburg and Nuremberg became flourishing.

While the long war of Frederick I with Milan and the cities of the Lombard League must have seriously deranged and impaired trans-Alpine commerce, there is nevertheless evidence that the commercial relations betwen Germany and Italy still continued. Italian merchants were certainly in Flanders by 1127, who must have traveled over the Alps and down the Rhine, and may have extended their operations into the cities of lower Germany, unless the "foreign merchants" reported as frequenting Goslar, Hildesheim, Brunswick, etc., were Flemings and not Italians. As for the southern German cities, the presence of Italian merchants in them must have been a familiar one after the middle of the twelfth century. The merchants of Lodi who appealed to Frederick I at Constance in 1153 to solicit his protection against Milan's commercial tyranny, presented their cause in the German language. Regensburg seems to have had a permanent colony of Italian merchants before 1200.

Of even greater significance, or at least of greater novelty, is the evidence that German merchants found their way into Italy during the twelfth century. In a toll record of Genoa for the year 1128, trans-Alpine merchants with balls of wool and linen are mentioned. These probably came from the Rhinelands or Flanders, where the weaving industry was developing. In a contract of 1168 signed by Como and Milan, each promised that it would not prevent German merchants from visiting the markets of the other. An agreement of 1193 between Lombard towns hostile to Milan mentions trans-Alpine merchants who doubtless were from Germany. A municipal statute of 1209 shows that citizens of Como often went security for trans-Alpine merchants. In 1220 a German merchant was plundered between Cremona and Ferrara, and two years later two merchants from Lille were robbed of their merchandise, consisting of cloth from Lille, Bruges, and Beauvais, and breeches from Bruges. The latter deed occurred near Como and the city paid an indemnity of ninety-seven pounds to the merchants. A toll register of 1228 mentions German merchants along with those of France and many Italian cities. Important to observe is the establishment of a German commercial connection with Venice in the twelfth century. But whether this development was due to the partial diversion of Lombard trade with Germany during the war in Lombardy, or due to the fact that Venice was a convenient port of debarkation for Germans on their way to the Holy Land as well as an important place of importation of Levantine wares, cannot be determined. Although no records remain to bear out the statement, German merchants had doubtless early visited Venice. The first authentic mention of the famous Fondaco dei Tedeschi is for the year 1228, but German merchants had shared similar quarters with German pilgrims in Venice before 1200. The

Brenner Pass was the route used commonly by the Augsburger and other merchants from southern Germany.

While North Italy was and remained through the whole medieval period *the* supreme region of commerce in western Europe, the increasing economic development of the countries of northern Europe is a fact to observe. What the Mediterranean was to the Greek and Romance lands of the south that the North Sea and the Baltic were to North Europe. And as the south had its focal point in Lombardy and Venetia, so the north found a focal point for the concentration and dissemination of commerce in Flanders and adjacent fiefs, roughly the Belgium of today. These "Low Countries" formed an agglomeration of feudal provinces wedged in between France, Germany, and the North Sea. The Flemish part of the county of Flanders, together with Brabant and Hainaut, pertained to Germany and the Empire. But they early inclined toward a large measure of independence, and culturally were a quite distinct entity. Broadly speaking, the provinces south of the lowest course of the Rhine were Walloon (French) or Flemish, while those north of the river were Dutch. The former class included Flanders, which held part of the Empire and part of the kingdom of France, Hainaut, and Brabant. The group north of the river was formed by the three counties of Friesland, Zeeland, and Holland. In the Walloon provinces the culture was predominantly French in form; in the others, German. The most powerful of these princes was the count of Flanders, less for the extent of his lands than for his wealth. As early as 1150 a chronicler described Flanders as *terra valde populosa*—a densely peopled land. The rich alluvial soil of this part of Europe, formed by the Rhine, the Meuse, the Scheldt, the Somme, which here converge and empty into the North Sea almost side by side, had early attracted occupation. These provinces, as we have seen, had once been the heart of the crown lands of the Carolingians. Here monasteries had flourished from early times in profusion, and around their walls had grown up a clustered population out of which, in the eleventh century, an intense town life had sprung, whose population increased owing to the stimulus given to commerce and industry during the Crusades, a prosperity enhanced by the remarkable accessibility of this part of Europe from all points of the compass on account of the river system which engrossed the territories, and the seaports along the coast. The complaints of the people of Bruges in 1128 against Count William Clito show clearly that the commerce of Flanders at that time was essentially an outside commerce. "We are shut up in our land," they said, "nor can we do business with what we own without currency, without foreign merchants coming to us."

We may distinguish two branches of production: industry and com-

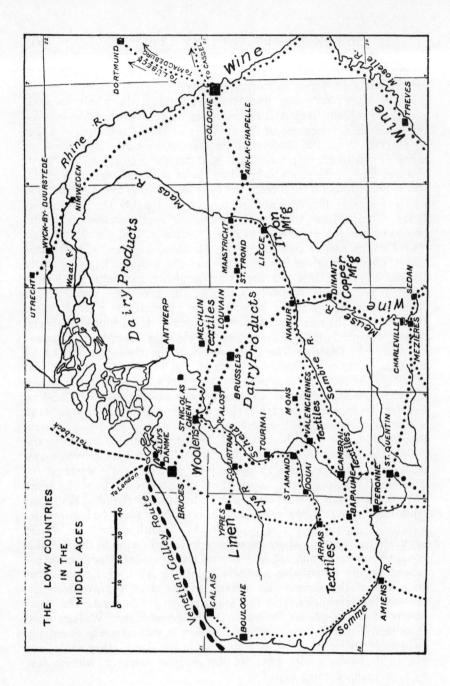

THE LOW COUNTRIES
IN THE
MIDDLE AGES

504

merce. Ghent was the industrial centre. In 1300 there were fifty different trades there. Bruges, connected with the sea by the canalized river Lys, was the chief emporium.

The chief industry of the Flemish cities was weaving. Ghent specialized in woolen cloth. Ypres was the linen centre. Almost every town had a particular weave, a particular pattern, a particular dye of its own, and the names of many medieval textiles are derived from these places. Arras gave its name to the hanging curtain called arras; Cambrai to cambric; Valenciennes created valence; the diaper pattern came from Ypres; the delicate linen known as lawn derived its name from Laon— a French city, it is true, but close to Flanders; the fair of St. Audrey created the word "tawdry," once a designation of quality which lost its first significance when shoddy was mixed with the long wool. Certain cities in the Low Countries excelled in metal work, especially Liège in iron and Dinant in copper ware. The French word for copper-smithing, *dinanderie,* was coined from the name of this town.

The Rhine was the most natural route of ingress into Flanders, but the flatness of the land made the overland road from Cologne through Aachen, Maestricht, where the Meuse was crossed, Louvain, where was the crossing of the Dyle, to Ghent and Bruges almost equally convenient. A toll schedule of Coblenz of 1104 shows the commercial intercourse between lower Germany and Flanders. In 1173 the emperor Frederick I, at the request of the count of Flanders, established fairs at Aachen and Duisburg.

Bruges was altogether a city of commerce and became the great middleman of North Europe. We have a remarkable list of foreign wares imported into Bruges about 1200.

One who attentively follows each of the streams of commerce converging upon Bruges from its separate source—the beer of Bremen and the Baltic products of the Hanse towns creeping behind the islands through the Zuider Zee, and threading a maze of Dutch waterways to avoid the Rhine tolls, the wool from England, the cloth of Picardy, the wine and salt of Rochelle, the cordwain of Barbary or Spain brought to the Fairs of Champagne by Provençal merchants, and the eastern argosies of Venice and Genoa venturing at length to face the perils of the open sea—will have become familiar with the essential features of international trade in the thirteenth century. . . . As the interruption of the English trade with Ghent and Ypres under King John enabled Bruges to establish its position as the centre of the wool trade, so the later disturbed condition of the land routes in France and Flanders assisted it to displace the Fairs of Champagne as the main and connecting link between North Europe and the Mediterranean. But it was not until the fourteenth century that Bruges became primarily an international dépôt and its citizens mere intermediaries in the transactions of foreigners whose permanent settlements gave their names to whole streets and districts of the city. . . . The healthier period of its prosperity was due to the active participation of its citizens in a commerce predominantly Flemish—English and Spanish wool for Flemish weavers being the main import and the cloth of Flanders the main export.[1]

In Hainaut and Brabant was little but an agricultural peasantry, and dairy products, grain, and live stock were the chief productions. Antwerp, on the estuary of the Scheldt in Brabant, was not important commercially until the late fifteenth and sixteenth century, and arose after the decline of Bruges.

The density of population in the Low Countries already alluded to had an important influence upon emigration. Lowland and eastern Germany was settled by Flemish and Dutch colonists in the twelfth and thirteenth centuries. Many Flemings also emigrated into England, where their skill as weavers was valued in wool-growing England. Floods and inundations of the sea were also causes of this emigration. The Rhine, the Meuse, the Scheldt, and many lesser rivers were liable to be flooded almost every spring by the head of waters from above pouring into them. But the sea was the greatest menace. It is true that dikes supplemented the natural barrier of the dunes in the most exposed places. But in a great storm these were often broken. The chronicles abound with tragic accounts of inundations, 1135, 1156, 1164, 1170, 1173. In the thirteenth century there were thirty-one. The Zuider Zee and the Texel were created by huge inundations. It is significant that there is a simultaneity between the occurrence of flood and Dutch and Flemish emigration. The connection is evident.

The commerce of Friesland and Holland was much less important than that of the provinces south of the delta of the Rhine. Most of the coast population was engaged in the herring and cod fisheries. The Rhine delta of the twelfth century, having practically the same course as it has today, owed its importance to its connection with the sea trade and the inland trade. Only a large map shows the names of the numerous branches that form the delta. On the left the Waal and the Leck extend westward from the main stream and flow into the North Sea. On the right the Yssel and the Vecht flow north into the Zuider Zee. It was impossible to enter the northern arms from the ocean, and in reaching this region traffic was compelled to enter the Leck and from this pass northward.

An important point was Arnhem, which lay at the point where the Yssel separates from the main course of the Rhine. A little below Arnhem lay Oosterbeek and Lobith, belonging to the count of Guelders. These were toll stations past which the traffic was compelled to go, and against these exactions there was more or less opposition. This was

---

[1] *English Historical Review*, XXIV, 774 (a review).

especially asserted at the diet of Frankfort in 1220. Duisburg, Doetchem, Arnhem, and Zutphen early acquired more than local importance, and from the end of the twelfth century foreign merchants were accustomed to visit them. A document of 1190 makes reference to Zutphen, which lay north of Arnhem on the Yssel. By the end of the twelfth century Zutphen was recognized as a central point for trade and commerce. The importance of the place and the extent of its trade relations are indicated in a commercial treaty of 1200 between the count of Guelders and the bishop of Utrecht in which it was provided that coins struck at Zutphen should not be the same as those coined at Utrecht. On the Vecht, which was the most eastern of the northern branches of the Rhine, lay Utrecht. Here was a toll station mention of which goes back as far as the tenth century. Through Utrecht passed fish and salt from the coast, and wine and grain from the inland. There was a regular trade between Utrecht and Cologne, wine being the most important article of commerce. Only a portion of this was for home consumption, as Utrecht became the centre of the wine market for shipments to England and to the north. Next to wine, grain was a most important article of the river traffic. The delta region was noted for its cattle breeding, but as no grain could be raised here it had to be brought from the south. As in the case of the wine trade Utrecht became the centre of the grain trade, which was brought from above and below Duisburg. The salt trade was especially carried on by the merchants of Friesland, who brought it in over the Zuider Zee. Their most important city was Stavoren, which lay far up the Zuider Zee at its narrowest point. There are no documents to show that any trade existed between this city and Utrecht; but it seems reasonable to suppose that there was, as this was the largest city of Friesland and its merchants were often found trading far up the Rhine. As early as the first quarter of the twelfth century Henry V had given protection to these merchants trading in German territory.

We now turn to the left arms of the delta. Here the Waal surpassed the Leck in commercial importance, just as the Vecht surpassed the Yssel in the north. There is no evidence that there was any commercial life at all on the Leck. On the other hand the Waal was dotted with a row of trading stations. On the left bank of the Waal not far below the point where it branched from the Rhine, was Nimwegen. This was the customs station for all imports coming in on this arm of the delta, but its importance for this period is not known with any degree of certainty. Tiel was another city on the Waal, which since the tenth century is mentioned along with the most important cities of North Germany as a place of toll. However, in the twelfth century the customhouse there was moved farther up the stream to Kaiserwerth on the Rhine, which gave great offense to Cologne. There is little that can be gathered as to the commercial importance of Tiel. Probably at the beginning of the eleventh century Tiel was the leading trading city of the Netherlands; but between 1134 and 1174 its commercial importance decreased. This is the reason why the toll station was removed to Kaiserwerth.

The Waal was the principal route of the left delta region. From the middle of the twelfth century, and even before, merchants used this route to reach middle and upper Germany. Wood was an important item. Rafts were brought down from the upper Rhine as far as Coblenz, but the exact point where the rafts were broken up is not known. Perhaps next in importance to the grain trade was the trade in fish. The delta was the door through which fish entered Europe. Ships came down the Rhine bearing wine and on the return voyage went back to Cologne laden with salted fish.

Through Flanders or Holland naturally passed all trade between Germany and England. We have seen in a former chapter that German merchants were accorded royal trading privileges in England as far back as the reign of Ethelred (978–1016). They were distinguished as "men of the emperor." "The great privilege seems to have been that they were, with certain exceptions, allowed to buy and sell on board their own ships, which doubtless exempted them from certain tolls to which others were liable." As the Norman Conquest quickened Anglo-French trade, so it also quickened this Anglo-German trade. William of Malmesbury, an English historian of the twelfth century, mentions the importance of the trade of the German merchants in London in his time. Henry of Huntingdon, writing in 1155, refers to the English trade with lower Germany as "extensive" and mentions as English exports lead, tin, fish, cattle, jet, and above all wool. German exports in return were chiefly copper, silver, and iron.

In 1157 Henry II of England granted extensive privileges to the gild or hanse of German merchants resident in London. The document distinctly mentions the house (*domus sua*) of the men of Cologne. These privileges were confirmed or extended by Richard I (1194), by John (1213), by Henry III (1232), by Edward I. The German House or Steelyard in London was an important place, a walled area enclosing warehouses, a weighing house, dwelling houses, a church, and was in essence not dissimilar to the *fondachi* established by the Italian merchant colonies in Constantinople, Alexandria, and the ports of Syria and the Holy Land during the Crusades. The trade between London and Cologne was the core of this cross-sea traffic, but one finds record of German merchants from other Rhine cities, from Lübeck and Bremen, not only in London, but in York, Hull, Boston, Newcastle, Lynn.

A letter from Frederick Barbarossa to Henry II hopes for security and freedom of commerce between England and Germany. In 1176 the men of Lübeck were freed from the law of wreckage. Richard I on his return from his captivity passed through Cologne and made additional grants to traders there. They were to be free from tolls; could buy and sell at all fairs on a payment of two shillings yearly for their Gild Hall in London. William of Malmesbury thus summarized the commercial relations of England in the twelfth century: "The noble city of London, rich in the wealth of its citizens, is filled with the goods of merchants from every land and especially from Germany, whence it happens that when there is a dearth in England on account of bad harvests, provisions can be bought there cheaper than elsewhere; and foreign merchandise is brought to the city by the famous river Thames." William of Newburgh records that a German nobleman said that if the emperor Henry VI had known how rich England was, he would have made her pay a much larger ransom for Richard I. John sent a letter to the citizens of Cologne in 1203 offering them the freedom of resorting to his dominions with their merchandise on paying the customary duties paid by their ancestors. This seems to indicate a temporary cessation of the Cologne trade after Richard I's captivity. In 1220 the merchants of Cologne reëstablished themselves in the Steelyard. In 1230 Henry III admitted the subjects of Otto of Brunswick to trade in his realm. In 1257, when Richard of Cornwall was chosen emperor—perhaps because of his fabulous wealth—he obtained from Henry III another charter for the burgesses of Lübeck. That same year the misery caused by the rapacity of the pope, the transportation of the earl of Cornwall's treasure to Germany, and further distress caused by a famine, resulted in a food crisis in London, which was relieved by the arrival of fifty large grain ships from Germany. Thus by the time of the early Plantagenets trade relations between England and Germany were well established—not through the initiative of English but through that of German merchants. The Hanseatic League was in embryo.

With almost all this internal and external expansion of German commerce and industry during the twelfth century the Hohenstaufen rulers had little to do. Even the princes were indifferent to it. The development was almost wholly due to the enterprise of the merchants and manufacturers themselves. Indeed, in the case of Frederick I (Barbarossa), he was so ignorant of the true nature of the age in which he ruled that he was hostile or indifferent to some of the most important of the changes. Much the same may also be said of the German feudality, both lay and clerical, of the time. The most brilliant exception is Duke Henry the Lion of Saxony and Bavaria, whose intelligent administration made his territories shining examples of prosperity. But in the main the material development of feudal Germany during the twelfth and thirteenth centuries was made independently of political authority and interest. The Hohenstaufen kings were deplorably devoid of that quick and sympathetic economic perception which characterized their French,

Angevin, and Norman-Sicilian contemporaries. Not one of them ever possessed a constructive economic policy.

The economic condition of Germany throws an important light upon the great feud of the two rival German political parties in the Hohenstaufen age. The Guelfs favored the burghers and the commercial and industrial revolution promoted by them. The Hohenstaufen, or Ghibelline, imperial party, on the other hand, was hostile to the change from the older feudal order of society. The shortsightedness and obstinacy of Frederick I in his burgher policy in Germany was of a piece with his policy toward the Lombard cities, and fortunately was just as ineffective in the end. His destruction of the walls of Mainz in 1163 reminds one of his treatment of Milan. Cologne in part owed her commercial preëminence to this setback of Mainz. Fortunately for German industry, the gilds had not yet become prominent enough to attract the wrath of the emperor and were unmolested.

The notorious prejudice of the Hohenstaufen emperors, especially Frederick I, against the burgher class encouraged seizure of existing tolls and the imposition of new ones by the feudality almost everywhere in Germany, in spite of Frederick I's boast that the Rhine was a "royal street." In 1155 the merchants of Mainz, Frankfort, and Bamberg protested in vain against "the new and unaccustomed and unreasonable tolls" exacted upon the Main.

The collections of charters tell a tale of tolls granted to bishops, to monasteries, to counts, with a liberality which seems almost profligate. . . . It is probable that during the whole of this period but an insignificant fraction of the tolls levied throughout the Empire found its way into the emperor's treasure-box. By the twelfth century the princes were probably all of them in possession of these rights. . . . In 1157, in 1209, in 1235, in 1290, the princes declare that their consent must be obtained to the imposition of any new toll. . . . To safeguard their own large pecuniary interests the princes combine with the emperor against the trifling bandit who pillages on the tow-path. One step further and they combine with one another to pillage the Emperor himself.[2]

Nevertheless, in spite of these deterrent factors there is no doubt of the steady growth of German commerce and industry during the Hohenstaufen epoch. In time, as we shall see later on, the cities by leagueing together managed to check these abuses.

Only one German prince of this time stood out prominently as an intelligent promoter of commerce and industry within his dominions. This was Henry the Lion (died 1197), the duke of Saxony and Bavaria. As such, Henry followed the example set by his father Henry the

[2] Fisher, *The Medieval Empire*, I, 278–79.

Proud in Bavaria. For during his struggle with Conrad III the burghers of Regensburg and Passau, who wished nothing so much as peace and commercial and industrial prosperity, had steadfastly supported him. When Henry the Lion inherited his father's possessions he continued his father's course in Bavaria and translated the same liberal economic promotion to Saxony, which he inherited from his mother. He founded Munich on the Isar, over which he constructed a bridge; the new city caught some of the Italian and oriental trade coming over the Brenner Pass and in time rivaled older cities like Augsburg, Regensburg, and Passau as a mart in southeastern Germany. Henry the Lion perceived the importance of this burgher movement in Germany as no other prince and identified himself with it. The Guelfs founded Brunswick, Göttingen, Münden, Nordhausen, Einbeck, and greatly developed Naumburg and Lübeck. Even Cologne, although never a Guelf or Saxon city, was Guelf in sympathy in the feud between the Guelf and Hohenstaufen parties. It was too closely attached to the metal industries of Goslar and Rammelsberg in the Harz and the Saxon hinterland not to be so.

The industrial development of the Saxon towns under Henry the Lion went hand in hand with their commercial prosperity. Not only the grosser industries but the fine arts were stimulated. His capital, Brunswick, became a German Florence because of its architects, artists, goldsmiths, silversmiths, wood, stone, and ivory carvers. Henry the Lion was not always just in his dealings, but he was ever keenly intelligent and alive to economic opportunities.

For nearly two hundred years the Danes had almost monopolized the commerce of the Baltic. Danish merchant colonies were established in Stettin, Wollin, Danzig, at the mouths of the Peene, the Oder, the Vistula rivers, amid the Slavonic population. Henry the Lion's ambition was to supplant the Danes and to establish German commercial supremacy in the Baltic. It is not too much to say that effective German commercial life in Baltic Germany begins with Henry the Lion's seizure of Lübeck, on an island in the little river Wochnitz, in 1158. The place had once been a formidable Slavonic stronghold, but in 1143 Count Adolph of Holstein established a community of Holsteiners there. The new town speedily began to compete with Bardowick, Charlemagne's old trading post and, except for Hamburg and Bremen, which were not under Henry's rule, was the principal German seat of trade in the far north. Thereupon Henry founded a new town, which he called Löwenstadt after himself, and nearer to Lübeck in the hope of competing with her. But it, too, declined like Bardowick. Henry, who was rapacious and domineering, then demanded of Adolph of Holstein the half of Lübeck for himself, and when it was refused, forcibly closed the market there. Hostilities followed, and in 1157 Lübeck was burned by the Saxon duke. When the count of Holstein refused to rebuild it Henry seized it (1158), rebuilt the town and its walls, established a market and a mint and proclaimed it a free port for all merchandise from Denmark, Sweden, Norway, and Wisby, on the island of Gothland, then the base of trade with Novgorod in Russia, and through Novgorod and Kiev with the Black Sea, Byzantine, and eastern trade. With the reluctant aid of Waldemar of Denmark, Henry the Lion then set to work to free the Baltic of piracy, and for the first time in history made the islands of that sea places of peaceable habitation.

Certain other elements of Henry the Lion's administration may also be briefly specified. He was a great road and bridge builder; he diked streams; he drained vast tracts of marsh and swamp, by importing lowland Flemings and Hollanders, used to laboring in that kind of soil.

The destruction of Saxony in 1181 as the climax of the feud between the duke and the emperor, the removal of the Hohenstaufen seat of power and political interest in 1190 to Sicily and southern Italy, the civil disturbances and internecine war into which Germany was thrown between 1198 and 1214 did not derange the commerce and industry of the country as seriously as might have been expected. For by that time the cities—the seats of greater material prosperity than the countryside—were walled and free towns and were able to protect themselves. Few of them seriously suffered except Goslar, which was sacked by Otto IV in 1206 because it adhered to Philip of Swabia in the conflict between these two aspirants for the throne. We have a picture, in the account of this catastrophe by Arnold of Lübeck, of the high degree of commercial development the German cities had acquired by the thirteenth century. "The enormously rich city (*civitas opulenta valde*) was devastated, streets and houses pillaged, the richest citizens made prisoner, during eight days. So great was the amount of pepper and spices that it was measured by bushels and divided into heaps."

Medieval Germany entered upon that long period of political disunity and feudal particularism in these fateful years. The power of the crown, the authority of the central government, was reduced to illusory dimension. The rule of the country was divided between powerful feudal princes, not the least of whom were the prince-bishops, and the burghers of the free cities. There was much money in the country owing to the expansion of German trade, but the power to tax the resources of the land escaped the crown. Otto IV dreamed of imposing a general tax, but feudal and municipal independence and fiscal autonomy were too great for him to enforce it. The policy of favoring the towns against the princes was initiated too late to be effective and both classes eluded crown control. The crown had permitted commerce, industry, and the very revenues of the soil to slip out of its grasp. "The mere rumor of an intended common imperial tax lost Otto IV some of his most influential supporters." The Hohenstaufen had looked so long to Italy for their money that when they lost rule over the Lombard cities they were unable to tax Germany and hence endeavored to recoup their fortune in Sicily, with the result that Germany was lost, too, and the kingdom dissolved into a complex of jarring petty feudal states and fiercely competitive city groups.

The commercial and industrial history of Germany in the thirteenth century is largely the history of conflict between feudally governed rural Germany and the towns. The bitterest source of this strife was the tolls by road and river, especially those of the Rhine. The cities fought for freedom of interurban trade. The feudality suffered from depreciation in their revenues from landed estates owing to the economic revolution in the twelfth century whereby the wealth derived from commerce and industry began to displace the wealth derived from agriculture—a condition aggravated by the migration of rural labor to the towns; and they sought to mend their fortunes by imposing all that the traffic would bear in the form of tolls and tariffs.

"The robber fastnesses multiply apace. . . . The steady multiplication of toll stations is in itself a sufficient indication of the growing anarchy, but though the smaller nobles joined in the pleasant task of relieving the merchant of his wealth, the lion's share went to the princes of the Church. The rich banquet of the Rhenish tolls was served up to the opulent archbishops of Mainz and Cologne." The Rhine was popularly described as "the priests' lane." The intelligent and constructive economic principle of Saxon and Salian times, whereby the revenues arising from these tolls were expended for improvement and protection of navigation, was succeeded by a selfish local and fiscal policy. In the late Hohenstaufen period the toll stations fell almost entirely into the hands of the bishops and barons along the Rhine. The number increased appallingly, from nineteen to sixty-two, and the rapacity of the barons and bishops was so great that the rates were continually raised, sometimes to as high as sixty per cent. It was a policy of exploitation and extortion greater than the traffic could bear and destructive of commerce.

The condition was a repetition of the condition in the early feudal age when every noble laid *péages* upon trade and converted the boundary of his fief into a tariff frontier. But with this exception: the condition was far more aggravated now by the great development of commerce and industry and the power and sense of independence of the burghers. The robber baron in the thirteenth century had to deal not with poor pack peddlers and small wandering merchants, but with a rich and united merchant class, commanding great resources and capable of acting with force in protection of its interests.

Out of this political and economic struggle between the towns and the feudality was destined to come a great and constructive movement in the middle of the thirteenth century, which was to have far-reaching influence upon the history of commerce and trade in medieval Germany. This was the formation of the city-leagues.

There seems to have been an effort toward the formation of a city-league in the Rhenish midlands as early as 1220. But nothing came of the movement until 1226, when Mainz, Worms, Bingen, Speyer, Oppenheim, Frankfort, Gelnhausen, and Friedburg united to resist the oppression of the robber barons. Archbishop Siegfried of Mainz complained to Frederick II. In answer Prince Henry, the regent of his father, declared the league must be dissolved. The cities refused to obey. They were in much the same position as the Lombard cities in the previous century, and the grandson of Frederick I had learned nothing and forgotten nothing. In 1231 the diet at Worms, in which burghers had no seat, formally interdicted the League of the Rhine. But the furious conflict of the emperor with the papacy prevented any imperial action to suppress it.

Other towns, in Swabia, Westphalia, and even Switzerland, soon joined it, and on June 25, 1255, an imposing league was constituted which ultimately included seventy cities and extended up and down the entire Rhine and covered a great part of central and western Germany. Recognized by William of Holland, these *civitates conjuratæ*—for such they are called in the *Formula pacis*—organized a constabulary on land and a flotilla on the water. Between Basel and the confluence of the Moselle with the Rhine at Coblenz this river fleet numbered a hundred armed boats. Only commercial barges were allowed to put in and out of those river ports pertaining to the league, and a *Bundzoll,* or official toll, was created to meet common expenses.

Having thus established security along the Rhine, the league attacked the arbitrary tolls imposed by the barons. In 1268 the cities obtained from the diet an act abolishing all tolls except those of ancient right and ordering the demolition of all collection bureaux between Strassburg and Cologne. Many of the castles were destroyed. But the most formidable of these, the famous Castle Rheinfels, constructed in 1216 and belonging to Count Dietrich of Katzenellenbogen, resisted all efforts to take it.

In 1253 the Westphalian cities followed the example of the Rhine cities. Münster, Dortmund, Soest, Lippstadt united. Sometimes only two cities arranged together for mutual protection, as Basel and Mühlhausen in 1246, Brunswick and Stade in 1248. In 1278 the towns of the upper Rhine and Alsace combined and in 1285 Strassburg, Basel and Freiburg.

Indubitably the healthiest and most progressive life of Germany in the Hohenstaufen epoch is to be found in these free cities. The number of them was very great, at least one hundred and fifty. As cities are estimated today they would seem small. But their influence for their time was equal to that of modern urban communities. Not only were they the focal points of commerce and industry, but as their wealth increased they also became of importance in the promotion of the higher arts and of literature. The architecture of later medieval Germany is preëminently a municipal and gild architecture, not, as formerly, ecclesiastical. In historiography it is now that town chronicles begin to supplant the older medieval form of monastic chronicles.

It is as suggestive to contemplate the trade routes of Germany as it is those of Italy and France, and to observe similarities and differences, ordained by natural resources and above all, by physical features. Italy is a long, boot-shaped peninsula whose axis is the Apennines, with three sides open to the sea and only one river of importance, the Po. France is a great hexagon open to the sea on south, west, and north and connected with central Europe all along its eastern frontier and easy of access from Lombardy, Germany, and Flanders. With the exception of the Garonne all important rivers of France flow from the centre to the circumference, or in other words, radiate as spokes from a hub. The centre of gravity of France is naturally in the Seine basin. Political France merely conforms to natural, physiographic France.

Medieval Germany, on the other hand, was rectangular in form; or rather, it was formed of two rectangular parts, upper or southern Germany, and lower or northern Germany. These two halves were separated from each other by the Main and Eger rivers, the former flowing west into the Rhine, the latter east into the Elbe through a great natural trough formed by parallel ranges of mountains. Except for the Elbe River (the long diagonal feature of physical Germany), all important German rivers flow along either horizontal or vertical lines. This makes the road map of Germany somewhat resemble a gridiron, at the intersection of whose bars one finds the cities. Careful scrutiny of the map will disclose the fact that there were five horizontal routes of commerce across Germany, and a like number of vertical ones. Horizontal routes: (1) the Danube Valley Route from Basel or Strassburg over Ulm, Augsburg, Regensburg, Passau to Vienna and Buda Pesth; (2) the Main-Eger Route from the middle Rhine to the upper Elbe from Mainz through Frankfort, Bamberg, Nuremberg, Eger, Prague; (3) Cologne, Cassel, Erfurt, Leipzig, Bautzen, Breslau; (4) Cologne, Dortmund, Soest, Goslar, Magdeburg, Berlin, Frankfort-on-the-Oder; (5) Cologne, Münster, Bremen, Hamburg, Lübeck, Stralsund, Stettin, Danzig. Vertical routes: (1) the Meuse, from Verdun to Ghent in Flanders; (2) the Rhine from Basel to Utrecht, in reality a triple route, for there was a road on each bank and the river between; (3) from the Brenner Pass to the Baltic, through Augsburg, Nuremberg, Bamberg,

Erfurt, Goslar, Brunswick, Hamburg, to Bremen or Lübeck; (4) from
the Brenner Pass through Munich, Regensburg, Eger, Leipzig, Halle,
Magdeburg to Hamburg or Lübeck; (5) from Venice through Villach,
Salzburg, Passau, Prague, Breslau, to Frankfort-on-the-Oder or to
Danzig.

In the twelfth century the texture of German society was greatly
changed from that of the eleventh. During the long War of Investiture,
which, so far as the emperor was concerned, was a revolt of the great
feudality, a swarm of lesser feudal lords had risen to power who
fortified themselves within their castles and exercised sway round
about them, and whose inclination was to set at naught both the authority of the crown and that of the great dukes. Thus, politically Germany
was given over to sectionalism and feudal particularism on a large scale
—a condition precisely the opposite from that which obtained in France.

The burgher population in the walled towns was able to protect itself
against the overbearing ways of this petty feudality. But the rural
peasantry had not such protection. The long civil strife, poverty, famine,
had reduced most of the free class in Germany to serfdom even before
the termination of the Salian epoch, and the dominance of the petty
lords who had arisen confirmed and continued this condition in the
twelfth century. And yet, although the general tendency was for small
freeholders to sink to serfdom and for serfdom itself to become more
aggravated, there were counterbalancing influences which ameliorated
this tendency. There was great competition among proprietors for laborers to clear forests, and to drain swamp lands as the price of land increased, and the consequence was that many of the proprietary class
were compelled to attract settlers by liberal offers. Moreover the rapid
growth of towns in Germany and the colonization of trans-Elbean
Germany tended to ameliorate the condition of serfdom. Labor was
so much in demand in the towns and in the new lands of the frontier
that the serf took flight to one place or the other if he were overworked
or abused. To avoid losing his tenantry the proprietor had to be considerate, if not kind. Thus the services of the peasantry gradually became definite and quasi-contractual in their nature; the peasant was
assured of his holding on reasonable terms. The "hard age" of the German peasantry was not in the twelfth and thirteenth centuries, but at
the end of the Middle Ages, when the "reception" of Roman Law for-
midably aggravated their condition.

CHAPTER XX

"THE great deed of the German people in the Middle Ages," it has been justly said, "was the expansion of the German race' eastward over the Slavonic nations, and the making of three-fifths of modern Germany."

There were two Germanys in the Middle Ages, and it is important to understand the distinction between them: Old, West, Feudal Germany, and New, East, Colonial Germany. The former was peopled by the ancient German tribal stocks, which preserved traditions of Roman and old Frankish rule and culture; the Church was a long established institution in it, and feudal institutions and civilization prevailed over it. New East Germany on the contrary, was a different world geographically, racially, culturally. It was the great zone beyond the lower Elbe, the Saale, the Raab, and the Leitha rivers, peopled by the Slavs and Magyars.

What Professor Turner has called "the common sequence of frontiers" in American history is true of medieval Germany. Rhenish merchants in the ninth century imported grain and cattle into the Rhine cities from the estates of the Hessian monasteries of Fulda and Hersfeld on the edge of the wilderness. Beyond these monastery ranches, conditions became more primitive, the thinly settled region shading off into patches of soil, crudely tilled by a German peasantry, and clearings in the forest, until the pure frontier was reached on the Saale and the lower Elbe. The stages in the eastward expansion of the German people are marked, though not so clearly (for lack of documents) as the same phenomenon here in the United States. In Charlemagne's time the frontier of settlement—for we must distinguish between the military boundary and the edge of civilization—was barely beyond the Rhine. The chain of fortified trading-posts along the course of the lower Elbe, the Saale, and the Nab rivers from Bardowick to Regensburg was far from civilization.

This parallel between American westward expansion and German eastward expansion in the Middle Ages is not a fanciful one. The line of the Elbe, Oder, and Vistula rivers as clearly demarked the eastward expansion of Germany as the "fall line" of the Atlantic seaboard, the Alleghenies, and the Mississippi delimited the successive stages of American

* MAP. Shepherd, *Historical Atlas,* 80.

westward expansion. That "return to primitive conditions in a continually advancing frontier line, and a new development of that area," which
is so manifest in American expansion, is just as true of the history of
the German border. The stages of transition are identical—from cattle-
raising and swine-herding to farming, to commerce, to manufacturing.
In the time of the Ottos, the Saxon peasant fed his cattle in the plains of
the lower Elbe and Saale rivers, and the Thuringian herded swine on the
pine-slopes of the Harz. The cowpens were not far from the town life
of old Franconia (Mainz, Worms, Speyer), as they were near the "fall
line" in the American colonies when tidewater cities like Baltimore, Rich-
mond, and Charleston had become staid communities. Erfurt, Hallstadt,
Forchheim, Priemberg, Schesel, Magdeburg, were fortified trading de-
pots with the Wends like Forts Granville, Shirley, and Bedford in
Pennsylvania, Cumberland in Virginia Chiswell on the Great Kanawha,
and Prince George above the Saluda. These German fortified towns
were often built on the sites of former Slavonic villages, as Indian villages were occupied over here. Beyond these posts the German pack-
trader, with whom furs were an important article of trade, threaded
the Slavonic wilderness as his American successor pierced the Allegheny
watershed into the plains of Kentucky and Ohio.

Nothing in history so resembles this history of German eastward
expansion and colonization as that of the westward expansion of the
American people from the Atlantic seaboard, first to the head of tidewater, then up the Mohawk or over the Alleghenies into the Ohio and
Mississippi country. At bottom both movements were a search for free
and cheap land by a farming people. For it is estimated that land values
in Germany rose forty per cent between 900 and 1300, especially in the
rich Moselle and Rhine lands.

The conquests of Charlemagne had been the first stage in this long
and bloody history of German expansion. In his reign Frankish expansion had reached the Saale and the lower Elbe, and in the Danube
Valley by the middle of the ninth century the German sphere extended
beyond the Enns, which had been the farthest east of German extension
in pre-Avar times, and had reached the Raab. What is now modern
Austria, with Carinthia and Styria, was not merely politically but culturally from now on affiliated with Germany.

But the break-up of Charlemagne's Empire and the evil days of civil
war and Norse and Magyar invasion arrested this eastward expansion.
The movement was not resumed again until the accession of the Saxon
dynasty in 919. Under Henry the Fowler and Otto the Great, German
trade and commerce increased, population grew, and with this development came the demand for more land. Moreover, the intimate alliance
between the Church and the Saxon crown entailed an obligation upon the

latter to back up by the sword the revived missionary activity of the Church. The result was renewed attack upon the Wends.

The Sorbenland between the Saale and the upper Elbe was the first territory wrung from the Slavs, and the first to be Germanized. In 928 Henry made a winter campaign across the frozen marshes of the Havel River and "by hunger, sword, and cold," as the chronicler says, captured the chief town of the Hevellians. It was called Brunabor. Henry converted it into a fortress—a *burg*. The town was built on a low hill, a remarkable thing in this land of marsh and fen, on the crest of which stood the famous Wend temple of Triglatt, which was transformed into a church dedicated to the Virgin. The little Wendish town doubtless was composed of the rude cottages of fishermen studding the river bank. The Wends were naturally a fisher folk, living as they did in a network of rivers and marshes. But bee-keeping was also a passion among them.

Such is the history of the beginnings of Brandenburg. The process of conquest and colonization went on under the ruthless margrave Gero, Otto the Great's "lord of the north." Magdeburg was made an archbishopric with power over the whole northeast, and seven new bishoprics established—Oldenburg, Havelburg, Brandenburg, Merseburg (notice the repetitious suffix "burg," for every one was half house of God, half fortress against the Wend), Zeitz, Meissen, and Prague. By the end of the Saxon period German ecclesiastical influence was dominant in Poland; the bishoprics of Breslau, Gnesen, and Posen had been founded. The Germans had reached the Oder River.

At the same time other Saxons crossed the lower Elbe into the Billunger lands (Mecklenburg) [1] and settled there. The frontier of settlement and the military border, however, were not identical. In Thuringia the frontier of civilization extended to the Saale, but in Saxony proper it stopped at the Aller and the Ocker. Along the middle Main civilization had crept up as far as Würzburg, as a charter of Otto III shows, which granted special privileges to settlers who would come and reclaim the forests and drain the marshes. Bamberg, which Henry II founded in 1007, succeeded Würzburg as the frontier outpost of the Main valley. The sources of the Saxon period show the large progress made in eastward expansion. Along the eastern edge of the kingdom,

---

[1] The province of Mecklenburg derives its name from the fortified town of that name. It was originally called "Wiligrad" or the "Great Town" by the Slavs. When it was captured by the Saxons and converted into a *Burg,* they prefixed the Old German adjective *mekel,* meaning "big" or "great," to the word *Burg.* Compare Middle English *mickle,* and Anglo-Saxon *micel,* which have the same significance Thus Mecklenburg is a German translation of Wiligrad. It was the key fortress in a line of frontier posts which extended from the Baltic to Lake Schwerin and included Wismar, Oldenburg, Ilow, Bukow, Schwerin on an island in the Schwerinersee, and Dobbin at the north end of that lake.

from the mouth of the Elbe to the mountains of Styria, German colonists annexed immense tracts of territory.

These pioneers were chiefly engaged in cattle-raising. Court judgments in this region were imposed in cattle fines under Otto I, and the legislation shows the prevalence of crimes of violence typical of frontier conditions. The country, like our own New West, began to be thinly settled with Saxon colonists, ranchers and farmers as ready to use the sword against the Wends as the American frontiersmen were to use the rifle against the Indians.

The Saxon population along the border (*Marcomanni,* or *Marchmen,* they were called), had need, as the chronicler Helmold says, to be of strong endurance and to be ready to risk their blood. These medieval German frontiersmen were resolute and hardy, hard-working and given to a rough hospitality toward strangers, provided they were Germans and "lived Saxon law" like themselves, but hating the Wend and detesting foreign incomers like the Dutch and Flemings.

Yet this subjugation was not permanent. In 983 the Slavs rose furiously and destroyed the German settlements. But the border warfare was renewed and colonization was resumed. In 1000 Nordalbingia was desolated for the second time by the Slavs. Again colonization was resumed, and again in 1018 a Slavonic uprising drove the Germans out. All the German villages and border posts were devastated; even Hamburg was threatened. It was an irrepressible conflict. For the third time German pioneers crossed the Elbe and for the third time in 1066 the Slavs, who this time found a bold leader in Kruto, whose stronghold was on the site of later Lübeck, drove them out. Brandenburg was lost until the first quarter of the next century, when once more the dogged determination of the Saxon people permanently recovered it. More than 600 families in Holstein left the country in 1066 and settled in the Harz.

The desolation was complete. In the twelfth century, when lower Germany under the leadership of Adolph of Holstein, Henry the Lion and Albert the Bear again recovered the "lost provinces," Helmold of Holstein, whose intelligent observation entitles him to no mean honor as an archæologist, found a melancholy charm in surveying the ruins of churches and monasteries in Schleswig and Mecklenburg— crumbled memorials of German power there in the days of the Ottos.

There still remain [he writes] many evidences of that former occupation, especially in the forest which extends from the city of Lütjenburg through the mighty tracts of Schleswig, in whose vast and almost impenetrable solitude yet may be descried the furrows which once marked out the plowlands. Even the lines of former towns and villages may be traced in the ruins. Along the streams in many places mounds of earth and silt, formed by the tributary waters, yet testify that every such site was once inhabited by Saxons—when Saxon valor was formidable.

It is the same even on the *left* bank of the Elbe between the great bend and the upper Aller (today the territory around Halberstadt, Salzwedel, and Stendhal), "where still may be seen the ruins of old levees which were constructed in the lowlands along the banks of the Elbe. When the Slavs over-ran the country the Saxons were cut off, and the land was possessed by them down to our own time."

When we sum it up, the Salian period closed with pitiably insignificant results so far as trans-Elbean settlement is concerned. In 1125 the linguistic frontier in the northeast was still where it had been in the reign of Charlemagne.

In the Bend of the Danube the history of German southeast colonization exhibits the same alternation between advance and retreat that characterizes the history of the northeastern frontier. Just as the Slavonic reactions of 983, 1018, and 1066 undid the work of Trans-Elbean colonization, and threw the Saxon pioneers back across the Elbe three several times, so in the southeast the labor of Bavarian settlement was undone by the Magyars, who by 896 were settled on both banks of the Theiss. In 900 the margrave Liutpold built the Ennsburg out of the stones of Passau's old Roman walls. Effective check to the inroads of the Magyars was not made until Otto I's smashing defeat of them near Augsburg in 955. After that date a steady stream of German colonists flowed into the wasted land of the Ostmark. The body of these pioneers probably came from Bavaria, but there is reason to believe that with them was a considerable proportion of Frank and Swabian immigrants from farther west.

After 955, in spite of obstacles and setbacks, the advance of German southeast colonization, if slow, was sure. The work of colonization was done by big "operators,"—namely, the high clergy and feudality. Unfortunately there is no general description of this movement by a contemporary observer, such as Helmold affords us for the history of the colonization of Mecklenburg. The frontier bishoprics of the southeast had no one to record their history as·Adam of Bremen did for Hamburg. The history is not found in any Austrian chronicle, for there is no chronicle of the Babenberger house.

The Wienerwald seems for several years to have retarded settlement. But more important than the resistance of the great forest was the hostility of the sparse but determined population (principally Magyar, but with some settlers of Slavonic blood), living east of the forest. This territory was a sort of No Man's Land where every man's hand was liable to be against another, and certainly against any encroaching pioneers out of Germany. The first positive evidence of German settlement east of the Wienerwald is found in 1002.

At some unknown date in the career of Duke Adalbert of Austria (1018–55), the site of Vienna had been occupied by him, probably as an advance-post to cover the German settlements which by that time had succeeded in penetrating the Wienerwald. Their appearance in this region was the signal for an intensification of the border strife in which the settlers were apparently the aggressors, and which soon led to intervention of the Magyar king Stephen. It was not long before the narrow strip of territory between the Fischa and the Leitha rivers, like the Scottish Border, was the scene of a strife which has left an indelible and picturesque mark upon medieval German literature in the greatest of German epics. Nevertheless, German settlers persisted in pushing into the land, and even some adventurous traders. Who made the first trading journey into Austria, no source tells us, but there are clear evidences of the coming of traders from the tenth century on. The Regensburgers were the first who came in any number. Austria, at that time, scarcely had a distinct trading class of her own. The progress of German culture toward the southeast during this period is no less important than the political development. By the time of Henry IV, under the able administration of Bishop Altmann of Passau (1065–91), this portion of the Danubian lands had begun to lose the shaggy frontier aspect of a border diocese, and to acquire some of the material amenities of civilization which might be enjoyed in older Germany.

The War of Investiture stimulated this extension of German colonization farther down the Danube, as it did that east of the Elbe. The anarchy in Germany led to an exodus of the population into the lands of the east. In the next century one finds a surprising number of German communities in these colonial lands. Further tangible evidence of German extension is found in the charters of the monasteries, especially in Austria. The colonizing activity of the bishops and the abbots in the March, in Steiermark, in Carinthia in the late eleventh, and through the twelfth century, was very great. The multiplication of German place-names shows it. This is when Melk, Klosterneuburg, Heiligenkreuz, Lilienfeld, St. Maria Zell, Zwettl, Seitenstetten, Geras and other abbeys began to grow rich and fat on gifts of land. At the same time families of the high feudality like the Ebersberger, the Schala-Burghausen, the Bogner, the Plaien-Pleisteiner, the Sulzbacher. the Falksteiner, who naturally brought with them a crowd of colonists, free and serf, began to rise up. Some of these probably drifted into the Danube lands during the early Crusades. North of the Danube the progress of German colonization was no less. German and Bohemian backwoodsmen clashed in the great Böhmerwald where their spheres of "squatter sovereignty" met.

With the accession of Lothar of Saxony to the German kingship in 1125 a new and formidable advance was made in German northeast colonization. Within the term of the next generation the entire fabric of Slav independence collapsed. Nordalbingia, Mecklenburg, Brandenburg, and Pomerania were settled by the German people. The speed and effectiveness of this rapid change is partly to be ascribed to the breakdown of the capacity of resistance among the Wends; more, perhaps, to the accumulated pressure of things economic and social in Germany, which bore down all barriers of opposition.

"Hard times" and feudal oppression were prolific sources of the migration of the small farming class into new regions. In the twelfth century, however, the feudal nobles began to show more enlightenment. They saw the economic value of promoting colonization in the vast stretches of forest and marsh land which they owned, and also were eager to dispossess the Slavs whose lands they coveted, and so began to hold out inducements to settlers. In 1106 the archbishop of Bremen imported hundreds of Dutch and Flemish settlers, used to deep plowing and ditching and draining in the low-lying lands of Belgium and Holland, and settled them in the great marshes of the Weser River around Bremen. Albert the Bear of Brandenburg did the same in the marshy region around medieval Berlin. Count Adolph of Holstein, one of the most intelligent and clear-sighted nobles of the twelfth century, "sent messengers into all the regions round about, even into Flanders and Holland, into Westphalia and Frisia, to proclaim that all who were in want of land might come with their families and receive the best soil— a spacious country rich in crops, abounding in fish and flesh and exceeding good pasturages."

The result of the reduction of the Wagri in 1143 was a large influx of colonists into the trans-Elbean lands, which were thrown open to settlement. After the Wendish Crusade of 1147 this drift of population toward the frontier became almost a "rush." Settlers thronged in *cum equis et bubus, cum aratris et plaustris et personis ad opus idoneis,* to the exasperation of the Wends who could do nothing but sullenly submit. Nothing so much resembles it as the American "rush" after the War of 1812 into the Western Reserve and the Ohio Valley. In the older parts of Germany the exodus was so great that manorial proprietors were compelled to ameliorate the condition of their peasantry lest they run away to the new lands beyond the Elbe.

It was a rough and uncouth frontier community, predominantly Wendish, but with a considerable sprinkling of a hardy, lawless pioneer element—Helmold says it was a *gens bruta*. But mixed with that negative ingredient found in every rough, frontier society seeking a way out of its discontent by change, was a very large element of the best blood and bone of the German race in this migration. A large proportion of the immigrants in the twelfth century were men of firm fibre, actuated by a determination to better their lot and ambitious to seize the opportunities offered in a new country.

The farm lands were distributed in an absolutely different way from the old method. The old manorial village community with its "strip" farming and its common ownership in pasturage and woods was not usual. Instead each man received a long oblong tract of from 60 to 20 acres like a modern farm. His house was built at one end of the tract facing the road and standing in the midst of a garden and orchard. Behind it, if the "lay" of the land permitted, were the farm acres, behind them the pasture, and last of all the wood-lot. This manner of settling new tracts spread to other parts of Germany later in the Middle Ages—into upper Bavaria, the Black Forest, the Odenwald; nearly one-quarter of Silesia was so colonized, as later the marsh lands between the Oder, the Warthe, and the Netze. The whole system goes back to the Dutch settlers first established in 1106 along the North Sea littoral and in clearings in the Franconian forest, and then *in extenso* in Brandenburg. A charter of Albert the Bear mentions these manors of Dutch measurement—*mansos Hollandriensis dimensionis*.

The picturesque variety of villages which one may still see in eastern Germany goes back to these days of early expansion and colonization. Where settlement was less formally regulated the old kind of "nucleated" village might have been established not far from those of the new type. And everywhere one might have seen the typical *Runddorf* or "round village" of the Slavs. For among the Slavs the houses, instead of being huddled together in a cluster as in the German *Dorf,* were placed in a circle or an oval around the edge of a green, enclosing it on all sides, leaving only a single gateway, so that the houses formed an enclosure into which the cattle of the villagers could be folded for safety. In a German Dorf the road ran through the middle of the village. Among the Slavs it passed outside of the entrance to the village. This difference points to the fact that the ancient Slavs were still in a pastoral stage, when the Germans had already developed agriculture, and combined cattle-raising and farming. When the Germans began to press eastward against the Slavs and to settle beyond the Saale and the Elbe, they carried their open village type with them, or established "street" villages, but sometimes imitated the Slavonic round-village.

There are other details also of German frontier history that ought to be luminous to the American student of history. Until the twelfth century the richest gold, silver, and copper deposits in medieval Europe were those of the Harz in Thuringia (the Nevada of the Middle Ages), and the art of mining was largely a Saxon monopoly. The Rammelsberg mine there was like the Comstock Lode, and Goslar was the most important mining town in Europe. But in the second half of the twelfth century, between 1162 and 1170, silver was discovered in the Erzgebirge, that barrier range of mountains dividing the March of Thuringia from Bohemia. Soon there was a "rush" from the old diggings in the Harz to the new El Dorado which reminds an American historian of the gold-fever of '49.

The discovery was first made upon the lands of the Cistercian monastery of Altenzelle, it is said, and the worldly-wise monks soon began to import Goslar miners. A cluster of German mining camps which gradually grew into towns rapidly arose in a ˙region hitherto wholly Czech in population, the most important of which was Freiberg, founded in 1171. In the thirteenth century it was said of Henry the Illustrious, the margrave of Meissen and lord of these rich silver lands, that he possessed towers full of silver, and if the kingdom of Bohemia had been for sale he could easily have purchased it.

Since general prosperity often attended the industry, mining became an important factor in German economic history from the twelfth century. Some mines belonged to the fisc, other pertained to the feudal lords. According to Inama Sternegg the ordinary freeman had no rights to the minerals found upon his property. Documentary proofs of German mining begin in the twelfth century and rapidly multiply between 1200 and 1400. Of these the charter of Trent (1185), of Goslar (1219–1301), the mining law of Iglau (1249–1300), the Kuttenberger regulations (1300), and the law of Freiberg (1296–1400) are the most important. Although Germany produced gold, silver, lead, iron, tin (after 1240), it is the history and technique of silver-mining that is of greatest importance. In spite of the paucity of sources for the twelfth century, one main point is clear. Even at this early period mining was conducted by an association (*Genossenschaftliches Betriebs*), a real principle of organization prevailed which developed a technically trained stock of miners from generation unto generation.

These alien colonies of Flemings and Hollanders established in lower Saxony in the time of Henry the Lion and in Brandenburg by Albert the Bear, the Angle colony about Merseburg, the settlements of Saxon miners in the Bohemian mountains, and the sixteen free "Zips" towns founded in the Hungarian Zipser-Erzgebirge were woven into the texture of medieval German society as the Dutch of the Hudson, the Germans of the Mohawk, and the Palatine Germans of the Shenandoah Valley and Piedmont were merged with the American people. In time these German settlements grew into towns which often retained their former Slavonic place-names, as Leipzig, Danzig, Berlin, Wollin, Küstrin, Kammin; for place-names with suffixes terminating in -*zig* and -*in* are a sure indication of former Slavonic villages. Even when the name of the locality is German it may be merely a translation of the original Slavonic name for the place. Thus, Oldenburg is a translation of Staragard (Slavonic, "Old Town"), the suffix *-gard* or *-grad* being a widely spread Slavonic place-ending signifying "town," as in Belgrade or Petrograd, and the prefix *stara* meaning "old."

With improved agriculture came the grape, and the vine was spread much farther than today over northern and northeastern Germany, in Mecklenburg, Brandenburg, Pomerania, and Silesia. More and more as the wilderness was subdued and the barbarian Slavs civilized, the old trade in furs, wax, amber, and forest products gave way before a larger commerce. Nowhere else in Europe was town-planting so energetic as in trans-Elbean Germany in the twelfth and thirteenth centuries. Stendhal, Breslau, Berlin, Dresden, Leipzig, Thorn, Marienwerder, Elbing are examples. These new towns were not like older medieval towns, which had narrow, tortuous and crooked streets, but were carefully laid out with rectangular streets and wide-open squares. In this they resembled the *bastides* of southern France, or new towns which arose in Languedoc and the southwestern provinces after the devastation of the Albigensian Crusade, and the havoc of the Anglo-French wars between St. Louis and Henry III of England.

Breslau   Leipzig
GROUND PLANS OF GERMAN TOWNS IN THE SLAVONIC LANDS

In the Danube lands the Slavonic population found in Carinthia, Carniola, and Styria by the incoming German settlers was less driven out than depressed, as was the case in the Thuringian March, Brandenburg, Mecklenburg, and Pomerania. But unfortunately such admirable chronicles as those of Thietmar of Merseburg, and Helmold, which cast so much light upon conditions in the northern colonial lands, are wanting for the history of southeast German expansion. In compensation, however, a considerable body of charters has been preserved. In the codices and cartularies of the monasteries founded in these lands peopled by the southern Slavs, Slavonic place and proper names are of frequent occurrence in the eleventh and twelfth centuries. The political and social overstratum in these provinces was German and aristocratic; the under-stratum Slav in ancestry and politically and socially a dependent population. In Austria, on the other hand, while there was the same aristocratic political and social organization, both the upper and the lower stratum was prevailingly of German blood; the dependent population was composed of German serfs brought eastward by their masters and established in the colonial lands.

The Magyars effectually checked German expansion in the southeast, while no force arrested it in the northeast until the Vistula was reached. In 1119 border warfare was especially fierce. In 1131 Styria was invaded by Hungarian forces, a raid in which the settlements established by the bishops of Salzburg suffered severely. In 1133 an allusion of Otto of Freising shows that Hungarian expansion north of the Danube had spread so far that Poles and Hungarians came to clash *in silva quæ Polunios et Ungarios sejungit,* as already Bohemians were in border strife with Bavarian pioneers in the Boehmerwald.

The expansion of German commerce naturally accompanied this expansion of the German people. In the twelfth century the Baltic became a German lake. Every year in November, at the time of the "big wind" a fleet of western craft came for dried fish and furs to the half-Slav, half-German towns on the Baltic coast. There is still a little village, now a watering-place, near Stettin named Heringsdorf. The Baltic herring trade was important. The Alt-Lübecker merchant group even penetrated into the Baltic and sought to capture the ancient Swedish-Russian trade of Novgorod and the Varangian route and had a "factory" or trading post on the island of Gothland. In 1134 the emperor Lothar II took them under imperial protection. The original charter of Lothar is lost, but it is referred to by Henry the Lion in a privilege dated October 18, 1163, granted to the merchants of Lübeck. We know little more about this distant commerce until the formation of the Hanseatic League and the incorporation of the Wisby group with it in 1298.

Pioneer traders, indeed, sometimes moved in advance of German colonization, but more frequently trade followed colonization. In the Obodrite country (it did not become the Duchy of Mecklenburg until after the conquest of 1147), at Staragard, which was the capital of the Obodrite duke Pribislav, there was a considerable colony of German merchants settled in 1129. German trading operations extended clear to the island of Rügen, whose inhabitants were still fiercely pagan, and where the famous Slavonic fane of Arcona was located. Before the storming and capture of this sanctuary by a joint German and Danish expedition in 1168, it was necessary for the merchants not only to avoid parading their Christianity, but also to offer substantial presents to the god in order to be permitted to buy and sell.

In the *Life* of the Bishop of Bamberg is a curious account of how the conversion of the peoples of the mainland of Pomerania interrupted for some time the trade with the Rugians, who would have nothing to do with the converted Slavs. Among the Rani, or Rugians, conditions of trade were so primitive that strips of linen cloth served for currency, like wampum among the Indians of America. This cloth currency was also once current among the Bohemians. In Czech the word for "linen" and the word "to number" come from the same root.

Of the trade of the Pomeranian mainland in the first half of the twelfth century we have interesting information in Ebbo's *Life of Otto of Bamberg,* who twice visited Pomerania (in 1124 and again in 1128), and also in the *Dialogues* of Herbordus. Twice Otto made the long and arduous journey down the Saale and the Elbe, and thence up the Havel, and so to the far Baltic coast towns of Stettin and Wollin.

Pomerania then was a land of marsh and fen, of sluggish streams and stagnant lakes, inhabited by a pure Slav people who still lived after the primitive manner of their kind and were absolutely untouched by Christo-German civilization. A fisher folk chiefly, they estimated wealth in "lasts" of dried fish and in hives of bees, for honey was a staple article of production. Their food was fish and rye and a few vegetables; they drank a mead of cherry and honey. Their textile skill was considerable, but they were poor farmers. The towns at the mouth of the Oder and the Poene had considerable commerce in raw products like dried fish, furs, tar, rope, etc., but were astonishingly squalid and miry. The only structures of prominence were the temples. Amid this population, which was spared the intolerance, bigotry, and greed which were so heavily inflicted upon the Slavs of the Elbe, Otto lived and labored, winning the confidence of the Pomeranians by gentle means. Pomerania and Poland were the only Slavonic lands under the domination of the Latin Church in the Middle Ages which made the transition from paganism to Christianity and from barbarism to civilization by transformation and not by force.

By the next century Stettin appears as the *totius Pomeraniæ metropolis,* although it could not possibly have had a population of from six to seven thousand, as said. Its chief rival was Kammin. The spongy, marshy soil upon which both towns were built was a serious drawback. Stettin was girded with swamps, and the streets in Kammin were so miry that bridges, which seem to have been nothing but planks, were everywhere. Otto himself fell off one of these planks and was pitched into the mud. The people were hospitable, though rude and crude in manners. Each town had a "forum" where business was done, and a certain degree of money economy obtained. There were warehouses, chiefly, one imagines, for the curing and storing of fish. Fishing was the main activity of the inhabitants, though furs and slaves were also articles of commerce. The herring ran in shoals in the Baltic; but there was a brisk trade in fresh-water fish, too. The coastwise trade must have been considerable, for Otto easily traveled by water from Wollin to Stettin.

By 1125 it is evident that there was a through route from the eastern parts of "New" Germany to the farther Baltic coast. Halle, on the Saale River, was the clearing-house and emporium of all this eastern German commerce. Both times when Otto of Bamberg made his trips to Pomerania he "stocked up" at the fair (*nundinæ*) in Halle, and thence traveled by boat down the Saale to the Elbe, down the Elbe to Werben at the mouth of Havel, and up the Havel and down the Peene to Stettin.

The founding of Lübeck in 1158 permanently assured German commercial domination in the Baltic. It soon became the emporium of the whole Baltic trade. Merchant vessels from England, Denmark, Sweden, Norway, and even Russia crowded the port. Stettin was Lübeck's closest rival. The Low German speech became the language of trade throughout the whole north, and the Elbean-Slavonic speech, which hitherto had been necessary for the conduct of Baltic trade, gradually died out. More than a hundred years later the records of the Hanseatic League began to be written in this Low German dialect. By the middle of the thirteenth century Lübeck was the chief commercial city on the Baltic coast and the trading centre of a swarm of lesser towns founded by the expansive and colonizing energy of the North German folk in the conquered Wendish lands, such as Rostock, Wismar, Greifswald, Stralsund, Mecklenburg, Ratzeburg, Schwerin, Oldenburg, the last four built (like Lübeck itself) on the sites of former Slavonic towns.

In the confederation of these cities in the thirteenth century for mutual protection of their commerce against coast and river pirates and robber bands along the roads we find the earliest beginnings of the Hanseatic League, although that name was not adopted before 1360. We do not know exactly when this process of coalition was begun. The earliest document preserved is an agreement of a very general nature between Lübeck and Hamburg in 1230. But in 1241, when it was renewed, the terms of this alliance have become specific. In 1259 Rostock and Wismar became members of the association, which by this time had formulated the rule that no city could become a member of the league which was not situated upon the coast or a navigable river, and which did not keep the keys to its own city gates. Between 1260 and 1265 we find the first recorded statues of the league, among which is a provision for an annual diet of representatives of every city "to legislate about affairs."

The greater history of the Hanseatic League is principally a chapter in the history of medieval commerce in the fourteenth century. We are concerned here only with the history of its formation. But the history even of its formation cannot be fully understood without knowledge of the history of German eastward expansion and colonization in the twelfth and thirteenth centuries. By 1265 the league had begun to alarm neighboring princes like the king of Denmark, the margrave of Brandenburg, and the duke of Schleswig. But fortunately for the cities, these princes did not agree. Denmark coveted Schleswig; Brandenburg looked with resentment upon the Danish settlements at the mouths of the Peene, the Oder, and the Vistula rivers, for the margraves coveted Mecklenburg and Pomerania. Between the years 1283 and 1293 the league successfully checkmated the Danish designs by adding Haddeby and Kiel to its membership and frustrated Brandenburg by taking the coast towns of Mecklenburg and Pomerania into its fold. Thus Brandenburg was kept back from the Baltic for many years.

Meanwhile the league also labored to create monopolistic commercial control in the waters in which it operated. Flemish and Frisian merchants were shut out from the Baltic, the Gothlanders from the North Sea, by the threat of boycott. A momentous step of the Hanseatic League was made in completion of this effort to convert the Baltic into a Hanseatic lake and to capture the rich Russian trade of Novgorod in furs, tar, hemp, wax, timber, in 1293 when Wisby on the great island of Gothland, the seat of the most ancient maritime trade of any German merchants, was seized and the merchants thereof compelled to join the league. This high-handed act was the sequel of an alliance made in 1280 between Lübeck and Wisby, joined two years later by Riga (founded by Germans in 1201), against pirates. Wisby thus lost its hold upon the Baltic trade, but it nevertheless continued to prosper enormously. Indeed, the wealth of the town became proverbial. It was said that "even the pigs eat out of silver troughs." The town walls of Wisby, built in the thirteenth century and still well preserved, are among the most imposing examples of medieval town walls anywhere in Europe, and the remains of four ruined churches are still beautiful and melancholy memorials of a vanished prosperity.

Under the name of *Osterlingi,* Hanseatic merchants invaded England, where bitter rivalry ensued between them and the merchants of Cologne —for each group had separate privileges—until the rival groups were united in the German Gild Hall or Steelyard in London in the reign of Edward I. In the middle of the same century an office of the Hanse was established at Bruges.

But home politics also occupied the league. Mindful of the time when Frederick II, in his struggle with the North German princes, had sought the support of Denmark and actually ceded to her all the territory of Schleswig, Holstein, Nordalbingia, and Mecklenburg (which is to say, the whole territory of Lübecker sway)—a loss of territory prevented by the crushing Danish defeat at Boernhöved (1227)—during the interregnum (1250–73) the Hanseatic League was resolutely Guelf in its politics, a policy which not a little contributed to the favor it attained in the cities of Westphalia, the lower Rhine and in England. The eastward movement of the German people, at first that of peasantry, clergy, and nobles, acquired new impulses with the rise of the Hanseatic League, with the expansion of which it became knitted in the thirteenth century, and the sway of German commerce was carried clear around the bight of the Baltic into Prussia, Livonia, and Kurland, where Memel, Elbing, Libau, Königsberg, Riga became the seats of mighty Hanseatic merchants.

In the middle Danube lands the political change by which the former margrave of Austria was made a duke, united with the double process of territorial expansion and political consolidation of the Austrian lands, had a notable effect upon commerce.

Lack of sources makes it hard to determine what the articles of trade were in this early time. However, we know that among the imports into Austria stood, first, salt, and, second, cloth; among the exports were honey, wax, hides, and, as time went on, wine in increasing amounts. Probably trade originated here, as Keutgen thinks it always originates, in the endeavor of foreign merchants to seek goods needful for them in exchange for their own products. The trade with Hungary, for example, may reasonably have arisen through the desire of upper Germany for precious metals, gold and silver. A complete change, however, from this small, unregulated commerce was brought about at the end of the twelfth century through the acquisition of Styria (1192) and Frederick II's (1230–46) ambitions for a political and commercial unity of this land. This gave Austria control of the routes in the southeast of the Empire, leading to Hungary and Venice. Now, for the first time, an energetic trade policy was possible with upper Germany on one hand and Hungary on the other. In Frederick's time, too, came the first laws regulating trade, the prohibition of the export of grain, the grant of "guest rights" to the Regensburgers, and the guarantee by charter in 1231 of a monopoly of Hungarian trade to Vienna. Foreigners were forbidden to trade, not only with Hungary, but among themselves. More important, perhaps, than the limitations placed by this and similar charters was the establishment by them of trade centres in which merchants could count upon a market. Under this policy of grants of privilege to towns, continued and extended by Rudolph of Hapsburg to Graz, Judenburg, Neustadt, and Freistadt, the towns flourished notably for many years. Its purpose was to give the Austrians a monopoly of the foreign trade. Perhaps it stimulated this too much, for there developed a certain unwholesome dependence of the Austrian merchant, especially the Viennese merchant, upon the trade abroad.

The tax records of Passau from the middle of the thirteenth century tell us something of the extent of Austrian commerce. From these we judge that the import from upper Germany exceeded the export to upper Germany two or three times. Much of the goods brought in, however, was not consumed in Austria, but carried by Viennese to Hungary. This was especially true of cloth. In the trade with Hungary the balance was always strongly in favor of Austria. This balance was paid chiefly in the products of the Hungarian gold and silver mines, though Hungary exported some cattle also. Besides this carrying trade to Hungary, the other main line of Austrian commerce for the whole of the Middle Ages was the trade with Venice. This had reached a considerable height by the thirteenth century. It appears, then, that Austrian trade to the thirteenth century depended somewhat upon the geographical position of the country, somewhat upon the ability of its people, but also somewhat upon privileges granted by its rulers. It appears, also, that the consumption of foreign manufactured goods in Austria was covered chiefly by the profit from carrying trade, while the equivalent for the import of salt and other raw materials is to be found in the export of wine and other products of the land.[1]

The earliest document referring to the passage of Venetian merchants through Austria is of 1244. The Baltic trade to South Germany was mainly up the Mulde and down the Nab to Regensburg, the former taking the place of the Saale when that stream was made the eastern edge of the German world in Charlemagne's time. In Bohemia a trade route ran from Prague up the Moldau and over the divide to Linz on the Danube. Another road was up the Eger—or through the Nollendorf Pass—and down the Nab to Regensburg.

By the thirteenth century, except in the Baltic lands of Prussia, Kurland, and Esthonia, German eastward expansion and colonization had reached its term. Hungary, Bohemia, and Poland, while not impenetrable to German colonists and German civilization, nevertheless were strong enough to preserve themselves from the fate of the trans-Elbean Slavs. Something with reference to the economic history of these three nations bordering upon the eastern frontier is now in place.

The first Christian king of Hungary, Stephen, who was baptized in the year 1000, was favorable to German incomers, especially knights and small nobles, yet cautious lest they acquire too much influence. His attitude is seen in his advice to his son: "Hold the 'guests' (*hospites*) in honor, for they bring foreign learning and arms into the country; they are an ornament and protection to the throne." German peasants also in this time began to emigrate to Hungary, and were settled on the royal lands and on those of the nobles and clergy. But while the Magyars accepted Latin Christianity and adopted much of German institutions and culture, the penetration and spread of that influence was strictly measured. King Geisa (1041–61) was the first Hungarian ruler actively to promote German colonization in the kingdom. He seems to have issued a proclamation similar to that of the

[1] Theodor Mayer, *Der Auswärtige Handel des Herzogtums Oesterreich im Mittelaler* (1909) (a review).

Fürsten of North Germany already mentioned, inviting German settlers into Hungary. Unfortunately the text has disappeared; not even the date is preserved. There is merely the statement that the German communities found in Hungary in the next century had originally come at Geisa's invitation. Almost all these immigrants were settled in the mountainous mining regions.

Ladislaus I (1077–95) and Koloman (1095–1114) labored hard to redeem their country from the bondage of barbarism and ignorance. The intelligence of these two early Hungarian sovereigns in promoting economic and social welfare is remarkable. The latter, who was highly educated for a layman of his day, when most learning was confined to the priest-class, had read history to some advantage. He quaintly observes in one of his documents: "The Roman Empire first grew, and kings were made great and glorious because many nobles and wise men met together from different parts. . . . For as strangers come from different parts and provinces, so they bring with them different tongues and customs. . . . For a kingdom of one language and one custom is weak and fragile." Koloman was at pains to induce immigration into Hungary from the more advanced lands of the West, and labored to promote trade and agriculture. At first most of these Germans came from Bavaria and Swabia—that is, from southern Germany, which lay nearest to Hungary. Budapest and Pressburg early had a German quarter, and many German settlers were to be found in the territory round about, as the place-names still indicate. To this day, in this part of Hungary, a German, no matter whence his origin, is often called a *Schwab*, or *Swabian*.

The commerce of the Danube basin and of the northern Adriatic which had been ruined by the pagan Magyars, revived under the first Christian kings of Hungary; the corn of the Hungarian plain became a valuable export to Constantinople, and furs and iron were exchanged for silks, gems, wines, and chased armor. Merchants and pilgrims from the West were again free to cross the ancient Dacia as they had not been for seven centuries, and the reopening of this new avenue gave an immediate and considerable impulse to the Crusades. As early as 1092 Mohammedan merchants are found in Hungary. Earlier than this an Hungarian colony is settled in Constantinople.[2]

But while Hungarian culture was thus predominantly German and Latin Christian, it is interesting to observe that a considerable amount of Byzantine culture poured into Hungary from Constantinople. Hungary in the twelfth century touched the large commerce of the Levant at two points: Constantinople, and Zara on the Adriatic. The quickened trade with Constantinople also brought missionaries of the Greek Church

[2] Beazley, *Dawn of Modern Geography*, II, 484.

into Hungary who competed with Bavarian Benedictines, Slovenes, and Italians from the diocese of Friuli and Aquileia.

In the twelfth century Hungary enjoyed great prosperity. The brilliant medieval German historian Otto of Freising, the uncle of Frederick Barbarossa, goes outside of his subject in order to describe the admirable character of Hungarian civilization at that time. He admits that Hungary was yet far behind Germany in material prosperity and moral culture, as well she might have been, and comments upon the rudeness of the manners in the country, the absence of towns, the wretched wattled houses in which they lived, their still semi-nomadic condition and rudimentary agriculture. Nevertheless, his account is a tribute to the advancement of the former utterly barbarian Magyars along the road of civilization.

One of the most influential agencies of colonization and culture in Hungary in the twelfth century was the French Cistercians. The influence which French civilization, largely through this order, had upon Hungary in the twelfth century is an interesting fact, King Bela III (1173–96) married Anne de Châtillon, daughter of the famous Crusader Renaud de Châtillon, and his two most intimate counselors were descendants of French families settled in Hungary. His ambition seems to have been to graft French institutions upon the nascent Magyar civilization, perhaps as a counterpoise to German influence. He founded a school at Veszprem for teaching *"prout Parisiis in Francia,"* created a royal chancery modeled on French lines, and personally appealed to the abbot of Citeaux, who visited him in 1183, to establish French Cistercians in his kingdom. The influence of this order soon became very great. Bela founded the abbey of Egresch on the bank of the Maros and called thither French monks from Pontigny in Champagne (1179); the abbey of Pilis (1184), which still exists and whose first members came from Acay near Besançon; and the abbey of Kerz in the district of Hermannstadt. After the death of Anne de Châtillon, Bela III married Marguerite, a sister of Philip Augustus. Some years after his decease, we find at the court of his son Emeric the French troubador Vidal of Toulouse who has left us some verses upon his hospitality. Everything demonstrates that French influence was very high in Hungary at the end of the twelfth century.

But the attempt of the Hungarian kings to limit the infiltration of outsiders into their country was largely rendered nugatory by the Crusades, for the valley of the Danube became an important route to the Holy Land. Even before that great military enterprise began, thousands of pilgrims were flocking through Hungary. It is impossible to think that these swarms of humanity did not leave an important residuum within the land. Indeed, we have the evidence of it in the Golden Bull of king Andrew II (1222).

The chief German communities in Hungary were to be found in the mining regions. Exploration of the Tatra and the Carpathians had followed the discovery of gold in the Erzgebirge on the edge of Bohemia. The Magyar princes held out inducements to these Saxon miners upon whose skill they were dependent for the working of the mines, and these latter flocked into Hungary by thousands in the twelfth century, bringing their own language, laws, customs. By 1150 the slopes of the Tatra, the valleys of the Waag and Popper rivers and the table-lands of Liptau and Zips were dotted with German villages whose names are reminiscent of Saxon origin. It is significant that the names of so many of these places terminate in -dorf, a common local suffix in Saxony. Commingled with these Saxon miners was a considerable element of Bavarian and Austrian incomers.

The greatest German colony was in Transylvania, whose rich ores attracted thousands of miners from the Erzgebirge, from the Tatra and Carpathian regions, and even from Thuringia in the twelfth century, commingled with whom was a considerable Frankish population from the region of the middle Rhine. In a papal document of 1191 these Germans are called *Teutonici ultrasilvani*. The place-names in this southeastern quarter of Europe are strikingly German to this day.

But military considerations simultaneously operated together with the gold-fever to induce this immigration of German settlers into Transylvania. For with the removal of the Hungarians from the plains of southern Russia to the great plain of central Europe, the evacuated space had been gradually filled, early in the eleventh century, by the Pechenegs and Kumans—Tartar or half-Tartar nations whose country vaguely extended around the Black Sea coast from the Don to the Danube. Hence we find German borderers colonized along this frontier for the purpose of defense. Finally, after the Third Crusade the Teutonic Knights settled here for some years before their removal to Prussia in 1224.

The permeation of things Germanic was not quantitatively or qualitatively in the same proportion in Bohemia and Poland, and was different from that into Hungary. In Silesia German influence was overwhelming after the twelfth century. In Bohemia, where the process was slower, and sometimes not without check, the spread of German influence continued until the Hussite wars in the fifteenth century. In Poland the degree of Germanization was never so great as in Silesia or Bohemia, and German colonization was of varying density in different parts of the country. The earliest and most widely spread German influence in these countries was that of commerce and trade. Already traders, probably German Jews, in the ninth century had become very active in Moravia, for we find the significant words in a chronicle:

mercatores undecumque sunt—merchants are to be found everywhere.
We have even a tariff list of the late Carolingian period.

The period beginning with the reign of Bratislav II (1061–1092),
marks the first nucleus of a permanent, predominatingly German,
community in Bohemia, settled within the country. Below the castle
of Prague on the Hradčany and in the Vyšehrad Street, besides the
rich and prosperous Jewish slave dealers, there gathered a medley of
merchants. This also was the place where the fairs were held. These
Prague fairs were widely famous by the eleventh century, and drew
to Prague traders and merchants from Poland, Novgorod and Kiev in
Russia, Italy, France, and, of course, from Germany. Many of these
traders remained in Prague and settled there permanently, especially the
Germans. They formed a compact community about the Church of St.
Paul. Bratislav granted them privileges, chiefly the right of self-
government under a magistrate of their own election, and the right of
living under their own laws. This grant was a most important privilege. In the course of time their settlement grew and extended by reason
of accessions from the ranks of other incoming merchants and by natural increase, so that in course of time the Germans formed an entire
quarter in Prague. The Prague community grew rich upon commerce,
and its population continually increased. By the time of Ottokar I it
occupied almost the whole of the present Old Town of Prague. When
in 1235 the quarter was circumvallated with a wall and a ditch, it formed
a veritable medieval town.

Bavarian and Swabian farmers overflowed the Bohemian border from
Southeast Germany as did Saxon settlers from the northeastward expansion movement. Situated as Bohemia was in an angle between the
two great projections of German power, this overflow was inevitable.
The anarchy of Germany during the long years of civil disturbance in
the time of Henry IV materially influenced this exodus of the peasantry
from Germany into Bohemia. Thus it came about that the German element in Bohemia was much more mixed than in the Baltic or Danubian
provinces.

The history of Bohemia in Hohenstaufen times is chiefly interesting
from the point of view of German town-planting. As in Silesia and
Brandenburg, so in Bohemia, we find the simultaneous operations of
town-planting, with the attendant development of trade and commerce,
and forest and moor redemption by German farming folk brought in
by churchmen and nobles. But Bohemia was not so heavily Germanized
as Silesia and Brandenburg, nor were the colonists so evenly distributed
throughout the country. The Czech population never lost its identity
as did the Slav population in Silesia. German historians have been inclined to disparage the culture of Bohemia in the Middle Ages before
the German colonization. But Bohemian civilization in the twelfth and

thirteenth centuries was superior to that of Poland, and it is historically unjust to include both in the same category. On the other hand it is an exaggeration of the self-sufficiency of Bohemia before the coming of the Germans into the land to say that all the usual trades were practised in Bohemia before the colonial era began, and that the Germans brought in only the German miners' skill and German craft gilds. Bohemia in every economic way was behind Germany, but superior to Poland.

The remoteness of Poland for a long time kept her shrouded in obscurity. The influence of this physical isolation upon the Poles was perceived as far back as the twelfth century by the earliest medieval Polish historian, known as Gallus, who wrote: *"Regio Polonorum ab itineribus peregrinorum est remota, et nisi transeuntibus in Russiam pro mercimonio paucis nota."* That sentence epitomizes much of early Polish history. The wide and distant plain of Poland, covered with lakes and swamps, was even more difficult to penetrate than the *"circuitus vasta horrens solitudo"* of the densely forested mountains of Bohemia. In a word, isolation was a more effective protection to medieval Poland against Germanization than to either medieval Bohemia or medieval Hungary.

The zealous catholicism of the Poles made monasteries of German foundation and German inmates the first important economic influence in Poland. For there, as in early western Europe, the founding of a monastery was usually an act of colonization. These monasteries kept in close communication with their mother monasteries in Germany, and spread their own culture and customs among the people of their districts. The monks brought over from Germany new methods of agriculture and horticulture, and by going out among the people and teaching them improved ways of farming, they exercised a beneficial influence upon the social and economic conditions of the peasantry.

Artisans and craftsmen also came to minister to the wants of the new monastic settlements. But the grants of land given to these foundations did not always include the right to reduce the local population to serfdom. Accordingly the monasteries were often compelled to import foreign labor, which as a rule was chiefly of the unfree class. "In this way the monasteries which at the time of their introduction into Poland were the only large private land-owners, supplied an example of organization of large manors and the utilization of the half-free class of foreign peasants who became attached to the soil."

In course of time German traders found their way into Poland and established themselves in "quarters" as they had done in Prague and other Bohemian towns.

The old Polish towns of Cracow, Lwow (Lemberg), Poznan (Posen), and Plock received a great influx of German merchants, and were regarded in Germany as the outposts of German commerce, civilization, and political influence. The native municipal law was supplanted by Magdeburg or Halle law, German silver money became the predominating currency, and even the municipal records began to be kept in the German language. Thus the cities became strongholds of German influence. The influx of masses of Germans was especially great with the extension of the Teutonic Order on the Baltic seacoast in the beginning of the thirteenth century.

Boleslaw V (Wstydliwy = the Bashful; 1243–79) gave this Germanizing process all the assistance he could. In his time colonization from Brandenburg east of the Oder was very aggressive. The German colonization on the Vistula also was given a powerful impetus. The land of the Prussians was wrested from them by the Teutonic Knights, and was slowly Germanized and Christianized. It was a peculiar blindness on the part of the Polish princes that this subjugation by Prussia received their aid; the last formidable Prussian native chieftain, Swietopolk, was defeated by the Knights, who were aided by the Polish Kings.

But there is another side to the culture history of these border states. While Hungary, Bohemia, and Poland for the most part looked toward the West, it must not be forgotten that their eastern edges were one with Russia. All along the eastern edge of these three nations bordering upon Germany, from the Baltic to the Black Sea, the Poles, the Bohemians, the Magyars touched hands with the trade of medieval Russia, of which the principal centres were Novgorod and Kiev. The mighty Mongol invasion in 1241 almost destroyed this communication. The sack of Kiev and the cutting off of Novgorod from its Byzantine and Baghdad connections is a turning-point in the history of medieval commerce so far as far eastern Europe is concerned. It helped Venice and Genoa by destroying the ancient and competing Varangian route and threw the transportation of almost all Levantine goods into the Mediterranean.

The great Tartar invasion of Russia also had another effect upon Poland. A large part of the population of Poland was either cut off or scattered, and a new influx of German settlers came into the country.

The country was in ruins and the population either scattered or exterminated. The refugees went north and helped to colonize the sparsely inhabited areas and to clear the forests to the east of the Vistula in Mazovia. On the heels of the receding Tartars came the Germans. Theirs was a movement along the line of least resistance. The new settlers were spared the hard labor of the pioneers, as the soil they occupied had been used for arable purposes centuries before. There was no need of clearing primeval forest or colonizing an utter wilderness.[3]

[3] Lewinski-Corwin, *History of Poland,* p. 36.

The manner in which the actual colonization was carried out was similar to that of Brandenburg and Bohemia. It was done by an agent (*Vogt*) who undertook to settle a stretch of land with colonists. Since the Polish nobles and land-owners were forced to offer special inducements in order to attract colonists to their deserted lands as quickly as possible, lands were offered exempt from taxes for a number of years. The only obligation was a rent, which was paid annually and was collected by the *Vogt*.

CHAPTER XXI

SCANDINAVIA *

DENMARK, after the time of Canute the Great, (1000–1035), was confined to Jutland, the islands of Fünen and Zealand, Scania (or Schonen) in southern Sweden, and parts of the Baltic coast of Germany. A Bamberg priest traveling through Denmark about 1100 has left the following description of the country: "The country has towns and villages without walls, only palisades and earthworks. The homes of the nobility and the churches are very poor and of bad taste. The inhabitants are engaged chiefly in hunting, fishing, and cattle-breeding, for with their poor system of agriculture all their wealth is measured in cattle."

The commerce and material and moral civilization of Denmark developed rapidly during the twelfth century. The towns increased. These were almost always situated upon the coast, for the Danes were far more a seafaring people than an agricultural people. When the towns were walled for protection against pirates we find the names of most of them ending in -borg and the merchants and craftsmen within them called burghers (borgere). Examples are Aalborg, Flensborg, Vordingborg, Faaborg. Other towns in Denmark, as in France and Germany, grew up around the monasteries. Still others owed their origin immediately and specifically to natural sites conducive to trade. The place-suffix -kjoebing, meaning "market," gives the clue to these towns of which Copenhagen (Kjoebenhavn, "Market Haven,") is the most striking illustration. Copenhagen was founded in 1165 by Absalom, the bishop of Lund, who erected a castle in the harbor in order to protect the merchants from pirates.

Ribe and Haddeby in Schleswig were the most important Danish towns on the German mainland. Adam of Bremen tells us that from Schleswig one sailed east to Jumna and from there farther east to Russia. From Ripen on the other side of Jutland, one sailed west to Saxony (Bremen), Friesland, and England. In the eleventh century the town of Aarhaus, farther north in Jutland, was connected in trade with the Danish islands, Scania, and Norway. Rosckilde on the island of Zealand was in early times the home of the kings. In Scania was the town of Lund, "at which town," Adam of Bremen says, "there is much gold, which they get from piracy on the numerous barbarous nations in the Baltic Sea: and for reason of the tribute paid to him the king of Denmark tolerates these piracies."

* MAP. Shepherd, *Historical Atlas*, 58–59.

Along the south coast of the Baltic, at the mouths of the rivers, there were settlements of Danish merchants in the ancient Slavonic towns such as Stettin, Wollin, and Danzig. These Danish traders looked with jealous eye upon those German merchants who had pressed beyond the Elbe and sought also to trade among the Obodrites and the Pomeranians. For many years a fierce competition existed between them. But the German conquest of Pomerania in 1124, the Crusade of Henry the Lion in 1147, and the founding of Lübeck in 1158 finally turned the scale and German commercial ascendancy excluded the Danes from the Baltic field. During these tumultuous years the Baltic and the Danish Belts swarmed with Danish, Slavonic, and German pirates.

Although excluded from Mecklenburg and Pomerania the Danes tenaciously hung on to Schleswig and were ambitious to extend their sway over Holstein, and thus to capture the two cities Hamburg and Lübeck, commanding the isthmus and an important trade route between the Baltic and the North Sea, which was shorter and safer from piracy than the long and dangerous route through the Belts, in which navigation was very difficult. In the early part of the thirteenth century we therefore find the Danes endeavoring to take advantage of the upset condition of affairs following the partition of Saxony, the fall of Henry the Lion, and the rival struggles which filled the first years of the reign of Frederick II. In order to make head against the pretender, Otto of Brunswick, the young emperor, made overture to Denmark and offered to yield Holstein, Lauenburg, and part of Mecklenburg to the Danes in return for support. Hamburg and Lübeck took alarm and were supported by many of the North German princes. The conflict was resolved at the battle of Bornhoeved (1227), which put a stop to Danish aggression upon German territory for centuries and enabled Lübeck without molestation to form the Hanseatic League and extend German commercial sway over the whole north.

In the thirteenth century, in the reign of Waldemar II, we find that Danish towns, all of which had their origin in fishing villages, harbors or market-places, or around a castle, were still small. Most of the trade between Denmark and England in the thirteenth century was with the town of Ribe. King John in 1208 took Nikolaus Marinellus, a citizen of Ribe, under his care. Another merchant from Ribe who lived about this time was Richervinus de Rippa, *mercator de Denemarch*. About 1300 Ribe was the only Danish town that sent ships to England. By that time the commerce of Denmark was controlled by the Hanseatic League.

From this brief consideration of the history of Danish commerce we may pass to that of Norway. Owing to its geographical situation most Norwegian trade was with England. It must be remembered that during this period Norway held sway over most of the western islands, Iceland, Greenland, the Orkneys and Hebrides, the Shetland Islands, the Isle of Man. It also controlled part of Ireland at times. Norway itself was a bleak and barren country. For a livelihood the population depended on cattle-raising and fisheries, with some hunting. Overpopulation and the almost incessant warfare of the more powerful nobles often forced the natives to leave the country. But in spite of these discouraging conditions we find times of peace during which wise kings tried to develop the resources of their country. Because the people had to depend so much on fishing, they became excellent sailors, and we find them doing an extensive carrying trade in the north until they were forced out of this lucrative industry by the German merchants.

Very early we hear of commerce in Norway. Viken as early as the eleventh century was visited by merchants from Saxony and Denmark, both summer and winter. The inhabitants of Viken themselves often made voyages to other countries: to England, Saxony, Flanders, Denmark. The towns had markets where foreign traders congregated to trade with the natives for their surplus wares. Among towns of this character Tönsberg was the earliest of importance. At nearly the same period we hear of Kongehelle, Stavanger, Steukiver, and Levanger. Nideras (Drontheim) was founded by Olof Trygversen, but did not assume any importance until the reign of Olaf the Pious (1015–30). Olaf the Pious founded Sarpsburg (near Frederickstad) and Harold Haardraade founded Oslo (Christiania) in 1050. Oslo became the capital, for it was less exposed to the raids of the Danish Vikings than other towns, and had been the harbor for the Viking ships of the most powerful nobles of Raumarike and Hedenmarken from the earliest times. It had also been a rendezvous of foreign merchants. Bergen, destined to become the most important of all the commercial cities of Norway, was founded by Olaf Kyrre about 1075. It had also previously been used as a harbor for the native Viking ships and foreign merchant shipping.

Some of the progressive kings of Norway, during intervals of peace, labored to develop the resources of their country, and especially to encourage commerce with foreign countries. During the time of Harold Haardraade (about 1050), in spite of the wars with Denmark, foreign commerce did not cease even with Denmark, but was carried on in neutral ships, as shown by the histories of Audun Islaendings and Sneglu-Halle. With the northern European countries, and especially with England, commerce flourished. It is related that Thore in his voyage to England, remained there a long time and brought home many costly wares to the king. When Sneglu-Halle, after an extended visit in England, wished to return home, he tried to get passage on a Norwegian ship (seemingly a common sight in the harbors of England), but so many Germans had secured passage with their numerous wares, that there was no room for him and he had to use intimidation to get room. Denmark, England, Ireland, Scotland, France, and Germany were the principal countries with which the Norwegians traded; and Danish, English, Saxon, and German ships frequented the Norwegian harbors, especially Viken. Norwegian ships found their way into Russian harbors also for the sake of the furs and the costly Asiatic wares. There was also trade with Greenland and Iceland.

In the twelfth and thirteenth centuries the trade of Norway became more extensive. King Eystein did much to encourage commerce and industry. He improved the laws and built churches. Through persuasion, gifts, and appeals to its self-interest, he regained the allegiance of the Swedish province of Jemteland, which had belonged to Norway under Haakon the Good. Knowing the importance of the fisheries as a natural resource, he had huts erected at Vaagen, for the accommodation of the fishermen, and also a church and monastery for their spiritual welfare. At Agdeness, where many ships were wrecked, he made an artificial harbor by the construction of a mole. He placed sea-marks and beacons on certain rocks and promontories to guide the sailors along the dangerous coast. In the reign of Sigurd Magnusson (1130) Bergen was a large and wealthy town. Orderic says that ships from all the corners of the world came there with riches. We also get the same impression of flourishing trade and growing cosmopolitanism from Ragnvald Jarl's impression of the town upon his voyage from Grimsby to Bergen. "The ship came to the town," the Saga says, "where there was a large crowd of people gathered from both the north and the south, as well as many foreigners, who brought many good wares to the country."

Bergen became the great fish market of Europe. It soon became the emporium of Icelandic commerce. The first foreigners to have special trading privileges in this new town of Olaf Kyrre's were the English. There was also considerable trade with the northern German cities, Scotland, and Iceland. In the twelfth century there were certain ships in Bergen that were called *Englansfarere*. These ships were Norwegian. They brought cargoes of honey, wool, cloth, and wine to Bergen. The wine must have come from the Rhineland or France and English merchants seem to have been middlemen in this trade. Trade was carried on between Bergen and the rich herring fisheries of Skanör and Falsterbo.

William of Malmesbury speaks of the commerce of York and says that the city was visited by merchants from Germany and Ireland (especially the Norwegian towns of Ireland, Dublin and Waterford). Another important commercial town on the eastern coast of England was Grimsby, which at the beginning of the twelfth century was visited by ships from Norway, the Orkneys, Scotland, and the Hebrides. Even in the reign of Henry I (1100–1135) the commerce of the Norwegians in

Grimsby is mentioned in the archives. The most important town on the western coast of England in the eleventh century was Chester, on the Dee. From the Domesday Book we learn that the northern fur trade was of great importance for Chester. The town paid an annual tax of marten to the king in the reign of Edward the Confessor. Chester probably stood in close commercial intercourse with Norway because of the Norwegian domination over the Isle of Man, the Orkneys, and the Hebrides. William of Malmesbury calls Bristol *vicus celeberrimus,* "a famous town, its haven being a commodious receptacle for all ships coming thither from Ireland, Norway, and other foreign lands." From another source we find that the chief export of Bergen in 1190 to the Germans was butter, and the chief import was wine, while from England came wheat, honey, wax, cloth, and copper kettles. We have an interesting account of Bergen of the year 1191.

Bergen is in its eminence one of the largest towns in this land, containing a royal castle and many relics. . . . There are many people and many monasteries for the monks and nuns. It is rich with resources. It is impossible to relate the amount of dried fish, which is called *skrejd.* One can see here a congregation of ships and peoples from all the corners of the world, Iceland, Greenland, England, Germany, Denmark, Sweden, and Gothland. There is a great surplus of honey, lumber, good cloths, herring, and other wares. One can buy almost anything.

In the thirteenth century Norwegian trade went exclusively to the eastern coast of England; to Grimsby, Boston, Yarmouth, Scarborough, and especially Lynn. King Sven of Norway made a treaty with John of England and received military aid from him. Soon after his coronation Haakon Haakonsson of Norway in the fall of 1217 made a commercial treaty with Henry III of England, which was later renewed in 1269 at Winchester. The archbishop of Nidaros and the monastery at Lyse near Bergen received certain toll exemptions and trading privileges from the English kings. The Norwegian commerce with England probably reached its height in the middle of the thirteenth century The peasant war which raged from the latter part of the twelfth century was ended by the fall of the Ribbungar in 1227. After this, trade and shipping could flourish. We find in the reign of Haakon Haakonsson a marked increase in commerce. At the end of June, 1224, fifteen Norwegian ships lay in the harbor of Lynn; this number was never reached in the fourteenth century. In the following year (1225) the number was greater. Henry III of England ordered the port officials at Lynn in August, 1225, to welcome Norwegian ships. He permitted these merchants in spite of the prohibitions on the exportation of grain, to export a thousand *malter* of wheat. German competition became too strong for the Norwegians in London, and in the thirteenth century they confined their commerce to the more northern ports of England. In 1215 we hear of the last ship from Norway in Bristol, the connection ceasing after the treaty of Perth, when the Hebrides and the Isle of Man were ceded to Scotland. By the middle of the next century the German merchants, by forcing certain trading privileges from the king, practically controlled Bergen and its commerce.

Sweden from 1000 to 1300 included only the eastern part of modern Sweden. Scania, the most fertile part of Sweden today, belonged at that time to Denmark. Sweden was perhaps the most barbaric of the Scandinavian countries, for it was the farthest removed from the civilization of Europe. Its connections were chiefly with Russia. Adam of Bremen, however, speaks of it as "a very fruitful country, rich in grain and honey, and cattle-breeding. The flow of the streams and the lay of the land was conducive to all kinds of foreign commerce." Another writer states that the exports from Sweden during the Viking period were slaves, furs, horses (for the Swedish horses were famous), wool, fish, etc. A little later lumber and iron were added to the list of exports. Travel by water was easier than by land, for there were no roads. The Swedes were, we may say, a people engaged in hunting and fishing and some cattle-raising. Toward the end of this period there was some agriculture, the raising of wheat, and some manufacture of iron and steel. The Swedes were specially skilled in making weapons and armor and in the building of ships. By the thirteenth century there were foundries in Gothland and copper works in Falem. Of the three northern countries of Europe, Sweden alone was badly situated for trade development except with half-barbarous Russia. For the Baltic was too nearly a closed sea and the only port at all giving upon the North Sea was Gothenburg on the Skaggerak, which was controlled by the Danes. For many, many years the only other Swedish place of commerce was Birka near Stockholm, but badly exposed to pirates.

The centre of foreign commerce in the Baltic was the island of Gothland, with its town of Wisby. It was the distribution point for the Baltic and North seas, for the oriental goods that came from the Black Sea by the way of the Russian rivers to Novgorod. In the Viking period Gothland was the most important commercial centre of the north, as is shown by the great number of Arabic coins that have been found on the island. The great number of English coins and the many runic stones that are memorials of those who have died in foreign lands, but especially in England, shows that the commercial intercourse between the Swedes and England must have been considerable during this early period. Wisby was not important in the tenth and eleventh centuries and did not become a town until settled by the Germans. After the rise of Wisby the native Swedish trade declined under the competition of the Germans, but did not fall entirely into the hands of these enterprising foreigners, for in the thirteenth and fourteenth centuries we still find in foreign countries, merchants from Gothland with genuine Norse names, who were not members of the Hanse. In London the Swedes enjoyed certain trading privileges as early as the Danes and Norwegians. The Swedes had established themselves in Novgorod as early as the eleventh century as traders and possessed their own church there in 1152. The German merchants of Lübeck, Hamburg, and Bremen were the strongest competitors for the Scandinavian shipping industry and finally destroyed it completely.

CHAPTER XXII

MOHAMMEDAN AND CHRISTIAN SPAIN (711–1284)

THOUGH joined to the European continent, central and southern Spain is geologically and climatically much like northern Africa. Andalusia, Murcia, Valencia have only two seasons, a wet and a dry. The annual rainfall is less than that of Italy, or Greece, which are in the same latitude. This oriental nature of the land and the climate probably accounts in part for the remarkable adaptability of the Moor and the Berber to Spanish conditions.

Spain was the earliest province of the Mohammedan Empire to shake off the authority of the khalif. Andalusia became an independent state under Abd-er-Rahman (756–788 A.D.). However, it was not until the reign of Abd-er-Rahman III, who died in 960, that the ruler took the title of khalif, and the kingdom became the Khalifate of Cordova. From the founding of the Spanish khalifate, the connection between North Africa and Andalusia was close. The Berbers formed a large part of the Mohammedan population of Spain, and they maintained intimate touch with their kinsmen across the straits. For the first half-century after the conquest there was bitter rivalry between the Berbers and the Arabs, the former claiming Spain as their conquest. Then began a general Arab migration into the peninsula with the coming of the Ommeyad prince Abd-er-Rahman I in 756, the effects of which were to introduce that brilliant Arabic culture into the West which so profoundly influenced it, and to unite Moslem Spain and Africa into a single state known as the Empire of the Two Shores.

During the three centuries following the Mohammedan conquest of North Africa and Spain, Arabic civilization in the West was of the highest quality. Agricultural products hitherto unknown to Europe were introduced and profitably cultivated. Rice, sugar-cane, cotton, dates, saffron, ginger, myrrh, mulberry trees, strawberries, lemons, quinces, figs, pomegranates, spinach, asparagus, buckwheat, and sesame constitute a variety of agricultural products which have been thought to have been introduced by the Moors. Olives, grapes, pears, and apples were produced in large quantities, and different flowers were raised for their perfume. Agriculture deserved the name of a science in Arabic Spain at a time when it was only manual labor elsewhere. The khalifs took a deep interest in the cultivation of the soil, and pride in their own gardens. The place held by agriculture in the minds of the Moors is shown by their proverb: "He who plants or sows, and who causes the earth to produce food for man or beast, does a service the account of which will be kept for him in the sky." Agriculture was studied as a science, as the number of Arabic treatises on horticulture shows. The royal gardens were in charge of distinguished botanists.

In the twelfth century Spain produced two notable writers on agriculture and husbandry, Ibn-al-Awam and Abu Zacaria. Both were natives of Seville, and both show the influence of the writings of Columella, the Romanized Spaniard. The former is so highly regarded in Spain that as late as 1802 his treatise was translated out of Arabic into the Spanish language for the benefit of Spanish farmers. The didactic poem of Ibn Loyon on the management of fields and gardens is a valuable commentary on the excellence of Moorish agriculture, while the treatise of Ibn Khaldun far excels any similar treatise of Christian Europe for centuries. He even developed a theory of prices and the nature of capital.

The insufficient moisture in much of the land required a high degree of engineering skill to construct the irrigating canals which parceled out the water of the melting snows of the mountains over the valleys. The khalifs expended large sums in the construction of aqueducts and canals of irrigation. Abd-er-Rahman III supplied Cordova with water by means of an aqueduct, bringing the water from the mountains through lead pipes. This is only one example from many; for the irrigation system of modern Spain is but what has survived of the work of the Arabs in the Middle Ages.

Stock-raising was an important industry among the Moors in central and northern Spain, especially sheep-raising. Even in Roman times Spain was famous for its wool, and the conquest of Spain by the Mohammedans in 711 increased sheep-raising in the peninsula, for the Moors and the Berbers were naturally a pastoral people. They improved the breed by importing new species from Africa. Abd-er-Rahman III, we are told, "constructed vast troughs of stone for the use of cattle, and watering-places for horses also." It seems likely that these were in market-places; but since the fields had to be irrigated in a large part of the country, it is possible that they were for watering the stock of the pasture lands. In some of the towns the watering-place became the local market-place. Attention was also given by the Moors to the breeding of goats, and to bee culture. The promotion of these rural industries made possible a dense population in the country districts. For years of drought, provisions were laid up, and grain was stored in large underground silos, where it would keep indefinitely, thanks to the dryness of the climate.[1]

[1] Bouchier thinks these silos were in use in Spain under the Romans. Others hold that they were invented by the Spanish Moors.

The most fertile provinces of Moorish Spain were Andalusia and Murcia. Andalusia with its half-tropical climate was the garden region of the Spanish peninsula, where dates, sugar-cane, cotton, olives, etc., were cultivated, while the plains of the Guadalquivir were a veritable granary. Wine also was an important production, especially in the Xerez (whence "sherry") district. Malaga also was a famous vineyard region and exported raisins in vast quantities. Murcia, like Andalusia, under the scientific farming of the Moors, produced wheat, olives, textiles, oranges, sugar-cane.

The Moors exploited the rich mineral resources of the country they had conquered. Gold, silver, tin, lead, quicksilver, copper, red and yellow ochre, alum, and iron were mined. The raw products of these mines were valuable in themselves, but many of these substances were more valuable in the industrial arts. The chief industry was the manufacture of sword blades. Those of Toledo had a reputation over Europe on account of their excellence, both in beauty and in temper. Near Cordova, Al-Mansur founded an establishment for the manufacture of shields, which was said to turn out twelve thousand finished shields each year. Murcia was a centre for the manufacture of all kinds of instruments of brass and iron. Almost every Moorish town was engaged in leather manufacturing. The so-called Cordovan and Moroccan leathers were the product of the best tanneries of the world. The Moors introduced cotton raising and the silk industry into Spain. Both raw silk and finished cloths fabricated by the Moors of Spain were in great demand throughout Europe. Sashes famed the world over for their brilliance of color and fineness of texture were manufactured in Almeria. Carpets were made at Teulala, and bright-colored woolens were manufactured in Granada and Baza. Vases of glass or pottery, mosaics, and jewelry were other commodities which were produced by Mohammedan workmen.

The revenue system of the Moors included taxes on personal and real property, quit-rents from tenants on domain lands, a tithe on agriculture, industry, and commerce, and customs duties. In the most flourishing period these assessments were based on a census, but with the break-up of the khalifate taxation became less just and more arbitrary.

During the period of the greatest prosperity of the Moors, the tenth century, the city of Cordova had many of the characteristics of a modern city. It contained many factories and workshops. The streets were paved, and there were raised sidewalks for pedestrians. At night, it is said, "one could travel for ten miles by the light of lamps along an uninterrupted extent of buildings."

The Khalifate of Cordova was on friendly terms with the Eastern Empire. As early as 839 it is recorded that the "king" of Constantinople, "a city situated beyond the Franks," sent presents to Abd-er-Rahman, at the same time soliciting his friendship. In the year 949

Greek ambassadors stopped several days at Cordova, and an envoy accompanied them home, bearing presents from the khalif of Cordova, consisting of Andalusian horses, decked with brilliant harness, and richly worked arms and armor from Toledo and Cordova, besides other rich products of Andalusia.

But naturally the bulk of the foreign commerce of the Spanish Moors was with the Mohammedan part of the world, rather than with Christian lands. Silk and wool, both raw and woven, were carried from Spain to the markets of Syria, Africa, and Egypt. Coral, cochineal, quicksilver, iron, and other metals, and weapons, also figured in this trade. In return for these products, spices, dyes, and unguents were brought from the East to Spain. In the twelfth century, it is said that as many as a thousand vessels were engaged in this Levantine trade. Until the twelfth century the commerce of the Saracens in the Mediterranean was much greater than that of the Christians. Trade relations between the Italian cities, notably Genoa, and the Moors in Spain appear by the middle of the eleventh century. The usual voyage extended along the Barbary Coast with the return by way of Cadiz and Provence. The trade brought to Genoa metals, especially copper, and alum. Almeria, in the kingdom of Granada, was the chief port of Spain; it was crowded with ships from Syria and Egypt, Pisa and Genoa, and boasted of a thousand inns for strangers and four thousand textile shops, besides manufactures of copper, iron, and glass. In 1149 and 1161 the Genoese negotiated commercial treatises with the Moorish kingdoms of Murcia and Valencia. Between 1155 and 1164 we find records of contracts of commercial societies relative to the commerce of the Genoese at Tunis, Tripoli, Ceuta, Bougia, and other places in Africa. The Genoese were on unusually good terms with Ceuta and Bougia, it seems, as they had permanent consuls in those cities. In 1133 an embassy was sent by the Almoravid Sultan to Pisa, which was well received. The Pisans valued the trade in figs from Granada. In 1186 a new treaty between Pisa and Abu-Yusuf-Yakub, son of Yakub-Yusuf, the Almohad khalif, is recorded in which provision was made for twenty-five years of peaceful commerce between Pisa and the towns of Ceuta, Oran, Bougia, Tunis, and Andalusia. In 1180 Norman Sicily made a treaty with the king of Morocco, in whose power was "all Africa and also the Saracens who are in Spain." Florence derived a large supply of raw textile materials from Malaga and Almeria. There was little commerce between France and the Spanish Moors. It was not a direct trade but was conducted through the Catalans and the Basques. Some Moorish goods found their way as far north as Flanders before 1200.

But in spite of the fair outward showing of material prosperity which Moorish Spain exhibited, its civilization was a brittle one and too readily liable to crumble. The political and religious contact with Africa twice brought about invasions of the country—in 1087 and again in 1146—by half-barbaric and fanatical sects of the Berbers, the Almoravids and the Almohads, which politically disorganized the khalifate and set back the high and enlightened Arabic civilization it had established. The Mohammedan provincial governors or emirs seized these occasions to localize their power and make themselves as independent as possible within their jurisdictions. In the eleventh century the Khalifate of Cordova was dissolved into almost independent Mohammedan states much as the Frankish Empire had been rent asunder in the ninth century, and these petty princes too often fraternized with what ought to have been the common enemy—the Christian princes of the north.

In addition to these adverse external forces there were forces of dissolution within, less of a political than of a social nature. Moorish Spain was "a confused medley of races and faiths subject to no guiding principle." The Mozarabs or Arabized Christians who lived under the Mohammedan domination, the *muladis* or former Christians who were descended from Visigothic serfs who had embraced Islam in order to acquire freedom, and the Jews, were distracting elements in the population.

Many of the Mozarabs were employed in the administration, some even rising to become viziers and army commanders. In time the Mozarabs so completely lost their knowledge of the Latin tongue that their Scriptures and church canons had to be translated into Arabic. They were far the most tractable element in the population and with time would have become completely merged with the conquerors racially and religiously. On the other hand, the *muladis,* or converted Mohammedans, were from the first a discordant group, regarded with suspicion by both Mohammedans and Christians. It was they who fomented the separatist inclinations of the emirs and even themselves established semi-independent petty principalities in Algarbe, Murcia, and Toledo. Between 853 and 933 Toledo was a seceded Mulad state. These renegades were frequently deserters to the armies of Castile and Aragon, playing fast and loose across the border. Ibn-Mardanich, king of Valencia and Murcia, dressed as a Christian, spoke Castilian fluently, and had an army composed chiefly of Navarrese, Castilians, and Catalans. His chief captains were two sons of the count of Urgel and a grandson of the Cid's most famous lieutenant, Alvar Fuñez. The Jews, who were very numerous, formed the third non-Moorish ingredient of the population. They had suffered much from Gothic intolerance and had materially assisted the Mohammedan conquests of Spain in 711, and were generally tolerated. Their commercial instincts and business acquisitiveness made them a valuable economic factor in the community. They were much employed in the Mohammedan civil service as farmers of the revenue and tax collectors. In the eleventh century two Jews, father and son, Samuel ha Levi and Joseph, were viziers of Granada for fifty years. But their wealth, their keen competition, their identification with taxation and fiscal policy in course of time gave birth to considerable economic prejudice against the race. Yet if it had not been for the irrepressible wars waged by the Christian Spaniards of the north, all these social ingredients—Moors, Mozarabs, *muladis,* and Jews—would in great probability have finally merged racially and religiously into a homogeneous nation. But the constant assaults of the Spanish Christians upon the Moorish state prevented peaceful fusion and aggravated the cleavages.

Turning now to northern and Christian Spain, we find conditions in general strikingly different from those in southern Spain—climate, physiography, soil, people, civilization.

In the Middle Ages, Christian Spain was the least favorably situated of all the countries of Europe. Located at the southwest angle of the continent, no international route crossed it. The huge barrier of the Pyrenees all but cut it off from communication with its northern neighbor, and the formidable sea-power of the Mohammedan states until the twelfth century jeopardized what maritime commerce it might otherwise have had. There was almost no commerce on the Atlantic side, and the drift of Mediterranean commerce out of the East was not toward Spain, but to Italy and Provence. Moreover, the orographic structure of the peninsula, its high plateaux, dividing mountain ranges and unnavigable rivers, seriously impeded commercial communication and the transportation and exchange of its natural resources. Since all the rivers of the peninsula have their sources in the mountains which almost completely ring these plateaux, and since their current is very swift, river navigation is impossible; they are quite as difficult to ford or to bridge. The physical dislocation of the land thus foreordained the formation of petty principalities, the union of which was never more than partially accomplished in medieval times. This great topographical variation is accompanied by marked climatic variation due to the many mountain ranges. Central Spain is a high, almost arid plateau, divided into two parts by the Sierra de Guadarrama. In consequence of this wide physiographic variation, broad generalization of medieval Spanish economic and social history is impossible. The truest statement is that physiography and climate especially favored pasturage and stock-raising.

During the universal dissolution of Charlemagne's Empire in the ninth century the Spanish Mark also had disintegrated, and the Moors again over-ran much of the territory north of the Ebro River from which they had been driven by Frankish arms. Much of the Christian population seems either to have been destroyed or to have fled into Gaul. Some sought the asylum of the few walled towns like Barcelona, Vich, and Gerona, which were able to resist the Moorish arms. The

Moorish horsemen, though they over-ran and devastated the valley country, were unable to penetrate the high and remote fastnesses of the Pyrenees where the inhabitants found refuge.

The Christian peoples of northern Spain, in the ninth and tenth centuries, formed tiny but furiously bellicose kingdoms, whose fusion ultimately was to form the Spain of today. But in the Middle Ages, although there was some tendency toward union, they never became wholly united. In the northwest the population was of Basque origin, and had never been completely Romanized or Gothicized. The Basques were a stubborn, hardy, fiercely democratic people of small farmers and cattle-raisers inland, and of fishermen and whalers along the Biscayan coast. In Navarre and Aragon the population was of Romanized Gothic origin, living almost entirely as cattle-raisers in the high valleys pocketed between the peaks of the Pyrenees and subsidiary ranges. Only the Catalonians of the northeastern coast—politically organized as the county of Barcelona—may be said to have had any commerce.

These earliest little states underneath the great mountain wall which extends across all northern Spain from the Atlantic to the Mediterranean, were (1) the principality of Asturias, a mountainous refuge never conquered by the Moors, a narrow strip bounded on the north by a range fringing the very coast, and separated from the interior by a tremendous barrier having only one pass, the great Puerto de Pájares, which Oviedo, the one important place in the Asturias, commanded. No invading army ever penetrated into this remote little territory in which the hardy Christian, but slightly civilized population, pastured their cattle, for the high humidity nurtured a heavy growth of grass. (2) East of Asturias in the angle of the Bay of Biscay around Pamplona sprang up the little kingdom of Navarre, a country rich in forests and mountain pastures where stock-raising was almost the only industry—except fighting the Moor. (3) East of Navarre, wedged in between it and the seaboard county of Barcelona, in the very centre of the Pyrenees in the valley of the Arga, an affluent of the upper Ebro, was formed the little county destined in course of years to grow into the kingdom of Aragon. In the ninth century the name "Aragon" was confined to the county lying in the upper valley of this torrent. Here again the economic resources were almost wholly cattle, sheep, and hogs, the last feeding upon the mast and acorns of immense forests of oak and chestnut. (4) The county of Barcelona, on the Mediterranean coast and possessed of an ancient Roman and Visigothic port, was the only one of this fringe of Christian states in northern Spain which may be said to have possessed any commerce; and that was slight in the ninth and tenth centuries, owing to the seapower of the Mohammedans in the Mediterranean.

The civilization of Christian Spain rose as that of Moslem Spain declined. When the latter was at its apogee in the tenth century, the small Christian principalities in the north were in a semi-barbarous condition. Their economic life was rude and crude, and was hardly manifest before the eleventh century, when the Navarrese, the Castilians, the Aragonese, and the Catalans began the "reconquest," piece by piece, of their country from the infidel. Unfortunately the early development of the material prosperity of these Christian kingdoms in Spain is very imperfectly known. As in other parts of Europe, in Spain, too, the economic unfolding was connected with the progress of political institutions. Material prosperity increased in some proportion to the growth of the royal authority. But the process is not nearly so visible in Spain as in Germany or Italy or France, and, speaking in the broad, Spain lingered from a century to a century and a half behind other countries of Europe. Castile in 1350 was relatively about where France was in 1200.

Christian power in the Spanish peninsula expanded from two centres, Asturias-Navarre and Aragon-Barcelona. The former was destined to create the kingdom of Leon-Castile, the latter the kingdom of Aragon. Backed by the free and fighting population of the Basques in the Asturias, the population of Galicia was the first to expel the invader. Between 739 and 757 Alfonso "the Catholic" overran and conquered the plains as far as the Douro, although the Moors continued to make annual forays into the land, more for plunder of horses and cattle than in hope of reconquest. By 910 the northwestern country was so far made safe from the enemy that the capital was removed by García from Oviedo to Leon, and the now enlarged principality of the Asturias erected into the kingdom of Leon.

But the frontier of Leon was exposed to perpetual Moorish attack, and hence a Mark was established there to guard the kingdom at the place where the plains of the interior began to run up into the high hills. This Mark, as elsewhere in Europe where similar conditions of danger existed, was protected by a line of castles, which in course of time gave their name to the territory. Not only Christian but Moor called the land Castile or the Land of Castles (*Kashtellah*). Into the protected area behind the long line of these *castillos* settlers flocked, and occupied the land as farmers and ranchers; and around the castles grew up a clustered population of colonists (*poblaciones*), which in slow lapse of time developed a town organization and were given charters, or *fueros*. Among the earliest of these groups we find Anaya and Santillan (about 882), Burgos and Ovierna (about 890), Coruña del Conde, Oca, San Esteban de Gormez and Sepulveda in the tenth century. The hero of this border and the creator of Castile was the half legendary, half historical Rodrigo, whose successors were never more than nominally subject to the kings of Leon.

It was natural that Leon, Navarre, and Castile should gravitate together, for they had a common foe, a similar economy, and a population essentially identical. The last heiress of Rodrigo married Sancho of Navarre, and in 1037 their son Ferdinand married the heiress of Leon. Hence in this eventful year Leon, Navarre, and Castile were united. The territory of Navarre later slipped into the hands of Aragon. But Leon and Castile, although before 1230 they were only loosely united, nevertheless formed a substantial and formidable state in the north and central portion of the Spanish peninsula. Ferdinand, realizing the manifest destiny of Castile to become the greater state, formally took the title of king of Castile and removed the capital from Leon to Burgos. The old order was reversed; Leon became a province of the younger state, which had absorbed the older territory into itself. The great victory of Calat Anazor in 1102 ruined the hopes of the khalifate of stemming the Christian advance into the heart of the peninsula. In the eleventh century Castile spread its sway across the Douro as far as the Sierra de Guadarrama, steadily colonizing the land with settlers, establishing castles and fortified towns and granting *fueros*. It is written of Sancho García in 1021 that "he gave good *fueros* and customs to all Castile." (*"Dedit bonos foros et mores in tota Castella."*)

Ranching was almost the sole occupation of the inhabitants, and the staple articles of trade were wool and leather goods. Even the monasteries, of which numbers were of French foundation, were great fortified ranch-houses on whose lands the dependent population were cowboys, shepherds, leather and wool workers. The border warfare was practically a constant series of cattle raids and sheep drives on both sides. Naturally the zone of territory between Christian and Mohammedan domination was a bitterly fought over border, almost wholly desolate. The war of Moor and Christian was chiefly an economic strife. Sheep, cattle, and horses were the prizes striven for. "Whenever the infidels withdrew from a district they deliberately devastated it so as to prevent their foes from following close upon their heels; they thereby created a wide neutral zone or No Man's Land, which, coupled with the natural poverty of the great *meseta,* opposed the most effective barrier to the Christian advance." The great *despoblado* of central Spain in its depleted population and its absence of towns is to this day a mournful memorial of those decimating conflicts. No living thing was safe within this intermediate zone. The familiar saying, "Castles in Spain" to signify a fantastic or chimerical idea, is as old as the twelfth century, and is cited in the *Romaunt de la Rose.* It meant that castles were impossible in such a land, for if not destroyed they would be seized by one side or the other and converted into strongholds against the other foe. Romance has cast its glamour over these border wars, especially in the case of the Cid Campeador. But the Cid of history was a desperado, a border ruffian, and a renegade, as often fighting on the side of the crescent as on that of the cross. Indeed, each side recruited its following to a large degree from the lawless frontier element.

Before the thirteenth century the medieval Spaniard was not greatly actuated by race antagonism or religious fanaticism; his ruling motive in war against the infidel was an economic one. "A Spanish knight of the Middle Ages fought neither for his country nor for his religion; he fought, like the Cid, to get something to eat." He coveted possession of the flocks and herds of his Moorish neighbor and necessarily had also to acquire the wide pastures on which these herds grazed. The root of the Spaniards' characteristic aversion to agriculture is perhaps to be found in the prevailing physiographic feature of the country whose dry plateaux were incapable of intensive cultivation. But the natural infertility of the *meseta* was aggravated by the interminable border warfare. Consequently, stock-raising was the only profitable industry, for pasturage could be found where crops were impossible. Moreover, in event of a raid there was always a chance that the stock might be driven to a place of safety, whereas standing crops were certain to be put to the torch by the invader. This condition of things in turn had a marked social effect. It made impossible in Castile the growth of a fully developed feudal system, such as existed in France. For feudal society was eminently an agricultural society. Castilian nobles, it is true, were large landowners, but their lands were grazing lands and not farms. They were ranchers, not proprietors. The dependents upon these ranches were herdsmen, and hence half nomadic, in winter living in wretched adobe huts, in summer in tents. In winter they dwelt on the plains; in summer, when the fervent heat dried up the pasturage, they drove their flocks to the cooler and moister pastures in the mountains. The manorial village as an economic and social unit, with its complex organization and immemorial customs, such as one finds in central Europe, hardly existed in Spain. On the other hand, the constant warfare, the ever-present insecurity, promoted castle-building and fostered the walled town to a far greater extent than elsewhere in Europe. "The problem of repeopling the conquered lands was in reality far more urban than rural. The boundaries were continually shifting; land which had been captured one day was likely to be raided and possibly recaptured by the enemy the next. The neutral zone between the rival forces could not possibly be occupied by a scattered and consequently defenseless agricultural population; it was essential for those who ventured to take possession of it to concentrate and intrench themselves in compact groups—in other words, to found cities." In France and in Germany country villages and rural communities abounded in the Middle Ages. In Spain they were few. In the rest of Europe the bulk of the population lived in the country during the feudal age. In Spain, on the other hand, the bulk of the population was urban and the country was sparsely peopled, and the distance between communities was immense. Country life in Spain was lonely, for the villages were few and isolated. In more feudalized parts of Europe villages were thick.

The intervention of thousands of French Crusaders in the eleventh century resulted in a new aggressive movement against Islam, and a new and great expansion of Castile. The war was now carried down into the centre of the country. Toledo was taken in 1085, and the Tagus was crossed. The capture of Valencia followed in 1094. In this wise a New Castile was created beteen the Sierra de Guadarrama and the Guadiana river, which was steadily advanced by successive lines of castles behind which the Christian population flooded in and settled. Alfonso VI (died 1109) liberally endowed the monasteries, protected merchants, and promoted pilgrimages, especially that to the great shrine of St. James of Compostella. The fair of Medina del Campo appears in the eleventh century, and those of Segovia and Valladolid in the twelfth. Yet the relative inferiority of the commerce of Spain, when contrasted with that of other countries of Europe at the same time, is shown in the existence of so few fairs, and also in the further and curious fact that these fairs were annual or even biennial, and did not last more than four weeks. In other parts of Europe at the same time fairs were held every spring and autumn, and sometimes even in summer.

Want of outlet to the sea was for centuries a serious deterrent to Castilian commerce. Cadiz and Seville were, of course, blocked by Mohammedan possession. The natural exit was by way of the Douro and Tagus rivers to Oporto and Lisbon. But unfortunately for Castile these ports were closed by the rebellion of Portugal from Castilian vassalage in 1139. Castile did not reach blue water until the conquest of Seville in 1248 and that of Cadiz in 1262. If the loss of Castilian control over Portugal had not taken place, in all probability Castile would early have become a maritime power like Aragon.

Commerce in Spain, as in other parts of Europe, grievously suffered from the imposition of provincial tolls, the variety of coin in circulation, and the confusion in weights and measures. In these respects medieval Spain was neither better nor worse than the rest of Europe in the same time. But from these inhibitions the inhabitants of the three Basque provinces of the northwest were exempt. The love of freedom among this hardy people, wholly made up of small farmers and fishermen, was proverbial. The Basques had always remained free, if not completely independent, and even Castilian pride had to bend before their rugged democratic spirit. So refractory were the Basques that the famous Gonsalvo de Cordova in the sixteenth century said he would rather command a troop of lions than one of Basques. In the three Basque provinces of Guipuzcoa, Vizcaya (Biscay), and Alava entire freedom of trade existed, both internal and external. The Ebro on the south was the line of limitation.

Evidences of industrial development in Castile are not great before the fourteenth century. The absence of gild organization among both merchants and craftsmen until late in the Middle Ages tells its own story of slight industrial activity. Most of the trades were plied by the Moors and the Jews. This backwardness of industry in Castile, when compared with industry in other European countries, made the kings jealous to protect and to stimulate the few local industries that existed. While one does not discover this protective policy in France before the fourteenth century, it is manifest in Castile in the thirteenth. The great weakness of Castilian industry was that it was chiefly founded upon the technical skill of the non-Christian element of the population, the Moors and the Jews, although the Mozarabs formed a considerable proportion of the industrial population. For contrary to a widely prevalent belief, after the conquest the Moorish population was generally unmolested and even induced to stay. Financially and industrially the Moors in Castile "formed a most valuable portion of the population. The revenues derived from them were among the most reliable resources of the state. . . . To the nobles on whose lands they were settled they were almost indispensable, for they were skilful agriculturists." They were allowed to retain their property, their own religion, their own laws, their own magistrates. It is true that the Moors and the Jews were compelled to dwell in segregated quarters of the towns and intermarriage with Christians was forbidden, but economically and socially they were more than tolerated, they were favored. Commerce and trade were largely in their hands. It was the very prosperity of the Jews and the Moors which finally provoked their ruin in the later Middle Ages. For the Spanish clergy and the Spanish nobles in course of time looked with covetous eyes upon their wealth and the spirit of religious fanaticism and intolerance—the poisonous flower of the Albigensian Crusades—fanned this covetousness into flaming hostility. The reign of Alfonso X (1252–84) marks the culmination of the prosperity of both Jew and Moor in Castile.

Unfortunately, the Visigothic tradition of ecclesiastical power and religious intolerance was carried down into the kingdoms of medieval Spain, especially in Castile, and the Church ceaselessly inculcated the doctrine of constant war against the infidel. Not unnaturally the Church got its reward in ample slices of land in the conquered territories and exemption from regular taxes. The Church performed a greater service to society of an economic and administrative nature in the repeopling and reclaiming of the devastated areas and reducing the arid soil of the *meseta* to tillage than it conveyed in its spiritual teachings. In less degree than the high clergy the great nobles also demanded and received reward for their military services. As a result of such loose and lavish grants the Castilian kings were chronically in financial straits owing to lack of sufficient crown lands.

The nobility of Castile seized the opportunity afforded by the "reconquest" to intrench themselves in privileges. The greatest nobles were *ricos hombres* or grandees; those of lesser rank were *hidalgos* and *caballeros*. The grandees were reputedly of lineage "beyond the power of the king to confer"; the *hidalgos* (the word is probably derived from the Visigothic *adalingi,* meaning "nobles") might be of ancient blood, but their distinction more usually rested on reward of service; the *caballero* answered to the knight of feudal France, a gentleman-at-arms. There was never a fully fledged feudal system in Castile, however. "Local conditions, particularly the constantly shifting boundary and the agricultural poverty of the *meseta,* were distinctly unfavorable to it." While much was feudal, there was no feudal system. The principle of primogeniture and entailed estates, with the effect of preserving the unity of landed possession and perpetuating the rights, powers, and immunities of a house, was of late introduction—nearly two centuries later than the same practices in France and England. A striking illustration of the exceptional condition of things in Spain when compared with other countries of Europe, is the fact that Spain alone possessed three indigenous military orders, those of Calatrava, Santiago, and Alcántara.

The most progressive social feature of Castilian history in these centuries of expansion is the fullness and intensity of city life. The communes of Castile were older than those of any other European country except Italy, and were endowed with an admirable vigor. Their charters, or *fueros,* compare favorably with those of Lombardy and Flanders in the large amount of municipal liberty accorded in them. Whereas town life was scarcely manifest in Europe at large before the twelfth century—Italy alone excepted—we find it strong in Castile in the eleventh century. Leon was chartered in 1020, Burgos in 1073, Sepulvada and Najera in 1076, Toledo in 1085, Logrono in 1095. Unfortunately the kings of Castile were too shortsighted to make intelligent and efficient use of this burgher class. They were "improvidently liberal" in granting charters, and in the end had as little control of the bourgeoisie as they had of the nobility. Spain never developed that third estate which was so progressive a factor in the history of the other countries of Europe. Moreover, the Spanish burgher was behind the same class in France, Italy, and Germany in natural aptitude for trade. The commercial prosperity of the cities largely reposed upon the enterprise of the Moorish population, which also paid the greater part of the taxes.

We have reminders of that municipal prosperity in the great cathedrals which were built in the centuries of the "reconquest," [2] but do not so easily perceive that the cost of their erection was very largely derived from the Moors. The poverty of Spain, the depletion of its population, the decline of its architecture, all date from the expulsion of the Moorish and Jewish population in 1492. Castile was incapable of perpetuating this prosperity.

The status of the Castilian peasantry was largely conditioned by the "reconquest" and the peopling of the devastated areas. Protection and security were primary objects naturally, and these could be secured only at the price of loss of, or at least great limitation of, liberty. Accordingly the mass of the population outside of the towns was serfs of varying degree, or even slaves. But as the Moors lost power and their territory shrank away, the condition of the servile population improved both economically and socially. The chief factor in this amelioration was the large number of towns, toward which the serfs gravitated in increasing numbers as war grew more remote and the opportunity for peaceful industry improved.

The agricultural problem was far the most important and the least solved problem of the realm of Castile. Pasturage was a natural form of exploitation, while agriculture required a patience and an intelligence beyond the Spaniard's power; moreover, the returns from it were precarious, both on account of the shallowness and aridity of the soil and on account of the hostile proximity of the enemy for so many centuries. In addition, the immense flocks of sheep in their migration were ruinous to what agriculture obtained. The farming peasantry and the cattle barons were alike hostile to the grazing of sheep, and strife between sheepmen and cattlemen was common.

We must now follow the history of the formation and development of that other Spanish kingdom, Aragon, which by the thirteenth century divided almost the whole peninsula with her rival. Between the ninth and the early twelfth centuries the little county of Aragon slowly and indefatigably crept down the valley of the Arga River to the upper Ebro and thence down that stream. Physically the territory was as inaccessible as Old Castile and it was protected by a broader river. Hence Aragon never suffered as much molestation from the common enemy as Castile. Like Old and New Castile, Aragon was an upland interior kingdom shut off from the sea. While Aragon obscurely expanded in

---

[2] San Isidore in Leon was dedicated in 1005, Santiago completed between 1082 and 1128; the cathedrals of Oviedo, Valladolid, and Avila date from the late eleventh or early twelfth century, the magnificent cathedral at Burgos from 1121. To these structures we must add enormous fortifications such as those of Ciudad Rodrigo and the walls of Avila, completed in 1090 and regarded by some as the most formidable erection of the Middle Ages.

the upper Ebro country, the Catalonians of the lower Ebro territory, which politically was the county of Barcelona, also expanded. The capture of Tudela in 1110, of Tarragona in 1116, and of Saragossa in 1118 created a greater county of Barcelona and one of a natural physical unity. The union of the two states was as natural and as inevitable as the union of Leon and Castile. The turning point in Aragonese history was its union with the county of Barcelona in 1137, exactly a hundred years later than the union of Leon and Castile. This gave Aragon an outlet for its produce and identified its own agricultural peasantry with the commercial tradition and maritime interest of Catalonia. Henceforth, although the state was called the kingdom of Aragon, the control of its destiny really lay with the maritime province of Catalonia and the commercial instincts of Barcelona. "It was at Barcelona that all the foreign and naval activity of the realm, both political and commercial, was centered; it was the Catalans who built the ships and manned them; it was the Catalans who cherished visions of expansion and a maritime career." Trade was an old story in Barcelona. The customhouse there is mentioned in the years 1029 and 1050. In 1068 Ramon Berenger published the *usages,* or customs, of Barcelona, in which there is evidence of commercial growth. The safety of merchants and security on the roads were especially assured. The growing sea-power of Aragon, Genoa, and Pisa together gradually got the upper hand over Mohammedan sea-power in the twelfth century. But the depredations of the corsairs who made the Balearic Islands their base of operations, were a constant menace to the commerce borne by sea, a danger not completely removed until the capture of Majorca in 1237.

In partial compensation for this Mohammedan restraint of Aragon's natural maritime development during the eleventh and twelfth centuries, Aragon found a wide and profitable field of commercial exploitation in southern France. For the ancient house of the counts of Barcelona was of French origin, and at the time of the union of Barcelona and Aragon it was possessed, thanks to adroit marriage alliances, of the greater part of Provence, Millau, and Gévaudan. These rich holdings were increased between 1137 and 1204 by the acquisition of Roussillon, Foix, Nimes, Béziers and—greatest of all—Montpellier. In the chapter upon France during the Crusades we saw how rich and varied the commercial and economic life of Provence and Languedoc was, and that Montpellier rivaled Marseilles as a port of entry for Levantine goods. Much of this prosperity was ruined by the destructive wars of the Albigensian Crusade, in which Aragon's losses were little less than those of the county of Toulouse; and when peace finally came to the ruined land political rule in southern France had passed to the French crown. In 1258, by the treaty of Corbeil, Aragon renounced to the French king all rights to Carcassonne, Agde, Béziers, Foix, Albi, Nimes, Narbonne,

Millau, Gévaudan, and all other territories north of the Pyrenees except Montpellier, which was retained by Aragon under French overlordship until the next century.

Undoubtedly the decline of Aragon's sway in southern France inspired James the Conqueror (1213–76) to new aggression against the Moors in order to get compensation for his French losses. In 1225 the Moorish king of Valencia was compelled to pay one-fifth of his revenues to Aragon. Thirteen years later James significantly proclaimed that he was going "to get the hen as well as the eggs," with the result that Valencia was besieged and captured, and all the territory north of the Guadalavir acquired. But Castile was now watching Aragon's expansion in the peninsula with jealous interest. For Castile in a peculiar sense had been formed by the "reconquest"; she was much more actuated by the crusading spirit than Aragon, and regarded the reversion of the two Moorish kingdoms still surviving in Spain as her residuary right. These two realms were Murcia and Granada. The latter was destined to be spared until the end of the fifteenth century. But Murcia, almost without a battle, was partitioned between Castile and Aragon, the former getting the lion's share.

But again, a new door of opportunity opened to Aragon. By this time, Castile was clearly the kingdom of the "reconquest" and the dreaded foe of all that was left of Moorish Spain. On the other hand no such hostility existed between Granada and Aragon, or between the Mohammedan states of North Africa and Aragon. What Aragon lost in future acquisition of territory in the peninsula was compensated for by the wider field of commercial action which opened to her with these states, which regarded Castile, not Aragon, as an hereditary foe. It now became Aragon's ambition to acquire commercial predominance in all the North African ports, especially Tunis, Bougia, and Ceuta.

Tunis was unquestionably the chief centre of European trade in North Africa, and regular Aragonese factories and consulates were set up during the reign of James the Conqueror. Vigorous competition not unnaturally ensued with the Genoese, Florentines, Venetians, and other Italian powers who were already on the ground; but the Aragonese were generally able to hold their own. . . . There was an elaborate set of duties and tariffs on this thriving trade; but in return European merchants were most effectively protected against fraud or maltreatment in the North African ports. . . . Much of this admirable organization was directly traceable to the needs and demands of the merchants of the Aragonese realms—for Majorca constituted a sister kingdom of Aragon—whose preëminence among the various foreign traders in the North African ports was unquestioned.

How keen the spirit of trade was in James the Conqueror is manifested in his jealousy of the competition of the Genoese, and the very interesting navigation law he proclaimed forbidding merchandise of Aragonese origin to be carried in foreign ships if national ships were available. In truth, unlike Castile which was almost wholly an inland and agricultural state, Aragon in the thirteenth century had become a fundamentally maritime and commercial state. Valencia supplied no more than one-third its need in wheat, while Catalonia imported almost all the cereals it consumed from the Balearic Islands and Sicily.

But Aragon also penetrated into the eastern Mediterranean in search of commerce. As we have seen elsewhere, although late in entering the Crusades, in the thirteenth century Catalan merchants are found in numbers in Alexandria, Cyprus, Constantinople, and Little Armenia. The tariff lists of James I mention spices, sugar, precious stones, rare dyes, and silks, as imports of Barcelona, and the records reveal the presence of merchants and shipping from Pisa, Genoa, Venice, Palermo, and Marseilles.

Aragon in the thirteenth century realized that her destiny was upon the sea and not upon the land. She left the rest of the Spanish peninsula to Castile. But her competition stirred up the intense resentment of Genoa, which hitherto had been without a rival in the western Mediterranean, and had handled almost all the African trade out of Tunis, Bougia, and Ceuta. From friends they became enemies, and Pisa, Genoa's other rival, and Aragon now made common cause together. The chief field of rivalry was southern Italy and Sicily. Here Aragon scored by a dynastic and commercial alliance with the Hohenstaufen, when in 1262 Constance of Sicily, daughter of Manfred, the emperor Frederick II's brilliant son, was married to Peter III of Aragon, and Aragon became the "favored nation" in the ports of Sicily and southern Italy. At this time Charles of Anjou and Provence, with papal support, was plotting to acquire Naples and Sicily; Genoa, which had large commercial interests in Provence, backed him with her fleet in hope of being restored commercially in lower Italy. The result, as we saw in Chapter XVII, was the fall of the Hohenstaufen, the establishment of Angevin power in Sicily and lower Italy, Genoa's commercial triumph and Aragon's discomfiture. But Aragon watched, waited, and intrigued, and when in 1282 she "underwrote," so to speak, the conspiracy of the Sicilian Vespers which wrecked Angevin political power and Genoese commercial supremacy in Sicily, she got her reward. The great and rich island lying in the middle of the Mediterranean, commanding the narrows between the two basins and possessed of the important port and city of Palermo, became a component part of the kingdom—an extension of Aragon. Thereby Aragon became and was to remain for centuries the foremost naval and commercial power in the western Mediterranean. Even Genoa's jealousy and her ascendancy with the restored Greek Empire could not keep the Catalans out of the Ægean and Byzantium.

Thus, of the two great states which divided almost all the Spanish peninsula between them at the end of the thirteenth century, Castile was the military and agricultural state; Aragon, the naval and commercial state.

CHAPTER XXIII

MERCHANT TRAVEL IN THE MIDDLE AGES. MARKETS. THE
CHAMPAGNE FAIRS. THE CONDUCT OF TRADE *

ALL medieval travel was either on foot or on horseback or muleback. Wagons were not in use even for heavy freight until the twelfth century and then their employment was limited to certain most favorable regions. Carts were used for transporting heavy stuff on farms and to the local market. The magnificent road system of the Romans had gone to pieces in the course of centuries and even if the ancient routes were still followed, the face of the highway had changed. Instead of the ancient paving blocks and cemented causeways were now mere dirt roads, heavy and miry in winter, deep with dust in summer; sinkholes were frequent, bridges few and poor. The roads had no "crown" and no ditches beside them to drain off the water. In the worst places rushes or boughs of trees made a "corduroy." Fords were used wherever practicable; if not, then a rude ferry was in vogue. When we add to these inconveniences the not unusual peril of highwaymen or robber nobles, insufficient shelter, and the trying influence of the elements like storm, snow, flood, it may easily be perceived that medieval travel was no light matter. There is a world of history in those words of the Litany: "That it may please Thee to preserve all that travel by land or by water, all women labouring of child, all sick persons and young children; and to shew Thy pity upon all prisoners and captives." It has been well said that "the persons thus interceded for are not mixed together casually or carelessly." Women were not peddlers and merchants in the Middle Ages, but many were wayfarers traveling of necessity or pilgrims en route to some shrine.

Keeping roads in good repair was regarded as one of the most meritorious of services. The monasteries were particularly distinguished for such works, especially the Cistercians, who built their houses in remote and isolated places, often in marshes or deep woods, and who perforce became road-builders. There is intimate relation between Henry VIII's destruction of the monasteries in England in 1537–39 and the bad roads of the Tudor period. However, when we reflect upon these evil conditions it must always be remembered that our knowledge of them is derived from records of complaint, of accidents and injuries, which illustrate the worse, not the better side.

* MAP. Shepherd, *Historical Atlas,* 98–99.

We read of Henry I of England that in 1102 he

issued orders for his army to march by the Hubel Heben (Evil Hedge) and laid siege to Shrewsbury. The road through a wood on this route is called by the English *Hubelheben,* which in Latin means *Malum Callem vel Vicum* (bad road or street). This road was for a thousand paces full of holes and the surface rough with large stones and so narrow that two men on horseback could scarcely pass each other. . . . The king gave orders that they should clear a broad track by cutting down the woods with axes so that a road might be formed for his own passage and a public highway forever afterwards.

Few nobles were intelligent enough to see the advantage of good roads. If one could get his produce to the nearest market he was content. There was little "through" trade, and what there was, was in the hands of wandering merchants, chiefly Italians, Greeks, and Syrians, for whom nobody cared and who were sedulously exploited by the baronage. It benefited no one to make good roads unless his neighbors did so, too. In consequence, until the commerce and trade of Europe increased during the Crusades to such a point that its volume became important enough to consider, the roads were largely left to themselves. Charlemagne had been careful in this particular and had made good roads and bridges. But the road system declined with the whole decline of Europe after his death.

What happened to a peasant boy, employed on the lands of a monastery, from his animal falling into a sinkhole, is amusing to read:

A boy from another monastery was sent by the prior to bring green hay from the meadow. The servants loaded this upon an ass which, on the way homeward, passed through a certain sunken way, where the load was caught between the banks on either side and the ass, slipping away, came home without the boy's knowledge. He stood by the hay, smiting it oftentimes and threatening the ass (which he did not know had got away) as best he could. Nor did he stir from the spot until the brethren came out to find him, who could scarce persuade him that the ass was clean gone and that the hay could not walk without a beast of burden.

The rule of the road was to turn to the left, a rule which still obtains in England. The reason lay in the fact that every one in the Middle Ages traveled armed, and by passing one he met on the left he had him at his right side, and naturally carried his sword or lance in his right hand. This precaution was necessary in a time when every person one met on the road might be hostile. It was the introduction of firearms which changed the rule of the road. A man with a gun naturally carries it with the barrel lying in the hollow of his left arm. Accordingly by passing on the right he had whomever he met off the point of the gun. In Colonial America the settlers in New England and Virginia and the frontiersmen along the forest trails always traveled in this way. In America the rule of the road has always been to pass on the right. In Europe it was not introduced until long after the invention of firearms. The earliest legislation I know of, instituting the keep-to-the-right practice, was in Saxony in 1736, when Augustus the Strong built the beautiful bridge over the Elbe at Dresden and introduced it there.

The improvement we might expect to have followed from the growing numbers of that class of travelers who had most to lose by the bad condition of the roads, is only slightly apparent. While Charlemagne and his immediate successors had employed measures to keep up the roads and bridges of the Frankish realm, the power of later kings to do so became restricted to their own personal domains, and the feudal nobles who took over the royal functions did not as a rule trouble themselves to fulfil their obligations in this respect. New roads were indeed opened from time to time, for military and market purposes. In the twelfth and thirteenth centuries there seems to have been some active administration of highways on the part of the more progressive princes and nobles interested in the gain they might derive from the passage of traffic through their domains. By the middle of the thirteenth century, land routes were used almost as much as water routes by the merchants seeking the great fairs. Yet the absence of a vigorous and thorough policy carried out by a centralized power prevented any widely extended and permanent improvement of the roads. As the feudality gradually lost their power of enforcing servile labor upon the roads, and as no other legal and regular means was provided for the maintenance of the highways, conditions in the fourteenth and fifteenth centuries seem to have been worse than ever before. Roads and bridges were patched and mended by the easiest method that came to hand. One bridge is mentioned the material of which was such a patchwork of wood and stone that it was impossible to tell of which material it had been originally constructed. The ruts in the roads were leveled up with fagots, and the mire was given some consistency by means of wisps of broom. If such accounts are, as they seem to be, illustrative of general conditions, it is not hard to agree with the statement that distances in the Middle Ages were equivalent to seven times our present distances, and we may wonder at the great development of interior commerce that actually took place.

To say that the roads lay in utter neglect, however, at this or any other time of the Middle Ages, would be an exaggeration. From 'the beginning to the end of the period, efforts at improvement were more or less continuously made; but they were chiefly local, and often were rendered ineffectual through lack of power of enforcement. Two principles seem to have held good throughout—that the proprietors along the course of the highways were responsible for their upkeep, and that the expenses of the upkeep should be provided by means of taxes, or tolls levied upon the users of the roads, especially merchants. The feudal lords generally took advantage of their power to levy and collect taxes, to draw from it as large a revenue as possible. Tolls were multiplied far beyond the requirements for the repair of highways. There were tolls for crossing the bridges, for traveling upon the roads, for the protection of an escort across the domain, etc. The customary exactions, however, would not have been as excessive or as illegal as often represented, if the revenues had been employed honestly for road upkeep. The evil of the situation lay in the fact that, while the traveler was stopped with annoying frequency for the payment of dues in consideration of good roads and protection, he quite often found neither.

The universal prevalence of local sovereignty subjected the merchant to an infinity of local taxes of many sorts. Every feudatory from dukes and counts down to viscounts and mere châtelains, not excepting the king himself, mulcted all traders and traveling chapmen who traversed his domains and assessed them with a multitude of exactions. The special names for these impositions varied from province to province and country to country, but they were all alike and may be classified under six different forms or types. The array of terms descriptive of them is amazing:

(1) Taxes on transportation. Such were *passage, pontage* (bridge toll), *charriage* (cart toll), *rivage,* river toll, *travers* (crossing a ford) and, most common of all, *péage.* The derivation of the last is illuminating. It comes from the Latin *pes, pedis,* foot, whence *pedaticum* or *péage,* a tax on chapmen and pack peddlers who carried their wares on their backs and traveled on foot.

(2) Taxes on goods or wares called *telonia* or tolls. Hundreds of tariffs survive from the twelfth century forward in which a myriad of commodities is enumerated, such as cattle, horses, salted or smoked meats and fish, wheat and other cereals, vegetables, wine, honey, oil, dried fruits, salt, metals, leather, furs, arms, dyes, wool, thread, millstones.

(3) Taxes on wine formed a class by themselves, and included caskage, bottling, measure (*galonnage*), *tavernage,* or sale in inns. The lord's ban gave him prior right of sale of the year's vintage, so that he sold his own wine when the market was "high," while the peasants could only sell later when the market might be glutted.

(4) The right of regulating weights and measures. Like the right of coinage, in the feudal age, the right of regulating weights and measures was a feudal prerogative. The units varied greatly. Almost every province, or at least region, had its own system. Even Charlemagne

had never been able to establish a uniform system of weights and measures and with the rupture of the Frankish Empire, local diversity grew apace.

(5) Taxes upon market and sale. These were license taxes and strictly an emanation of feudal sovereignty, not domanial in nature. In seaboard countries port and harbor dues were of this classification. Of all produce the selling of wheat was most jealously supervised, a fact quite natural when one considers the prevalence of famine in the Middle Ages.

(6) Douanes or tariffs, in medieval parlance usually known as *maltôtes* (bad taxes), because of their great unpopularity and often burdensome nature. They do not appear much before the end of the twelfth century—that is to say, they were coeval with the rise of the towns—and are again an interesting evidence of the growing volume and variety of trade during the era of the Crusades. This form of taxation had long been familiar in Mediterranean countries, in both Arabic and Byzantine lands. Its adoption in the West is therefore significant of the commercial and economic awakening of western Europe.

A lord frequently compelled an itinerant merchant to follow one road rather than another in order that he might subject him to toll, or force him to cross a bridge when he might have taken a ford. In Germany this was called *Strassenzwang*. Even Charlemagne had to legislate against such practice. The local lord claimed the right to any pack which fell from the load; if a cart upset he might claim the whole load; but the roads were usually so bad that most merchandise was carried on muleback. Sometimes a group of merchants for greater security traveled together in caravan. The most vexatious of these baronial taxes and the worst abuse of them, however, tended to diminish with the growth of stronger and more centralized governments. In the twelfth century a systematic or customary fixation of tolls began to be developed and arbitrary exactions gradually fell out of use, except in Germany.

The following query made to the princes under Frederick II, in 1236, sheds light. "The venerable archbishop of Salzburg asked: When merchants are going along the public highway to a market, may anyone force them to leave the highway and go by private roads to his market? The decision of the princes was, that no one has a right to compel merchants to leave the highway, but that they may go to whatever market they wish."

The interest of the medieval public in good roads expressed itself in various ways. The care of roads was looked upon as a pious and charitable duty, and to endow a bridge or a stretch of highway, or to labor upon the same, was efficacious in absolving from sin, just as the giving of alms or the making of a pilgrimage. Frequently, when a local situation became desperate, indulgences were granted by neighboring bishops to those who would give either means or labor for the repairing of the highways. Even indulgences, however, did not always awaken sufficient response to bring about the end desired, and public authority supplemented the measures of the Church. Bridges seem particularly to have been objects of interest for the medieval public, probably because their scarcity and their tumbledown condition often made the passage of the rivers as formidable as that of the mountains. Sometimes there was other danger in crossing a bridge. The incident is told of a bondman in the service of Enguerrand de Coucy who was set to collect the tolls paid for crossing the bridge at Soord and used to watch until a lonely traveler appeared, whom he would murder and rob, sinking the body in the river. Charlemagne had wisely imposed upon the monasteries the obligation to maintain roads and bridges, and it is to the credit of the monasteries that they adhered to this rule down into the feudal age. With greater perception than the laity they recognized the benefit to commerce arising from good roads, although, of course, the interest the monasteries had in collecting local tolls was an incentive to maintaining roads and bridges. It was often the case that certain families, tenants, or individuals, were grouped in responsibility for the care of a neighboring bridge. In 1174, two brothers in Italy received certain immunities from the government on condition that they would keep a stone bridge over the Mella in such a shape that convenient passage of the river would be possible.

Gilds and associations were sometimes formed with the express purpose of keeping highways and bridges in repair. Toward the close of the twelfth century, a young priest of Vimarais believed he heard a divine voice directing him to build a bridge over the Rhone at Avignon, the rendezvous of the pilgrims to Rome. His enthusiasm over the suggestion spread to others, and resulted not only in the building of the bridge (1177–89), but in the organization of the "Fratres Pontis," consisting of both lay and clerical members. The order of the Bridge Brothers was popular, and in a short time appeared in various other countries of Europe. Four arches of this famous bridge still stand. Pont Saint Esprit, farther up the Rhone, is still in use. The Pont de la Guillotière at Lyons was subventioned by Pope Innocent IV by indulgences. There is a tradition that the first wooden bridge built across the Thames in London was built by a religious order founded by a ferryman's daughter named Mary. It is a matter of record that the first stone bridge over the Thames was begun in the latter part of the twelfth century by the head of such an order—Peter of Colechurch. This work was thirty years in the building; the faithful monk died four years before its completion and was buried in the bridge chapel of his own construction. Bridges were sometimes fortified with castles at each end. A wondrous example is still preserved near Rome, and the bridge at

Cahors in France is another. Bridges in cities, as London Bridge, the Ponte Vecchio in Florence and the Pont-Neuf in Paris, were lined on either side by small shops, giving them a most picturesque effect.

From the twelfth century on we find many instances of the activity of governmental authority in behalf of road improvement. In 1135, Henry I of England issued an order that all highways should be broad enough for two wagons to pass each other, or for sixteen soldiers to ride abreast. In 1285, a statute ordered that highways connecting the market towns should be cleared of woods and bushes for two hundred feet back on either side, that robbers might not find lurking places along the way. In many German states there were laws determining the width of both main roads and by-roads, as well as the privileges of using and the duty of maintaining them. In Italy, neglect of the highways was not so common as in other countries. The communes took special pains to keep the trade routes in good shape. Pisa and Piacenza in the twelfth, and Verona, Padua, and Pavia in the thirteenth century, passed many decrees for the laying out, maintenance, and repair of roads, ways, and bridges.

Besides the dangers and inconveniences due to bad roads, the traveler of medieval times was constantly exposed to robbery and pillage. So numerous are the accounts of highway robberies, that one might well doubt whether any journey could have been taken without some experience of the kind, or at least without constant fear of such. The great number of highwaymen infesting the roads of every European country in the Middle Ages was perhaps due in the main to the weakness of government and the lack of economic pursuits adequate to the employment of all the population. The class was greatly augmented by, if not mainly composed of, criminals and debtors fleeing from justice, dismissed soldiers, and others for whom society did not furnish sufficient occupation to assure a livelihood.

The robber feudal baron of the iron age of feudalism gradually became an anachronism in the twelfth and thirteenth centuries, owing to the enforcement of the Truce of God and increase of royal power. His place was taken, however, by the fugitive criminal and above all by the *routiers,* those mercenary soldiers who, when dismissed from service, took to brigandage. Late in the Middle Ages a newcomer was the impecunious, impoverished knight whom the change in economic condition, fixed rents and rising prices, increase in cost of living, had so to speak caught between the millstones and ruined. Rather than face poverty and too proud to work, this class became the ruffian road-men dear to romance. There is a record of two counts who in 1308 negotiated with the Venetians for delivery to the latter of many bales of cloth, which they had seized from Venetian merchants and had carried off, with the owners, to their castles. They declared that their poverty had driven them to highway robbery, and offered to restore the goods at half their actual worth! Other nobles, who did not so boldly take to the road themselves, allowed their castles to be used by robbers as hiding places from justice, and storage places for stolen goods. Yet it is not impossible that modern writers have exaggerated the perils of travel in the Middle Ages, when we remember that chroniclers then as now recorded crime, accident, and calamity far more than less uneventful matters.

By the twelfth century, political authority grew more active in measures for the protection of merchants on the highways. These measures sometimes took the form of decrees, such as the peace ordinance of Frederick I, in 1156, which included the provision that "a merchant who is traveling through the country on business may carry a sword bound to his saddle or on his wagon, but he shall use it only to defend himself from thieves, and not against innocent persons." Cities and princes coöperated with one another in the work of protection, and there are instances of a city's contracting with a great noble along the route for his aid in the policing of the highway. Even the services of dwellers along the roads within the jurisdiction of Piacenza were requisitioned for this purpose. These people were put under oath that they would keep watch, and hasten to the aid of any they heard cry out upon the highway for help.

Growing interest was shown by German rulers in the safety of Italian merchants traveling to the fairs of Flanders and Champagne. Rudolph of Habsburg, near the close of the thirteenth century, ordered the nobles of his dominions to assure protection to all merchants traveling through their territories, and made each of them responsible for any robbery committed upon his land. King Albert in 1301 made a compact with certain bishops and nobles of his realm, to keep the peace of the ways. This was the first time, says Schulte, that a king, in order to make the peace of the land effectual, strengthened his position by a compact with influential subordinate powers. The ordinances of the German princes seem to have been not wholly without effect. In France, also, the kings tried to make the feudal lords responsible for crimes committed on their territories, but with little success until the thirteenth century.

Another method by which the Middle Ages sought to protect the traveling merchant was the system of reprisals for robbery committed by citizens of one state against those of another. The natural inclination of the injured man to indemnify himself from the goods of the one who had done the injury, or of the latter's countrymen, was recognized by government, and carried out with its sanction. This policy can be traced from the twelfth century. The custom came to be carefully regulated by law, and the merchant who had been robbed was obliged to apply first to his government, which took the matter up with the authorities of the robber's country. In case no satisfactory restitution could thus be provided for, then the complainant was given written permission by his government to make good his loss from any available property of the offender's countrymen, by violence or otherwise—a regulation which was a hardship for the mercantile compatriots of the robber, who happened to be passing through or sojourning in the country of the one robbed.

Gradually there developed a broader governmental policy of protection and relief to foreign merchants. Many instances of such occur in the thirteenth century. Commercial law was, however, intermittent in passage and enforcement, often partial and unjust, or restrictive and unwholesome. But a gradual evolution of a kind of international law, the *jus mercatorum,* is found, by which foreign merchants in all lands were subject to similar regulations, and which princes tried to enforce justly, in order to induce merchants to frequent their markets and fairs.

Next in importance to the legal security of trade was the shelter afforded to the person and wares of the traveling merchant. Inns existed from a very early day; but in the first centuries of the Middle Ages they were scarce enough to compel travelers to carry along provisions and tinder box, and sometimes to sleep in the open. It had always been the self-imposed duty of the Church to house wayfarers, and provide shelter especially in lonely and dangerous places along the routes. The cloisters were numerous. There were hospices in the high passes of the Alps probably as early as the eighth century. Schulte mentions one destroyed by the Saracens in the tenth century, which had probably existed more than a hundred years. Other hospices were founded in the Alpine passes after the expulsion of the Saracens. Before the close of the eleventh century, there were stations or refuges on the St. Bernard and Mont Cenis passes, and six others on the road of Mont Genèvre. There were also hospices in the passes of the Pyrenees. In Sweden, the law required inns on main roads within half a day of each other. Public inns managed for profit were not slow to follow the increase of commercial travel along the main roads. Jusserand writes that in England the "common inns" were used by the merchant class generally, the monasteries receiving only the rich and the poor, the one from policy, the others from charity.

The conveyance of merchandise on land during the Middle Ages, as has been said, was by means of pack animals. But in the late medieval period rude, solidly built wagons came into use. They are pictured in contemporary drawings, and often mentioned in the regulations for taxing merchants for the purpose of repairing bridges and highways. The medieval wagon or cart was constructed with an eye to the roughness of the roads. It was heavy and cumbersome, and solid enough to bear heavy jolting. In Germany, small wheels were used, in order that the vehicle might not so easily lose its balance in the ruts of the highway, and thus expose its contents to the operation of the *Grundruhrrecht,* the law by which a local feudal lord seized all goods which accidentally fell off to the ground. The difficulties and dangers of transportation upon the roads led to the use of rivers wherever available, especially for the carriage of the heavier forms of merchandise. Waterways furnished a cheaper as well as an easier conveyance, since a single boat might carry the burden of five hundred pack animals. Incorporated gilds of "keelmen" or "watermen," who made a business of freighting goods, were to be found in many river towns. We have already seen such at Rouen, Paris, and on the Yonne above Paris. The merchants of Amiens, Abbeville, and Corbie controlled the Somme. The Loire in like manner was divided into "reaches" under separate associations of rivermen, which, however, were not united until the fourteenth century. At Bayonne was the *societas navium Baionensium* upon the Adour. Upon the lower Rhone, Arles by 1150 had an elaborate series of statutes for police of the river and exaction of tolls. There is fragmentary evidence for the existence of gilds of bargemen upon other French rivers like the Saône and the Garonne. In like manner in Germany we find gilds of keelmen on the Rhine, at Strassburg, Mainz, and Cologne. In Lombardy there were many on the Po and its affluents.

It was usual, especially in the earlier centuries of the Middle Ages, for the merchant to accompany his goods on the journey. If he were wealthy, he might take with him a band of hired men for a guard; but the more common method was so to arrange the time and place of starting that he might join a caravan of other merchants and travelers going in the same direction or to the same place as himself. The greatest travelers of the time were the pilgrms and the traders, two unarmed classes who gladly joined each other's company to increase security with numbers, the purse of the merchant and the arm of the pilgrim supplementing each other in dealing with the demands of highwaymen and robber barons. The necessity of fellow travelers prevented the free choice of the trader as to the time of transporting his wares; but this was not so disadvantageous to commerce as might be inferred, for the periodicity of the fairs made possible a more or less periodical regularity in the movement of caravans. Not infrequently, however, the merchant traveling unaccompanied attached himself to the retinue of a noble who happened to be journeying the way he wished to go.

The speed of travel in the Middle Ages is a difficult matter to determine. Merchant travel must necessarily have been slow, with frequent stops. But courier and messenger travel was as fast, perhaps, in the twelfth and thirteenth centuries as it was in the sixteenth and seventeenth centuries. It was steam power which wrought the great revolution in this particular. The news of Frederick Barbarossa's death in Cilicia in 1190 required four months to reach Germany. That of Richard I's capture in Dalmatia in 1190 reached England in four weeks. The average time from Rome to Canterbury was seven weeks, although there is a record of the journey having been made in 29 days. The great Italian banking houses which did business at the Champagne Fairs had a courier system whose efficiency is shown by the fact that the trip was customarily made in from 20 to 25 days. Perhaps 18 miles *per diem* was considered a fair distance. But couriers sometimes made as much as one hundred miles. In 1421 a messenger covered the distance between Barcelona and Perpignan, 210 kilometres, in 30 hours. In the fourteenth century a merchant traveled from Montauban to Rome via Avignon, Embrun, Susa, Pisa, Viterbo in 23 days, or at the rate of 56 kilometres *per diem*. When Charles VII died in 1461 three messengers were dispatched from Meung near Bourges, where the king died, to Louis XI, then at Genappe in Brabant. They rode three horses to death but covered the distance, 530 kilometres, in less than 48 hours. The news of the Mohammedan conquest of Syria and Persia in 635 reached China eight years afterwards, and is mentioned in Chinese annals in 643.

The need for a responsible person to attend the wares to market, and for another to supervise affairs at home, made association in commercial business very common in the Middle Ages, the merchant usually taking as his associate a son or other relative. Associations were formed also with other purposes in view. The numerous tolls levied by nobles upon the river traffic, and the fact that these tolls were not used for the improvement of the rivers, or even for keeping them open and navigable, caused the great merchants of the river cities to associate in order to perform the duties neglected by the lords. They took over the toll rights of the seigniors, and kept up the tow paths, dredged the rivers, and constructed magazines and quays. By the thirteenth century adequate law for regulating the carriage of goods had been developed, so that it was not always necessary for the merchant himself or his associate to go with his goods to their destination. Carriers were sometimes entrusted with the transfer of the wares to the market, where the merchants awaited their arrival. These carriers were bound by stringent contracts, which they took oath to maintain, to guard the goods faithfully and deliver them intact, bearing as they did the trade-mark of the owner, at the fair or other destination. If, however, the goods were lost by act of violence or other casualty that the carriers could not prevent, they were not held responsible for the loss.

On the whole, the conditions of inland travel were comparatively little changed for the better during the Middle Ages. The physical hardships and dangers of the highway were scarcely mitigated, and the means of transportation were not much improved. Chief alleviation came in the better regulation of the toll system, the increasing number of inns and hospices, and the higher efficiency and better agreement of governments in safeguarding mercantile rights at home and abroad.

An inconvenience not obsolete yet, experienced by the medieval traveller, arose from the multiplicity of languages in Europe. In the Middle Ages almost every province had its own peculiar dialect. These patois, it is true, still survive as vernacular forms of expression; but every nation in Europe today has a national speech understood by almost all its people. No such uniformity of speech obtained in medieval times. St. Bernard in the twelfth century complained of "the isolation not only of distance, but that due to difference of language." On the other hand the all-prevailing sway of the Church made Latin a uniform language at least of the clergy throughout all Europe and must sometimes have mitigated the inconvenience of the numerous dialects. For the great merchants kept their accounts in Latin until late in the Middle Ages, and if they did not know Latin, a clerk at least understood it.

The life of the seagoing merchant from the tenth to the fifteenth century was in general one of great peril, if not of greater hardship, than that of the land traveler. The incidents of his voyage were likely to be of a more disastrous kind and accidents on a greater scale than those of a journey on land. There is seen, however, in regard to the methods and means of navigation during these centuries, a more marked improvement than is disclosed by the study of travel on land.

At the beginning of the period, no ship captain ventured out of sight of land, for the danger of shipwreck on the rocks or shoals was not so terrifying as the thought of being lost in the open sea. The terrors of the sea diminished after the beginning of the Crusades, yet the safer and customary way to voyage was within sight of the friendly shore. The galleys and the ships more heavily laden with men or wares, throughout the period did not venture into the open sea. The Genoese, Pisans, and Amalfitans, as also the French voyagers of Montpellier and Marseilles, and the Catalans, went usually along the west coast of Italy toward the south; after resting at Messina, the fleets were accustomed to take the course around the Greek peninsula, along the north coast of Candia to Rhodes and Cyprus, where they also often rested; then they made from Cyprus for the Syrian coast, following this in a southerly direction until they came to Tyre and Acre. Travelers from the North Sea regions, coming through the Straits of Gibraltar, owing to piracy would not take the chances of a direct route east, but made the detour along the coasts of Spain, France, and Italy. In the thirteenth century, the more adventurous captains took a straight course from Candia to the Syrian coast. It was not until the fourteenth century that the compass was applied to navigation and so enabled sailors to cross the Mediterranean without fear of the unbroken circle of the horizon.

The shipping of the Mediterranean was more rapidly developed in size and efficiency than that of northern Europe. Daenell suggests that the shallowness of the harbors on the Atlantic, North Sea, and Baltic coasts, discouraged the building of greater ships in the northern waters. The Normans in 1066 crossed the English Channel in boats of about 30 tons burden, which carried 50 or 60 men each. English vessels of the early thirteenth century are mentioned as carrying from 8 to 15 horses, placed amidships, although these ships are called in the records *naviculæ*. In the time of Edward III, the average ship was about 200 tons, the largest mentioned being 300. They were manned with 65 men for each 100 tons burden, besides archers and soldiers to the number of about one-half the crew. The North Sea ship rose high above the water at stem and stern, the Mediterranean vessel being lower and longer.

The accounts handed down of Mediterranean vessels indicate that these far excelled northern craft in point of size. The Spaniards are said to have built huge ships after the model of those of their Arabic neighbors, and to have been distinguished for the size of their vessels till their loss of sea-power in the sixteenth century. The government galleys of Venice during the Crusades are recorded to have averaged 500 tons of cargo "under hatches, besides a large cargo upon their decks." The transports of the Mediterranean cities carried, according to accounts, from 800 to 1000 persons, including the crew. These numbers will, perhaps, not serve us as a just criterion of the size of the vessels; for the indiscriminate way in which passengers were crowded in cabin and hold would increase the capacity of the ship relative to its size, if anything like a modern standard of comfort or safety were used. A ship furnished by Venice to Louis IX, in 1268, measured 108 feet long over all, and carried 110 seamen.

The method of propelling vessels was by means of both sails and oars. A single mast with a square sail seems to have been customary before the thirteenth century. In the contract for Venetian vessels to be furnished to the king of France in 1268, it was provided that the larger vessels were to have two masts and two square sails each. The Venetians also had vessels during this period with three and with four sails. Vessels did not depend on sails alone, unless they were very small craft, but were furnished with oars according to the size of the ship. The larger vessels had three rowers on a bench, each with a separate oar, the oars passing in a bunch through the same oarlock port; the smaller had the oars in pairs. The rowers' benches were ranged from stern to prow, at one elevation as a rule, although in the late thirteenth century there were galleys with two or three banks of oars. Sanudo the Elder, writing in the early fourteenth century, states that a galley had 60 benches, 30 on each side, worked by 120 rowers. Felix Fabri, in the late fifteenth century, voyaged in a galley which had 60 benches, with three rowers to a bench. The number of benches and rowers varied with the size of the vessel, and with the speed required, the number of oars sometimes reaching 200. The toil of propelling the vessels was tremendous. Yule has concluded that the oars were worked by freely enlisted men until after the period of the Middle Ages. This statement is made in regard to Venetian galleys by other authors also, Venice not employing convict labor at the oars until 1549. Felix Fabri, sailing in 1483 in a Venetian galley, learned that the "galley slaves are for the most part the bought slaves of the captain, or else they are men of low station, or prisoners." "Whenever," he adds, "there is any fear of their making their escape, they are secured to their benches by chains." It must be inferred from this that galley slaves were not unknown before the sixteenth century, even though not made use of by governments. The description of excessive cruelty in the treatment of the rowers given by Felix Fabri makes it hard to believe that, unless his picture is exaggerated, freely enlisted men would have entered such a service. Yet he says that merchants "sometimes became voluntary galley slaves in order that they might ply their trade in harbors."

In the tenth and eleventh centuries ships were of simple contruction, the larger ones having deck and forecastle. I have found no mention of vessels with cabins before the thirteenth century. In the early part of that century cabins were constructed in certain English ships for the special use of the king and queen. Of the vessels furnished by Venice to Louis IX in 1268, the two largest had several cabins in bow and stern, and each had two decks five and one half feet high. In the early fourteenth century, the Catalans were using ships with three decks each, probably running the full length of the vessel. The "berths" were spaces the length of a man and the width of a cot, marked off on the floor with chalk and assigned to the passengers "for sleeping, sitting, and living in." Between the benches of the rowers, on the upper deck, was a space used for the storing of chests of merchandise. Below this deck was the cabin, a spacious chamber without light or air except through the hatchway, where Felix and his companions dwelt in their six-foot plats, but which in a galley of burden was used for stowage of cargo.

Vessels were not very distinctly classified as to use. The "large and strong" ship in which Saewulf sailed to Joppa in 1102, and many others lying in the harbor there, were burdened "with corn and merchandise, as well as with pilgrims coming and returning." There were vessels especially constructed for the transportation of horses. They had a door in the stern through which the horses were admitted, and which was then closed and calked, "being under water when the vessel was at sea." The distinctive war vessel was not generally known, vessels being employed for war or commerce as occasion demanded, and frequently for both at once, as it was not uncommon for a merchant ship to meet a pirate or other hostile ship. Throughout the Middle Ages merchant ships were depended on for war purposes, being requisitioned by the government when needed. All that was required to put them on a war footing was a fuller equipment of men and arms. Yet from early times there was this much distinction, that vessels meant primarily for burden were often built with broad hull, and called "round ships," while "long ships," lower and swifter, were meant primarily for war.

Life on a medieval ship was regulated by strict laws and severe government. There prevailed a different régime on shipboard from that on land. The vessel was a little world in itself, with its special customs, courts, and penalties; bargains and contracts made on the ship could not be enforced on land, and quarrels among fellow passengers or crew were not to be carried ashore. Coulton quotes an extract from an account of a Hanse voyage written in 1590, which, he says, represents features of ship life handed down from very early times. When half a day out the skipper called all on board together, and said to them: "Seeing that we are at the mercy of God and the elements, each shall henceforth be held equal to his fellows, without respect of persons. And because, on this voyage, we are in jeopardy of sudden tempests, pirates, monsters of the deep, and other perils, therefore we cannot navigate the ship without strict government." When they came within half a day's sail of their port, they were again called together and instructed that whatsoever had passed and befallen on shipboard all this time, each man should "forgive to every man his fellow, overlook it, and let it be dead and gone."

The customary regulations on shipboard in medieval times, as set forth in the "Laws of Oléron," were derived directly or indirectly from the Rhodian maritime code. As the Mediterranean maritime codes came generally from the same source, these Laws of Oléron must represent the customs and ideas not only of England, but of other seagoing peoples of the time. They became the basis upon which the Hanse towns and Baltic nations erected their system of maritime justice in the thirteenth and fourteenth centuries. By the code of Oléron, harbor regulations were well defined, provision being made for proper mooring, the use of buoys, and other means of promoting safety. Harbor pilots were held severely to account, and any loss sustained through inexpert or treacherous piloting must be paid for by the pilot, with his goods if he were possessed of enough but, falling short, with his head. The master of the ship was obliged to consult the ship's company as to what they thought of wind and weather, before starting out on a voyage. If he failed to do this, and damage was caused by the elements, he was held responsible. If there were any merchants on board, they, as well as the ship's company, had to be consulted by the master before any act was undertaken affecting the ship's course, or place of stopping. By Mediterranean rules, a merchant, or a group of merchants, chartering a vessel for the shipment of goods, and embarking upon it themselves, had almost complete authority upon it, the majority, in case there were several, governing the management and movements of the vessel, the master being responsible for damages only if he acted contrary to the advice of a majority of the merchants.

The loading of a cargo was carefully prescribed by the laws of Oléron. It was performed by "stowers," who were to be paid for their work by the merchants. They were "to dispose the cargo properly, stowing it closely, and arranging the several casks, bales, boxes, bundles, in such a manner as to balance both sides, fill up the vacant spaces, and manage everything to the best advantage." Men called *sacquiers* (sack carriers) were employed to load and unload grain, salt, and fish, to watch that the merchant was not defrauded by the ship's crew. The Italian republics had strict rules to prevent the overloading of a ship. The capacity of the vessel was measured by inspectors at the time of launching, and her sides were marked by a painted line, above which the water was not allowed to rise. Nowhere in Europe was the technique of loading and unloading a vessel so highly organized as in Venice. The famous Arsenal is described by a traveler as "like a great street on either hand with the sea in the middle." Warehouses, each with its special kind of materials and goods lined the long waterfront. A galley making ready for sea was towed from warehouse to warehouse, from each of which stevedores handed out bales, cordage, arms, food, etc., "and so from both sides everything that might be required, and when the galley reached the end of the pier she was equipped from end to end." In like manner an arriving galley was unloaded.

When in storms at sea it seemed expedient to throw a part of the cargo overboard, the master had to ask the advice of the merchants, but was not required to conform to it if he felt that the ship's safety demanded his disregarding it. Any loss incurred by the merchants through this "ejection" of cargo was, by English law, made good to them from the property on shipboard of master and seamen, and the master lost the freight on the goods thrown into the sea.

The increased dangers of the sea at certain seasons of the year, as well as the constant dangers of piracy, caused the organization in Mediterranean ports, from about the middle of the crusading period, of two great fleets annually, for the trip to the East. One made the voyage near Easter time, and the other in the summer after St. John's Day (June 24), though the time of starting might vary. Merchants much preferred this way of voyaging, especially if they were transporting very valuable wares. It was usually planned to avoid the sea in stormy seasons. Ludolph von Suchem suggests some features of Mediterranean travel in 1350:

> The ship always flies, as it were [he writes] from west to east with a fair wind, making more way in the night than in the day, and traveling fully fifteen miles in every hour of the day. . . . Great ships going from the West to the East are wont to return in the months of September and October, but galleys and vessels of that sort begin their voyage thither from hence in August, when the sea is smooth; for in November, December, and January no vessels can cross the seas because of storms. Howbeit, no vessels can, except very seldom, return without toil, fear, and tempest.

In the fourteenth and fifteenth centuries it was impossible for the ships of the period to make the voyage from Italy to the Baltic and return in the same season.

The fear of shipwreck was augmented by a common-law practice known as the law of wreck, which persisted throughout the Middle Ages. Vessels, as we have seen, were seldom in the course of their voyage far from shore, and wrecks were frequent. One of the trials of a mariner's life was this custom of wreckage by which all the goods washed from a wreck, or which were in a stranded vessel, became in whole or in part the property of the owner of the shore The lord who owned a dangerous stretch of coast was likely to reap a goodly harvest in the sailing season. A lord on the coast of Brittany boasted of a dangerous rock on his shore as the finest stone in his crown. Mariners were sometimes lured by lights placed upon the rocks by peasants, and it can be imagined that this was often done with the connivance of the lord. The French were very active as wreckers on the coast of the Bay of Biscay. In most of the Mediterranean states there were severe laws against those who tried to plunder a ship in peril, and any one convicted of such an offense was thrown into the sea, and then dragged out and stoned to death, "just as a wolf should be stoned to death." The law of wreck was early recognized as an injury to commerce, but it was very slow to lose its rigor. Prutz says it was in the crusading states that the law was first abrogated, in regard to Christian mariners only at first; later it was applied to Mohammedans also. From early in the twelfth century there are compacts between the various crusading states and certain commercial cities of southern Europe, which contain renunciations of the "strand right" by the former in favor of the latter. In 1170, the Eastern Empire agreed to punish any exercise of the strand law within its jurisdiction against the Genoese, and to compel a restitution of property thus lost. Many instances of special dispensation from the burden of the law of wreck, as well as complaint of the exercise and abuse of the custom, in the thirteenth century show that it was still a considerable factor in the life of the Mediterranean mariner.

In the first part of the twelfth century there began in England a movement for the mitigation of this practice. Henry I ordained that if any person escaped alive from an unfortunate vessel, it should not be considered a wreck. A law of Richard I was leveled against the "accursed custom" and the abuse of it by rapacious lords, and provided that a pilot who wilfully directed a vessel toward a dangerous coast where it was wrecked, if in the pay of the lord of the land, should be hanged on the spot on a high gibbet, which was "to abide and remain to succeeding ages on that place, as a visible caution to other vessels that sail thereby." If the lord appropriated any of the goods of a wreck, he was called "accursed," and punished as a robber. Another article declared that when a lord was guilty of aiding the wreckers or connived with a treacherous pilot who caused the ship to be cast upon his shore, he was to be burned in his own house, the site of which was to be turned into a market-place "for the sale of hogs and swine to all posterity." In spite of these frightful penalties, the practice seems to have been continued in England as elsewhere. In 1236, King Henry III provided, in a charter "for the abolition of unjust customs," for the restoration of the property of a wreck in case a man escaped or a beast were found alive on board. A similar law was made in 1275, according to which a ship was not to be considered a wreck, if man, cat, or dog escaped from it alive. The Hanseatic League exerted itself to eliminate the law of wreck from the custom of the sea; in 1287, the merchants who frequented Wisby met and agreed that shipwrecked property should be restored to its owner, and the cities of the league were to be held to this rule under penalty of ejection *"ex sodalitate mercatorum."* That the custom of wrecking prevailed more or less generally, with the force of common law, up to the close of the Middle Ages, is indicated by an act of the Scottish Parliament, in 1430, providing that, in case vessels were wrecked on the coasts of Scotland, the restoration of the property to the owners or its confiscation by the king should be determined by the "law respecting wrecks in the country to which they belonged."

The loss of life and property by shipwreck was not the only peril of the seaman's life. Travel on the sea as on land was enlivened by the ever present dread of attack and robbery, and ships always went well armed, with such a casualty in view. In the ninth and tenth centuries piracy was the chief trade of all the northern nations. Venice at the same time was hampered in her growing commercial activity by the Croatian and Dalmatian pirates of the Adriatic, and the Saracens were harrying commerce in the western Mediterranean. The Venetians in 870 defeated the Saracen pirates who were attempting to enter the Adriatic, and before the close of the tenth century they had destroyed the power of the Dalmatians, and fairly cleared that sea of piracy. But the nuisance, though abated in the Mediterranean and Adriatic, was by no means abolished. Professional piracy continued to be practised, and the seas were infested from first to last by such groups as the "Victoral Brothers" of the Baltic, who had for their motto, "God's friend and all the world's enemy," and whose power was broken by the Hanseatic League early in the fifteenth century.

Besides the lawless professional piracy practised against all ships indiscriminately, there was another form of the evil which was legitimized by the connivance or instigation of governments, and used as a means of warfare against a hostile state. In the twelfth and thirteenth centuries, Genoa, Pisa, and Venice tolerated if they did not encourage piracy as a commercial weapon against each other. The mariners of the Cinque Ports were commissioned by Henry III in 1242 to make reprisals upon the French. The Hanseatic League, although the repression of piracy in the North and Baltic seas had been one of the objects for which it was formed, did not scruple on occasions to employ the aid of pirates when convenient, to injure the commerce of a rival. The practice of legalized reprisal under letters of marque very often developed into full-blown piracy, without particular regard as to nationality. It was common for commercial seamen of one country to turn corsairs and ravage the shipping of another country, or even sometimes of their own. Matthew of Westminster says "that in those days there was neither king nor law for sailors, but everyone called whatever he could plunder or carry off his own." The Cinque Ports took advantage of their commission to harry the French and made themselves so pestiferous in the English Channel in 1292, to friend as well as foe, that the government made efforts, without entire success, to suppress them. In general, however, the principle held good among corsairs that fellow countrymen were not to be disturbed. Northern maritime commerce flourished in the reign of Canute, because the people of his Danish empire, being fellow subjects, did not prey upon each other's shipping. The corsairs of the Mediterranean cities of Europe refrained from injuring their compatriots.

Governments were slow to recognize their responsibility for protecting their subjects on the high seas, and slower still to acquire the power of doing so effectively. The half-respectability of piracy, as well as its usefulness in time of war, made rulers lenient toward it when practised by their own subjects, and more or less helpless in exacting redress from the pirate subjects of other states. The story of Alf, the Norwegian nobleman, shows us how difficult the problem sometimes was. The sea, like the land, did not lack its robber baron, and Alf was famous as a Baltic pirate in the thirteenth century. At one time thirty cogs belonging to German merchants were scouring the sea for him. He escaped and returned home, where his sovereign raised him to the rank of earl, and looked upon the pursuit of Alf by the German merchants as an act of hostility to himself.

Security upon the seas rested generally, in the early days, with the merchants themselves. They formed associations by means of which they could send their ships in fleets, the vessels being armed against attack by pirates, and sometimes having convoys of vessels specially armed and manned for war. Lively engagements often took place, and if the merchants were defeated and lost ships and goods, they had recourse to reprisal, and a sort of private warfare ensued. When governments began to interest themselves more in the security of the seas, they sought to regulate this practice of reprisal by providing that redress should first be demanded through governmental channels, and only on the failure of such action was the plundered merchant to take the matter in his own hands.

The Italian maritime city republics, whose prosperity and even existence depended upon commerce, interested themselves from before crusading times in ridding the sea of pirates and in regulating and safeguarding the passage of their ships. They were the first states to assume sovereign jurisdiction over neighboring seas, Venice laying claim to the whole Adriatic before the close of the thirteenth century. This assumption, while due in the main perhaps to other motives than protection, involved the responsibility for making those seas safe, and in fact did much toward that end.

As medieval life became more settled and more civilized, the mechanism of business improved. Bartering and peddling vanished except in the more rural regions and established markets and fairs came into being, as they had been before in the Roman Empire. Fairs and markets in the Middle Ages played a far greater economic part than they do today. They were the chief and often the sole means of distribution of local products and purchase of necessities from the outside. So lucrative was this right of market that in Carolingian times it was a crown prerogative. In the ninth and tenth centuries the baronage, wherever they could, usurped this prerogative and asserted it as a right of local sovereignty. Many monasteries and bishoprics enjoyed it by royal grant, however. As the feudal form of government became more settled in the twelfth century the great feudatories deprived the small baronage of the right of fair but usually left them the right of local market. Thus the fair passed under the political administration of the high nobles, while the market remained under manorial jurisdiction.

Market right in the Middle Ages was a feudal right. The market was part of the fief. It was a domanial institution, confined to the manor or collection of manors of a single lord. Such local markets often must have been close together and served a small locality. The *Sachsenspiegel*, the local code of Saxony compiled in the thirteenth century, but of earlier origin, forbade markets to be within less than a mile (German) of one another. Ordericus Vitalis, a Norman chronicler of the twelfth century, instances a countryman driving home a cow from market, and elsewhere speaks of "the common talk of the vulgar in the market-places and churchyards about the death of William Rufus." The churchyard was frequently the market-place, and Sunday afternoon a common market day. Thus Guibert de Nogent, another writer of the twelfth century, writes: "On Saturdays the country folk would flock in from divers parts round about for purposes of trade, carrying around for sale beans, barley, or any kind of corn, and in the town the stalls of cobblers and other craftsmen were open." If a peasant found a buyer who wished a larger quantity or amount of grain or cattle than he had brought to market he would often take the purchaser home with him to view the stock on foot or the grain in his barn. What kind of merchandise was offered for sale in these local markets? First of all, provisions. The market, therefore, had a bucolic character and was much frequented by the peasantry of the region. As life developed, as taste became more refined, the market became quasi-permanent. It became a weekly institution where on certain days of the month—the second Wednesday, the third Thursday, etc. —special markets were held, for grain, wood, wine, horses, cattle, etc.

As the great feudatories extended their sway and as territories became more consolidated, naturally the seats of the mighty became the most important centres of trade; and as many of these in turn developed into towns, at last the towns became the chief places of commerce and trade, where the princes, as Philip Augustus in Paris, erected *halles,* stores, warehouses. "The establishment of a market," as Maitland has pointed out, "is not one of those indefinite phenomena which the historian of law must make over to the historian of economic processes. It is a definite and legal act. The market is established by law, which prohibits men from buying and selling elsewhere than in a duly constituted market. To prevent an easy disposal of stolen goods is the aim of this prohibition. . . . He who buys elsewhere runs a risk of being treated as a thief if he happens to buy stolen goods. . . . A by-motive favors this establishment of markets. Those who traffic in safety may fairly be asked to pay some toll. . . . Perhaps also the use of . . . weights and measures known and trustworthy is another part of the valuable consideration." [1]

When the towns were formed, these markets became more numerous and assumed an importance much greater than in days previous. In the twelfth century the enormous stimulation of trade caused so great an increase in the number of markets that we find complaint of their excessive number. However, one must discount this dissatisfaction in some

[1] Maitland, *Domesday and Beyond,* 194.

degree, for it was chiefly voiced by the clergy, who resented the competition of secular commercial activity due to the rise of the towns. An energetic letter of Pope Eugene III to Henry II of England, protesting that the market of the bishop of Bayeux was being ruined by the new town markets which the king had authorized, is illuminating on this head. In the twelfth century revival the Italians—Venetians, Lombards, Genoese, Pisans appear as the first conductors of "through" traffic from one country to another. But, as we have seen, the Provençaux, the Catalans in the south, and the Flemings and Germans soon got into the game. Von Below has shown, so far as Germany is concerned, that the texts do not enable us very often to draw an exact line of separation between the wholesale merchant and the retail dealer. If in one place wholesale commerce is in the hands of foreigners, who seek the authorization of the municipal authorities to sell at retail, in another place we find it is active and exploited by the citizens themselves, the distinction being a vanishing one between the two kinds of merchants. The small trader shared in and was interested in wholesale importations, exactly as the big merchant disposed of his goods indifferently at wholesale or retail, either within or without the town.

The three chief distinctions between fair and market were: (1) the fair was under higher feudal jurisdiction than the market; (2) it was not domanial, but served a far wider public (the greatest of the fairs were international in scope); (3) it was seasonal, not weekly or biweekly. It should be added that merchants resorting to fairs were assured not only special safe-conducts which provided special penalties for violation of the merchants in person or goods, but also reduction of tariffs and tolls, conveniences for sale, and special courts for adjustment of disputes and to enforce collection of debts. In England this court was known as the court of piepowder, from Norman French *pied de poudre,* "dusty foot." The opening day of the fair was always an important fête day (*feria*), whence the word "fair."

Every country and every great fief had its fair. In the *Chronicle* of Lambert of Ardres is an account of how Count Baldwin of Guisnes established a fair, in which the distinction between the two institutions is clearly expressed. He writes:

The market also which in the days of his predecessors had been at Sutkerka not for any special cause but because of chance, he changed to Alderwicum, but following the advice of the Church did not change the day; where assembled and came to reside those living round about as citizens. Also the count of Guisnes, as much for heavenly glory as for a virtuous deed, to all the people, as much merchants as other peoples, because of the abundance of merchandise which came there from all parts, ordered to be held each year in that place during the feast of the solemnity of Pentecost a public fair, and this decree he confirmed by oath. The villa he surrounded by a double ditch and rampart in the midst of which he built halls and necessary buildings, and as was fitting he built with diligence and reverence a chapel at the entrance of the first enclosure, to the honor of St. Nicholas (the patron saint of merchants) : where he placed a holy man named Stephen as chaplain, with sufficient books and various ecclesiastical ornaments, to the glory of the town.

In these markets foreign merchants and strangers to the town entered into competition with the local trade. Thus at Paris on Saturday, which was "great" market day, the drapers of St. Denis, Beauvais, and Cambrai came to sell their cloths; they had a special room in the Place des Métiers, only it was provided that all these merchants must not sell until the clock gave the signal for the opening of the market, and when the clock sounded the hour of closure all sale had to cease and the foreign merchants retire. Permanent commerce, i.e., everyday commerce, was the privilege of the local bourgeois. On the "great" market day of Paris, merchants who had stores in the city had to close them and sell in the market under penalty of a fine of forty sous, which was doubled for each offense. Merchants and artisans were compelled to go to the king's market and were forbidden to sell in their shops. Only a few *métiers* obtained the privilege of selling at home on market day; and they paid the king a fee of forty sous annually for the privilege. But as a rule the obligation to sell in the market was maintained. These measures were taken for fiscal interests chiefly. It was easier to make the merchants pay their dues in the market than to go around and collect them. In Paris the market was royal. In these *halles* the king rented the stalls; and therefore had an interest in seeing that the *halles* were thronged on market days. In France, in the reign of St. Louis the crown claimed the right over markets as part of the regalia. It asserted the principle that no one could start a market anywhere in the kingdom of France without the king's consent, and what is said of markets is also true of fairs. When application was made to the king for the establishment of a market, an investigation was made by his agents, bailiffs, or seneschals. If the investigation was unfavorable the request was refused. In 1265 a decision of the *Curia Regis* abolished the market created by a feudal lord.

In the twelfth and thirteenth centuries the awakening of commerce and industry enormously increased the number of fairs, so that every country had many. Most of these, of course, were relatively local in nature, but still served a wider zone than the old markets. The towns quite naturally became the important seats of the fairs. The most famous fairs in Italy were at: Pisa, Venice, Genoa, Pavia, Modena, Padua, Milan, Bergamo, Viterbo, Piacenza, Bari, Capua, Gaeta, Salerno, Manfredonia, and Brindisi. Significantly, Rome had none. In Germany we find: Cologne, Erfurt, Naumburg, Brunswick, Leipzig, Hamburg, Magdeburg, Regensburg, Frankfort-on-the-Main and Frankfort-on-the-

Oder. In Flanders and the Low Countries were: St. Omer, Bruges, Courtrai, Lille, Thourout, Douai, Cambrai, Orchies, Ypres, Alost, Audenbourg, Axel, Malines, Poperinghe, Mons, Ghent, and Antwerp. France was thick with them, among the most important in Normandy being Rouen, Caudebec, Elbœuf, Harfleur, Caen, Evreux, Montmartin-sur-Mer (Cotentin), Avranches, Mont St. Michel, Coutances, Carentan, Valognes, Bernay. In Brittany were St. Malo, Rennes, Pontorson, Guingamp (whence the word gingham) Tréguier, Quimperlé, Plouescat. In the Ile-de-France one finds: Paris, Dreux, St. Denis, Orleans, Puiseaux, Morigny, Étampes, Mantes, Montlhéry, Melun, Beauvais. In Anjou: Verger, Beaupréau, Marillais, Brissac, Saumur and Angers. In central France: Bourges, Nevers, Poitiers, Angoulême, Gourville, Périgueux, Chalon-sur-Saône, Dijon, Auxerre, Autun, Tonnerre, Beauvray, Tours, Chartres, Château-du-Loir, St. Aignan, Chinon. In the English provinces, Bordeaux, Bayonne, Agen, Châtillon. In the Midi far the most famous were the fairs of St. Gilles and Beaucaire. Among Spanish fairs of importance were Medina del Campio, the greatest, Seville, Cuenca, Valladolid, Segovia, Toledo, and Burgos. In England the fairs of Stourbridge and St. Ives were very famous; others were Chester, Winchester, Boston, Stamford, Portsmouth, Abingdon, Northampton, Bury St. Edmunds.

Paris, in the Fair of St. Denis, possessed the very oldest fair whose history can be traced without interruption in the Middle Ages. It was founded by Dagobert I in 630 and was held for the four weeks following October 3, the day sacred to the memory of St. Denis. Thus it was an autumn fair. But when commerce and trade began to increase about the time of the Crusades and Paris to grow in population and political importance under the Capetian kings, the monks of St. Denis wanted a summer fair also. Hence in 1124 Louis VI set aside the tract of ground north of Montmartre for a new fair called the Foire du Lendit.[2] It began the second Wednesday in June and ended on St. John's day (June 24). Religious formalities always accompanied its opening, a sermon being preached to the people by the bishop of Paris, who received ten *livres parisis* from the monks of St. Denis for the service. The Lendit Fair was popular with the merchants of Paris, Normandy, and Flanders. In fact it was the chief rendezvous of the merchants of North France. The chief articles of sale were cloths, leather, parchment, furs, and horses. The abbots of St. Denis derived a revenue from the rent of stalls and were responsible for the police of the fair. In the fourteenth century the crown, however, began to trespass upon the abbatial privileges and extended royal jurisdiction

---

[2] The word was derived from the Latin *indictum*, which originally signified a religious gathering at a fixed (*indictum*, Old French *endit*) time, and by extension a fair, a *feria* or holy day being also a holiday.

over the fair. The *Foire du Lendit* is almost as famous in the chansons as those of Champagne, especially in the *Chanson du pélerinage de Charlemagne à Jérusalem*, the *Fierabras,* and the *Dit du Lendit.*

We have the right to insist upon the commercial, legal, civilizing part played by the great fairs in the Middle Ages. A great quantity of articles—wheat, linen, silk and cotton goods, alum and dyestuffs, arms and metals, and many other objects besides, fed a traffic on land and sea which far surpassed the limits of urban and mere market economy. Is it necessary to recall the character, not only national, but even worldwide, of the wool trade of England and the vast field of expansion, the extent and the power of the cloth trade of Tuscany and of Flanders in this epoch?

Far and away the most famous fairs in medieval Europe were those of Champagne. Lying to the east and southeast of Paris was the remarkable collection of fiefs ruled for most of three centuries by the counts of Champagne, a line or succession of rulers rivaling the strong royal house itself in its best days in energy, wisdom, power, and affluence. Of the five counties ruled by these powerful seigniors, those of Champagne and Brie formed the most important part. Physically undivided, they occupied the great elevated plain beginning a few miles east of Paris, extending from the valley of the Seine and the Oise to the border of Germany. To the south lay the great duchy of Burgundy, to the north the counties of Hainaut, Brabant, and Flanders.

A glance at the map is sufficient to convince one of the wonderful natural advantages of the Champagne country. This great fertile plain of France is blest with one of the most marvelous river systems, or rather groups of river systems, to be found anywhere in the world. Through it flows the upper Seine, giving outlet to Normandy and the Channel coast; along its eastern border from south to north flows the Meuse on its way to the Low Countries and the North Sea. A few miles to the southeast, across what was in the Middle Ages the duchy of Burgundy, are the Moselle and ,the Saône, the latter the chief tributary of the Rhone and hence an important outlet to the Mediterranean and the whole world of medieval commerce. Almost as close on the southwest and flowing through the county of Blois, also a possession of the counts of Champagne in the Middle Ages, is the Loire, chief waterway to the western sea. Two other rivers, the Marne and the Moselle, furnished an almost complete water transportation from east to west through the Marne gap, thus connecting the Rhine and the Seine. The Great and Little St. Bernard, the Mont Cenis, the Mont Genèvre passes of the Alps, supplemented by the admirable river system, connected Champagne with North Italy. And those Italian merchants who did not cross the Alps, like the Genoese, Pisans, Sienese, found the way to Champagne as easy up the Rhone and the Saône.

Another striking fact concerning the Champagne country is its central location. Lying midway between the thriving towns of the Low Countries, the English wool-growers, the fisheries of the North Sea, and the bankers and merchant importers of Italy and Languedoc on the south, between Germany on the east and all of the realm of France

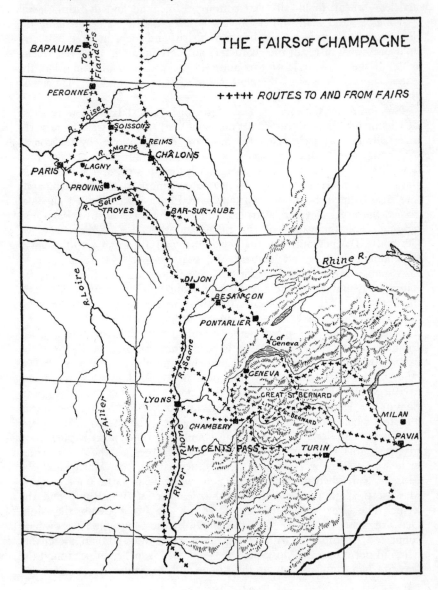

THE FAIRS OF CHAMPAGNE

++++ ROUTES TO AND FROM FAIRS

to west and south, it is no wonder that Champagne became the meeting-place of the nations in the new age of commerce and industry opening up in the eleventh and twelfth centuries. Champagne was the focal point of central European trade where all routes from north and south, from east and west converged.

Moreover, in addition to being middleman and place of distribution of all of this commerce, Champagne was a goodly land in itself. For ages its well watered and well drained valleys have been famous for rich yields of grain and wine, live stock, wool, and dairy products. Its climate is moderate and mild. Thanks to its natural fertility and intelligent government, Champagne very early became the home of a numerous and happy population. The counts of Champagne were eager promoters of the material welfare of their territories. The records abound with evidences of their surveys of woods and waters, the drainage of marshes, the peopling of thinly populated areas. They were notably active in seeking to exterminate wolves, whose considerable presence testifies to the existence of much forest land in the twelfth and thirteenth centuries, in a region now almost destitute of timber.

The precise date of the foundation of the famous Fairs of Champagne is lost in obscurity. Probably as far back as there has been a movement of peoples and goods across the continent, just so long has there been a mart at this point. Roman records show that there was a fair at Troyes in the fifth century. But no organic connection can be shown between Roman fairs and the great Champagne Fairs of the twelfth and thirteenth centuries. A French chanson makes Charles the Bald the founder of the Champagne Fairs. But we must cast this theory aside. The fair at Provins is said to have arisen in the ninth century. Tradition relates that because of fear of the Norsemen the relics of St. Ayoul were carried from their resting place at St. Benoît-sur-Loire to Provins, where Count Etienne conceded and confirmed a fair for the benefit of the church of St. Ayoul. The earliest certain date is 963, when a fair at Châlons-sur-Marne is mentioned. Another was at Lagny-sur-Marne in 996. The slave dealers of Verdun were at the Champagne Fairs in 996. The fairs of Bar-sur-Aube and Troyes appear in 1114. How early Italian merchants appeared at them, we do not know. As far back as the reign of Philip I of France, Pope Gregory VII (died 1085) unwarrantably accused him of despoiling Italian merchants going to the Champagne Fairs.

A whole series of official documents authentically dated, beginning in the early twelfth century, proves conclusively that the Champagne Fairs were established and flourishing institutions at the opening of that century. These documents are of various kinds: grants from the counts to a near-by abbey or church of the taxes or revenues on certain kinds of merchandise, of a certain share of all revenues, or

permits to rent their houses to sojourners at the fairs. Papal bulls
and various charters from ecclesiastical authorities, as well as grants
from lesser lay lords, refer to the fairs and their importance. A charter of Count Hugh of Troyes in 1114 granted to the abbey of Montier-
en-Der the taxes on horses and other beasts sold at the fairs of Bar.
and another of the same year gave similar favors to the abbey of St.
Pierre-de-la-Celle at Troyes. Charters of 1137 and thereafter show the
fairs of Provins to be well established. In 1157 a charter of Count
Henry of Champagne in favor of the church of St. Etienne proves
the existence of the fairs of Lagny and shows their organization and
protection to be a thing well developed and of long standing. From
1157 on the charters of the Fairs of Champagne and Brie are frequent.
By the middle of the twelfth century they were in a highly organized
state and long before the end of the century their fame was international, and their activity and magnificence of wealth became an object
of universal admiration.

The Fairs of Champagne were really a series of fairs, and in the
later days at least, the tendency was toward a constant increase of their
number. Yet from the beginning certain centres were preëminent,
and the fairs held at these places were of an international character.
Six fairs in particular, of the more than fifty markets existing at one
time or another, had assumed such prominence as to become known as
the "Fairs of Champagne." One of these was at Bar, one at Lagny,
and two each at Provins and Troyes every year. Other fairs were held,
even at these places, and in later years repeated grants were made for
markets and fairs at other towns in Champagne, but these six remained
the leading fairs. The most important of the lesser places were Eper-
nay, Vitry, Nogent, and Châlons. Once the natural advantage of these
special points became apparent the counts set them apart by special
legislation, regulation and safeguards, so that soon all outside interest
was concentrated in them. Other fairs might have local importance
as markets and exchanges, but none could hope to win great international
patronage.

At first the duration of the fairs was rather short, but by repeated
grants and concessions they were extended until each of them covered
a period of something over six weeks, so that, with the intervals required for settling up affairs and moving on to the next stand the six
fairs gave Champagne an almost continuous market throughout the year.
The fair of Bar-sur-Aube in 1160 lasted but fifteen days, but by 1250
it was somewhere around five weeks long, and ultimately it was still
longer. Something of the same kind of process occurred in the cases of
Provins, Troyes, and Lagny, only much earlier. In the heyday of the
fairs that of Lagny commenced on January 2; on Shrove Tuesday the
fair of Bar was opened; the May fair of Provins commenced the last

of April or early in May, depending upon the fair of Bar, which followed the movable calendar of the Church. The fair of St. John, or the "hot" fair of Troyes as it was called, opened the Tuesday after a fortnight from the nativity of St. John (June 24), in any case during the first two weeks of July, and lasted until September 14. The fair of St. Ayoul of Provins began on the day of the Exaltation of the Cross (September 14) and lasted till All Saints' Day (November 1). It was held in the lower city, while the May fair of the same city was held in the upper city. Finally the fair of St. Rémy, or the "cold" fair of Troyes, began on November 2, and practically closed the year, lasting until the week before Christmas.

Of these fairs, that of Lagny belonged to the monks of St. Pierre de Lagny, and the proceeds of the first seven days of the autumn fair, or fair of St. Ayoul of Provins, were the perquisite of the monks of St. Ayoul. The rest belonged to the counts of Champagne, save as they granted portions of them to others for a time. All were dependent for support and protection upon the administration of the counts.

The order of business in the fairs seems to have varied somewhat in early years, but tended to become fixed and uniform for all the great fairs as the regulation of the counts was extended over them. Eight days of entry at each fair were allowed the merchants in which to arrive, install themselves, unpack and place their goods on exhibition. During this time no taxes or dues were collected from them. Then came ten days of the fair itself, called the *foire de draps* or fair of woolens. During this time only cloth was to be sold or bought in the premises of the fair. On the evening of the tenth day of the *foire de draps* the cry of "Haro, Haro!" was sounded by the sergeants throughout the city and the cloth disappeared. The next day the fair of hides, peltries, and furs opened, and it likewise occupied ten days of the fair. When the cry of "Haro" closed this fair, there began the fair of *avoir de poids,* or things sold by weight and measure, which covered an innumerable variety of articles. This was also the time of paying fees to the officials and government of the fair. During most of this time the fair of horses and other beasts brought from near-by places and even remote counties of France went on. Four weeks from the close of the cloth fair the final cry of "Haro" closed up the booths of the money-changers and the fair was over. Five days of grace were allowed for the completion of inventories, settlement with the count's officials, obtaining "letters of change," and having the seal of the fair placed on all important contracts to insure their validity. The ringing of the bell each morning was the signal for the opening of the booths, and when it rang at nightfall they were closed. There was no selling except between these hours.

In appearance the fair differed very much from the markets of Paris and many other cities, in that the fair instead of being confined to a single hall was spread all over town. These towns had their own local markets for fish, meat, and other staples of local consumption, but the fairs occupied the towns, dominated them socially and economically, and it was natural that the town should largely be given over to them. In particular at Provins, the two fairs occupied at one time or another both the upper and lower town.

The counts provided commodious halls and great storehouses in each of the towns. At Provins these magazines were largely underground, connected by subways, making a veritable subterranean city. Many communities or groups of communities trading at the fairs owned their permanent halls in one or more of the four towns. These houses, booths, stables, and storehouses served as hotels and places for displaying and selling goods. In the great throng were merchants from the chief provinces of France—Normandy, Flanders, Languedoc, Picardy, Provence, and foreign merchants from Italy, Germany, the Low Countries, England, Spain, Portugal, and even Poland. German merchants are first mentioned in 1178. The Sienese were frequent visitors. The merchandise was as varied as the merchants. It consisted of cattle and produce, cloth of every kind—silks from the Far East, woolen goods from Flanders and Tuscany, linen from Brittany, canvas from Cahors, furs from Scandinavia and Russia, iron and leather goods from Germany, wines from the south of France and Spain, and a complex variety of condiments and spices brought by Italian and Provençal merchants from the Orient.

Of the goods exchanged at the Fairs of Champagne, cloth, and especially woolen cloth, stood first in importance. Not the least of the sources for this commodity were the Champagne towns themselves. Provins early became well developed in this industry. In 1230 it is said that in this town of 5000 hearths there were 3000 loom workers, with fullers and carders for the manufacture of wool. Cloth of many kinds from the very finest to the coarsest and for every purpose was woven. Dyeing was far advanced. The gilds were highly organized and the business of cloth-making was minutely regulated by the counts and the kings who succeeded them. At Troyes, Bar, and Lagny there were cloth industries, though not so extensive as at Provins. At Châlons-sur-Marne and Rheims were weaving industries. From many towns in France came woolen goods, among them Rouen, Arras, Beauvais, Paris, St. Denis, Toulouse, Montpellier, and Limoges. From Flanders—Malines, Ypres, St. Omer, Diest, Ghent, Valenciennes, Lille, Bruges, Namur, Douai, Dixmude, Cambrai, Louvain, and other places—came still more. Linens came from the four towns of the Fairs and Rheims, from Germany, especially from Ulm, and very famous ones from Burgundy, as well as from Besançon and Lorraine. Silks from far-off countries, and especially from and through the Italian towns, were important.

Lucca's silk products had a great reputation at the Fairs, as they did throughout the western world. Besides, there were other textiles of a rarer sort. From the Levant, Syria, Persia, and Egypt came wonderful cloth of gold and silver for the vestments and garments of the great folk and for the ceremonial robes of the priesthood.

Abundance of hides, furs, peltry, came to all of the Fairs, but especially to the fair of Lagny. Some hides, especially sheep skins for which it was famous, were furnished by Champagne itself. Cordovan leather came from Barcelona or Lérida in Spain or from Montpellier, Aurillac, Limoges, and Toulouse in southern France; for this famous product was imitated more or less successfully in many places. Paris itself sent some hides to the Fairs of Champagne. Peltries and furs came from every direction and were of many and varied types, skins of sheep, goats, rabbits, hares, squirrels, the lerot (a species of dormouse), ermine, marten, otter, civet, sable, deer (this not valued highly), beaver, cats both wild and tame, fox, polecat, wolf, and others.

Under the name of *avoir de poids* were sold every kind of spices from the Orient, drugs of all kinds, dyes such as indigo and cochineal, the latter from Provence, salt, silk, hemp cord, ointments, lard, tallow, honeycomb, sugar, wax, dates, lemons, and fruits.

Provisions and drinks included many things. Many of these were of local production and were brought to the fairs for the necessities of the inhabitants and the crowds of strangers drawn to the fairs. Provins alone had two great halls for the selling of wheat and taking of tolls thereon, one in the lower and one in the upper town, and two halls for butchers and two for fish stalls hardly sufficed for her needs. The butchers' halls each contained an abattoir as well as stalls for the sale of foods. Among the foodstuffs sold were cereals and vegetables—wheat, beans, peas, cabbages, garlics, leeks,—cattle, sheep, hogs, and kids, and the flesh of each. Salted and fresh-water fish of every kind were sold in the great fish stalls. The cheese of Brie was already renowned in the Middle Ages. Though much of this foodstuff came from Champagne and Brie, evidence is not lacking that much also, particularly such things as cattle on hoof, came from Flanders, Brabant, and Hainaut as well as adjacent French counties. Native and foreign wines played an important part in the grand exchange of the fairs, as the numerous tolls and taxes placed upon them would indicate. The wines of Champagne were famous in story and verse, as was *cervoise,* or beer brewed there and consumed principally in Flanders and Picardy. The tariffs contain many references to this merchandise.

The Champagne Fairs powerfully stimulated the local economic activities of the region. Sheep-raising and the manufacture of woolen goods became an important industry of Champagne; iron-working was largely carried on along the upper Marne and in Lorraine; a whole quarter at

Troyes was occupied by the tanners; the dyers of Provins, the fullers of Bierges, and La-Ferté-sur-Aube, were famous. Rheims made woolen cloths, bunting, serges.

Gold, silver, precious stones, iron, steel, incense, wood of various kinds, charcoal, raw wools and silk, silk floss, hemp, linen, cotton (to be mixed with wool, silk, or linen), salt and other articles are enumerated by Bourquelot as of chief importance and frequently mentioned in the tariffs. Beasts of burden—horses, mules, and asses—came in great numbers and at each of the Fairs was a great square for the sale of them which went on during most of the time of the fair. A portion of the *tonlieu* from these sales of beasts was frequently given to the local abbey.

Manufactured objects of various kinds besides those already mentioned as being at the Fairs were pots and pails of copper and brass, especially the latter, from Dinant; firkins and tubs from Alsace; vases of various metals, basins, kettles, and caldrons. The *"pots et pailles"* of Dinant were famous. Saddler's products, haberdashery, and even old clothes found a market at the Fairs. Tassels, purses, headdresses, gloves, hats, hose, mirrors (not glass but bits of highly polished metal), baskets, cushions, parchment, wheels and carts, and cutlery were on sale. Of cutlery, Provins itself became in later days a leading centre. Jewels, precious stones, and the work of goldsmiths and silversmiths were bought at the Fairs, as many a literary reference shows. Ink stands or ink horns, beads of amber, bells for cows, horsewhips, steel anvils, whetstones from Ardennes or England, wooden spoons, and many other articles were there to find buyers.

A study of the weights and measures and the kinds of standard of money used at the Champagne Fairs would be too complicated to enter into here. Measures in particular varied very much in various parts of France and many different units were used. Almost every province had its own system. The hogshead, the *setier,* which was generally one-twelfth of a hogshead, and the bushel for grains, with the hogshead for liquids, were the most common measures. But the weights and measures of the Champagne Fairs tended to set a standard for the country. One standard has survived to this day—troy weight, so named from Troyes. Of course there were many subdivisions of each measure. The variation of weights was not quite so wide as that of measures, but the same lack of uniformity is to be observed. Here again the weights of Champagne came to be a standard over a wide area. The weights were originally the property of the counts, but were frequently granted in part or in special fairs to abbeys or other organizations as a sort of revenue, since the goods sold must be weighed and a fee paid for the service. The *aune* was the measure for cloth. This was a measure that varied widely but in Champagne came to mean nearly three feet and eight inches. The *aune* of Provins, still preserved in the form of an iron ferrule formerly in the care of the monastery, measured three feet, seven and one-quarter inches. It tended to become the standard, even being adopted in Burgundy. The memory of it survives in the "cloth-yard."

The part played by the counts of Champagne in the development of the Fairs at international marts was important. This remarkable line of rulers remained unbroken from 1010 until 1284, when the heiress of Champagne married Philip the Fair, who in 1285 became king of France, thus joining the administration of the counties of Champagne and Brie to that of France. This long line of Étiennes, Henris and Thibauts, aided and supported by able and broad-minded wives, with occasionally a woman ruler, conceived and carried out a statesmanlike plan of internal regulation and external support and protection for these Fairs. Feudal annals present few such instances of breadth and consistency of view.

The glorious period of the Fairs of Champagne was under the rule of the brilliant count of Champagne known as Henry I, the "Liberal" (1152–81). In the third year of his reign he issued a notable ordinance in restraint of private war, and formally assured the security of the peasantry and merchants within his dominions. He was seconded in this policy by the archbishop of Rheims, who was a brother of King Louis VII. Under Henry's rule the fairs of Lagny, Bar-sur-Aube, Provins, and Troyes acquired an international importance.

The Fairs gave the towns what renown they had and it was fitting that the town should be given over to the fair. As one of the chief sources of revenue to the counts and the principal object of their solicitude, it was but natural that the fair in its administration should overshadow the local arrangements or even completely displace them during the period of the fair. Since under the regulations all fees not otherwise disposed of belonged to the count, and since merchants established outside the limits of the fair paid no fee, it became vital to make the limits of the fair approach those of the town, so that there could be no advantage from staying outside the fair. The control of the town by the count's officials became analogous to the control of other towns by merchant gilds. Not only were the boundaries of the fair thus definitely laid out, but even the locations of merchant groups, individuals, and the very goods themselves were controlled by the count's officials. The minutely ordered daily, weekly, and monthly programme described above was part of the same scheme. All of this was for the purpose of police supervision and to the end that nothing due the count should escape his officials.

For this administration an elaborate system of officials was developed. Of these the "guards of the fair" seem to be the earliest. The first documentary record of them is in 1174; after that they appear in records throughout the history of the Fairs. Generally the guards were two in number, though in 1225 there appear to have been three. They were paid a fixed salary, a thing unique for such officials, and showing how careful was the personal attention of the counts. Their functions were manifold, comprising the judicial, the execution of the police power, and the promulgation of regulating ordinances, in a word, the general direction of the Fairs of Champagne.

The clerks of the Fairs, often called the "lieutenants of the guards," are first mentioned in the second half of the thirteenth century. They were originally persons of note called occasionally to take the place of guards who were absent or removed from office. Somewhat after the fashion of the old Frankish Mayor of the Palace, the lieutenants of the guards tended to absorb the functions of the guards until finally they became the real directors of the Fair. The chancellor, or "guard of the seal" of the Fairs had the important function of attaching the count's seal to all important contracts made during the Fairs. This seal guaranteed the validity of the contract and assured the contracting parties that the power of the count would be used to enforce it. The sergeants of the Fairs were the police officers chosen by the guards and chancellor to maintain order and peace in the Fairs and to execute the multifarious orders of the guards. The number of these varied, but in the best days of the Fairs it was necessarily a very respectable force. In 1317 it consisted of 140 men, 120 on foot and 20 mounted. After 1344 the number was reduced to 100, but by this time the Fairs had gone far towards their decline. Something like 40 notaries were needed to act as recorders and draw up contracts for the merchants.

Besides this organization of the counts, the local mayor shared in the administration. Church officials, especially the Benedictines of St. Ayoul of Provins and the abbot of Lagny, exercised a wide jurisdiction, fiscal and judicial in particular, over the part of the Fairs committed to their keeping. Certain classes of cases were exempted from the jurisdiction of the count's courts and these were handled in Church and local courts. The *baillis* of the king and later the *prévôts* often shared with the count's officials in local supervision.

The courts of the Champagne Fairs call for at least a passing notice. Somewhat after the fashion of the Court of Pie Powder of the Normans, there were local courts in the Fairs for the settlement of disputes that arose. These were in the hands of the guards of the Fairs and their assistants, with the Church officials, or in rare cases apparently in the hands of local officials. At Troyes what was known as the *Cour des Grands Jours de Troyes* was attached to the count's administration and became a sort of court of appeals for the Fairs of Champagne and Brie. From this court appeal was had to the supreme court of the realm, the Parlement of Paris.

Outside the limits of the counties of Champagne and Brie the activity of the counts was still further responsible for the growth of the Fairs. By treaties and conventions with the many countries through which the merchants trading at the Fairs passed, a large part of the usual tolls of passage was remitted for traders to Champagne. The power and fame of the counts served to protect the merchants even where there were no treaties. Further, the counts endeavored to protect their clients, not only from feudal exactions, but from robbers and brigands of all sorts. When this *conduit des foires* was violated along the road the counts did not hesitate to protest most vigorously to the governing powers of the offending community, even though it were to the Capetians themselves, as in the well known case of Thibaut the Great, who in 1148 protested to Suger because the money-changers of Vézelay had been robbed in the county of Sens with the connivance probably of the son of the viscount of Sens. A powerful weapon in the hands of the counts was the threat of exclusion of the merchants of an offending community from the Champagne Fairs until redress had been made by the offending individuals or some one else for them. This was used to enforce the collection of debts and thus the merchants dealing at the Fairs were compelled to make good the guaranty of the count. Even when not used as a threat, this power to exclude communities from a share in the rich business of the Fairs was sufficient to compel obedience.

But the *conduit des foires,* while it served to protect the money-changers and merchants from violence and from many of the tolls along the road, could not wholly bring free trade. Powerful seigniors could not be expected to forego such rich sources of revenue. A notable instance of this was the system of *péages* collected by the kings of France on the border line of the Low Countries, at Bapaume in Artois, and at Péronne, Roye, Compiègne, and Crépy-en-Valois. Of these points, by far the most important was Bapaume, and frequent charges were made that the royal collectors at that place monopolized the tolls on merchants coming into France. The enforcement of these tolls was a serious blow to the Champagne Fairs, where the bulk of Flemish goods was destined to be sold and in 1262 we find bitter complaint of the French king's extortion at Bapaume. In 1293 Philip the Fair, then in authority over the Champagne Fairs through his marriage with the heiress, issued an order exempting Hanseatic merchants if they were bringing to the Champagne Fairs goods from Germany, but compelled them to pay if they carried Flemish goods. This legislation of the French kings in the thirteenth century in restraint of Flemish trade is very interesting to observe. They ardently coveted possession of the rich and populous territory of Flanders and adopted this method of restraint of commerce in order to starve Flanders into submission. By the end of the thirteenth century "trade" had entered politics, and we can discover evidence of tariff wars and intimations of the future great mercantilistic policy of the seventeenth century.

The merchants trading at the Champagne Fairs did not usually travel alone but grouped themselves in some sort of organization, choosing a leader or "captain" who performed the duties of director of the body, and consular duties in dealing for the company as a whole and obtaining commercial privileges from the count of Champagne or other rulers. Such a group was that composed of the merchants of Languedoc and Provence in the thirteenth century, who called themselves the "Society and Community of the Merchants of France." Montpellier had the privilege of naming the captain, who was put on oath as the "Captain Consul of France and Merchants Trading in France." Similar organizations existed among the Lombard and Sienese merchants.

No port in the world whose commerce was worth much failed to touch in some degree these great inland markets. Naturally the progressive industrial and commercial towns of Italy and southern France and those of Flanders made the greatest use of the Champagne Fairs. Thus there came to the Champagne Fairs a cosmopolitan crowd of every race, language, and costume, from Scotland to Sicily and from Castile to Damascus. Egyptian, Syrian, Armenian, Greek, Italian, Frenchman, Spaniard, German, Hollander, Brabanter, Fleming, Englishman, and Scot mingled and jostled each other through the great halls or added their voices to the eager, humming babel that rose and fell around the pillars where the bargaining and chaffering was going on. And the omnipresent Jew from everywhere added his individuality to the throng.

The Champagne Fairs had a profound influence upon the conduct and technique of business. As the Fairs emerged from obscurity a money economy was more and more established. Various kinds of money were used, corresponding in diversity almost to the heterogeneous throng that gathered to Champagne from the ends of the earth. Money of Tournay, of Paris, of Poitou and other parts of France, "easterlings" from England, bezants, and every sort of Italian coin appeared. In Champagne itself were many different coinages, lay and episcopal, but the most famous were the coins of Provins, which made a standard for the Champagne Fairs. An interesting fact is that the monetary system was well developed along the line of "money of account." The denier with its subdivisions was actually struck, while the sou and livre were theoretical coins used in accounting and credit. In the fourteenth century, Pegolotti, a Florentine who dwelt in Cyprus but traveled much, "judged it necessary to prepare a table of moneys and of weights and measures in use at Alexandria, on the one hand and in ten places in Italy, in Provence and the Fairs of Champagne."

The assembly of so many merchants at the Fairs naturally drew much money to Champagne. In addition men took this opportunity to carry on transactions having no connection with commerce—the payment of debts contracted in distant lands, even arrearages in rents. The payment of tolls and charges of all kinds created further demands for money. Hence there were many reasons why money should flow to Champagne. Exchange of goods and money was facilitated by the important institution of the *changeurs* who performed the operations today done by bankers. This institution was of very early origin. In fact it grew up with the Fairs. Documents of the thirteenth century often mention the money-changers. In the fourteenth century, under the kings, they were officially recognized as public officers. Their establishments at the Fairs were simple booths, containing each a table covered with a checkered cloth, a pair of scales, and leathern bags filled with coins or ingots. Their business was to change money, for which they received a regular rate of exchange, to receive deposits, to loan money on interest, and to issue *lettres de foires,* or bills of credit, in order to obviate the danger and trouble of transporting bodily the ever increasing quantity of metal money. They were allowed to take interest on their loans, and loaned money often to the counts and countesses themselves. The Italians from Lombardy, a strongly organized group, were the earliest to seize any large part of this business, and they were long the most noted of the *changeurs* at the Fairs, but others came, especially the Cahorsians and the Jews.

Closely connected with the ordering of the Fairs is the question of the revenues. It will be remembered that the fair of Lagny and the first seven days of the fair of St. Ayoul of Provins were given over to the local abbeys. Of the rest of the fairs which belonged to the counts, it was customary for them to make certain specific grants to local orders, monasteries, Templars, or others. Sometimes the special grant was the right to a certain *tonlieu* or tax on beasts sold, or on certain other articles. Sometimes it was the right of weighing or measuring. In the main the revenues of the cloth and peltry fairs, as well as from much of the *avoir de poids,* the counts reserved for themselves. The variety of fees and tolls paid by the patrons of the Fairs is a monument of ingenuity. One of the most important as well as the most common was the *tonlieu* or tax made on each sale, a small fee prescribed for every sale and collected at the time of the transaction. Theoretically it was paid, half by the seller and half by the buyer, but probably as a practical thing the buyer paid all. In addition there were fees for the rent of houses, fees raised on the habitations and stalls of merchants, fees for entry and departure, for stallage, for *salage* or the preservation of food by salt, for measuring and weighing everything, special taxes on wines, special taxes on the Jews and Lombards, fees for the attaching of the seal of the Fairs to contracts, besides fines and defaults, which tended to increase under the kings.

To the foreign merchants from many lands were added the local merchants of the various Champagne towns, the small retailers and peddlers, who came to replenish their stocks. The neighboring lords and their families came to see and to buy and enjoy the diversions of the Fair. The monks from the abbey and secular clergy mingled with the throng. No doubt many an artisan and many a runaway serf from the neighboring manors was drawn hither by the strange sights and sounds and the gay-colored crowd. Mountebanks, jugglers, and musicians of every description vied in their efforts to attract the crowd, men with trained monkeys, dogs, or dancing bears, wrestlers, wandering minstrels singing ancient lays, fakers without number were there to entertain and astonish the populace. There were gathered as in modern fairs the thief, the pickpocket, the cut-purse, the thug, the prostitute, beggars. Often the sergeants were hard pressed to maintain order in this heterogeneous mob. "In the evening when the trumpeters with their escort of torch-bearers had sounded the curfew, the vagabonds, the drunkards, the thieves, the whole world of beggars, of male and female debauchees for whom the Fair was a rendezvous, gave them more trouble than the crowd during the day." Many of the *fabliaux* of the twelfth and thirteenth centuries, as the story of *La Bourse pleine de sens,* the *Dit des Marcheanz,* and the romance of *Hervis,* another fragment of the *Loherain* cycle, throw interesting light upon the life and activities of the Champagne Fairs.

The Fairs of Champagne and Brie seem to have begun to decline even during the latter days of the counts, partly because of the creation of onerous fees and partly because of the coercive commercial policy of the kings of France. The chief cause of decay was the constant increase of royal taxes and imposts indirectly imposed upon the Fairs. As early as 1262, as we have seen, the Flemish merchants had threatened to forsake the Champagne Fairs if the tolls charged them at Bapaume were not lowered. The marriage of Jeanne, heiress of Champagne, to Philip the Fair in 1284, which brought Champagne and Brie at once under the actual control of the French crown, was a body blow to the Fairs. The notorious fiscal measures of the French king soon led to such oppressive taxation that the merchants began to avoid them. In 1296 the Florentines removed to Lyons. In the same year Philip IV began his war with Flanders, and the long involvement of Flanders in the war between France and England thereafter seriously injured the Fairs. Finally, when the Venetians opened the famous all-sea galley route to Bruges and London *via* the straits of Gibraltar and the Channel in 1317 the Champagne Fairs received almost a death-blow. They shrank to mere provincial markets.

CHAPTER XXIV

THE NEW MONASTIC ORDERS—CLUNIACS, CISTERCIANS, PREMONSTRATENSIANS, FRANCISCANS, DOMINICANS

THE influence of monasticism reached its height in the tenth, eleventh, and twelfth centuries, and indeed, was so great that a somewhat close study of the institution in this period is necessary. Even contemporaries were struck by the wide and rapid spread of monasticism then. This multiplication of new orders is a singular testimony to the faith of the Middle Ages. For every new order without exception was founded to reform the corruption of the older orders. "The history of monachism is one long record of corruptions and reforms." So the Cluniacs followed the Benedictines in the tenth century, the Cistercians followed the Cluniacs in the twelfth, the Franciscans and Dominicans followed all three of the previous great orders in the thirteenth. The remedy for monastic corruption always was more monks—the founding of a new order to redress the evils of the former, to reintegrate the system. It rarely seems to have struck the medieval mind that perhaps the proper remedy was not more, but fewer monks; any more than today, with the evils of unrestricted democracy so evident, few suggest the remedy of endeavoring to make the world less democratic.

Yet now and then one finds a voice of protest raised against the increase of monasticism. "The world is full of monks and monasteries," wrote a German thinker in the twelfth century. "To what use?" Dialogues between monks and seculars as to the relative merits of the two classes of clergy, and virulent tirades against monasticism are not uncommon in medieval literature. But usually one must discount their arguments because there was political, social, and economic rivalry between the two clerical classes amounting to bitter antagonism. Each competed for possession of land, each intrigued with and against the reigning feudality and feudal kings. The orders were not slow to utilize the popularity which they enjoyed. Statistics of the number of monasteries founded in each century are illuminating and suggestive. The following figures pertain to France in the Middle Ages: fourth century, 11; fifth century, 40; sixth century, 262; seventh century, 280; eighth century, 107; ninth century, 251; tenth century, 157; eleventh century (the age of Cluny), 326; twelfth century (the age of the Cistercians), 702. At the end of the tenth century there were 543 abbeys in France. From the time of the Franciscans and Dominicans there is a sharp falling off in the number of new monasteries. In the thirteenth century we find 287; in the fourteenth century (the period of the English wars in France and the beginning of the Great Schism), only 53. In the fifteenth century the number drops to 26. No wonder that Trithemius in 1493 complained, "Once princes erected and endowed cloisters; today they plunder and destroy them"; and later in 1496 mournfully wrote: "The days of building cloisters are past. The days of their destruction are coming." Forty years afterwards Henry VIII abolished the monasteries in England.

Sharing in the feudal world, an abbey was a lordship, vassal or suzerain, but suzerain in its own rank, possessing vassals and having serfs by whose labor on its lands it was enriched. The abbey of St. Riquier, which did not pass for being very rich, had 117 vassals holding in fief of it; it owned 2500 houses of the town in which it was situated, or rather of the town which had grown up around it, whose tenants paid a money rent and in addition were required to furnish 10,000 chickens, 10,000 capons, 75,000 eggs, and 400 pounds of wax to the monastery. "The inventory of the rents and dues owing to the abbey of St. Riquier shows us, as early as 831, a numerous population of lay artisans grouped in streets according to their trades around that abbey, and in return for lands which are granted to them, furnishing some, tools, others, binding or clothes or articles of food."

No medieval institution was a greater object of popular piety than the monasteries. Not unusually they were enormously endowed at the time of establishment. The nunnery of Gandersheim, the favorite foundation of the Saxon house, was started in 956 with an endowment of 11,000 manors; Hersfeld in thirty years accumulated 2000 manors scattered in 195 localities; Tegernsee in Bavaria, before Duke Arnulf despoiled it early in the tenth century, owned 11,866 manors; Benedictbeuren, which suffered the same fate, owned 6700 manors. Fulda possessed 15,000; Lorsch, 2000; St. Gall, 4000. As early as 787 St. Wandrille possessed 4264 manors; St. Bertin owned more than 100 villages in the ninth century; St. Riquier, 2500 manors; Charles the Bald endowed Avenay with 1150 manors for the support of 40 nuns and 20 clerks. In 1023 Henry II deprived St. Maximin of Trèves of 6656 manors and still left it rich. By 1030 it possessed over a thousand manors scattered in 140 localities. By the twelfth century Fulda had so far picked up again after deprivation that it had 3000 manors in Saxony, 3000 in Thuringia, 3000 in the Rhinelands around Worms, and 3000 in Bavaria and Swabia. St. Ulrich, accounted as very poor indeed, owned 203 manors, on each of which was located from one to six villages.

On the other hand, there were many small monasteries occupied by a mere handful of monks. But the tendency was for the smaller to disappear through absorption by the greater abbeys—Cluny largely grew in this way—or engrossment by a local feudal noble to whose depredation their small size and isolation exposed them. The isolation of such small houses is remarkably illustrated in an incident related by Hermann of Tournay. The abbey of St. Martin in Tournay was a rich one and possessed a charter given it by Charlemagne. During the Norse invasions in the ninth century, in order to preserve its treasures and manuscripts from their ravages, the abbot of St. Martin sent them away

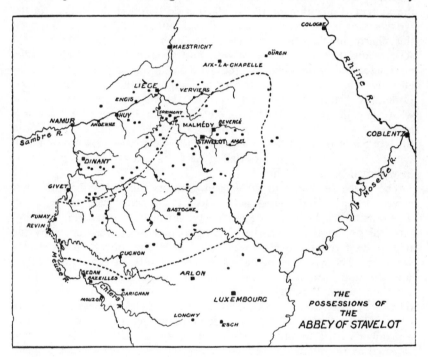

THE POSSESSIONS OF THE ABBEY OF STAVELOT

to Ferrières in the diocese of Paris. At that time Ferrières was an important house and made distinguished by the scholarship of its famous abbot Lupus. But the ravages of the Norsemen in the basin of the Seine, combined with the feudal anarchy of the tenth century, impoverished it, reduced its numbers, so that it ceased to be generally known. St. Martin lost trace of its charter and even was ignorant of where Ferrières was situated. Nearly two hundred years later it so happened that a monk of Courtrai, who had visited Ferrières was one day at St. Martin's and remarked to the abbot that he had seen a charter of Charlemagne belonging to St. Martin's at Ferrières. But the visitor got away before the abbot could ask him where Ferrières was. More years elapsed. Finally at the council of Rheims in 1119 the abbot fell in with a clerk from Paris who revealed its location and the lost charter was at last reclaimed and restored. Imola, though it had a bishop, and was located on one of the principal roads of Italy not far from Bologna, was not well informed about public events. Thus for more than two years after the accession of Henry V in 1106 it was believed that the emperor was named Charles.

Monastic life possessed great allurement for the medieval mind, especially for men who were studiously inclined or who shrank from the violent civilization of the feudal period. Guibert de Nogent in his *De vita sua,* one of the very few medieval autobiographies, has described this charm in eloquent language. The quiet life of cell, library, and scriptorium, the opportunity to read and to study, the sheltered walks in cloister and garden, excited the derision or contempt of lustier men-at-arms, who ridiculed the literary and academic labors of the monks. Ordericus Vitalis bitterly records this contempt of the feudality for what they did not understand and what was far superior in worth to their own violent activities. In the epic poem *Girart de Roussillon* this contempt of the warrior class for the cloister is very pronounced. One of the characters swears that if he finds a coward among his sons he will make a monk of him.

The anecdote points to an evil in monasticism not sufficiently perceived. In the Middle Ages a man had to be either hammer or anvil. The outside world was rude and lusty, no place for weaklings, either physical or moral. Hence the path to a monastery was for many the line of least resistance. The weak, the timid, the infirm, found shelter within it. The average mental and moral quality of most monasteries was probably low, and it was this condition which largely accounted for their constant deterioration and constant efforts at reform. Sometimes too, an energetic man might be made a monk against his will because it was a matter of family pride or family property interest to have a member of the family a monk. Such an inmate was bound to be dissatisfied or rebellious. A medieval satire tells the fable of such a monk sent on an errand by the abbot into the outer world. "He returned in the evening mounted on a foaming steed. He wore a bearskin on his head, his gown was cut short and divided behind and before to make riding easier. In his embroidered military belt he carried bow and quiver, hammer and tongs, a sword, a flint and steel, and an oaken club. He wore wide breeches and as his spurs were very long, he had to walk on tiptoe." From the pen of such a worldly brother we have an interesting little work entitled *The Delights of Chivalry.*

Contrary to what is generally thought, most monks in the Middle Ages were not priests entrusted with the cure of souls or spiritual duty to others.

As monks they neither preached nor heard confession, nor administered sacrament, nor exercised any spiritual function whatever. They were lay-men and nothing else but laymen, bound, indeed, by vows of poverty, chastity, and obedience; vows spontaneously assumed and such as any layman might take upon himself now, and yet in so doing would not cease to be layman. . . . They were associations of laymen appointing their own chaplains and possessing ecclesiastical property, but not ecclesiastics on that account. . . . Though these monks were in fact laymen and nothing more than laymen, . . . their purely laical character was forgotten by the world and their lay employments considered by their enemies as irreconcil-able with the strictness of their profession. Yet what it may be asked, was the essential difference in itself as distinct from its consequences, whether a monk labored in the fields as St. Augustine commanded, or superintended those that did? whether the abbot, as in earlier centuries, handled the trowel and stooped his back to mortar, or arranged with his tenants and others for the performance of such drudgery by deputy? [1]

The Benedictine Rule had approved of actual manual labor for all monks. But the old ideal of labor was soon obscured. The monks in feudal times had ceased to labor with their own hands. Their revenues derived from leases were sufficient for their wants. Labor was performed vicariously by serfs. This change was inevitable as the monasteries in-creasingly became peopled by sons of the feudal aristocracy to whom manual labor was repugnant. Men from this class devoted themselves to teaching, copying manuscripts, or administration.

Only in times of intense religious emotion, as during revival seasons, do we find monks in a sort of self-humiliation and for a short time performing actual manual labor. William of Jumièges records with some surprise, of the monks who founded the great monastery of Bec, that "you would have seen them after the office of the church going into the fields to spend the day in agricultural labors, the abbot carrying the seed on his head and holding tools in his hand, some clearing the land, others fertilizing the ground, no one eating his bread in idleness, and then all returning to the church at the hour of divine service." Again one Julian, in visiting a monastery, reports: "I found there some old men writing. I asked them where the abbot was and they replied: 'In the valley beneath the monastery. He is cutting grass'!"

But the blame for constant deterioration of the morals of the mon-asteries is not wholly to be attributed to internal conditions. The feudal conditions of the outside world had a large influence upon them. From the inception of the movement, monasteries were private foundations; that is to say, the proprietary class endowed them with lands and re-tained thereby a large measure of control over them. The local mag-nate often was a "lay abbot," enfiefing the abbey's lands and using a portion of its revenues for his own advantage. Hincmar of Rheims in the

[1] Giraldus Cambrensis, *Opera*, IV, introd. xxxiii, lx (Rolls Series).

ninth century wrote of Hugh the Welf, lay abbot of several rich monasteries: "Tonsure is the only thing which distinguishes him from the life of the laity." Kings, nobles, bishops, founded monasteries out of mixed motives of piety and self-aggrandizement. For, once established, the monastery's endowments increased rapidly owing to the largess of the pious who gave or bequeathed it lands, and the revenues derived from these increments in part accrued to the original founder or his family. Thus, the founding of a monastery in the Middle Ages was a lucrative form of investment. For the founder was the overlord. Abbeys created by laymen were the hereditary property of the founder's descendants, their revenues formed part of his estates, they were bequeathed, devised, partitioned among his heirs. The only restraining fact was that they could not be wholly secularized or abolished.

In the darkest and most violent days of feudalism the monasteries, in common with all other institutions, declined. Ruined by the invasions of the Northmen in France and the lower Rhineland, by the inroads of the Hungarians in Germany and North Italy, by those of the Saracens along the Mediterranean coast and far up into the Alpine passes, by the trespass of the feudality upon their lands and the seizure of their property, many of their inmates fled the cloister and resorted to a life of pillage like that of the baronage. The serfs upon the monastery lands had run away or perished in the anarchy, and those that were left were often numerically so reduced that the monks themselves were compelled to till the glebe farms. In the tenth century complaints are common against the monks, who are accused of licentiousness, of neglecting their vows, of eating meat on fast days, of drunkenness, and of refusing hospitality. The plight of the monasteries was so bad that they seemed incapable of reforming themselves.

From this depth the monastic reform movements of the tenth and eleventh centuries rescued them. New orders arose, like the Cluniacs, the Cistercians, the Carthusians. And with their rise Europe entered upon not only a new spiritual, but a new temporal improvement. Manors, fields, forests, vineyards, pastures, mills, dairies, were showered upon them. The abbeys opened regular markets for the sale of their produce; their shops manufactured wooden, leather, textile, iron, and copper materials. The abbots, like lay nobles, even coined their own money. Guibert de Nogent has vividly described this monastic revivalism:

When nowhere but in the oldest monasteries was there room for many of the monks, new structures were begun everywhere, and as they flocked in from all sides, great store of provisions was made. And when the means did not exist for building on a large scale, they arranged for food and shelter of the monks by twos and fours in the neighborhood. Consequently in manors and towns, cities and garrisons, and even in the very woods and fields, there suddenly appeared swarms of monks spreading in every direction. . . . Therefore the nobles became eager to submit to voluntary poverty and, scorning their possessions, to give them up to the abbeys they entered, and ever in a pious kind of hunting they strove to capture others to do the same. Moreover, the noble wives of well-known men forsook marriage and putting from their hearts the love of children, bestowed thereon their wealth. . . . And those men or women who could not wholly surrender their property supported those who had done so, by many a gift from their substance.

The establishment of a monastery was usually an act of colonization of waste, forest or swamp lands, in remote regions, whether in the interior of a country or upon the frontier. The bulk of land so redeemed was waste and wild land never before subjugated by the axe and the plow. It was virgin area now only acquiring value under pressure of increasing population. The natural resources of a locality, of course, often particularly conditioned the kind of exploitation employed. Swamp and marsh lands were convertible into fat and fertile meadows and fields; forest land provided timber, charcoal, and if of oak or beech, pasturage for swine; rivers, lakes, and seashore provided fish and seaweed for fertilizer. In maritime Europe a stranded whale was usually the prize of the local abbot. Bury St. Edmunds paid four thousand ells as rent for certain lands.

The beginnings of a monastery in Brittany are thus described: "Conuoion, accompanied by five brethren who desired to live in solitude, left the episcopal residence. After having searched for some time for seclusion, Conuoion selected a place at the confluence of the Oust and the Valaine, where high hills served as protection." A Norman historian relates how in 1100 one Bernard withdrew from the abbey of St. Cyprian in Poitiers because it had ceased to be a quiet place and "after much journeying he and his monks settled on some land pertaining to the bishop of Chartres in a wooded region called Tiron. Soon

a multitude of the faithful flocked to him, and in the new monastery practised the occupations which each had learned. In consequence there readily assembled about him workmen, both smiths and carpenters, sculptors and goldsmiths, painters and masons, vine dressers and plowmen, with skilled artificers in various branches of industry. Thus where lately robbers sheltered themselves in a frightful forest, a stately abbey was by God's help quickly reared. . . . Count William made a road to the monastery by a sharp and difficult ascent to the steep hills, cutting the rocks with hammers and pickaxes and other iron tools, and with the fragments laid the base of a causeway along the river.

Elsewhere the same chronicler narrates how "the venerable Vitalis retired into solitude and remarking the village of Savigny near Mortain, where he found vast ruins of some ancient building, erected a monastery to the Trinity." The annalist of Zwifalten relates how, in the twelfth century, all Germany was covered with thick forests. "But after the servants of God had become powerful here, they began to hew down the unfruitful trees and to root out the thornbushes. They turned the wooded land into fruit farms, erected houses and domiciles for man, seeded the fields, and planted vineyards. . . . They built an aqueduct, set all kinds of fruit trees and established gardens in the woods with its budding trees." Conrad III in 1147, confirming a gift of Ludolf of Rümelingen to a monastery, makes the statement: "I add thereto some waste land belonging to the crown, namely, a wood . . . and will that the monks of the said house of God root it out, hew it down, cultivate it, and settle husbandmen there, who shall cut it down and root it out, until they can employ it for their daily use."

The great forests of Europe before the thirteenth century, when their denudation began to excite some alarm owing to the increasing cost of building timber and charcoal, were regarded as an enemy to be hewn down. Men treated them exactly as the pioneers in America treated the forests. The abbot of St. Mary's in Trèves wrote to a correspondent: "I believe that the forest which adjoins Fellarich covers the land to no purpose and hold this to be an unbearable harm; therefore I have allowed the inhabitants of Tomblet to clear the forest under the condition that they deliver to me and my successors annually for this three kegs of wine." One cloister, that of St. Trudo, still had thirteen forests early in the eleventh century. By 1120 practically all were destroyed.

The "new monasticism" of the feudal age wrought an economic revolution in agriculture by the reduction of forest and the redemption of waste and swamp. In this practice the Cistercians played a preëminent part. Founded in 1098, the new order set itself against the luxury of the Benedictines and Cluniacs. The Cistercian Order, with its austere practices, its simple and plain churches with bare whitewashed walls devoid of decoration, its avoidance of rich adornment and imposing ritual, came as a protest against the extravagance and magnificence of the Cluniacs. St. Bernard time and again in his letters inveighs against the current display of his time. Similarly in the next century St. Francis wanted to pull down the new and imposing church structures at Bologna and Assisi. The Cistercians and the Friars were the puritans of the Middle Ages. Stained glass, elaborate ritual, grand processionals, to them savored of worldly pomp. The Cistercians resolved to restore again the dignity of toil, to keep themselves unspotted from the world.

The question of land ownership early arose. The Benedictine Rule had originally prohibited acquisition of "lands beyond the actual precincts: granges, serfs, mills, or any possessions a seignior might have." This regulation, however, had become obsolete during the feudal age. An attempt was made by the Cistercians to restore it and to assure the new order independence of seigniorial authority from the beginning. The solution was a new departure in monastic organization. In order both to remove temptation to worldly wealth from the monks and to avert extension of proprietorship over the community, it was ruled that the lands of the house were to be just sufficient for sustenance, but not great enough to provide riches.

The Cistercians deliberately sought out remote and isolated regions in Europe, and these naturally were in forest or marshy localities, for the better farming regions had long since been acquired by the earlier orders and the bishops. Hence we find Cistercian houses established in the wilds of Northumberland, which William the Conqueror had so wasted, in the moors of the Biscayan coast of France, in the gorges of the Vosges and the Alps, and above all in the far eastern frontier lands of Germany. Second to them in colonization were the Premonstratensian canons, who followed the same policy. "Give these monks," wrote Gerald of Barri concerning the Cistercians, "a naked moor or a wild wood; then let a few years pass away and you will find not only beautiful churches, but dwellings of men built around them." Undrained valleys, unreclaimed wastes, the hush of dense forests were the favorite haunts of the order.

Seeking out the desert places of the wilderness [writes a contemporary observer] and shunning the haunts and hum of crowds, earning their daily bread by manual labor and preferring uninhabited solitudes, they seem to bring back to one's eyes the primitive life and discipline of the monastic religion, its poverty, its parsimony in food, the roughness and meanness of its dress, its abstinence and austerities.

Of the Cistercians of Yorkshire it is said that "they turned the waste land into good land; they planted the trees; they improved the streams; they made corn grow where thistles had sprung unchecked; they filled the meadows with cattle and stocked the uplands with sheep." This disposition on the part of the Cistercians and Premonstratensians to seek out places of settlement in undeveloped lands rather than to establish themselves within the older historic regions, made these two orders preeminent as colonizers.

It is a very striking fact that as the Elbe was the frontier between the Old and the New Germany, so it was a dividing line between these new orders of monks and the Benedictines. Except for Bohemia and Poland not a Benedictine foundation existed east of the Elbe River save a few convents of nuns. The old order of things had passed away. With the conversion of the Slavs even missions had become obsolete. The great Northeast had been conquered, and the land lay open to settle-

ment and exploitation. The future of the Cistercians and Premonstratensians lay along the line of agriculture, forest and swamp redemption,
cattle-raising, and trade. Their monasteries in this New East were farm
schools, not mission stations nor places where letters and the arts were
cultivated. They left "higher" culture to the Benedictines, who vege-
tated within cloisters and fastidiously shivered at the very thought of
the rough life of the German border.

Land was given the Order generously. Lavish grants were common
in the twelfth and thirteenth centuries. Once possessed of the land, the
Cistercians had no great cost of upkeep, for they were exempted from
all taxes on land, whether unimproved or improved, as well as from taxes
upon their flocks and herds and work animals.

Moreover, the rule of Citeaux imposed actual manual labor upon
members of the Order and discountenanced the work of serfs as an
abominable evasion of the principle that physical work was good for the
soul as well as for the body. Its puritanism even went so far as to prohibit the possession of feudal fiefs in order that the monasteries might
be kept aloof from feudal entanglements. The more secluded the spot,
the harder the struggle against nature, the more alluring the locality to
the Cistercians. A novice of Clairvaux wrote enthusiastically of finding
the monks there employed "with hoes in the garden, forks and rakes
in the meadow, sickles in the harvest fields, and axes in the forests."

It was not long, however, until with the Cistercians, as with the earlier
Benedictines, the hard manual labor in every house came to be performed
by lay brothers, and the monks only labored vicariously. The Rule of St.
Benedict had permitted the introduction into the monasteries of laymen
who, without being "religious" in the sense in which that word is used
by the Church of Rome, yet lived there. Among these, two classes were
distinguished: those capable of theological instruction were educated
and in time became full-fledged monks; the rest (*illiterati, idiotæ*)
formed an inferior category of monks who performed menial tasks.
Finally a new class of *conversi*, or lay brothers, was admitted as
house and farm servants (*famuli*). They were taught the creed, the
paternoster, and the "Ave Maria"; they were forbidden to marry, and
silence was enforced among them. They were entitled to food, clothing,
and shelter from the monastery, in return for which they labored long
and hard either on the farms, in the forests and quarries, or in the
shops. They were a species apart from the agricultural and industrial
serfs.

These *conversi* acted as a medium between the monastery and the outside world. The institution was foreign to the Benedictine Order. They
first appeared in 1038 in the Order of Vallombrosa, founded by St.
John Gualbertus. In Germany Hirsau first adopted the practice. They
were subject to all the obligations and observances imposed upon the

illiterati, but they could not become priests. Their special function was with reference to the material affairs of the monastery. They farmed the granges, they did the heavy work in the interior of the abbey, and they plied those crafts which were necessary to the material life of the community. The *conversi* also acted as commercial agents, going to market with the produce of the abbey lands.

This combination of the ideal and the practical made the Cistercians eagerly sought after as colonizers in the waste lands. They were as truly pioneers in the eastward expansion of the German nation as were the Saxon, Eastphalian, Westphalian, and Thuringian settlers, who at the same time were flocking from the more thickly populated regions of older Germany into the newly conquered and sparsely peopled lands beyond the Elbe. They cleared the forests, they reclaimed the swamps, they drained the marshes, they built levees and dikes to confine the streams, and they made roads and bridges. When the redemption of the wilderness was accomplished they brought new settlers in from the "Old West," conducting these emigrants upon the journey and seeing that they were comfortably housed along the road in the numerous monasteries *en route,* which served as taverns or hostels.

Bishop Otto of Bamberg, the apostle to the Pomeranians, and a friend of Norbert, the Premonstratensian whom Lothar II made archbishop of Magdeburg, recognized the economic possibilities of Pomerania as a place of colonization for the overflowing population of North Germany, when on his first missionary trip.

Monasteries might certainly be established in this country [writes Herbordus, his biographer]. An incredible number of fish may be obtained there from the sea, also from the lakes and rivers. For a penny one might get a huge quantity of freshly pickled fish. . . . As for wild animals, the country abounds with stags, deer, wild fowls, bears, wild boars, swine, and all kinds of wild beasts. Butter is also to be obtained from cows, and milk from sheep, together with the fat of lambs and rams, and there is great abundance of honey and wheat, of hemp and of poppies and all sorts of vegetables. If the land possessed the vine, olives, and fig trees one might regard it as the promised land in view of the abundance of its fruit trees. The bishop, being unwilling that the land should be without the vine, brought a case of cuttings with him on his second journey, and had them set out so that the land might bring forth wine.

The founding of Kloster Leubus in 1175 is the initial date in the history of Silesia. In that year Boleslav the Lanky of Poland (1163–1201), aiming to colonize the upper valley of the Oder, invited the Cistercians to settle there. It was the farthest eastern post of German culture in the twelfth century.

As farmers the Cistercians surpassed all other orders. A brother of the Order, writing at the beginning of the fourteenth century, describes in detestable verse but with genuine and justifiable enthusiasm the work of the Cistercians in civilizing Silesia. He pictures the country as a land of forest and fen inhabited by wretchedly poor and lazy Poles, who used the forked trunk of a tree for a plow, drawn by a pair of scrawny cows or oxen. The people lived without salt or metal or shoes and were pitiably clothed. Nowhere was a town to be found. Markets were held in the open air, where barter took the place of coin.

Although the German Cistercians were determined partisans of the papacy in the conflict between the popes and Frederick Barbarossa, owing to the influence of French Cistercianism over them, many German nobles, even when themselves of Ghibelline persuasion, were favorable to the German Cistercians, for they appreciated the nature of their services as colonizers. But Frederick I himself was less wise.

When Roland, the redoubtable chancellor of Hadrian IV, succeeded to the pontificate and became the formidable Guelf pope Alexander III, the emperor countered by putting up as anti-pope the cardinal Octavian, who took the name of Victor. The Cistercians naturally sustained Alexander, and for that reason Frederick decreed the exile of the Order from Germany. Where the Hohenstaufen arm could reach, their lands were assimilated to the royal fisc, their granges sacked, and the monks themselves driven out of the land, not to return until 1177, when peace was made between pope and Emperor. Then the Cistercians came back in flocks to Germany, where they were popularly hailed as *Friedensengel,* or angels of peace.

One is tempted to think, unless he knows past history, that the policy of conservation of natural resources is a wholly modern movement; that intelligent engineering perished with the Romans until it was revived in the sixteenth century; that the study of soils and geological conditions, the appreciation of economic botany, animal husbandry, plant culture, etc., were utterly unknown until relatively recent times. Swamp reclamation, crude ditching and draining, forest clearing, a little mining and a simple, if not wholly primitive, agriculture are usually believed to have been the limits of man's exploitation of natural resources in the Middle Ages.

But the history of the labors of the Cistercian monks in Germany in the twelfth and thirteenth centuries belies this snap judgment. Almost without exception the Cistercian cloisters in medieval Germany were located in swamp or marsh regions, so that a system of drainage had to be worked out. The ruins of many of their foundations in North Germany still retain traces of these improvements. In the Harz and the hill country of Thuringia the tourist will come upon these remains. The swamps were drained, and the redeemed land (known as polders in Holland) was made fit for tillage and grazing. The water was impounded in reservoirs by dams and walls and used for both irrigation and milling purposes. The ditches were used as fishponds.

As interesting as their use of engineering was the German Cistercians' effort to utilize the forest. Much of the face of the country was covered with dense forest. But instead of the former haphazard way of making clearings without reference to the value of the soil underneath, the Cistercians studied both the timber and the soil. They knew, or discovered, that where hardwoods grew there good land was to be found. They never wholly denuded the forest, but left patches of standing timber. Moreover, they studied plant life for food purposes, seed germination, grafting of fruit trees, and mayhap even cross-fertilization. We know that in 1273 Dobberan had a glass-roofed house for purposes of plant experimentation. When a brother went on his wanderings he always took with him plants and seeds and slips of trees and brought home whatever herbs and seeds he thought might flourish in the locality of his monastery. In this wise the culture of the grape was extended from the Rhinelands into central Germany. The monks of Altencampen imported the prized vine slips of the vineyards of Basigny around Morimond to Cologne, whence other shoots were taken to Walkenried in Thuringia, and thence to Pforta and Leubus.

The particular history of a few of the more notable Cistercian enterprises in medieval Germany may be of value as illustrating the nature and extent of their labors. One of the most famous of their achievements was the creation of the Goldene Aue, or Golden Meadows.

The traveler who today traverses by railroad the fertile region from Naumburg to Artern would not know that the broad tract, waving with corn in the summer wind, lying between Rosaleben and Artern, was once one of the most terrible swamp lands in all northern Germany. For these Golden Meadows are in the very bottom of the Thuringian Basin. Until the coming of the Cistercian monks hither in the middle of the twelfth century, this region was a wilderness of bog, morasses, and tree stumps. In prehistoric times a lake had been here. The lake had now degenerated to a huge marsh whose sluggish waters found a partial exit through the little river Helme into the Unstrut and thence into the Saale. It was in the shape of a three-pointed star, one extension reaching from Sachsenburg to Meuthen, another, Untere Helmerieth, from Brücken to the Unstrut, and the third, Ober Helmerieth, from Brücken to Sundhausen.

In 1144 Count Christian of Rothenburg an-der-Saale gave a portion of this boggy area near the village of Görsbach to the Cistercians of Walkenried and later much enlarged the tract by subsequent grants. At the same time the archbishop of Magdeburg exempted from payment of the tithe all the land which they might redeem. Within four years there was meadow where once there had been morass only. The monks then turned their attention to the lower Rieth. In the last years of his reign Frederick Barbarossa, who had learned to esteem those whom he had once persecuted, gave permission to Jordan, a monk of Walkenried, to drain the whole region of the lower Rieth. Not many years afterward the monks of the Goldene Aue had mills in operation at Riethof, Bernigen, Görsbach, Windelhausen, and Kaldenhausen.

In Brandenburg the monks of Zenia had absolute control of the water power round about their monastery, with which they ran their mills. In 1269 they purchased the village of Burchstall, near Prettin, which had to be protected by levees. It was the monks of Zenia who discovered the valuable limestone quarries near Rudersdorf on the Spree, now in the environs of Berlin, and constructed a grange there for exploitation of the stone.

Count Adolph III of Holstein (1164–1203), whose father had been a pioneer in promoting Dutch and Flemish colonization of the marshlands of lower Germany, in 1186 established a colony of Cistercians from the monastery of Lokkum, near Hanover, which had originally been founded by Henry the Lion, in the marshes of the Trave River between Lübeck and Oldesloe. Before the end of the century this fenland became known (and is still locally known) as *"Die Heilsaue."* The Cistercian monastery of Dünamunde, at the mouth of the Düna, owned the island of Ramesholm in the estuary, and erected a mill there in 1226. Dargun in Mecklenburg-Schwerin, founded by Bishop Berno in the ancient land of the Wendish Circipani, after the Wendish Crusade of 1147, was much interested in fishery in the Baltic; in 1270 it was given freedom from tolls for twelve fishing smacks.

As early as 1154 Wolkenrode, in the Thuringian Forest, owned mills at Germer and at Graba, and in 1282 is found negotiating for three additional mills. From the numerous references to Wolkenrode's arable lands and her constant endeavor to acquire new fields it is evident that this monastery was largely engaged in the milling business. In 1229 a farm was purchased at Mühlhausen (the very name is significant) with the proviso that the Cistercians should have the monopoly of the making of beer and the sale of cereals in that locality.

The German Cistercians were both millers and maltsters on a large scale. Reinfeld in Holstein is a typical example of a Cistercian milling corporation. In 1237 four hides of land and a mill in Badow were bought; in 1258 another mill at Börzow, for 244 marks; in 1275 a *conversus* was sent to Nelitz to manage a mill there. In 1272 mention is made of a house in Parchim (near Neu-Brandenburg) which Reinfeld was using as a granary. The count of Schwerin at one time, being hard up for funds, sold the milling monopoly of the city to the local Cistercians for the sum of 1264 marks. It is interesting to notice that the deed mentions both water-mills and windmills. Dobberan in Mecklenburg bought the mills at Parchim and Plau for 885 marks in 1282; between 1287 and 1292 those at Güstrow for 2050 marks; in 1298 the mill at Guvien for 310 marks, the deed in each case giving the monks a milling monopoly.

By monopolistically controlling such a local need as a mill the Cistercians controlled the cultivation of grain in the neighborhood round about. The farmer had no other way to dispose of his produce; and in order to prevent establishment of other mills which might compete with them in localities where they did not enjoy complete monopoly the monks "cornered" the water rights. The cloisters at Mecklenburg and Neuencampen successfully did this and farmed out the water rights for a good revenue. The damming of the streams sometimes worked serious damage to adjacent property owners. For example, as a result of the damming of the Plöne River, the Madü See (a lake twelve miles long and two miles broad in Pomerania) rose eight feet and inundated many farms round about.

Wherever natural salt springs occurred the Cistercians were not slow to get their hands upon them. The abbot of Altencampen, on a visit to the abbot of Neuencampen in 1298, discussed with him the exploitation of the salt pan at Lüneburg. Already Reinfeld, Dobberan, and Scharnebeck were working "claims" there, and between 1326 and 1329 Amelungsborn entered into the competition. In 1301 Riddigshausen paid 140 marks for right to work the salt pits at Magdeburg. By the middle of the fourteenth century nearly a dozen Cistercian cloisters were working the Lüneburg salt deposits.

In addition to grain-farming and milling the Cistercians everywhere were much given to stock-raising. Hay and fodder was raised and cut for cattle, meat was pickled or salted down, bacon smoked, sausage made, and the hides dressed and tanned. From these enterprises shoemaking, saddlery, and wool-carding naturally developed. In the far north of Germany along the Pomeranian coast and on the island of Rügen, where the cultivation of crops was limited by the cold, the great forests of beech trees afforded mast for feeding swine. In 1241 Barnuta, a brother of Wizlaw I, gave the little island of Koos, which was covered with beech and oak, to the monastery of Hilda in Rügen. Lokkum had a hog farm on the Büchenberg, near Detmold, where there were 133 swine.

The Cistercians seem to have developed animal husbandry to a high degree. In 1300 two armed nobles invaded the premises at Walkenried and drove off numbers of the horses and cattle there. In 1302 the count of Wernigerode and Gebhard von Arnstein robbed a cloister of horses, oxen, sheep, and grain. In 1309 Walkenried was again plundered. Johann von Beberstadt robbed Rufenstein one night and took away thirty-four horses. A few years later it was again despoiled by the vagabond baron Dietrich von Echleben, and in the scuffle two of the lay brothers were killed. Horse-raising was an important business among the Cistercians. As early as 1157 we find complaint that they had more horses than could be disposed of. Fixed regulations prevailed, governing their sale. All purchases had to be made within the monastery walls, and no colt was sold until it had grown four teeth. The contract of sale provided that the animal was to be used for *"Nutz-thieren, nicht zu Rennern, Ritterpferden oder Prachtrossen."* Himmelspforte, in the Barmin region, had on one of its large farms 80 head of cattle, over 60 hogs, and more than 800 sheep. The cartularies of the monasteries afford interesting evidence as to cattle and sheep, which were raised in large numbers. The abbey of St. Froidmond near Beauvais sold 7000 fleeces in a single year.

Even in older parts of Germany, like the Rhinelands, where a more intensive agriculture prevailed, the German Cistercians improved upon conditions and introduced new methods of farming. As early as 1140 their stock farms along the Rhine were famous, if we may believe the story told of Eberhard von Altena of whom it is told that in remorse for the number of men he had slain in war with the duke of Brabant he wandered away from home and after much traveling arrived at the Cistercian monastery of Morimund near the Rhine, where he became a shepherd and swineherd. A servant of the count, who by accident visited the cloister, recognized his former master and exclaimed: *"Graf Eberhard hütet die Schweine von diesem Klosterhof."*

Schmoller, in his classic monograph upon the weaving industry in Strassburg, gives high praise to the Cistercians for their promotion of this technical industry. But they not only promoted industry; they also helped to develop better commercial methods through regulations which governed the sale of raw wool, restraint of reselling at higher price, precautions taken against sale of imperfect or shoddy goods, etc.

In Pomerania, Mecklenburg, Brandenburg, and the Plattland generally of northern Germany, flax was extensively grown and was manufactured into a sort of canvas cloth. This industry was an old one among the Baltic Wends which the incoming Germans adopted and increased. The peasantry wove a rough, unbleached homespun in their cottages, which they brought to the market to sell. But they had neither the skill, the apparatus, nor the technical methods for the making of high-grade textiles such as the monasteries were able to turn out through possession of fulling mills, dyeing processes, better looms, and, above all, better operatives.

Grape-culture and wine-making was also an extensive industry of the German Cistercians, especially in the Rhine and Neckar valleys. If the grape could not be grown in the locality of the monastery, ground was acquired elsewhere. In Tübingen, where the hills made grape-growing easy, the arbors were thick. Before 1193 Walkenried had planted the vine

at Bodenrode and built a press and a wine cellar; later on, it built a
new cellar at Thalheim near Frankenhausen. In 1202 it purchased a vineyard near Würzburg for 150 marks. Each of these establishments was
superintended by an expert lay brother. Walkenried had so many vineyards around Würzburg that in 1206 it purchased a site in the town, built
a cellar, and opened a store for the sale of wine. At Pforte, where the
valleys of the Saale and the Unstrut united, scarcely an acre of the surrounding hills was without its vineyard. We find reference made to vineyards at Borsendorf, Gernstadt, Hecherdorf, Odesrode, and elsewhere.
The long arcade which extended from the monastery to the bridge at
Almerich was covered with vines. It cannot be precisely ascertained what
the extent of Pforte's wine industry was, but the fact that in 1202 Pforte
disposed of two hundred tuns of wine in Flanders is interesting. The
grape was more widely cultivated in medieval Germany than it is today.
It was grown even in Brandenburg and Saxony. In Thuringia, as in
Normandy, apple-growing and cider-making was a profitable activity
of the monasteries. Here Kloster Georgenthal was famous for its orchards. In 1227 it accepted in liquidation of a debt from a local knight
the manors of Haingrupe and Hundsborn, both abounding with apple
trees. Pforte had apple orchards as well as vineyards.

Most of the land of the Cistercians, like that of other monks before
them, was either rented out or else worked by "lay brothers." The rent
was paid partly in money, partly in produce. These dependents of the
cloister were subject, like serfs of lay proprietors, to various manorial
dues, such as the *zins* (French, *cens*); they paid a death due or *heriot,*
which was graduated according to circumstances. If the deceased were
married to a serf woman not belonging to the cloister, his heir had to
pay one-half of the estate to the monastery. If, however, the wife of the
deceased were also a dependent of the cloister, only his best garment
had to be surrendered. If the deceased had been a property owner, the
house had to be given up as fee to inherit the land; if there were no
dwelling upon the land, then half the land. The arm of the medieval
Church was long and its heart hard.

As the economic system of the Cistercians prospered modifications
ensued. In course of time it was found impracticable for the lay
brothers to do all the work, and a new type of dependents grew up
(*mercenarii*). These dwelt outside the monastery walls, though on monastery land. The original plot of ground was given to them, but any
additional plot had to be leased. The *Lohnarbeiter* took no vows, nor
was he bound to the glebe like an ordinary serf. If he was dissatisfied
with the terms he was free to remove, although in practice he probably
was seldom able to do so for the reason that he was often in arrears for
the rent, so much so that his lot outwardly differed little from that of
the real serf.

In addition to these servile or semi-servile dependents, there was another and higher class of what might be called pensioners (*familiares*). These were people who in their old age had wished to come to the monastery to live, and who had bestowed upon it their property, receiving an annuity from the cloister. They were recruited from the class of small free proprietors and lesser gentry, who found it hard to protect themselves against the pressure of the great feudality and sought the protection of the Church in this way.

The farms of the monastery were not a contiguous tract, but formed a complex of scattered possessions, frequently several miles apart, on each of which was a village of peasantry and a resident petty bailiff or steward. These holdings were acquired in one of four ways: they might have been formed by natural agglomeration of people around the cloister; they might have been former free villages which had been reduced to dependency (this was especially true of the Wendish villages); they might have been landed gifts made by local proprietors; or they might have been purchased by the monks.

In addition to these farms there were the granges, usually single and often isolated farms. The grange at Wintirbach in Lorraine was worked by four *conversi* and nine servants; we do not know the area of it, but there were 28 head of cattle and 20 goats upon it at one time. Riddigshausen in Saxony had three granges at Remtheim, Mascherode, and Ahlum. Buch about 1352 is found using its grange at Amelgostewitz as a central storehouse and trading-post. Here were a monk who acted as priest and manager, a cook, 2 lay brothers, a farm bailiff, a shepherd, a throng of dependents, and 24 plow horses.

It is clear that the Cistercian monasteries were formed for agricultural exploitation; they expended little on churches or other edifices; few of them maintained any school; they were even indifferent to ministering to the villagers. Instead they farmed especially the staple cereals, as wheat, rye, and barley, and monopolized the milling rights of the community; they cultivated the grape and made wine; they raised flax for linen and sheep for wool; they were orchardists; they were ranchers and stock-raisers.

It is interesting to observe the changing economy. In the beginning the monasteries were wholly occupied in agriculture; then they branched out gradually into industry and finally became engaged in commerce. At the same time, in the course of these changes, the physical radius of the monastery's action enlarged.

Before 1157 no inmate was permitted to go beyond one day's journey from the cloister for the purchase or sale of commodities. In that year the rule was relaxed so that a four days' journey was permissible. At this time the economy of the monastery still was predominantly agricultural. But a little later we see the effect of the production of a surplus in the seeking for a market. Instead of mere barter or exchange of commodities which the monks possessed for those which they needed, a money economy came to prevail, and real trade ensued. The cloisters along the Baltic are discovered in the thirteenth century to be shipping their goods by sea to Lübeck and the Danish ports. The order was so well established in Livonia that in 1204 Innocent III took occasion highly to praise it. By 1209 the Cistercians had several prosperous colonies in Russia.

By 1241 Eldena had the right to hold a weekly market in Rügen. Lübeck and Schwerin were both important Cistercian trading centres; Rostock was another. Dobberan trafficked with Mecklenburg. As early as 1229 the Cistercians in Livonia must have tapped the trade of Russia, for in that year Pope Gregory IX ordered the bishop of Riga, the abbot of the Cistercian monastery there, Dünamunde, and the provost of the city to discontinue trade with Novgorod unless the Russians ceased molesting the Finns, who had lately embraced Christianity. In this century we find grain and wine shipped from the Baltic ports to Norway, and wheat sent from Lübeck to Holland. Some of this produce must have come from the Cistercian foundations in Mecklenburg. Most of the market grants made to the Cistercians date from the thirteenth century, when their cloisters were at the height of their power and affluence, but morally were in decline.

The development of their wine trade illustrates the stages already noted in economic change. In 1134 no wine could be disposed of to outsiders. Late in the twelfth century the vineyards of the Cistercians had become so flourishing that their surplus was seeking a market where it could be found. Some of the cloisters even peddled drinks, erecting booths outside the walls, where lay brothers dispensed the beverage. Later, we find wine sold openly within the precincts of the cloister, it being stipulated, however, that the sale should not be accompanied by any unseemly words or conduct; dicing was particularly forbidden.

The strength of the Cistercian Order was in its adaptation of means to the changed economic conditions in the twelfth century. The Benedictines and Cluniacs had been content with a simple agricultural economy which proved ill adapted to the new times. Hence they gradually lost out. But the Cistercians developed special production according to local conditions, as wine-production, horse-raising, etc., and moreover displayed great activity in marketing their products. The Cistercian houses, too, were in close association with one another. They maintained strict supervision of their enterprises and were careful bookkeepers and accountants. Each house was responsible for the efficiency of all new houses which it founded and both supervised their discipline and audited their accounts.

That the Cistercians soon came to live on the fat of the land is evidenced by the following complaint of the abbey of Leubus (1280) concerning the incessant begging of the community round about or the blackmailing tactics of the neighboring nobles. We may read in the *Monumenta Lubensia:*

Scarcely a month passes by, nay, scarcely a day in which it is not necessary for the abbot to give away something. His monastic garb does not protect him. This one implores, that one threatens. One demands money in mark and pence, another grain, the one bread, the other hay, and he takes at the same time 100 head of sheep. . . . There is hardly a thing to be thought of that is not demanded of the cloister. . . . The third begs for wood, the fourth for hay, the fifth wants to hear the beautiful choral music, the sixth demands that his horse be shod; the seventh would like to have his jug filled; the eighth demands fish; the ninth requests a measure of large cheese; the tenth, seed-cake; the eleventh, apples; the twelfth comes year after year to get cloth for his clothes . . . the thirteenth wants a pair of socks or shoes; . . . but it is far worse when the huntsmen come with their servants and dogs. . . . They are as hungry as wolves and a loaf of bread for one of them is too small. One demands a drink and swears that he will lay waste the cloister; another goes to the cellar door and demands wine, and, cursing, says that he will give not a penny to Christ, still less to the monks.

By the thirteenth century the monks of Citeaux, like the Benedictines and Cluniacs before them, were sunk upon the lees. Wealth, idleness, vice had gradually worked their corruption and decay like that of all the others. The evidence is manifold. Cæsar of Heisterbach, one of the Order and intensely loyal to it, admits this condition time and again. They no longer were actuated by a pioneer spirit, and they shunned the hardships of frontier conditions. Instead they began to cluster in the old and more densely populated regions, where they ousted the peasantry or enclosed their farms to make granges and sheepwalks. Whole villages disappeared in this way.

Donations to monasteries were due to a mixture of religious and worldly motives. One of these was clearly economic. Great tracts were granted in the wilderness because under the Rule of St. Benedict it was known that the monks would clear the forests, drain the swamps and marshes, drive back the savage beasts that menaced the lives of the little hamlets, repair the roads and bridges, and reclaim the waste land. Not only tracts of land, but entire villages, were given to the monasteries, as were other grants, such as right of market, right of collecting tolls and tithes, toll and tithe exemptions, coinage privileges, right of administering justice, use or ownership of mines and salt springs, free use of wood from the forests. The lands were held in fief and subinfeudated by the monasteries. This practice of course deeply involved the monasteries in the feudal régime—war, lawsuits, political ambition, political conflict.

For the guarding of their broad acres the monasteries imitated the nobles, and in the feudal age converted their retreats into castellated piles of buildings with frowning battlements, moats, bastions, barbicans, and the architectural paraphernalia of the warlike, castle age. These huge stone structures were as expressive embodiments of monastic proprietorship as the feudal castles. The change wrought a revolution in the monastic spirit and ideal; it assimilated the monks with the military feudality. The more spiritual in the Order deplored the new condition. Witness this protest:

Behold how far we are departed from the simplicity of the ancients in this matter of buildings. What means this loftiness of your structures?. Thou shalt not thereby be better defended against the devil, but all the nearer to him. St. Bernard wept to see the shepherds' huts thatched with straw, like unto the first huts of the Cistercians, who were then beginning to live in palaces of stone, set with all the stars of heaven for adornment. You have lost all your freedom for the sake of rich granges and lands.

Another medieval writer deplores the heavy services exacted by the monks from the serfs and villeins upon the monastery lands:

The innocent must die of hunger, with whom these great wolves [i.e. the covetous monks] fill their maws. This grain, this corn, what is it but the blood and bones of the poor folk who have plowed their lands?

Medieval governments, in general, looked askance upon the great growth of the monasteries. Their vows and manner of life alienated the monks from secular activities. The abbots could not be used as freely as the bishops in secular administration or in military affairs owing to the greater isolation and less compact form of government which prevailed in monastic organization. The material wealth of the monasteries was even greater than that of the secular clergy. The monasteries were not only relatively, but absolutely, richer than the bishoprics. They owned a greater proportion of land, and withdrew a greater amount of it from the taxing power of the state through privileges and immunities. Neither the military nor the financial burden upon the monasteries was so heavy as upon the episcopate. Under these conditions the monasteries were of less practical benefit to either the state or society than the secular clergy. Their wealth was out of all proportion to their material needs, such as the daily support of the inmates, the maintenance of schools and hospitals, and poor relief. The "dead hand" kept much of their surplus wealth from free circulation for the advantage of so-

1. Entrance to the church from outside the monastery walls.
2. Church: notice the double apse and many altars.
3. Main cloister, showing the arcades and fountain in the middle.
4. Dormitory, on second floor with heating apparatus underneath.
5. Refectory, on ground floor with wardrobe above.
6. Cellar, with storage room over.
7. Hostelry for pilgrims and wayfarers with bake-house and brewery adjoining.
8. Scriptorium, with library above.
9. Living-room and dormitory for visiting monks.
10. Schoolmaster's apartment.
11. School-room with apartments for teachers adjoining.
12. Porter's lodge.
13. Apartments for notable visitors.
14. Brewery and bake-house pertaining to 13.
15. Towers with circular stairways, the tops of which commanded a wide view.
16. A large structure, the use of which is not clear.
17. Sheep-stall.
18. Quarters for servants.
19. Goat-stall, with quarters for herdsmen.
20. Hog-house, with quarters for swine-herds.
21. Cattle-shed, with quarters for herdsmen.
22. Horse barn, with quarters for hostlers.
23. Stable for mares and oxen, with servants' quarters and hay-loft above.
24. Workshops of woodworkers, coopers and turners.
25. Storehouse for grain for brewing.
26. House for drying fruits.
27. Brewing house and bake-house for resident monks: notice the mortars and handmills.
28. Workshops of leather workers and smiths of various crafts.
29. Granery and threshing floor.
30. Poultry-keeper's house with hen-house and goose-pen adjoining.
31. Gardener's house with kitchen garden adjoining.
32. Cemetery.
33. Cloisters and living-room of the oblates.
34. Church for the novices and for invalids.
35. Hospital.
36. Hospital garden.
37. Physician's office and apothecary shop, with rooms for patients adjoining.
38. Another building for medical purposes.
39. House of the abbot, showing entrance into the church and the main cloister.

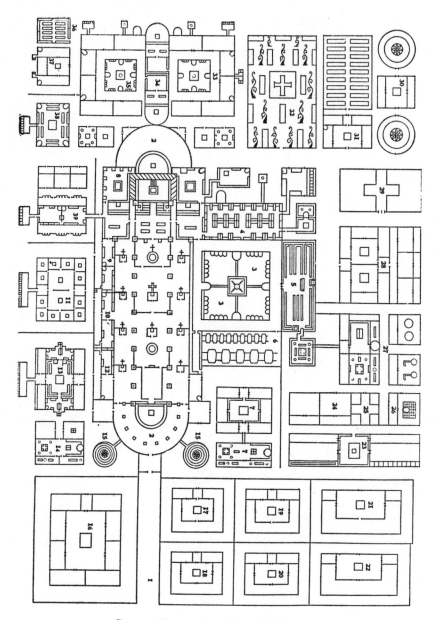

GROUND PLAN OF AN IDEAL MONASTERY

Reduced from the original now preserved in the library of St. Gall in Switzerland and made in the ninth century. The entire area measures about 400 feet by 300 feet.

ciety, and it was not forced out into the open, as was the case with the Church's wealth, through government use of the Church.

The incongruity between the enormous wealth enjoyed by many monasteries and the vow of poverty taken by the monks is apparent. The Rule was evaded by the legal fiction that the monastery was a corporation. Individually the inmates possessed nothing; as a group their incomes were very great and—unless a stern abbot rigidly enforced the Rule—the monks lived in luxury. The Rule was more honored in the breach than in the observance. Cæsar of Heisterbach says some Cistercian houses were so rich that they could have fed 5000 persons every day if they had so wished.

The older Benedictine houses almost all strenuously resisted monastic reform. At La Réole the monks killed a prior sent by the abbot of Cluny. In Germany the Benedictines continued to support Henry IV against Gregory VII in spite of papal anathema. The Cluniacs, an order never disposed to do manual labor, became famous for their refined luxury, their delicate table, the elegance of their costume. Avarice, the love of wealth, is a frequent and often just charge made against the monasteries in medieval literature. The hundreds of spurious charters forged by unscrupulous abbots in order to increase the lands of their monasteries, are evidences. Often they turned adversity into benefit. For example, during the invasions of the Norsemen in France and the Magyars in Germany, the monasteries were much despoiled, for the invaders soon discovered that the abbeys were seats of great wealth. But after the tempest of spoliation had passed, their wealth rapidly increased. They were amply compensated for their losses by new endowments by the faithful who were deeply moved by their pathetic appeals. And when gifts were slow in coming in, "with the aid of false charters they got more than they lost." The passionate veneration of relics was sometimes adroitly utilized by the monks in order to secure new grants of land. For it was the usage to parade the relics around the countryside, and wherever the procession stopped the land was claimed as appertaining to the saint. "When the founder and first prior of Grandmont after his death in 1124 commenced to show his sanctity by curing a paralytic knight and restoring sight to a blind man, his single-minded followers took alarm. The saint's successor interceded with the spirit of the deceased, or rather remonstrated: 'Thou hast preached solitude, and now thou seekest to convert our solitude into a market-place and a fair.'"

Moreover, trade brought corrupting influences. In 1223 the council of Béziers complained that the taverns maintained by many monasteries attracted jugglers, strolling players, mountebanks, gamblers, thieves, and lewd women. Rich and powerful abbeys were used to provide lucrative and easy living for younger sons of noble houses. Odilo, the abbot of Cluny, had a nephew who was abbot of Novalesea in North Italy, and who, instead of living as a monk, surrounded himself with a jovial band of cronies, enfiefed the monastery lands to them, and lived a life of riotous excitement as a warlike baronial cub.

The personnel of an abbey was organized in a businesslike way. Under the abbot was a prior, and often one or more subpriors, who directed the duties of special administrative officials. The chamberlain was responsible for the lands, the revenues, and the movable property of the monastery. Under him was a cellarer or overseer of the storage and the shops, a treasurer or bursar, and an *œconomicus* who was auditor of incomes and accounts.

The arrangement of buildings and lands of a medieval monastery is illustrated by the plan of St. Gall in Switzerland. The abbey included a cloister court, adjacent to the chapter house, with the sacristy between it and the church, separated by a staircase; a cellar for beer, wine, and oil was under the dormitory; on the opposite side of the church were the refectory and kitchens; the lavatory was located in the south cloister walk; an inner court contained an infirmary, a guest-house, kitchen, servants' hall, library, and scriptorium (the writing-room for making and copying books). There were also a common court, with double gateway for carts, surrounded by granaries, bakehouses, stables, storerooms, servant-rooms, tribunal, prison, and barn; in addition were mills, workshops, brewing-house, gardens, fish-ponds.

Like a modern business, the capital of the abbey consisted of fixed and working capital. Fixed capital included the lands, buildings, and equipment. Working or circulating capital was formed of the products of land, labor, commercial profits, market dues, taxes, etc. A medieval abbot was required, if a successful one, to be a man of affairs and keen judgment. Guibert de Nogent, himself an abbot, writes of an efficient abbot who "know how to adapt himself to the manners of the outside world, being courteous and liberal in his dealings with others and in the management of their legal business, in the details of which he spent much care in their behalf. . . . This man was considered shrewder than most abbots in legal business and was well known in towns and cities." Jocelin of Brakelonde's *Chronica* gives a graphic picture of life in and around a medieval abbey, in this case that of St. Edmunds at Bury St. Edmunds, between 1182 and 1202. The minute account of the activities of Abbot Samson is illuminating:

The abbot caused inquisition to be made throughout each manor, touching the annual quit rents from the freemen, and the names of the laborers and their tenements, and the services due in respect to each, and reduced all into writing. Likewise he repaired the old halls and rickety houses where kites and crows hovered round; he built new chapels and likewise inner chambers and upper stories in many places where there never had been any dwelling-house at all, but only barns. He also enclosed many parks, which he replenished with beasts of chase, keeping a huntsman with dogs; and upon the visit of any person of quality, sat with his monks in some wood, and sometimes witnessed the coursing of dogs. He improved much land and brought it into tillage. . . . In managing these manors as well as in all other matters, he appointed keepers who were far more careful than their predecessors. . . . After Easter the abbot surveyed every one of the manors of the abbey. . . . He built barns and ox stalls, being above all things solicitous to dress the land for tillage and watchful in preserving the woods, in respect whereof either in giving or diminishing, he was very chary. . . . He often became hoarse from exposure to the weather.

Jocelin tells us of Abbot Samson that "he seemed to love the active rather than the contemplative life, and he gave more praise to good office-bearers than to good choir-monks; he seldom commended any one merely for his learning unless he had a knowledge of secular affairs; and when he heard of any prelate's retiring from the care of souls and becoming an anchorite, in this he praised him not." He also relates in lively fashion a quarrel between the abbot of St. Edmunds and the bishop of Ely about timber to be cut for building. The woods to be cut belonged to St. Edmunds and the bishop asked permission to cut the timber. Owing to a confusion of names it was necessary to make a second request. Meanwhile the abbot had selfishly cut the wood and marked it for his own use. At the same monastery, Abbot Samson built many useful, many pious edifices, dwellings, churches, church-steeples, barns, also the Hospital of Babwell, fit houses for the St. Edmundsbury School. Roofs thatched with reeds he caused to be thatched with tiles.

The new monastic orders, one and all born of reforming tendencies and revivalism, like Cluniacs, Cistercians, the Dominican and Franciscan Friars, while they often aided to relieve certain evil conditions in society, nevertheless themselves in time created new evils or repeated old ones. The growing emancipation of the monasteries from both episcopal and secular control, from the inception of the Cluniac and Gregorian reform, tended to make the monastic orders dangerously independent of the state and worked against both nationalism and monarchy. It is in the very time when these orders were most popular and most flourishing that we also discover incisive criticism of not only the abusive practices and corruption of monasticism, but criticism of the very principle of the institution. The great multiplication of monasteries and convents, the great increase in the number of inmates in them disrupted families, and the undue diversion of private property to them often reduced families to poverty. The protest against monasticism does not come entirely from the laboring peasantry upon the lands of the monasteries. It comes from intelligent (though sometimes jealous) bishops and nobles, government officials, courtiers. Cæsarius of Heisterbach has written at length of the virtues of Ensfrid, dean of St. Andreas in Cologne, and quotes him as saying: "A good tree cannot spring from an evil root. There be few monks in these days who have entered by canonical ways; few who are not either blood-clerks [that is, foisted by their families] or jester-clerks [that is, those who have been imposed upon the monastery by influence] or simoniacs, who had purchased membership in the order." Guibert de Nogent, himself a monk, had that rare quality of mind which enabled him to look upon both sides of a question. While a true and honest monk, he was not blind to the evils of the institution. He complains of the "enormous number of men living a pious life"; of the "congestion of several monasteries, noted for their huge size, in which the zeal of the brotherhood fell away"; of the abuse arising from infeudation of abbey lands; of the practice among noble families of finding an easy place for a ne'er-do-well in a monastery; of the pride which made monks refuse to labor with their hands since manual labor was considered base by the aristocracy; of "slack morals and waste of moneys." But Guibert was human. When he observes that rich men are learning to look askance upon monasticism, closing their purses and no longer giving land as formerly, he is incensed. "In the old days," he rails, "men with a generous desire to found monasteries, bestowed on them lands and money, spending their substance on such works more freely and gladly than their sons favor us now with buttered words."

The vulgar charge frequently made that medieval monks were gluttonous, wasteful, extravagant, and profligate is belied by the hundreds of cartularies or inventories which have been preserved, and which show care, intelligence, and honesty in management. The enormous economic betterment of medieval Europe which the monks achieved proves them as a whole to have been intelligent landlords and agriculturalists. Agriculture was the chief economic activity of the monasteries, but the necessity of marketing their surpluses drew them into trade and commerce. The rich abbey of Maubuisson is a type of the time. The accounts of the abbey reveal the abbot augmenting his resources by selling hogs, charcoal, leeks, iron, building stone, timber. The cost of its erection is spread out in detail in the records. The enumeration of its luxurious furnishings throws interesting light upon what it was possible to purchase at the fair of Lendit. In 1110 the abbot of St. Ives in Huntingdonshire procured from Henry I the grant of a fair at St. Ives to begin shortly after Easter and last for a week.

Two types of markets specified in the records were weekly and annual markets. In many grants the day upon which the weekly market could be held was stated. St. Denis was granted a Tuesday market for its village of Cormeliæ near Versailles; Lorsch at Weinheim, St.

Ghislain at Horna, and Andlan for its village in Alsace were granted Wednesday markets. But Thursday was the favorite day for many monastery markets. There are no records for Friday markets (the day of the passion) and very few for Saturday. Many monasteries received grants for conducting both weekly and annual markets. The annual markets were usually held on the patron saint's day and for several days or weeks after it. St. Denis held its annual market in October, opening it on the ninth, the feast of St. Dionysius, and continuing for four weeks to accommodate strangers who came from foreign lands. Monastery St. John at Bishopsburg opened its market on June 24, St. John's Day; St. Matthias, on the feast day of its patron saint. The monastery at Essen conducted its annual market three days before and three days after its saint's day, the feast of Cosmas and Damianus, September 27.

If the market was not held upon the feast day of its patron saint it was held upon some other great holy day, the aim being to buy and sell at the time when the greatest number of people assembled. Complaint was made that it was difficult to get the crowds into the church for the mass after they had assembled at the market. Fulda conducted its annual market on Palm Sunday, extending it on to Easter Day. Metten opened one of its markets on Whitsunday, the other in the autumn, on St. Michael's Day, September 29. Kauffington held its annual market on St. John's Day.

Proximity to a church edifice gave added protection, especially after the enforcement of the peace of God. The neighboring graveyard or cemetery was a favorite location, although often the church edifice itself was used. The chronicler relating the miracles of St. Philibert tells of a market belonging to St. Denis that was held within the church itself. When the merchandise was not actually present at the market the buyer was compelled to assume the risk of transportation, that is to say, to protect it from the thieves that infested the highways and the pirates on the rivers. A record shows that the abbot of St. Gereon bought wine at the monastery market in Cologne but was obliged to go to Worms for it. This was one of the peculiarities of the monastery trade of the Middle Ages.

A few records only specify just what trade was to be carried on at any given place. Otto I permitted several monasteries to establish cattle markets on their possessions. The merchandise of the monastery markets was the surplus of their agricultural products and the products of the various industries. The Benedictines and Cluniacs, when secular markets and fairs developed, also disposed of their products in these as well as in their own abbatial market. But the rules of Citeaux forbade the Cistercians to sell their products in secular places. Produce and wares were sold directly on the monastery's estates and cash payment was invariably exacted. No deferred payments or partial payments were allowed, nor were articles bartered or exchanged for other articles. The prevalence of a money economy in their time—the twelfth century—made this rule more easily enforceable than in earlier centuries.

In theory the monasteries, in disposing of their surplus, were supposed to use their gains for religious purposes. When we read of the vast amount of charitable work done by these monasteries and see the beautiful buildings that were erected during this period, we realize that much of their gain was used for this purpose, but the monasteries also heaped up vast treasures as a result of their commercial activity.

The amount of surplus at the disposal of the monasteries can be judged only by the extent of their holdings. A few records mention specific things in connection with some of the monasteries. Pabo at Regensburg and St. Emmeran on the left bank of the Regen near Unter Mensbach had permission to cut down timber for two days each week from the Nord Wald. The chronicler states that the neighboring secular lords tried to prevent the monks from driving across their land with this wood, thus making it hard for the monasteries to conduct their lumber trade.

The manors furnished a surplus of wheat, rye, oats, barley, and spelt; hogs, sheep, lambs, goats, fowl, ducks and geese, etc. Only a small part of the monastery lands was under cultivation by the monks, the remainder was allotted out to laborers, dairymen, foresters, serfs, etc., all of whom paid their dues and rents in kind. Eggs, cheese, mustard, shingles, posts, torches, kegs, casks, etc., are among the articles enumerated in the records. Women spun and wove linen cloth and sewed garments for the monks. The serfs worked in the forest, made charcoal, conducted the fish hatcheries and the bee culture for which the monasteries of the Middle Ages were noted. They tilled the fields, cultivated the vine, furnished oxen, horses, and carts for transport service, and propelled rude craft along the waterways.

The aggregate of their own surplus products, tolls and tithes from their holdings, quit-rents, etc., must have been a large amount. Tegernsee received annually from its possessions 6288 measures of grain, 14,529 cheeses, 2025 eggs, and 33 wagonloads of wine. It required fifty-five oxen and wagons to haul the grain of this monastery from Funsing to the granaries. Prüm received annually, according to ninth century records, 432 measures of salt, 300 of wheat, 177 of rye, 473 of spelt, 1631 of barley, 4525 of oats, 469 of grain, 4382 chickens, 20,896 eggs, 4277 hogs, 207 sheep, etc.

The monasteries had their trade well organized. They used the by-paths for the packhorses, and the highways for the oxen and carts. The paths and short cuts for foot travelers were well known to them. They had their own boats upon lakes and rivers. They acquired places of deposit in seaport towns and in bends of rivers, and when necessary built warehouses to hold their merchandise. They organized caravans and sent escorts to convoy back to the monastery the goods bought by their "negotiators." The practice of using agents was a common one. Regino, abbot of Prüm, stated to his monks that it was not within their province to travel about conducting their trade in person, since this detracted from the high esteem in which the Order should be held because of its spiritual character. Prüm was one of the most important trading centres of the Middle Ages. It regularly employed six agents in the wine and salt trade. Later it increased the number of its agents to twelve.

Monasteries which did not possess markets of their own established warehouses or *halles* at neighboring markets. Here they stored their surplus until a chance to make a good profit came. Several warehouses were erected in the outer market at Cologne on an island in the Rhine. Fulda erected its own scale in a market at considerable distance from the monastery.

"The situation of a monastery upon the banks of a navigable river contributed materially to the development of its capabilities, affording an easy communication. . . . Yet to a considerable extent it was independent of these advantages since it enjoyed the valuable privileges of a fair within its own town. The keenness with which the exercise of this right was attacked, and the pertinacity with which it was defended afford proof of the value at which it was regarded." [2] Almost all monasteries received immunity from toll along highways and rivers. Many records of such toll exemptions exist. These exemptions grew out of the feudal conditions under which the monasteries were conducted. The abbot kept under his control all the various scattered holdings and sought every possible means to render his control effective. As the monasteries entered more and more into trade as a means of increasing their incomes, a closer connection between the central organization and its dependents became necessary. Markets were established at the monastery itself and at convenient points near its most valuable holdings.

As a result of donations the monasteries came into possession of widely scattered lands. The monastery St. Gall not only had possessions in Switzerland on Lake Constance, but owned vast tracts in Swabia, Neustria, Austrasia, Alsace, and even Italy. Such gifts, while making the monasteries great economic factors of the feudal régime, carried with them the germs of their disintegration and the break-up of feudalism. With their possessions so widely scattered it became increasingly difficult to maintain a strong centralized organization and to manage their holdings so as to make them profitable to the monas-

[2] *Chronicon Monasterii de Abingdon,* II, introd. lxxvii.

tery. Strenuous efforts were made to overcome this condition of decentralization and to regulate the trade and commerce of the monastery in such a way as to bring the highest returns possible from its possessions. Exemptions from tolls, market rights at the monasteries themselves or at central places located near their most productive holdings were obtained, and the right of exploitation of mines or salt springs was leased to responsible parties. The most important means at the command of the monasteries was to exchange possessions widely scattered for those more centrally located. This was, however, difficult to accomplish, chiefly because most donations had been given with a stipulation making it binding on the monastery to retain the land in its possession and also because the rule of the Church demanded that all exchanges should be of advantage to the monastery, and such an exchange was not easy to obtain.

An example in point to show how widely scattered the possessions of the monasteries were, and how vital it was to the monastery trade to secure toll exemptions is Werden on the Ruhr. In 880 it owned vast holdings in the former crown lands of Fremersheim on the Rhine. These were well stocked with cattle. A little to the south on the Erst it had a fine manor adjoining the royal demesne land. On the middle Rhine it owned several large vineyards. At the Rhine mouth it had great stretches of meadow land including eight manors on which were immense herds of cattle and of swine. On a strip which reached from the Yssel to the Zuydersee it had a large number of tenants who paid quit rents to the monastery; also the village of Wachszinsige. In Westphalia it owned four or five villages and about 330 hives of bees that paid quit rents, all widely scattered. In Friesland it had 82 smaller manors, also widely scattered, most of which brought in an income in money. It had here also under its control several tracts of forest land and several churches. It also possessed several places supplying salt, one of these being located in the vicinity of Werl in Westphalia, where salt is mined today. In all it owned over 200 villages, and 420 large manors as well as hundreds of smaller tracts. Yet it is listed later as one of the poor monasteries.

The advantage of exemptions from toll in bringing merchandise from scattered territories to the monastery itself or to one of its great central markets can be readily seen. Werden succeeded in gaining toll exemption for the Neuss district in 877. In 898 it gained from Zwentibold exemption from tolls on the Rhine, and a little later exemption for the entire kingdom.

There are records of exemptions for the late Merovingian period. In the eighth century the abbots of St. Germain-des-Près and St. Denis were granted exemption from toll or other royal tax. In 716, Corvey had not only privileges of free transport from the monastery to its seaport Fos, but also the right to requisition ten horses and twelve wagons to carry its merchandise. The abbots of Corméry near Tours, St. Mesmin near Orleans, Fleury and St. Benoist, were all given free navigation of the Loire. St. Aigrain in Orleans kept six boats on the Loire in the time of Pepin, and was released from paying toll along the entire length of the river. Pepin further decreed that all monastic merchandise that was transported through his kingdom without use of wagons, oxen, or horses should be exempt.

Not only did the monasteries strive to obtain exemption from toll for their produce on the great highways leading from their fields and vineyards or to their markets, but they also sought a monopoly of specific trade in the districts in which their markets were located. Reichenau received the exclusive right to sell its wines throughout the district in and about its market at Allenbach. Its tenants, dependents, and small farmer neighbors were prohibited from marketing wine, although they were at liberty to market their surplus in other products at the monastery market. At some markets the rival producers were permitted to sell in small quantities for immediate consumption, but could not sell it by the cask. In some districts the monasteries had the monopoly of vine-growing and could lay a ban against any infringement of this monopoly except for private consumption, while the small producer was forced to use the monastery wine-press and pay a generous toll in wine for the privilege. Many monasteries controlled not only the amount of wine produced in their regions, but also the time and methods by which their competitors disposed of their surplus. St. Maximin had the exclusive right of sale during several weeks following the feast of St. John. It not only pressed this advantage to the limit, but went so far as to threaten traders at its market who neglected to purchase a goodly supply of wine, and a quantity which the market master deemed suitable to supply their needs would be charged to their account and be shipped by the monastery at the buyer's risk to his home.

The extent of the cattle and live-stock trade of the monasteries cannot be accurately determined. During the period of purely natural economy cattle were raised for the specific purpose of providing for the needs of individual sections rather than to supply a medium for exchange. Only in the large towns did the butcher ply his trade. Many monasteries, however, sought and received the privilege of handling meats at their markets.

The salt trade of the monasteries ranked in importance with the wine trade. The salt deposits of Reichenhall in Bavaria, Marsal in Lorraine, and probably Salzburg in the Tyrol had been profitable during Roman times and had continued throughout the migration period. The monasteries early recognized the great advantage accruing from the possession of salt deposits. Throughout the Middle Ages there was an ever increasing demand for salt, and the possession of various privileges assured the monastery of a definite and lucrative income. During the manorial period, almost every salt spring was owned wholly or in part by some monastery.

The monasteries operated these salt mines themselves whenever possible. If, however, the distance from the monastery to the place was great, the privilege of operation was farmed out, and operated on shares, the monastery agreeing to furnish the necessary equipment. Two methods were used to bring the salt to the surface from the mines, one by means of underground shafts, the other by the use of water wheels. Monastery Weissenburg sunk shafts in its salt mine at Marsal, while Prüm and Metlach used water-engines. These engines were used throughout Bavaria also. The salt on reaching the surface was placed in small iron vats or kettles and heated over a slow fire. Many of these kettles and stoves were required and gifts of this kind were eagerly sought by the monastery.

Forest grants in connection with the ownership of salt privileges were most necessary; hence there are recorded many donations of forest lands near the salt mines or of the privilege to cut wood at stated times and to haul this wood to the settlement near the salt mine. These settlements were usually fair-sized colonies of serfs from the monastery lands over whom one or more overseers were placed in charge. Little huts were erected for their use, and they were allotted strips of land for cultivation. Tegernsee kept twenty serfs permanently located at its village of Achselmannstein in Reichenhall.

The salt was packed in sheets or layers in small tubs of various sizes. It varied in quality and price. Every care was taken to safeguard it and to expedite transportation. The salt belonging to Altaich at Reichenhall was transported by wagons to the Salzoch, sent by boat via the Inn River to Passau, carried by pack animals across to the Danube River and by boat on the Danube to Altaich. The roads were carefully safeguarded, right of way being obtained from the various lords, with exemption from tax and toll wherever possible. The income received from the salt trade became the basis of the vast treasure that many monasteries succeeded in accumulating during the eleventh and twelfth centuries. Both raw and skilled labor existed in plenitude in a medieval monastery owing to the thousands of serfs upon its glebe lands.

Agriculture was, of course, the main occupation of these laborers, but many were employed as artisans, manufacturing utensils and articles which were by-products of agriculture, like harness, saddles, shoes, woolen and wooden goods. In a large abbey these workers lived in "quarters" outside the monastery walls, each "quarter" being devoted to a fixed occupation. The abbey St. Riquier is an interesting instance of this kind. In the economy of a monastery specialization of occupation was carried out very far. We find gardeners, drivers, herders, plowmen, hostlers, butchers, foilers, fullers, carders, weavers, copper and iron smiths, wheel-wrights, carpenters, masons, tile-makers, millers, fishers, fowlers, bakers, bee-keepers, foresters. The monastic system was favorable to the development of malting and brewing, and for several centuries the monks were renowned for the excellent malt they made and the ales they brewed. The brewing qualities of the Burton water appear to have been discovered by monks in the thirteenth century. Up to the twelfth or thirteenth century the preparation of beer on any large scale was done by the monks.

The finer arts also were represented by men of superior talent or technique, as wood and stone carvers, gilders, painters, goldsmiths, silversmiths, parchment makers. Those manorial communities adjacent to the walls of a monastery were often wholly composed of industrial artisans. Sometimes, though, the shops were within the precincts, installed in basements, alcoves, and cloisters for greater convenience or security. A regulation of the twelfth century advised this practice as conducive to greater protection.

All this labor, as said, was servile, and it must also be remembered that the monks enjoyed many privileges and exemptions. Hence the cost of production of articles of manufacture and the cost of merchandising natural produce was less for the monks than for free artisans or merchants. The latter not unnaturally regarded clerical competition as unfair competition, and with the rise of the towns and the organization of craft and merchant gilds a bitter animosity arose. The anticlericalism evinced in the economic legislation of the towns had its root in this feeling. The sentiment is manifested in the thirteenth century, but in the fourteenth and fifteenth it became widespread and pronounced, so much so that economic anticlericalism may be regarded as a factor in promoting the Reformation.

The avarice and covetousness of the clergy, especially of the regular clergy, is an object of wide and bitter denunciation in medieval literature. While some of this vituperation must be taken with reservation because of the widespread envy of the wealth of the monasteries, enough of truth remains to justify the charge, Good old Richard de Bury thus fulminates against the monks:

Flocks and fleeces, crops and granaries, leeks and potherbs, drinks and goblets are nowadays the reading and the study of the monks. . . . Alas, a three fold care of superfluities, viz., of the stomach, of dress, and of houses has seduced them. . . . Forgetting the providence of the Saviour, who is declared by the psalmist to think upon the poor and needy, they are occupied with the wants of the perishing body, that their feasts may be splendid, their garments luxurious, against the Rule, and the fabrics of their buildings, like the battlements of castles, carried to a height incompatible with poverty.

Of the convent of Canterbury in the twelfth century we read:

The influx of wealth produced a corresponding lavish and luxurious outlay. The hospitality of the convent became famous in all the western church, from the crowds of pilgrims who returned from the shrine of the martyr. The internal expenditure was also immense. The refectory was the scene of the most abundant and tasteful feastings. Seventeen dishes were served up at the prior's table. The servants and equipage of a hundred and forty brethren were numerous and splendid.

Giraldus Cambrensis, a caustic critic yet an honest observer of the Cistercians in the days of their plenitude, offers some apology for their corruption:

A good intention [he says], I suppose, is the occasion of this greed of theirs which is denounced throughout the world; it arises from the hospitality which the members of this order, although in themselves the most abstemious of all others, indefatigably exercise, in their unbounded charity to the poor and to strangers. And because they have no revenues, like others, but live entirely by labor and the produce of their hands, they greedily seek for lands with so much effort, in order that they may provide sufficient for these purposes, and so they strive to get farms and broad pastures with unabated perseverance.

We have observed in the history of the development of monastic economic enterprise that successive stages are manifest. At first the monasteries were agricultural colonies; then they began to market their produce; then to manufacture commodities like wooden and leather goods, textiles, and metal wares. Inevitably, as the economic and social life of Europe grew more complex, new forms of investment were found. Hence it is no surprise in course of time, when a money economy had largely supplanted the old natural economy, to find the monasteries developing a mortgage and loan business and finally becoming the earliest banking corporations of the Middle Ages.

The famous canonical prohibition against the exaction of "usury" or interest was a dead letter; for it was readily evaded by fictions and subterfuges. For example, a common argument was that, as the monastery was a corporation and not a person, no sin was attached to the taking of usury; or at the time a loan was made the collateral was so large that the monastery would make a handsome profit in event of default of payment; or when the loan was made the grantee was required to make a "gift" to the monastery apart from the collateral he might put up; or when the loan was paid the borrower was expected to make an additional "gift." By loaning the money for a short term the monasteries made it practically impossible for the borrower to redeem his property. Very frequently the monastery canceled a loan on condition that the tract of land which was held as security should be donated to the monastery.

In time the loan business of the monasteries became so extensive that the abbots were compelled to seek the assistance of trained officials to handle the various transactions of this character. Jews and Lombards were hired for this purpose since they were the skilled money-changers and brokers of this period. The extent of this monastic loan business and the importance that it assumed in facilitating the conduct of business fully justifies one in calling the monasteries the first bankers of the Middle Ages.

The Crusades especially promoted the mortgage business of the monasteries, for in the sudden call for ready money the nobles eager to take the road of the cross either sold their lands for a low price or mortgaged them at exorbitant interest for cash in hand. The ransom of King Richard I in 1192 and that of Louis IX of France in 1248 required his subjects to raise coin or bullion in great quantity, which the monasteries largely furnished, taking a mortgage upon the lands of the nobles as security.

From mortgages and the profits of their markets and trade it was a natural transition to actual banking.

The ecclesiastical foundations during the eleventh and twelfth centuries were the only money-lenders; they alone possessed well-kept barns; they alone were masters of a surplus, and even in the last decade of the thirteenth century, as is shown by an analysis of the debts contracted by a Lotharingian knight, a man might fall into the clutches of confiding nuns and monks.[3]

But many an abbot found that dabbling in the high finance of the epoch of the Crusades, with its multitude of complex and fluctuating values, was perilous practice. The growth of royal authority, the rise of the towns, the enfranchisement of the serfs, the development of commerce and industry from the twelfth century onward, diminished the sources of political power and the opulence of the monasteries. With shrinking incomes the abbots sometimes had recourse to financial expedients which often proved disastrous. In the second half of the twelfth century, there is a visible decay of monastic revenues. Some stewardships became hereditary. Attempts failed to put stewards on salaries or

[3] Fisher, *The Medieval Empire*, I, 257–58.

in some other way restore their older economic dependency. The crusading orders of the Knights Templar, the Knights of the Hospital, the Teutonic Knights, caught the popular favor in the twelfth century so that donations to the older monastic orders began to fall off. Landed wealth began to suffer from the competition of new forms of wealth derived from an awakening commerce and industry, so that many abbeys found themselves "land-poor." And this peculiar form of poverty was aggravated by the scattered nature of a monastery's landed holdings. In vain the abbots endeavored to consolidate their lands by exchange for others, or purchase. The long distance often to the abbey market made it impossible for these outlying domains to send their produce thither, and hence the priors or bailiffs of such farms marketed their produce in a secular market which deprived the abbey of much of the profit it would otherwise have derived from the transaction. Moreover, these local managers, as the grip of the abbot relaxed, tended to make themselves more and more independent, so that finally the abbey was practically deprived of all income from such lands.

The possession of large estates and the necessity of studying economy in all its branches, had converted abbots and priors from simple religious men exclusively devoted to God's service into great land-owners with all the troubles and annoyances of land-owners, surrounded by grumbling and refractory tenants.[4]

The failure of many abbeys to consolidate their lands was undoubtedly an important cause of their economic decline.

As distant farms and manors fell into the hands of different monastic bodies, either their engagements to provide for the erection of some religious foundation, or the necessity of looking after their estates, made it necessary to despatch one or two monks, generally under a prior, to take possession. Removed from the stricter discipline of the larger house, often without the means of carrying it on, no longer under vigilant supervision, the tenants of these cells, as they were called, soon abandoned, under various pretenses, the rigid rules of their order.[5]

Moreover, the cost of living increased greatly during the twelfth century. Protracted litigation to recover debts and to foreclose defaulted mortgages consumed revenues. The rise of the towns and the Crusades drew the serfs away from the domains of the monasteries, so that frequently resort had to be made to casual hired labor at high wages. Too great expansion in the earlier era, when land was a profitable investment, in the purchase of land which brought inadequate returns in the next

---

[4] Giraldus Cambrensis, *Opera*, IV, introd. viii (Rolls Series).
[5] *Ibid.*, IV, introd. xxiv–xxv.

century, compelled monasteries caught in such plight to mortgage their own lands, usually to Jews. Bad or unwise management of monastic property was a common cause of decline and even of bankruptcy. Abbot Hugh of Vézelay was deposed in 1206 for having put the abbey in debt to the amount of 2220 livres silver. St. Omer was nearly bankrupt at the end of the thirteenth century. The abbot of Bury St. Edmunds borrowed money from a Jew named Benedict in order to make some repairs to the abbey, but was unable to repay it. When his creditor pressed him he went on a futile pilgrimage to the shrine of St Thomas à Becket in the hope of recruiting his fortune. He died en route and there were not pence enough in the coffers of the abbey to defray his funeral expenses. The debts of the monastery when Samson became abbot amounted to 3952 pounds, which must be multiplied six or eight times to arrive at the present value of money. Jocelin of Brakelonde gives a vivid account of the penury of the monastery at the accession of Abbot Samson. "Hugh the abbot was old and his eyes were dim, a pious and kindly man, yet not wise in worldly affairs. . . . Everything got worse and worse. There was but one resource and relief to the abbot and that was to negotiate a loan on interest [notice that he is paying, not collecting interest], in order in some measure to keep up the dignity of his house." He borrowed 880 pounds—an enormous sum—from a Jew of Norwich (the same who later brought the downfall of the abbot of Bury St. Edmunds). Fortunately. Samson was an able manager and within twelve years had paid off the debt.

The commonest financial device to effect recuperation of a monastery thus involved was the sale of annuities, pensions, and corrodies, which were mere food pensions. But unless the capital thus acquired was wisely employed or invested, these measures were a precarious resource.

The fundamental cause, however, of the economic breakdown of the monasteries was certainly the passing of the manorial system upon which the economy of every monastery was based. The monasteries had arisen during the epoch of a natural economy and they were ill-adapted to adjust themselves to the new economic revolution which began early in the twelfth century, and which, by the time the thirteenth century opened, had wrought an economic and social revolution in medieval Europe. The lands which they had extensively acquired by mortgage could not be profitably worked according to the old economic system, and the monks could not readily adapt themselves to the new conditions. The monasteries in last analysis were the victims of their own once excellent but now obsolete economic system.

Economic involvement quite curiously made the monks papalists. For the high pontificate of Innocent III and his successors enjoyed enormous revenues, as will be shown in the succeeding chapter, and the popes were quick to take advantage of the impoverishment of the monasteries to bind the monks more firmly than ever to the throne of St. Peter. This they accomplished by themselves making loans to them or underwriting the loans which they might succeed in negotiating. For by the thirteenth century investment in monastic property was everywhere regarded as unsafe. The monks of Canterbury in 1188 bitterly complained because the Roman bankers looked with suspicion upon any loan unless it was backed by papal security.

Far-reaching political results were destined to flow from this state of things. As the new national monarchies arose and resented with increasing indignation the papal claims to temporal sovereignty over them, "the monks looked to the court of Rome for sympathy and assistance." On the other hand, "as the bishops and secular clergy opposed themselves to Roman centralization, the monasteries became colonies of Roman partisans. Their sympathies and antipathies were all in common with Rome, and their national spirit evaporated. . . . When the pope and the king quarreled, the nation sided with the king, the monks with the pope; hence the monasteries became more papal as the state became more national." [6]

Under Philip II (1180–1223) the French crown broke away from monastic tutelage and pinned its faith upon the allegiance of the bishops, with the result that the bishops became props of the monarchy and the power of the abbots was greatly reduced. So far did the French kings carry this repression of the monks that even the abbeys themselves were destroyed, which accounts for the few examples of well preserved abbeys found in northern France. In Norman and Plantagenet England, on the other hand, the kings played the two branches of the clergy against each other and so maintained the balance of power in their own hands. Hence England preserved its abbeys until Henry VIII abolished the orders.

But this breakdown of the monasteries which is manifest about 1200 was not wholly due to economic adversity. The constituency of the monasteries experienced a profound social change in the twelfth century. The older orders had been largely—the Cluniacs wholly—recruited from the families of the feudal aristocracy. The upper class in the feudal age represented the stronger, the more intelligent, the abler element in medieval society. The feudal system with its concepts of the nobility of service, fidelity, honor, coupled with the wealth which the upper class possessed, on the whole bred men of stronger physique, stronger mental ability, and stronger moral fibre than were found among the lower classes, whom generations of hard labor and servile bondage had made heavy and gross. The physique and the intelligence of the peasantry were generally on a lower level than those of the aristocracy and the peasants were wholly without the tradition of service and long experi-

[6] Stubbs, *Introductions to the Rolls Series*, 371.

ence in administration and public affairs which the feudal aristocracy possessed.

Accordingly, as serfdom declined and towns began to rise, the new monastic orders began to be invaded by monks of peasant birth, who, though they might be actuated by the best intentions, were unable to continue as successfully as their predecessors the management of the monasteries. This breakdown of aristocratic control of the monasteries coincides, it is significant, with this invasion from below. It first became apparent in the Hirsauer monasteries, the popular offshoot of the Cluniacs, and was continued in the Cistercians, Premonstratensians, and other minor orders which grew up in the twelfth century.

I am aware that this sort of argument may be repugnant to those who are deeply imbued with a reverence for and a faith in democracy. But what is "progress"? and of what criteria does "progress" consist? History shows many examples of advance side by side with conditions of stagnation or retrogression in other things. The current conception is rarely analyzed.

The decadence is most strikingly manifested in the deterioration of education and intellectual pursuits in the monasteries. Every student of medieval history is familiar with the fact that by the twelfth century the schools of the monasteries were far inferior to the cathedral schools, which were under the management of the secular clergy. The catalogues of monastic libraries, too, afford important information in regard to this intellectual decay of the monasteries. Many of the manuscripts of these libraries went back to the ninth and tenth centuries, and the production of manuscripts was an important occupation of medieval monks. What do we find? Taking two typical monastic houses, each once famous for its school and the cultivation of letters, we discover a significant decline in the production of manuscripts, as the subjoined table illustrates:

		Reichenau	*St. Gall*
9th	century..	100	237
10th	"	29	86
11th	"	7	49
12th	"	4	54

A more sinister evidence of monastic degeneracy than economic decay or intellectual decline, was the tendency to suicide in the monasteries. Accusations of mere immorality, although abundant, must be somewhat discounted. As a class monks were certainly not more dissolute than other classes of medieval society. It must always be remembered that public opinion in the Middle Ages judged the monks by the standard of perfection, not by the standard prevailing in secular society.

By the end of the twelfth century the Cistercians, Premonstratensians, and lesser orders which had appeared in the previous century were verging toward decay. As the Cluniacs had followed the Benedictines in the tenth century, as the Cistercians had followed the Cluniacs in the eleventh, so in turn the Cistercians themselves were followed in the thirteenth century by the Franciscans, or Begging Friars, and the Dominicans, or Preaching Friars. Time had antiquated them. Their luxury and avarice estranged them from sympathy. They were incapable of adapting themselves to the new, anti-feudal drift of things toward town life, commerce and trade, and the development of a bourgeois civilization. Not only were the isolation and provincialism of feudal conditions broken down; the very ideal of monastic isolation had become obsolete.

Instead of being recruited from the feudal aristocracy as was the case with the Cluniac foundations, the Franciscans and Dominicans were recruited from the common people. Instead of dwelling in remote localities "far from the madding crowd," the friars established their houses within the towns. Instead of seeking land and material wealth, they scorned endowments and lived upon alms. Instead of practising agriculture and industry vicariously through the labor of serfs upon their lands, the friars devoted themselves to teaching and preaching and charity relief. Instead of mulling over manuscripts written in a dead language, at least so far as the popular classes were concerned, the friars preached in the vernacular, the speech of the common people, wherèver men might be gathered together, in city squares, at markets and fairs, even at country crossroads. Instead of being ministered unto, the friars ministered. The old monastic ideal had been isolation, to keep one's self unspotted from the world; if the monks ministered unto others it was not for the sake of others, but as a duty imposed upon them, as a means of acquiring credit in heaven, as a species of humiliation—they had no intentional ideal of social service. The friars on the other hand introduced a new ideal: that only by saving others might one save himself. Their charity was genuine and real, not egocentric as that of the monks.

It is indispensable to remember that the rise of the Franciscans was contemporary with the spread of the town movement in Italy and the formation of a bourgeois class in society. The Friars were manifestations of the economic and social revolution in medieval Europe which spelled the passing of feudalism. They were distinctly urban, not rural, monastic groups; democratic, not aristocratic, in spirit and organization. When they could not settle within the town walls their houses were situated in the faubourgs as close to the heart of the town as possible. In purpose and in practice the Franciscan and Dominican houses were city missions and social relief societies.

As in our own times the cities under the impulse of modern industrial and transportation conditions have grown so fast that acute economic and social problems have arisen in them, so in the twelfth and thirteenth centuries the towns grew rapidly and without intelligent direction. The streets were narrow and noisome, the housing conditions deplorable, poverty and vice widespread, often aggravated then as now by sickness and unemployment. Neither the town authorities nor the Church was alert to these new conditions and these new problems. While the population had greatly increased, there were few or no new churches built in many towns and local priests were often no more numerous than two centuries before. When St. Norbert came to Antwerp about 1100 he found one overworked parish priest laboring in a community which had been transformed from a little fishing village into a town by increase of its trade. St. Francis scathingly declared that the cities of Italy "abounded with heathen without God and without hope in the world" owing to the worldliness of the clergy and the neglect of its great mission by the Church. It was with reason that the Catholic poet Francis Thompson compared the Franciscan Friars to the Salvation Army.

The enormous popularity of the Gray Friars, always traveling in pairs —"one before, the other behind," as Dante describes them—never riding horse or mule or vehicle, always shod in sandals with bare feet, clad in rough woolen garments, cheerfully living on what was given them and lodging where night befell, may be easily understood. For the contrast between their simplicity and the luxury and haughtiness of the old orders of monks was striking. They were beloved both in town and in country, whither their wandering might lead them as they journeyed from town to town. Merchant, trader, artisan, peasant loved them as heartily as the monks and secular clergy and the feudal aristocracy hated them for their sympathy with the masses, their open advocacy of the communal movement, even of revolution, their condemnation of irresponsible wealth, their contempt of the feudality and high worldly clergy. The Franciscans were popular not only with the people of the towns but with the university students. For "the poverty of the infant universities presented a disagreeable contrast to the riches of the monasteries."

It is true that in time—and that rapidly—the Franciscans, too, declined and went the way of decrepitude and corruption like the preceding orders. But the fact must not blind our eyes to the substantial ethical and social ideal and practice which they initiated. The Franciscans in their rebellion against the evils and abuses of wealth went to the other extreme, and as with the Cistercians, their sins arose from the very poverty which they idealized. They carried in their bosom the seeds of their own ultimate failure. But they were the victims quite as much of prevailing economic conditions as of degeneration of character. Waiving the question whether mendicancy be not a false ideal in itself, certainly dependence upon casual charity was more difficult to adhere to as a principle of livelihood in the thirteenth century than today, for recurrence of famine and pestilence was far more common then than now. In consequence the friars' scorn of property and proprietary attachments soon became a hypocritical attitude, and the friars became whining syco-phants and artful beggars, employing questionable methods for the ex-tortion of funds, and rapidly delivered themselves over to avarice. As legacy hunters and hawkers of indulgences they became notorious. Roger Bacon, himself a Franciscan, who died in 1292, mournfully wrote that already in his time the friars "were horribly fallen from their former worth." St. Francis has been truly described as "the most spontaneous and unconventional genius of many ages." His followers were unable to sustain his almost superhuman ideal of purity, poverty, and devotion to humanity. The causes of the failure of the friars are inseparable from human nature. Their downfall was as certain as that of all their prede-cessors.

It is pleasant to turn from these gloomy reflections inseparable from monastic history to a lighter side of monastery life. In the Middle Ages the monasteries were "the sole depositories of news, the only places of entertainment when kings and nobles visited their estates. Without the monasteries a country life would have presented to men, especially to the laborer, one dreary round of unalloyed and hopeless drudgery, of fasting days without festivals; of work without mirth or holidays." In a medieval monastery after harvest, often a motley group of jugglers, musicians, and amusing vagabonds broke the dull monotony of rural life. When the harvest and fruits were gathered monasteries and priories were often the scenes of meetings and shows (*conventicula, spectacula*), in the form of miracle or mystery plays by the monks, while wrestling matches and rough games amused the peasants of the manor. It is true that no scholar has yet succeeded in tracing the ancestry of the miracle play back as far as the thirteenth century, but we know that later in the Middle Ages such representations were not uncommon. In these dra-matics the Franciscans seem to have been very active, probably because they saw in them a means of popularizing their preaching and bringing home to the masses the history and the teachings of the Bible. The fa-mous Coventry Plays were wholly in the hands of the Minorites. In time the gilds also began to present mystery and miracle plays, but with them there was a tendency toward horseplay and broad farce which was absent from those presented by the friars. In music, too, the friars introduced innovation by adapting popular airs, as the Salvation Army does today, to their hymns, which, unlike the hymns of the Church, which were in Latin, were written and sung in the vernacular tongue.

CHAPTER XXV

THE CHURCH AND FEUDAL SOCIETY

EVERYWHERE in Europe today, except in England and Spain, the Church has been disestablished and has no connection with government, while in America a state-supported church never existed except in Virginia during the colonial period. Hence it is difficult for a modern person to grasp the reality of a State Church system such as existed in all Europe in the Middle Ages.

The medieval Church differed enormously from modern churches, whether catholic or protestant. It exercised everywhere not only spiritual dominion, but great political, administrative, economic, and social sway. Its jurisdiction extended over every kingdom in Christendom; it was not only a state within every state, but a super-state as well. "The unity of the Church and its official language produced throughout the Middle Ages a cosmopolitanism which has never prevailed again since the Reformation." Unlike secular kingdoms, which were each an independent entity, the medieval Church was a united and universal institution, whose jurisdiction prevailed over all dividing lines of race, nation, language. All Christians were at once subjects of some state protected by natural laws and the laws of their country, and subjects of the Church. The Church made no claim to abrogate feudal law, but it insisted upon the imposition of a higher law as well. It drew a sharp distinction between feudal law and this higher code of right and wrong. It must always be kept in mind that every one in medieval Europe except the Jews, who were tolerated or persecuted, according to time and circumstance, was a subject of the Church, allegiance to which was exacted and rebellion against which was punished. Whatever a man's country, whoever his ruler, every one was subject to ecclesiastical jurisdiction; and in the case of hundreds of thousands who dwelt on church lands, whether as vassals or as serfs, those persons were also temporal subjects of the Church.

The Church's administrative organization was like that of a state, but a firmer and more united one than that of the feudal realms. Its ruler was the pope; its provincial governors were archbishops and bishops; it had its own legislative assemblies in synods and councils; it made its own laws and possessed its own courts of law and its own prisons. The Church had enormous endowments of land, and it imposed a regular tax, the tithe, upon all persons in every community, besides which it collected innumerable fees. For many centuries these fees were derived from the multifarious activities of the Church's administrative bureaux and law courts and were not unsimilar to those which a modern government, whether national or local, exacts for the despatch of business. But in course of time, as we shall see, the practice of exacting fees was enormously extended.

The Roman Church in the Middle Ages was a governor, a landed proprietor, a rent collector, an imposer of taxes, a material producer, an employer of labor on an enormous scale, a merchantman, a tradesman, a banker and mortgage-broker, a custodian of morals, a maker of sumptuary laws, a schoolmaster, a compeller of conscience—all in one. So universal was its sway, so various its activities that in a very large and true sense it is often said that medieval history is primarily the history of the medieval Church. Certain it is that the Church combined in an amazing degree the spiritual and the temporal, the ideal and the practical. If its head was in heaven, it always kept its feet upon the ground. The key to an understanding of this peculiar temporal interest and temporal power of the medieval Church is to be found in the grants of privilege, exclusive jurisdiction, and immunity made to it by the later Roman emperors and continued and extended by the barbarian kings. Still another source was in the growth of the Church as a landed proprietor. Land was not only the most widespread form of material wealth, it was for many centuries almost the sole form of wealth production. Proprietorship and temporalities in course of time carried with them political authority, preferred social status, economic resources, the power to regulate and control society, not merely religiously but temporally. What Sir William Ramsay has said of the Church in the Roman Empire is just as true of the medieval Church:

The administrative forms in which the Church gradually came to be organized were determined by the state of society and the spirit of the age. . . . These forms were, in a sense, forced on it; [but] . . . they were accepted actively, not passively. The Church gradually became conscious of the real character of the task which it had undertaken. It came gradually to realize that it was a world-wide institution, and must organize a world-wide system of administration. It grew as a vigorous and healthy organism, which worked out its own purposes, and maintained itself against the disintegrating influence of surrounding forces; but the line of its growth was determined by its environment.

It is not right to dogmatize when considering the part played by the Church in the feudal age. Institutions, social structure, ideals were very different then from what they are today. It is not always easy to distinguish the line of division between the use and the abuse of the Church's institutions in the history of medieval Europe. An instance may be cited from the reign of Henry II of Germany which serves to make this point clear. The empress Kunigunde had a brother named Adalberon, who was a typical robber baron, a headstrong, quarrelsome Lorrainer. His depredations in the archdiocese of Trèves were so great that he nearly reduced the country to a desert and drove the archbishop to seek refuge in Coblenz. The situation required a man of war, not a man of peace. "I will send a man," wrote the emperor, "who will put a stop to your wild deeds." He was as good as his word. For he chose as the new incumbent of the see not a pious churchman, but a hard-headed, hard-fisted young Franconian baron by the name of Poppo of Bamberg, whom he rushed through the various grades of the hierarchy until he emerged as archbishop of Trèves. Poppo distributed sixty prebends of the see to as many knights, and with this miniature standing army besieged Adalberon's castles and finally brought peace and order into the land again.

Even in the early Middle Ages the proprietary growth of the Church was so great that it alarmed secular rulers. Already in the first half of the eighth century the Agilofinger dukes of Bavaria and Charles Martel in Gaul forcibly deprived the Church of many holdings. But the Church was soon indemnified for its losses by new and larger gifts. For the Carolingians found the employment of the clergy in secular affairs an indispensable necessity as counts, *missi dominici,* diplomats, and even as army commanders, and recompensed them in the only way possible when "natural economy" was all-prevailing—that is to say, by endowments of land. Charlemagne treated the bishops and abbots of his Empire exactly as he treated secular dignitaries and was as cautious in dispensing favors to them as he was to the great lay nobles. The Monk of St. Gall records:

He would never give more than one county to any of his counts unless they happened to live on the borders or marches of the barbarians; nor would he ever give a bishop any abbey or church that was in the royal gift unless there were very special reasons for so doing. When his counselors or friends asked him the reason for doing this, he would answer: "With that revenue or that estate, with that abbey or that church, I can secure the fidelity of some vassal, as good a man as any bishop or count, and perhaps better."

Piety increased what necessity required. It would be an error, however, to infer that all "piety" was generous or disinterested. The avarice of certain of the clergy frequently exacted as a gift what could not prudently be refused. Charlemagne complained that gifts to the Church were so frequent that freemen were reduced to poverty and compelled to take to a life of crime. In 817 Louis the Pious was obliged to legislate to prevent clerks from taking gifts which might disinherit the children or near relations of the giver, and the measure was reënacted by Louis II in 875.

As early as 816 the council of Aachen classified the clergy into three degrees, according to wealth: those having from 3000 to 8000 holdings; those having from 1000 to 3000 holdings; and those having fewer than 1000 holdings.

Most of such holdings were probably real manors, i.e., whole villages of dependent peasants embracing at least a thousand acres of farm land in each; but many holdings were smaller and more detached granges or *curtes*, having no village community upon them, but merely a grange-house in charge of a *villicus* or farm boss, with a few cottagers; while still other holdings may have been isolated patches (*prædia*) with only two or three laborers upon them, who dwelt there only in the spring and summer and returned to the village in winter.[1]

As the manor was not a fixed area, but an economic unit, and allowance must be made for lesser holdings than manors, it is difficult to estimate what these amounts mean. But one of the greatest of modern historical students, striking the average of all the manors possessed by one of the richest abbeys in France, whose book of accounts for a series of years in the ninth century has been preserved, has estimated that the richest clergy in the ninth century possessed from 75,000 to 140,000 acres; the medium rich clergy from 25,000 to 50,000 acres; and even the poorest bishops and abbots from 5000 to 7500 acres. The same historian further estimates the annual revenue of the richest clergy at from $85,-000 to $225,000; that of the medium rich at from $28,000 to $56,000; that of the poorer bishops and abbots at from $5000 to $14,000. In the tenth, eleventh, and twelfth centuries, owing to the improvement in farming methods, lavish gifts, and the redemption of waste, swamps, forest, etc., the landed wealth of the clergy, especially that of the monastic orders, enormously increased.

The rivalry between the secular clergy (episcopate) and the regular clergy or monastic orders for possession of land in the Middle Ages was so keen that it amounted to a permanent feud between them, especially when the so-called "new monachism" or monastic revival wrought by the Cluniac, Cistercian, and Carthusian Orders in the tenth, eleventh, and twelfth centuries arose. In the competition the monks in general were the more successful. For their cloistered, ascetic life impressed popular imagination and their profession of "otherwordliness," gave them a reputation for sanctity which was denied to the secular clergy. Medieval wills which have come down to us show that the abbeys were beneficiaries of private endowment far more than the bishoprics. Other reasons

[1] Coopland, *The Abbey of St. Bertin.*

also had influence. The bishops were identified with secular rule much more than the monks, and were state-supported in considerable measure, whereas the monasteries were proprietary or private foundations. An illustration may make this observation clearer. Here in the United States we have many privately endowed colleges and universities, and state universities in every state. Legacies and bequests to the former are common. The state universities have to look almost wholly to legislative appropriation for funds. So in the Middle Ages the abbeys, which were always of private foundation, found friends and supporters, while the bishops, as part of the system of Church government, were regarded as sufficiently provided for in the possessions and prerogatives which they had. Naturally the bishops endeavored to adjust themselves to this condition, and sought to compensate for the lack of private endowments by reorganizing their properties. In addition to introducing greater efficiency in the management of its lands, the Church also strove to consolidate its scattered buildings into compact complexes, and thus to gain by more scientific management and reduced cost of administration what it lost from the failure of private munificence. The last half of the tenth century and the early part of the eleventh witnessed many sales or exchanges of scattered or remote parcels of land owned by the Church for other holdings lying nearer to the bishopric or monastery. From the data preserved, the success of the experiment was considerable.

But in addition to the rivalry between the bishops and abbots for lands, there was another source of feud in the zeal of the monasteries to acquire right to lay and collect tithes. As originally instituted in the time of Charlemagne tithes were leviable only by the bishops, and the revenues arising therefrom were strictly apportioned. One quarter went to the bishop; the other three portions were assigned to maintenance and repair of churches, the support of the parish clergy, and the relief of the poor. In course of time, since they were imposed upon land, like other real property of the Church, the tithes became feudalized and the object of purchase and sale, enfiefment, patronage, inheritance, mortgage, etc., —to such an extent that by the eleventh century so large a part of the tithes was sequestrated for secular and feudal purposes that the parish clergy were often in a state of poverty and compelled to eke out their petty stipends by dues and oblations and even to labor as field-hands in backward rural parishes. In France and Germany this laicization of tithes went far and was widely sanctioned by custom. In England, however, the practice was hardly known. St. Louis himself was a tithe-owner, and in France the law decreed that all tithes which had been in lay hands before 1179 were to be regarded as secular property, and as such might be sold, entailed, exchanged, devised, or given in dower. In 1789, when tithes were abolished by the French Revolution, it was as lay, not as ecclesiastical property.

The alienation and abuse of the tithe gave the monks a plausible reason to protest against episcopal monopoly of them, and to demand that they should have the right to lay and collect tithes like the bishops. The claim was made on the ground of "reform," but closer scrutiny will reveal that the word reform was usually a cloak to conceal the monks' own desire to aggrandize themselves, without offering any guaranty either of honesty of administration or of relief from abuses. Moreover, the monastic orders had less reason for the tithes with only themselves to support, while the episcopate had the whole care and maintenance of public worship to sustain. In the issue the monasteries usually secured a writ of exemption from Rome, which conferred the right upon them to levy their own tithes, thus putting them on a parity with the bishops in this matter. Indeed, in the high Middle Ages, when the influence of Cluny and Citeaux was at its height and many of the popes were themselves monks, this practice was very common. Incidentally it may be observed that the practice of granting immunity to monasteries from episcopal jurisdiction was a lucrative one for the papacy, which exacted a liberal fee and annual tribute for this grant of papal favor. The notorious controversy over the Thuringian tithes during the reign of Henry IV, in which the archbishop of Mainz was involved in a feud so bitter that it became a war, with the abbots of Fulda and Hersfeld and with Dedi the margrave of Thuringia, is a case in point. The welfare of the Thuringian peasantry, who suffered heavy exploitation, was the last consideration of any of the contestants.

As administered by the Church

the tithe constituted a land tax, income tax, and death duty far more onerous than any known to modern times. Not only were the farmers and cottagers bound to render a strict tenth of all their produce—theoretically, at least, down to the very pot-herbs in their gardens—but merchants, shopkeepers, and even the poorest artisans were by the same theory bound to pay from their personal earnings this same tax of two shillings in the pound. . . . Tithes of wool were held to include even the down of geese; the very grass which he cut by the roadside was to pay its due toll; the farmer who deducted working expenses before tithing his crops damned himself thereby to hell.[2]

A characteristic feudo-ecclesiastical practice—and one frequently of gross abuse—was the right of patronage or advowson, by which the founder of a monastery or the builder of a parish church retained control of the monastic or parish property. The roots of the institution of patronage are to be found as far back as the fifth and sixth centuries. The fifth article of the acts of the council of Châlons (639) shows that laymen already controlled parish property. By the end of the seventh

[2] Coulton, *The Medieval Village.*

century most rural churches were regarded as private property and by slow degrees patronage was often converted into actual proprietorship.

The patron grew in much the same fashion in which the lord grew, and of course in most cases the character of lord and patron would be united in the same person. . . . The advowson of a church was looked on as a matter of property which could be granted, sold, divided, or unjustly occupied in exactly the same way as any other property. . . . Spiritual preferments, great and small, were ceasing to be looked on as offices with an endowment for the maintenance of those who held the office; they rather became benefices, livings charged, like a temporal benefice, with certain duties, but duties which might be discharged at pleasure in person or by deputy. The endowment of a church thus became a benefice, a property, and the right of the patron came to be looked at chiefly as a right to bestow that property, a right which was a property itself.[3]

This conquest of the parishes by the proprietary class was recognized and legalized by the Frankish kings. It became a public institution. The council of Frankfort in 794 permitted freemen to own and possess churches, to alienate them, to sell them, provided that the church edifice itself was not destroyed nor services interrupted. Charlemagne in the *capitulare de villis* carefully regulated the management of parish churches situated on the crown lands. A capitulary of 810 enjoins that the bishops shall see that rural priests "render to their overlord the honor that is due." It is true that in principle such a church was still under the spiritual authority of the bishop, and a crowd of legislative enactments attest it, but the theory and the fact were far from coinciding. A proprietary church in fact was part of the lord's domain. The only real limitation upon his authority was the prohibition that he could not use the income of the land—the *mansus integer*—set aside for the direct support of the parish priest for himself, nor destroy the church building. It was in vain that an element in the Church protested against this prevailing condition. The letters of Agobard of Lyons, the events of 829, the False Decretals, witness to the existence of this opposition. In the reign of Louis the Pious there is marked opposition of the episcopate to seigniorial control of churches. But the protest was ineffectual and after 840 there was merely querulous complaint, nothing more. The spirit of the age and the condition of the times confirmed and sanctioned the system. The letters of Hincmar of Rheims abundantly show how far the Church acquiesced in the condition. He does not deny the right of private proprietorship over the Church, even over the episcopate; he merely limits it. In the tenth century the council of Trosly (909) acknowledged the principle and the practice in canonical decree. A purchased benefice was a form of investment.

[3] Freeman, *Norman Conquest*, V, 501-02.

Thus by the end of the ninth century and the beginning of the tenth, instead of a Church divided into dioceses and parishes, each administered under a spiritual authority of its own, bishop and priest, we see in actuality that many ecclesiastical divisions had become converted by feudal process into a confused agglomeration of feudo-ecclesiastical proprietorships of greater or less extent. In a word, the Church was feudalized like government and secular society. There was no appreciable difference between proprietorship of a church and proprietorship of an ordinary domain. From the end of the ninth century onward real estate transactions in respect to private churches are as common as real estate transactions in respect to manors. Even the Carolingian prohibition against division of the patrimony of a seigniorial church became obsolete. We find cases of church property being halved, quartered, sixthed, etc. And these partitions were not simple assignments of revenue, the capital remaining undivided among the proprietors. The texts show that the partitions were actual and real. The very altar of the church was sometimes divided, so that one finds four or more priests, each the appointee of a separate patron, officiating at the same altar, and each conducting a separate service.

It goes without saying that under such conditions the lands of the Church were subjected to the same economic exploitation as lay lands, and that *cens, corvées, redevances,* etc., were imposed and exacted in precisely the same way that manorial dues were imposed and exacted in the secular world. In some instances the lay proprietor reckoned among his sources of income the rent exacted of merchants who bought and sold in the church porch. The local graveyard, too, was often appropriated by the lord of the manor, whose was the right of advowson, and used as a source of revenue, the land not actually required for burial being rented to peasants as garden plots or cottage sites. This manorial appropriation of the revenues of a church went so far that even the offertory, baptismal fees, penitential fines, burial fees, were appropriated.

It was often shrewd business in the Middle Ages to found a monastery or college of canons or convent, and the piety of many donors was far from being disinterested. For such foundations remained under the control of the founder and his heirs, who pocketed a portion of the revenues, and as gifts, legacies, new endowments of the faithful multiplied, the profits of the heirs might become prodigious from such increment. By their donations to the local church, vineyard, field, and farm, the faithful of the neighborhood enriched the founder. Their wealth increased his wealth; his church drained the private fortunes of those around into his pockets.

The lord of the manor in whose hands lay the right of presentation to the living could treat the incumbent, who not infrequently was one of his own former serfs, with impunity. Jonas of Orleans in the ninth century complained that "poor priests" were compelled to serve as varlets. Agobard of Lyons echoed the complaint, citing instances of priests attached to oratories being compelled to wait at the table, to trim vines, to take care of dogs, to dress ladies' hair, etc. The council of Metz in 888 complained of a priest having been mutilated by his patron because the priest had had the courage to reprimand him for his immorality.

It is not surprising that one of the aims of the Hildebrandine Reform was the suppression of such abuses and the emancipation of church property from lay ownership or control. Many churches and monasteries, in order to protect themselves from feudal spoliation, gradually fell into the way of putting themselves under the patronage of the papacy. Through this practice the pope often became the eminent proprietor of lands of churches and monasteries widely scattered in Europe. These foundations, thus liberated from any other human control, lay or clerical, and protected against spoliation by apostolic anathema, recognized this protection by paying an annual sum (*cens*) into the papal treasury. Under various forms the papal patronage was spread over hundreds of churches and monasteries in Germany, France, and Italy. Gregory VII saw in the practice both a means to extend his authority and a means to reduce the power of the bishops, and a lucrative source of papal revenue as well, and so widely extended the system. Not only ecclesiastical establishments, but private nobles and even towns appeared upon the revenue rolls of the papacy as "wards" paying for papal protection.

But patronage also grew up in another way. In the hard and violent period of the early Middle Ages bishops and abbots often found it expedient to have an official guardian of their property, whose service was rewarded with some share in the estates of the house. Thus arose the *advocatus* (French *avoué*, German *Vogt*). The advocate represented his ecclesiastical superior in the administration of the purely secular affairs which fell to the bishop or the abbot to perform in pursuance of his double rôle of an ecclesiastic and a landed proprietor. He pleaded the causes of the bishop or abbot in the courts of the suzerain; he administered justice in their name among the church's vassals; he represented his principal in the judicial duel, participation in which was forbidden to ecclesiastics; he presided over cases of trial by battle between the bishop's or abbot's vassals, and, most important of all, he commanded the *milites ecclesiæ* when the church was called upon to do military service.

In the anarchy of the ninth century, when the churches began to wall their houses, the office of advocate acquired great extension. Protection was the crying need of the time. Often, though, the bishop or abbot had no choice in selecting the incumbent. The post was eagerly coveted by the lay feudality, since it gave the holder control of certain ecclesiastical revenues and the use of certain church vassals for military purposes. As a consequence, in practice, the bishop or abbot had frequently to appease the greed of a neighboring noble by purchasing his protection, for otherwise his lands were liable to be pillaged by the noble. Under this form of blackmail the remedy became worse than the disease. The Capetian kings of France made themselves "lay" abbots of half a dozen of the richest abbeys in France. The counts of Flanders so built up their power. In Germany the practice was carried to an extreme by Frederick Barbarossa, whose Italian campaigns were largely fought with church vassals.

As proprietorship and patronage tended to manorialize the Church, so feudalism tended to militarize it. Church lands inclined to fall into much the same relation to the state as lay lands, to become converted into fiefs and bishops and abbots to be transformed into barons. Bishoprics became baronies, which in event of vacancy were under the guardianship of the crown to be conferred afresh upon some new holder, who did homage and swore fidelity to the king as every other vassal. Like a fief, the bishopric was often kept vacant by the king, sometimes for three or four or five years, for it was feudal law that a suzerain had the right to the incomes of vacant benefices, whether secular or clerical. Such a tendency naturally resulted from the magnitude of the high clergy as proprietors and the political importance of the Church in the Middle Ages. Bishops and abbots enfiefed nobles and knights with ecclesiastical lands, just as the baronage provided their vassals with fiefs. The feudal system of the Church was a replica of that of the secular world. "The status of the bishops was based upon their possession of real property, and consequently their ecclesiastical status depended upon their status as territorial lords."

The Carolingians in the eighth century, under whom landed proprietorship formally entailed military service, had instituted this practice, which became universal in feudal times. From that time onward fighting bishops—abbots less so—are to be found in every age, and the art of war became a necessary episcopal accomplishment. In a battle fought in 880 two bishops perished. In 955 the prowess of the bishop of Augsburg in the battle of the Lechfeld against the Magyars won him wide renown. The armies of the Hohenstaufen were chiefly composed of church vassals. Bishop Adhemar of Puy, the papal legate on the First Crusade, enjoyed a reputation second only to that of Godfrey de Bouillon. Odo of Bayeux, half-brother of William the Conqueror, fought at Hastings, *"un baston tenait en son poing"*—swinging a mace instead of a battle-ax, for it was against the rule of the Church for a churchman to shed blood. When, in the Third Crusade, Richard Lion-Heart found the blood-stained hauberk of Bishop Philip of Beauvais upon the battle-field, he sent it to the pope with the message: "This we have found. Know now whether it be thy son's coat or no." Guerin of Senlis was the strategist of the French in the battle of Bouvines (1214). Even popes took the field, as John VIII, John X and Leo IX. Church lands were used without any reminiscence of the original purpose of the endowment by kings and princes for state and secular interest. In Germany three-quarters of the contingents enumerated in the muster-roll of 981 (1482 out of a total of 1990) were drawn from ecclesiastical lands. The Church furnished 74 per cent of the forces for the Italian campaign of Lothar II in 1136. The German kings gave lands to the Church in order to increase its military effectiveness, and the grants were made subject to this stipulation. This is the reason why the kings so resolutely held fast to the right of ecclesiastical appointments, for it was the surest way of controlling the Church's resources, both of men and of money.

Under these conditions the hierarchy tended more and more to become a military caste like the feudality. "In your kingdom," Pascal II wrote to Henry V, "bishops and abbots are so occupied in secular affairs that they are compelled to frequent the county courts and to do soldiering. The ministers of the altar have become ministers of the court." "Lo, what lusty and warlike archbishops there are in Germany," wrote Richard of Cornwall to Prince Edward of England during the War of the Barons. "It would not be a very bad thing for you if you could create such archbishops in England." Bishops and abbots exercised a temporal sovereignty analogous to the powers they had long practised within their ancient immunities. In the name of churches and monasteries they granted fiefs, ruled vassals, distributed tenures, and governed serfs. Side by side with the secular feudatories grew up an ecclesiastical nobility composed of archbishops and bishops, who were at the same time dukes or counts, and cathedral chapters and abbeys which as corporations controlled immense territorial possessions. The practice of infeudation penetrated the whole body of ecclesiastical offices and functions. The Church's lands, offices, altars, prebends, tithes, became feudalized. The Church, in order to sate the land hunger of the feudal nobles, was often compelled to effect an accommodation with them by enfiefing its lands to them. In an age of blood and iron such an arrangement was frequently of mutual advantage. The bishop or abbot did not give nor the baron get something for nothing. The baron might have bullied the bishop into making the enfiefment, but he was subject to the feudal contract which always required the rendering of military service by the vassal to the suzerain. Thus originated that class of *milites ecclesiæ* which played so great a part in the period of the Crusades; thus the Church entered more deeply than ever into the feudal polity. Vassals and revenues of the Church were regarded as part of the military and fiscal resources of the crown and were used by the king at his discretion. The bishop or abbot (if the abbey were "royal") was as much the choice of the king as a local priest was the creature of his lord, and the conduct of the hierarchy was assimilated to the condition, if not the status, of the secular feudatories. Bishops and abbots were held to the performance of *auxilia* [feudal aids] in the same way and to as great—or even greater—a degree as dukes and counts.

The domain of a bishop or abbot in the Middle Ages was rarely, if ever, a compact, contiguous area. On the contrary it was composed of a vast ensemble or complex of scattered parcels which had been acquired by gift or purchase during years of time, and was therefore widely located. The unity of the whole was not a physical but a moral one. The bishop or abbot was the proprietor thereof, whose legal position was guaranteed by the immunity which exempted him from any lay jurisdiction or authority. No duke nor count could lawfully enter within this circumscription, which, in spite of the agglomerated nature of the lands, nevertheless formed a closed circle. Within and on his own lands a bishop or abbot was a feudal official.

Both in law and in practice these ecclesiastical lands were regarded as a particular kind of barony. This was the view of the Church as well as of the State, and neither party looked upon the relation as either incongruous or unusual. Vacant sees and vacant abbeys were treated as knights' fees. After the analogy of lay fiefs the king attached the incomes of ecclesiastical office in the interval between two occupations; the new appointee paid what answered to a "relief" in the secular world in order to qualify for the office; the lands and offices of the Church were let to farm, enfiefed, or sold exactly as was secular property. "Church preferment was indeed throughout the Middle Ages the usual way of paying civil servants who were in orders."

The society of the Church was as sharply divided as lay society into an upper and a lower class, an independent and a dependent class. The hierarchy was very generally closed to any but those of noble blood, while the parish priests were usually recruited from the servile villagers. Formal emancipation by the lord was necessary for a serf priest to enter holy orders. In the eighth and ninth centuries there was such an influx of monks of lowly origin into the monasteries that the law stepped in and arrested the tendency in the interest of the proprietary class, "lest the fields become deserted." Thegan, the biographer of Louis the Pious, deplores the practice of elevating serfs to even the lowest grade of the hierarchy. As early as the ninth century the aristocratic nature of the upper clergy is apparent. Louis the Pious was reprimanded for appointing Ebbo, the son of a serf, as archbishop of Rheims. When Otto II made Gerbert of Aurillac, whose parentage was servile, pope (Sylvester II) outcry was made; and Benno II of Osnabrück was the only German bishop of lowly origin in the reign of Henry IV. Archambaud of Sens in the tenth century, who had a passion for horses and hunting dogs, removed the altar of the cathedral out of doors into the porch, and converted the interior of the church into stables and kennels. Manasseh of Rheims is alleged to have said that "the office of archbishop would be a fine job if one did not have to say mass." Helinand of Laon, "being a man of poor family and humble origin, as he knew he would have no influence through respect for his birth, placed his hopes on the acquisition of great wealth." It was lodged against Suger, the famous abbot of St. Denis, that he was of servile birth. Bela of Hungary refused to receive a bishop at court because he was of servile family. "In Germany a mass of evidence shows that in the feudal age the most important offices of the Church were normally almost confined to men of noble blood. From that class were chosen bishops and abbots. Only in the later Middle Ages did this exclusiveness begin to break down when members of the ministerial and unfree classes were admitted."

The union of spiritual authority and temporal power in the medieval Church, however incongruous it may seem to us today, and however incompatible with modern conditions and ideals it may appear, was unavoidable and necessary in the feudal age. Indeed it was good that it was so. For no great historic institution can be effective if it does not reflect the dominant ideas of its time and embody in its economy the customary practices thereof. The Church's function was to lead and not to follow; to guide and to teach; to be of its age but to be better than its age; to use and not abuse the civilization of which it was representative; to invest for the benefit of society the capital of heritage, tradition, culture of which it was the legatee or depository. The Church's successes and the Church's failures were alike the result of its close identification with the institutions and the civilization of its time. The evil lay not in the use of things of the age, but in the abuse of them. It is easy for one to be critical, even harsh in one's judgment of the medieval Church. But it is not so easy to be just. For justice partly depends upon a clear understanding of both an intricate organization and a complex civilization. It must ever be remembered that the Church faced a condition which in many ways was repugnant to its theories and its ideals.

The character of the Church in these centuries is to be found, not so much in the doctrines which it professed, but in the organization which the Church possessed. That organization, like every other institution in the Middle Ages, was feudalized through and through, so thoroughly that the primary function and spirit of the Church by the eleventh century seemed to be in danger of destruction owing to the long and at last intolerable tyranny of things material and worldly over things in origin and essence of a spiritual nature. He who understands feudalism has in his hand the key to an understanding of the tremendous issues involved in the Hildebrandine reform movement.

The Church, in common with secular government, rested upon land as its base. The stipends of the clergy were derived from landed endowments, as prebends and the like. They were not fiefs, but they tended to follow the customary tendency of fiefs, and hence to become hereditary. It was difficult in such an age to distinguish between the corporate Church as possessor and the personal incumbent of the stipend, for men thought in concrete terms, not abstract ones.

In the eleventh century the increasing invasion of the high offices of the Church by the aristocracy, the growth of family control of church offices and church property which frequently culminated in the actual hereditability of church offices and church endowments, the intrusion of local jealousies and family feuds into ecclesiastical matters, reached a pitch. Rather of Verona in the tenth century declared hereditability of church offices was almost the normal condition in Italy. Benedict VIII deplored the universality of the evil in 1020 at the council of Ticino. A biographer of St. Bernard in the twelfth century says that marriage of priests and hereditability of church offices and church property was general among the Norman clergy.

It is difficult for the modern mind to understand or to appreciate the danger which thus threatened the Church.

An hereditary caste would have been established, who would have held their churches and lands of right; . . . In an age when everything was unsettled, yet with tendencies so strongly marked, it thus became a matter of vital importance to the Church to prevent anything like hereditary occupation of benefices or private appropriation of church property, and against these abuses its strongest efforts were directed. The struggle lasted for centuries, and it may perhaps be fortunate for our civilization that sacerdotalism triumphed. . . . It became an absolute prerequisite that the Church should hold undivided sway over its members; that no human affection should render their allegiance doubtful; . . . that the immense landed possessions of the Church should remain untouched and constantly increasing as the common property of all, and not be subjected to the incessant dilapidations inseparable from uxorious or paternal affections. . . . Perhaps in this there may have been an unrecognized motive urging Gregory VII to action. Sprung from so humble an origin, he may have sympathized with the democratic element, which rendered the Church the only career open to peasant and plebeian. . . . All this would be lost if, by legalizing marriage, the hereditary transmission of benefices generally resulting, should convert the Church into a separate caste of individual proprietors, having only general interests in common. . . . To us, retrospectively philosophizing, it further appears evident that if celibacy were an efficient agent in obtaining for the Church the immense temporal power and spiritual authority which it enjoyed, that very power and that authority rendered celibacy a factor not devoid of advantage to the progress of civilization.

It is easy to show how the churchmen could have selected matrimonial alliances of politic and aggrandizing character; and as possession of property and hereditary transmission of benefices would have followed on permission to marry, an ecclesiastical caste, combining temporal and spiritual power to a dangerous excess, might have repeated in Europe the distinctions between the Brahman and Sudra of India. The perpetual admission of self-made men into the hierarchy, which distinguished the Church even in times of the most aristocratic feudalism, was for ages the only practical recognition of the equality of man.[4]

The surest, although the most difficult way to prevent alienation of church property and the entailment of its offices, was thus to prohibit the marriage of all priests and create a celibate priesthood. The intensely radical nature of such a remedy is manifest. Yet, again to quote a very eminent historian: "Any real familiarity with the early Middle Ages will lead an unprejudiced student to the belief that the celibacy of the clergy was at that time essential to the setting apart of the ecclesiastical order, to the purification of the Church and to its influence upon the world; that clerical celibacy was in fact a necessary stage of the spiritualization of European society."[5] If the Roman Church today is still justified in maintaining a celibate priesthood, it was ten times more justified in so insisting in the days of feudalism. It requires a profound knowledge of medieval conditions to understand the necessity of celibacy and the popularity of the doctrine with the masses. "It is hardly possible for us, even in imagination, to conceive a danger to modern civilization similar in kind to that which threatened the men of the eleventh century from feudal brutality with its contempt for mental thought and its hatred of the bonds of morality. Yet it is only by steadily keeping before us the existence of this danger that it is possible to pass a fair judgment on the drastic remedies proposed by the medieval churchmen." For "as soon as the clergy began to provide for their offspring by gifts of ecclesiastical property, the temporal possessions of the church were in danger of becoming completely alienated; and in the second place, a married priesthood would naturally tend to become a hereditary caste little inclined, as its local power increased, to subject itself to the supreme pontifical authority. . . . Possibly Gregory VII was the first to realize just how important the enforcement of celibacy would be to the power of the papacy. Whether his predecessors had seen the situation as clearly as he did or not, it can never be argued that they, any of them, were prompted solely by the desire to extend the monastic ideal."[6]

Perhaps the Church in the eleventh and twelfth centuries would have acted more wisely if it had gone more slowly and been more moderate in

[4] Lea, *Sacerdotal Celibacy*, 3d ed., I, 165–66, 267–68.
[5] A. L. Smith, *Church and State in the Middle Ages*, 83.
[6] S. R. Gardiner, *Introduction to English History*, ch. III, secs. 9–10.

its demands for celibacy, beginning with the higher clergy and gradually enforcing the rule upon the lower clergy until all, even parish priests, had been brought to adherence, and at the same time have not made celibacy retroactive, and so slowly reduced and finally eliminated the evil of alienation and misuse of church property. There were wise churchmen who so advised, like Lanfranc in England, who refrained from molesting the parish clergy, but forbade canons to have wives; and for the future refused to ordain deacons or priests who were married; but did not compel those clergy already married to put away their wives or stigmatize the latter as concubines and their children as bastards.

But the papacy and the Cluniacs would have nothing to do with so temperate a policy, and urged the radical course, with the result that the clergy was broadly divided into two camps, the secular clergy, led by the bishops, being moderates, the regular clergy being radicals. The feud between the two classes was a long and bitter one, for each was jealous of the prerogatives of the other, envious of the political influence of the other, covetous of the wealth of the other. And the popes of the eleventh and twelfth centuries, most of whom were monks, played the two parties against one another, and one or the other, depending upon conditions, against the kings and the feudality in order to depress secular political authority and establish the supremacy of the papacy over the State everywhere. Monks were appointed to vacant sees, secular and regular canons supplanted married clergy in cathedral staffs; even parish priests were displaced by monks who assumed holy orders for the express purpose, unless the local patron resolutely fought to preserve his right of advowson. "As to priests," an instruction of Anselm provides, "if any can be found who are leading regular, *i.e.,* celibate, lives, let them act for the others, *i.e.,* married priests. But if none or few such are to be found, give orders that in the meantime monks shall say mass for the people. . . . The same clergy shall receive confessions in place of the others and bury the bodies of the dead. All this you may enjoin upon even monks of advanced age until this obstinacy of the married priests shall yield. It will not last long providing we persist in what has been begun. . . . If those expelled rebel let all Christians be against them and exclude them not only from their own society but also from the lands they hold, together with their *female belongings* [!] until they come to a better mind." It cannot be denied, in admitting the fundamental justice of the Church's policy, that much injustice and much inhumanity was committed in the enforcement of the Hildebrandine reforms; that thousands of innocent men, women, and children suffered contumely, abuse, social ostracism; that true wives were declared concubines and children born in lawful wedlock stigmatized as bastards.

In 1059 the Lateran Council for the first time formally legislated in regard to clerical celibacy and ordained it. The alienation of property thereby threatened, the impending rupture of priests' familes and the taint thrown upon their children produced a tumult of opposition. The bishops of Turin, Asti, Albi, Vercelli, Novara, and Lodi refused to promulgate the decree. At the same time the proletariat in the Lombard cities, notably in Milan, began to agitate against married priests under the leadership of a demagogue named Landuiph.

While some of these violent and radical partisans were honest in their purpose, many of the agitators were actuated by an ignoble self-interest, their primary aim being the spoliation of that portion of the priest class who were luckless enough to be married.

Availing themselves of the mass of discontent existing among the inferior clergy of the diocese and the small respect entertained by the commonalty for their superiors, the confederates soon collected around them a numerous party consisting chiefly of hedge-priests and rabble. . . . Landulph began operations by collecting crowds in the streets and public places and haranguing them in terms of the bitterest and coarsest scorn against the metropolitan clergy. . . . "Let their wealth be impounded, their property put up at auction, and if they resist, let their houses be given up to pillage and they and their bastards be hounded out of the city." . . . While Landulph was agitating the rabble of the city, Ariald was busy goading on the rustic population against the country clergy. . . . Within a year . . . a new set of puritan reformers had arisen among the populace of the Lombard cities. . . . The new party became known by the name of Patarini . . . according to tradition derived from a quarter of the city inhabited by the poorest and most discontented class.[7]

Even in the great struggle over the question of lay or clerical investiture, as in the conflict between Gregory VII and Henry IV, between Alexander III and Frederick I, there is to be found a whole group of economic phenomena which are little understood by the student. It is vastly important for one to perceive that one of the conditions of the papacy becoming a sovereign power was the Church's enormous possession of landed property. In the so-called War of Investiture the issue was as much one of property as it was one of dominion. Peace with the emperors and the other sovereigns of Europe would have been easy to procure provided the Church had been willing to renounce her feudal revenues, her temporalities. Keen-witted men like Abelard, Arnold of Brescia, and Gerhoh of Reipersberg already perceived this in the twelfth century. Even St. Bernard, in spite of his deep hostility to Arnold, was one with him in the opinion that the great wealth of the Church was an evil to it. Like the certain rich man in the New Testament, the medieval Church was too rich to make the sacrifice.

The Church was amply possessed of free alodial endowments long be-

[7] Greenwood, *Cathedra Petri*, Bk. X, p. 176.

fore the spread of feudalism. Most of the donations made after the death of Charlemagne (814), however, were fiefs. Hence the effect of renunciation, if it had taken place, would have been to reduce the Church to the proportion of land which it had possessed at the accession of Louis the Pious. This would have been far from cutting the Church to the quick, for even early the Church's landed wealth, as we have seen, was enormous. There is little doubt of the justice of requiring the Church to evacuate its purely feudal lands, although it may have been going too far, in an age of natural economy, to expect the Church to renounce, too, its endowments in the form of tolls, market rights, etc. These were the very sources of income which tended to emancipate it from the natural economy of the earlier medieval period, and enabled the Church to keep abreast of the economic changes of the time. The question was not a doctrinaire one, but one of practical interest. The feudal state contended that the properties of the Church having been acquired by it in and under feudal conditions, the Church was bound to perform service in fulfilment of the obligations assumed. The Church contended that its possessions could not be severed from it and that ecclesiastical endowments were indivisible and inseparable constituents of the Church; that all Church property was "holy unto the Lord" and could not be used or controlled or diverted by any other authority.

It is obvious that there is here a difference between endowment for spiritual purposes and endowment for temporal purposes; that two different titles and two different conditions obtained. Could they in theory or law or fact be separated? The Church in the tenth and eleventh centuries, particularly in Germany, had accepted huge endowments of land on condition of performing the feudal services to the crown attached to their possession. In accepting and profiting by feudalism the Church assumed the obligations of feudalism. But the Gregorian reform confused temporal and spiritual together, or rather adroitly sought to evade the obligation of its temporalities by ignoring the essential difference in the nature of the Church's holdings, some of which, especially the earlier endowments, were for legitimate support of the Church, while the later ones were largely feudal and temporal. But the Hildebrandines declared that all church property was spiritual.

For the secular governments such an interpretation everywhere was a challenge to their independence and their sovereignty, and only by a stretch of truth may it be said that lay investiture of a bishop or abbot *for his temporalities* was "simony" or corrupt practice and government intimidation of the Church. One who purchased or used the temporalities of the Church but gave nothing for consecration, was not simoniac. The sacramental functions in such a transaction were not, or at least need not, have been the object of barter, for a layman could not make a priest. The just and logical remedy for the evils of abuse in the Church arising from its identification with feudalism, and a way out of the impasse lay in the Church's renunciation of its temporalities. But the Church was too rich to make the sacrifice and took refuge in the argument that spiritual and temporal endowments were indivisible and inalienable constituents. Twice the proffer was made that the Church give up its feudal lands, *i.e.,* all the lands feudally acquired and feudally held since the death of Charlemagne (814), and twice it was refused. The Church replied that no distinction was possible between the species of its holdings, and further argued that such a renunciation would be the betrayal of a great trust and sacrifice of "the heritage of the poor." Was the Church sincere? Or was it avaricious?

Since in the Middle Ages the separation of Church and State was impracticable and the idea was cherished only by visionaries and dreamers, and since the Church refused to accept the parity of State and Church, and instead found the solution of the controversy in the doctrine of supremacy of Church over State, conflict was unavoidable. A party had gradually grown up within the Church which was eager to establish, not only ecclesiastical independence, but even ecclesiastical supremacy; which denied that the grants of the emperors had been made conditionally, or that the Church had ever willingly entered into such a relation with the State. This party stigmatized all secular control of church offices as "simony," and found the readiest means to attain its end in a denial of the legality of lay investiture. The War of Investiture was at bottom a contest for control of church patronage, and the root of the whole matter was the temporalities of the Church. The contest was not without economic interest. Gregory VII and his successors strove to repudiate those feudal duties and obligations to both government and society which the Church's possession of vast landed property naturally and legally entailed, and at the same time to keep the Church's lands. Whatever the weight given to the influence in Gregory's mind of Augustinian ideas of a *Civitas Dei* on earth, whatever the arguments of papal legists and proponents, the papacy never would have attempted to translate these vague, abstract aspirations into actuality if the wealth of the Church had not stimulated the papal ambition and created the opportunity. The popes and emperors fought the issue on other grounds, but the object of the struggle between them was largely wealth and power, in the chief form in which wealth and power were embodied in the feudal age, namely, *land*.

Gregory VII may have been a magnificent idealist in advocating the supremacy of the Church over the State. But there can be no doubt that that way also promised enormous material aggrandizement to the Church and stupendous political prerogative for the papacy. In the issue the victory was not with either the papacy or the kings. For in the struggle control of the Church's temporalities largely fell into the hands of the feudalized bishops themselves, who became ecclesiastical princes and regarded their episcopal lands as their own feudal possessions. As early as the twelfth century in Germany we find bishops designating the lands of their sees as *"terra nostra"*—our land. Except that they combined a spiritual office with temporal power, and could not transmit either office or temporalities hereditarily, the bishops of medieval Europe differed little from the great nobles of the time.

While both the merits and the principles involved in the War of Investiture are a matter of controversy and of difference of opinion even unto this day among historians, there can be no doubt of the forward nature of many other of the Church's reforms. One of the most striking examples of the Church's effort to suppress the abuses of feudalism was the institution of the Peace of God and its later correlative, the Truce of God. "History records no such triumph of intellect over brute strength as that which in an age of turmoil and battle was wrested from the fierce warriors of the time by priests who had no material force at their command and whose power was based alone on the souls and consciences of men." [8] Private war was one of the worst oppressions of the feudal régime and was a derivative of the ancient German feud-right. In the feudal period, when kingship had become attenuated to a mere overlordship and central authority was wanting, the practice reached enormous proportions. Personal injuries or grievances, conflicting property claims, rival claims to inheritance, real or alleged wrong done by vassal to suzerain or suzerain to vassal, were redressed not by courts of law but by the swords of the principals in the case. And often these grievances were shallow pretexts for base self-aggrandizement of the strong by spoliation of the weaker. Such were the robber barons who robbed merchant and pilgrim, who gained a thievish living on the highways.

The worst sufferers from private war, however, were not the baronage, but the peasantry. No one need pity the nobles who battened on war, with whom warfare was an heroic accomplishment, and who more often than not welcomed the fray. But the women and children in the castles, the peddler, the traveling merchant or monk, the pilgrim, and above all the peasants of the lord's manors were innocent sufferers from this baronial indulgence in private war. For the first act of each combatant was to destroy the farms and manors of his opponent. Medieval chronicles abound with instances.

Such a condition of things could not have gone on indefinitely, else the peasantry of feudal Europe would have been destroyed. It is not strange, therefore, that already in the tenth century—and more in the eleventh—we discover signs of protest and rebellion against the worst evils of the feudo-manorial régime and attempts to regulate, if not to

---

[8] Lea, *History of the Inquisition*, I, 1.

suppress, the worst abuses, such as the movement to establish first the Peace of God and later its more developed and effective restraint, the Truce of God. It is of immense credit to the medieval Church that it stepped in and used its spiritual authority and its temporal power alike to suppress such violence. The first suggestions of it are to be found in the ninth century, when civil power was going by the board and the weak descendants of Charlemagne began to lean upon the Church for support. Charles the Bald made every bishop a *missus* in his diocese and every parish priest a constable. Excommunication of brigands became the order of the day. The "pacts of peace" which this king required of his vassals, in which the barons swore to suppress brigandage, to renounce the right of personal vengeance, to protect the Church, embodied the principle of maintenance of law and order which the futility of the crown compelled the Church to enforce in its stead. The employment of church vassals by the bishops in this manner is of frequent occurrence in the ninth and tenth centuries.

But what makes the Peace of God so interesting and important is that, while the Church took the initiative in it, the movement was really a spontaneous one which appealed to all classes of feudal society, clergy, baronage, and peasantry, and which associated them all together in a common enterprise for the benefit of society. It was the manifestation of group spirit in feudalism, of coöperative social consciousness so strong that, while it lasted, it to a certain degree canceled the antagonism which existed between the classes. Nothing better shows the organic and constructive nature of feudalism, the essentially formative forces at work in it, slowly laboring with much trial and error, but also with much success, for the regulation of feudalism and the founding of a truly feudal form of government in Europe. It fell to the Church to initiate the movement, not because it was the chief sufferer from anarchy, but because both the innocent who suffered and the violators who perpetrated these atrocities were members of a Christian society of which the Church was the moral leader. The function of the Church was a spiritual one, an ethical one, a social one. More than any other institution, more than the State, more than the kings, it appreciated the principles of law and order, justice, protection of life and property which inhere in every body politic.

The initiation of the Peace of God, then, must be visualized from two points of view: from the actual violence and strife and injustice which it strove to suppress, and from the viewpoint of the development of a new social conscience and new social consciousness. It was not mere police power which the Church assumed. It was social leadership. The real greatness of the Church manifested itself in the latter capacity. It enunciated a new ideal, it proclaimed the doctrine of better laws and a higher ethic; of a feudal society based not on might but on right, on justice, on protection of the laws, on the inviolability of person and property.

The history of the origin and development of the peace movement shows various and important phases of growth. It was initiated in the far south of France, in the synods of Charroux (989), Narbonne (990), and Anse (994), and was then a purely ecclesiastical movement. The resolutions declared that church property was not to be treated as the property of the warlike laity and threatened violators with anathema. There was nothing new in this, for such menaces were as old as the ninth century. The novel feature was anathema upon those who ravaged the property of the poor and the peasantry. The Church in the earliest stage of the movement, therefore, did not prohibit private war, but it endeavored to protect its property and the peasantry everywhere from being made the victims of such strife. The Church created a category of a specially protected class. It asserted that a defenseless peasantry, however weak, still had rights before the law which the baronage, however violent, would be compelled to respect. The following is a typical example of the oath exacted. It was imposed by the bishop of Beauvais in 1023.

I will not carry off either ox or cow or any other beast of burden; I will seize neither peasant nor merchant; I will not take from them their pence, nor oblige them to ransom themselves; I do not wish them to lose their goods because of wars carried on by their seigniors, and I will not beat them to obtain their subsistence. I will seize neither horse, mare, nor colt from the pasture; I will not destroy nor burn their houses; I will not uproot their vines or gather the grapes under pretext of war; I will not destroy mills and I will not take the flour therein, unless they are on my land, or unless I am on war service.

But if the Church most fully represented and expressed progressive opinion in the feudal world, it would be an exaggeration to think that such sentiment was wholly of the Church's creation. The better element of the laity must be given some credit, and even the opinion of the masses was not so immobile as is customarily thought. For it was not long before the laity, both noble and unfree, were participating in the movement to repress private warfare. The baronage itself began to perceive the evil of the *faida* or feud, and voluntarily offered to renounce it and to restrain others from appealing to it. Physical compulsion was added to the threat of church penalty. This new phase was first manifested in Aquitaine, whence the movement spread into Burgundy (1016). King Robert of France in 1025 took it up, and it soon spread over all of central and northern France, becoming more and more defined and more and more acquiring the form of a positive institution. Fraternities of Peace were formed. At the same time the sanction became more rigor-ous. To simple excommunication the Church added the interdict (Synod of Bourges, 1038), a sort of ecclesiastical "strike" by which the offices of the Church were stopped until the offender yielded. The very resort to such drastic practice indicates the power of public opinion, for in the end it was public opinion as much as fear of the Church which compelled an offender to yield to "peace."

At this time the Peace of God went through a profound change both in spirit and organization, and merged into the Truce of God, a far more effective institution. We discover "a conscious endeavor to mark off by general definitions a sphere of peace from the surrounding sphere of feud, so that peace for itself and for its own sake now becomes the object that is aimed at." For two weaknesses had become apparent in the Peace: it was not upheld by the civil law, and no time-limit was imposed upon the practice of private war—a baron might wage it any and every day in the year. The only prohibition was with reference to churchmen, church property and the peasantry. But the Truce of God, which we find first proclaimed at the council of Elne in Roussillon in 1027, declared certain days in every week and certain seasons in the year to be "closed" seasons, when private war was made illegal. At the same time the secular arm stepped in to aid and reënforce the penalties. It is obvious that this new form was a more thorough policy of restraint than the old form. The Truce of God was both an ecclesiastical and civil movement. In some places popular support of the Truce of God had the psycho-social characteristics of a camp-meeting revival. Thus, in Guienne in the late twelfth century a carpenter gave out that Jesus and the Virgin had appeared to him and commanded him to preach peace among all men. The organized nature and the consecrated idea in these local peace associations come out in that at Puy, where clergy and barons formed an association called the "Brotherhood of God." Like the earlier "Peace," the *Treuga* spread with great rapidity, synod after synod, council after council ordaining it in the latter half of the eleventh century until finally at the council of Clermont in 1095 Pope Urban II proclaimed it as universal law. Already even before this date, the *Treuga* had been declared in Germany and Italy. In England, where the Norman kings were always strong, it was never proclaimed because it was never needed.

The progressive development of the Peace and the Truce into an institution is suggestive to observe. At first only the persons and property of clergy and peasantry, especially women and children, are declared inviolate; then merchants and wayfarers, and their property, are included; the penalties are both ecclesiastical and secular, extending even to exile or banishment with forfeiture of goods; the "closed" days at first were the three days of the passion (Friday, Saturday, Sunday), and later were extended from sunset on Wednesday to sunrise on Monday; the "closed" season at first was only Lent; later it included the whole period of time from the beginning of Lent to the Sunday after Easter; later still it was extended to Whitsuntide, and then to St. John's Day (June 24). Similarly, as the planting season was protected, so was the harvest and vintage season protected, and private war made illegal from the Feast of the Assumption of the Virgin (August 15) to St. Martin's day (November 11). In the aggregate a violent baron thus had left to him only the hottest summer months and the coldest winter months as fighting days. At the same time with these changes the repressive legislation tended to become a code—the articles increase from three to eight, to eleven, to fourteen, to nineteen, etc., and other forms of crime besides robbery are included in them, as making or circulating counterfeit coin, receiving stolen goods, sheltering criminals and fugitives from justice.

Such formidable extension of police power by the Church did not go without protest, on the ground that it was usurpation of the prerogatives of secular princes and the State. Even some churchmen protested, arguing that it was not the business of the Church and that the exercise of police power by the Church would tend to confound the Church with the world and secularize and demoralize it. Undoubtedly there was truth in this objection, yet the argument was more doctrinaire than actual, for the Church and society in the hardest period of the feudal age were face to face with a condition and could not afford to give ear to theoretical objections. The situation was too real. In the issue the question solved itself. In the twelfth century the legislation of the Truce passed into the *Decretals* of Gratian, into the canon law, into the legislation of the kings and the emperor; it became the municipal law of Europe, and lasted as a force until the formation of the national monarchies with effective systems of administration made it obsolete. When modern government and the modern State appeared, civil law alone was sufficient to maintain law and order.

Other manifestations of new social and group consciousness in the eleventh century, when Europe began to stir universally as never before, are interesting to observe. Among such group phenomena, besides the Truce of God, one finds the habit of making pilgrimages en masse to popular shrines, relic worship, the first manifestations of chivalry among the feudal caste, the formation of gilds and confraternities, religious revivalism, often culminating in the formation of heretical sects.

Among the most interesting of these popular group manifestations is the enthusiasm—one might almost say mania—for building new churches. It is one of the most striking evidences of psycho-social emotionalism in all the Middle Ages. The construction of these new and more beautiful church edifices coincided with this social awakening and this new consciousness of power in Europe expressed in the establishment of better government, better laws, and the formation of new religious and social ideals. The phenomena all hang together as parts of one whole in the centuries of recovery and restoration which followed the prostration and anarchy of the ninth and tenth centuries.

Before this wave of church-building swept over Europe many of the churches, even great churches and cathedrals, were made of wood, or at least the fabric was largely constructed of wood. Little or no glass was yet to be found in them. The age of stained glass was to come, and glazed linen sheets covered the windows. Many churches were unpaved, or else the pavement was only in the choir and around the altar. Very many parish churches were flimsy timbered edifices with beaten clay floors. All were damp and dark, and all were liable to fire. Indeed, almost every great church in Europe was burned once, many several times within a few hundred years.

And then came new religious revivalism, sweeping up out of Italy and over the Alps into the Rhineland, France, Flanders, and southern England, on the crest of which was borne the first Romanesque architecture in Europe. The new structures were made out of cut stone, materially safer and esthetically susceptible of far greater artistic adornment. Again (in parenthesis) observe the advancement in industrial skill and technique. These new, clean white stone structures in the space of a few years in the first half of the eleventh century became so numerous, especially in northern France, that a Burgundian monk of artistic feeling beautifully recorded that one might think that God had snowed churches down upon the land. They were, it has been well said, "the outward sign of the coming of peace and piety"—the Peace of God given real embodiment. The plans for many of these early Romanesque churches were drawn by Italian architects and Italian stone-cutters, and masons were imported to work upon them. Those of Como were the most famous craftsmen of this kind in Europe. Upon church decoration the growing material wealth of Europe was lavished in the form of adornment, wall frescoes, paintings, sculpture, carved screens, altars, and exquisitely wrought vessels of gold and silver. Colored marbles were imported from Italy, even whole columns from old Roman basilicas, tin to make bronze from England, lead from Spain, precious stones from the Orient. Although the general effect was Romanesque as a form of architecture, and although certain styles predominated, yet there was much freedom of composition. The architects vied with one another to express originality. Local conditions, as the kind of stone available, contributed to diversity. In Auvergne a local colored stone gave a local stamp of distinction to the churches there. The provinces of France and the Rhineland differed as much in architectural details as the dialects of the language differed.

The new religious zeal became so fervid that it actuated all classes of society to labor together without reference to caste or class. Noble and peasant, serf and freeman labored side by side in the common cause of the community, and over the whole movement was spread the Church's garment of light. There are many examples of the participation of the whole village or community, priests and laymen, peasants and nobles, men and women. A real rivalry existed between the architects of one district and those of another, between churches here and there, between monasteries of this place and of that. *Corvées* were self-imposed by the people to further the work. Sermons were preached to stimulate the enterprise and gifts were lavished by rich and poor. Encyclical letters were circulated asking for help, miracles and legends were told about workmen who fell from scaffolds and were miraculously saved; concessions, often very liberal ones, were made to the builders.

We fortunately have preserved for us several very vivid letters of the eleventh century depicting this enthusiasm for church building. At Chartres it was so intense that it took the form of a crusade. The archbishop of Rouen, who saw the movement and described it to his friend the bishop of Amiens, wrote:

The inhabitants of Chartres have combined to aid in the construction of their church by transporting the materials. . . . Since then the faithful of our diocese and of other neighboring regions have formed associations for the same object; they admit no one into the company unless he has been to confession. . . . They elect a chief under whose direction they conduct their wagons in silence and with humility. Who has ever seen? Who has ever heard tell, in times past, that powerful princes of the world, that men brought up in honors and in wealth, that nobles, men and women, have bent their proud and haughty necks to the harness of carts, and that, like beasts of burden, they have dragged to the abode of Christ, these wagons, loaded with wines, grains, oil, stone, timber, and all that is necessary for the construction of the church? . . . They march in such silence that not a murmur is heard. . . . When they halt on the road nothing is heard but confession of sins, and pure and suppliant prayer. . . . When they have reached the church they arrange the wagons about it like a spiritual camp, and during the whole night they celebrate the watch by hymns and canticles. On each wagon they light tapers.

Even the oxen which labored in hauling stone and timber were sometimes taken into a sort of fellowship. When Laon cathedral was completed the grateful people set up four huge stone oxen in each of the two great towers in grateful recognition of the dumb beasts which had done their part in the achievement, and these eight stone figures still stand looking out toward the four points of the compass and across the plain below this fascinating old medieval hill town.

By the time that Gothic began to succeed and supplant Romanesque architecture we discover a significant change has taken place in the status of the craftsmen employed. Formerly most of these, except the imported Italian masons, were of servile condition. By the twelfth century skilled artisans had largely become free craftsmen, organized into gilds. Social liberation and elevation therefore accompanied this religious revivalism. Before its destruction during the late war, the great castle of Coucy-le-Château interestingly preserved the evidences of this social development. The mighty stone structure, the hugest of its kind in France, was begun when serfdom was the prevailing condition. The lower courses of stone were laid by serfs, but as the château was more than a century in building, by the time the upper courses began to be laid, stone masons, stone cutters, etc., had become freemen and were gilded, and these upper courses preserved the mason's marks or emblems of these gilds. Similar workmen's marks may be found in many Gothic cathedrals.

Among the famous architects of the day were Ingelbert, Guillaume de Bellême, Louis de Bourbourg, Aimon, Guillaume de Sens, the builder of Canterbury Cathedral. These architects would make a contract, submit a plan, often in competition with other architects and supervise the erection. Sometimes several architects were called in and conferred together as to the best mode of procedure. The architects traveled much and spread their ideas everywhere. They received all payments made and in turn paid their men. Five hundred *solidi* are mentioned for five feet of elevation. Wages were paid in clothing, lodging, food, and money. Agreements were made as to the weekly, monthly, or yearly payments. The architect guaranteed his work. The completion of some important piece of work like a tower or the roof was a sign for joyous festival and merrymaking.

A medieval cathedral was an object of civic pride to a city, and a community enterprise of vast dimension in which all classes of society and all conditions of men were interested both spiritually and as contributors to the cost of its erection. The same is true of lesser structures down to the humble parish church. As the largest and best building in the community, and one in which all had a common share and a common interest, it was used for many secular purposes. In time of war the villagers sought asylum within—they, their cattle, and their belongings. In time of peace it was the social and trade centre. The traveling merchant and itinerant peddler set up their booths within the porch of the church, and sometimes spread their wares upon the flat tombs in the graveyard in the dark and bloody days of private war, before a settled feudal government became established. Later, when times became more secure, the market spread over the square in front of the church, and even after the conduct of trade and commerce had become so secure that the Church's protection was no longer necessary, the market cross still preserved the reminiscence of the earlier condition. Sometimes the local weights and measures were graven upon the wall of the church, that every man might know them, as in Freiburg cathedral, where one may yet see the ordained measures of length and size of loaves of bread.

The men of the Middle Ages had larger—perhaps looser—ideas about the use of churches than we moderns. Corn-grinding and brewing were sometimes done in them; winter grain and hay were stored in them; barrels of wine and beer were housed in them. The city authorities of Milan appropriated the galleries of the basilica of San Ambrogio for the storage of grain. As early as 1022 Brescia used the cathedral for local public meetings. On festal days masques or mysteries were given in the church. To a world without secular art, without secular music, except of the crudest kind, the frescoes, the stained glass, the music, the lights of lamps and tapers, the colors of the priests' robes, which differed according to time and occasion, the odor of incense in a great cathedral furnished emotional and esthetic enjoyment.

It is true that sometimes the invasion of the outside world created untoward and abusive conditions. Feudal lords often despatched local business in their pews. Henry Plantagenet complained that petitioners "pester me even in the mass." the burgomasters of Strassburg regularly heard lawsuits during service in the municipal pew, and it was counted unto St. Louis for righteousness that he refused to conduct administrative matters during divine service. But in spite of such abuses, it must be admitted that the Church in the Middle Ages socialized its edifices and humanized its religion, while at the same time preserving the dignity and the mystery of worship. The Roman Church always has shown a remarkable and profound psychology and social sense, and never more so than in these splendid centuries between 1000 and 1300, when a great and original material and moral culture reached its zenith.

But while the Church thus modified the excesses or moderated many of the abuses in secular feudalism, the fact that the Church itself was a feudalized institution opened the door to the growth of excesses and abuses within it. Privilege protected ecclesiastical property, not merely land devoted to positive spiritual endowment, but all lands of the Church, so much so that an additional burden was thrown upon secular society for the maintenance of government. The Church paid nothing in recompense for what it received in the form of police protection from lay government. Yet the exempted lands of the Church included from one-third to one-half of all the real property in medieval Europe. Mortmain, or the "dead hand," illustrates this grievance of the governments against the Church. The Church was a perpetual corporation; it never died, hence land once passed into the hands of the Church never changed title and the governments were deprived of the inheritance tax in this particular. An anecdote related in the *Life of Meinwerk,* bishop of Paderborn, shows that even the saintly emperor Henry II could use sharp language in regard to the evils of mortmain. He was plied diligently by the bishops of Saxony for grants of land, and once he exclaimed to Meinwerk: "May God and all his saints confound thee, for that thou never ceasest to pluck at my estates, to my serious loss and the great detriment of the government." The evil effects of mortmain became so great by the end of the thirteenth century that civil law was invoked to restrain the practice. The frequent violent attacks on church property by the baronage in the twelfth century attest not only the envy of the proprietary class, but the dangerous degree to which ecclesiastical property had come to overshadow secular property. There is awful irony in the satire of an antipapal priest during the war of investiture, who attacked the covetousness of Urban II for temporal wealth.

It requires an effort of imagination in this unfeudal age to realize how profoundly feudalized the medieval Church was. Its temporalities conferred rights and powers upon the clergy exactly similar in kind and degree to the rights and powers attached to lay seigniorial lands, extending even to the power over life and limb. Its taxes were of both a temporal and a spiritual nature. The former differed in no whit from those of the feudality. As lay lands and secular offices were feudalized, so the tendency was for church offices and church lands to be regarded as fiefs. Gregory VII unsuccessfully endeavored to convert episcopal offices and episcopal lands into fiefs held of the Holy See. In the Lateran Council of 1139 Innocent II actually proclaimed that all ecclesiastical dignities were received from and held of the pope like fiefs.

Yet hierarchized as the Church was, and despite the fact that its higher clergy was largely recruited from the feudality, two practices preserved the Church from becoming a wholly aristocratic institution like feudal society. Celibacy prevented the clergy from becoming an hereditary caste, and the Church always practised what might be denominated "selective democracy." With superb wisdom the preferments of the Church have always been open to a man of talent, no matter what his birth or socal status may have been. The Roman Church has always believed in the democracy of opportunity. Merit has always counted with Rome.

The Church offered the only career open to men of all ranks and stations. In the sharply defined class distinctions of the feudal system, advancement was almost impossible to one not born within the charmed circle of gentle blood. In the Church, however much rank and family connections might assist in securing promotion to high place, yet talent and energy could always make themselves felt despite lowliness of birth. Urban II and Hadrian

IV sprang from the humblest origin; Alexander V had been a beggar-boy; Gregory VII was the son of a carpenter; Sixtus IV, of a peasant; Urban IV and John XXII were sons of cobblers, and Benedict XI and Sixtus V, of shepherds. . . . The Church thus constantly recruited its rank from fresh blood.[9]

The medieval Church was a feudalized Church; it was in and of the feudal world. But it never indolently accepted conditions as it found them; it never was content to let things drift; it never passively tolerated abuses and corruption either in itself or in secular society. It possessed in an eminent degree the quality of leadership and the strength to initiate reform. It labored with magnificent courage and industry— although it did not always practise what it preached—to make a better feudal Europe, to redress the wrongs, excesses, and abuses of feudal government and feudal society. It did not seek to overthrow feudalism, but it sought to regulate feudalism; to make a "new" feudalism out of old traditions and customary practices. It was often anti-feudal in the constructive sense of endeavoring to make a better feudalism. Illustrations abound: the effort of the Church to stamp out the ancient German blood-feud, the *faida,* or right of relatives by personal retaliation to avenge real or fancied wrongs or grievances; to abolish the judicial duel and trial by ordeal of fire or hot water; to ameliorate the abuses of feudal wardship, or the custody of widows and minor children of a vassal by the suzerain, which frequently resulted in the appropriation or dissipation of the ward's inheritance by the guardian; to curtail the intolerable tyranny of property over the relation of husband and wife, and the corruption of the family as an institution by the practice of the feudality of arranging monstrous marriages, as of a young girl to a man in his dotage, or a mere youth to an elderly woman, for reasons of property. The battle which the Church fought in Germany (though this was later than our period and in the fifteenth century), against the "reception" of the Roman law for the protection of the peasantry from worse exploitation than ever manorialism at its worst had practised, is another example. "The canon law, Roman in form, was yet Christian in spirit and infinitely more in accord with the Christianized folk-law of the German people." Historically the ancient Germanic codes were the product of a free people, whereas Roman law had been the creation of a slave state.

The medieval Church was so universal in its extent, so unique in its authority, so complex in its interests, that it was a bundle of inconsistencies, some actual, some more apparent than real, spiritual yet temporal, feudal yet anti-feudal, aristocratic yet democratic. In its regulation of society the Church sometimes went beyond accustomed social legisla-

[9] Lea, *History of the Inquisition,* I, 4.

tion and pierced to the quick of things. While preserving and profiting by feudalism it sometimes sought to regulate it drastically, and sometimes apparently sought even to destroy its integrity. The motive of such policy is not always easy to fathom: whether it was motivated by a truly moral purpose, or whether it was actuated by ambition for power while protesting the moral or high social purpose of its course.

A case in point is the Church's opposition to the law of primogeniture. Was it done in the interest of social justice, *i. e.*, of securing equal division of land among the sons, or was it done in order to break the power of the great feudal houses by dissipating their heritage? Similarly, was the Church's opposition to hereditary monarchy and its advocacy of elective kingship in the interest of popular sovereignty, or was it in order to subordinate secular power to ecclesiastical sway? Did Gregory VII support the rebellion of the feudality and the Saxon insurrection against Henry IV because he believed in the social justice of their contentions, or in order to discomfit his antagonist? Did the Church advocate the right of female succession to fiefs, or inheritance through the female line, *e.g.*, in Tuscany and Saxony, with Countess Matilda and Duke Lothar, because it believed that in justice women should have equal property rights with men; or, since feudal government and property control was exclusively in masculine hands, did it advocate the change in order to break down the feudality? It is significant that in both these cases just cited the Church immediately and enormously profited. Did it insist on the finality of its courts as courts of appeal in so many cases in the interest of justice, contending that secular courts were too often unjust and venal in their findings? or was it in order to diminish the power of the secular governments and increase the volume of its fees?

Whatever the reasons for these policies, the Church at times went far in upsetting customary law and overthrowing tradition. For example, feudal law favored not merely primogeniture, but also family marriage alliances for the purpose of preventing the splitting up and distribution of fiefs and maintaining the power and wealth of the great families in as compact form as possible. Hence the frequency of marriage between blood-relations. But in 1066 the Church condemned the age-long practice of the Roman civil law with regard to consanguinity and established a new series of prohibited degrees. Marriage according to the civil mode of calculating relationship was declared to be incestuous and the rite null and void. The second, fourth, and sixth degrees of the civil law were made to be the first, second and third degrees, and marriage within them forbidden. Even spiritual affinity was a bar: that is, godfathers and godmothers and their children were supposed to be related within canonical prohibition. Again: the Church contended that marriage between two persons legitimated their already born offspring.

The feudal contention was jealous to preserve the distinction in order to preserve the integrity of house lands, and resented legitimation of bastard children.

Were these changes made by the Church in the interest of improved social morality, to protect the integrity of the family, to prevent in-breeding in castle and manor? or in order to break up the great princely families? or in order to make dissolution of wedlock, when necessary or desirable, easy of accomplishment? Or was the motive a mercenary one, since for a fee the Church might waive the canon law through dispensation? Or was it in order to multiply occasions for the Church politically to interfere in society to its own advantage? There is no positive answer to these questions. But the fact remains that the Church initiated much and far-reaching legislation of a social nature, the effects of which upon society were profound.

The influence of the Church by a process of social erosion, so to speak, tended to break down the great feudal houses, and even to extinguish them. It was always detrimental, except in a social way, and sometimes fatal to the continuance of a family when one of its members entered the Church. When the only brother of Henry II of Germany became bishop of Augsburg it doomed the Saxon house to extinction, for the emperor himself was childless. From calculations necessarily imperfect yet significant it has been estimated that in medieval Germany in the space of three hundred years 12 per cent of the princely houses, 36 per cent of the counts and 80 per cent of lesser noble families failed to perpetuate themselves owing to so many of their sons having entered holy orders. The effect was a form of birth control culminating in the actual extinction of many distinguished feudal families.

But other effects flowed from this tendency and condition. In the ninth and tenth centuries, as has been said before, the feudality, owing to the bond of proprietary interest between it and the high clergy, began to monopolize high Church offices. The episcopate was aristocrat-ized. But from the eleventh century forward there is observable a steady increase among the bishops of men of servile origin. The feudal aristocracy first lost its monopoly, and then even lost its preponderant control of high Church offices. The Hildebrandine Reform, by its blows at lay investiture and patronage and secular right of presentation to church livings, by its work to separate the right of advowson from proprietorship, promoted this democratization of the Church, and un-doubtedly these effects helped to popularize the Church with the masses and to antagonize the aristocracy. In the twelfth and thirteenth centuries the new monastic orders like the Cistercians, Carthusians, Pre-monstratensians, and above all the Dominican and Franciscan friars were recruited almost altogether from the ranks of the common people, as the bishops also tended more and more to be. The Church went through a social revolution as all Europe did at the time. It is not an accident that this growing democratization of the Church synchronized with the decline of serfdom and the rise of the towns.

Yet curiously enough, while the Church kept step with, and even walked in advance of most of the liberalizing tendencies of the age, and more and more opened the door of Church preferment to men sprung from the common people, in the matter of serfdom itself the Church was conservative to the point of being reactionary. Anselm, the father of scholasticism, writing about 1100, formulated the orthodox theory of hereditary serfdom in words often approved by other publicists after him:

For if any man and his wife . . . commit in partnership a grievous and inexcusable fault, for which they are justly degraded and reduced to serfdom, who would assert that their children whom they beget after their condemnation should not be subjected to the same servitude?

The Church in the Middle Ages never objected to the slave trade of the times. Its protest—even then often a gesture of profession and not a conviction—was only against the traffic in *Christian* captives with Mohammedan lands. It made no demur against the sale of heathen Danes and Slavs—thousands of Wendish captives were distributed to German monasteries after the great campaigns across the Elbe; Saracen captives in the Moorish wars in Spain, Corsica, Sardinia, Sicily, and on the sea were sold not only to lay, but to clerical Christian masters. Chattel slavery existed on church lands in Italy, even in the papal states, in the eleventh century and later.

In the matter of emancipation of serfs, the Church lagged behind secular Europe and even retarded emancipation. The Church least yielded to the pressure of economic revolution, and was more disinclined to free the serfs upon its glebe lands than secular proprietors were. Of great interest is the discovery made by Salvemini that the Florentine decree of August 6, 1289, abolishing serfdom was the direct result of the action of a few serfs of the Florentine chapter, who petitioned not to be sold to the Ubaldini on the ground that it would be to the detriment of the commune, which would thus lose the right to receive personal and pecuniary services from the petitioners. This shows that the abolition of serfdom by the Church was due to practical reasons and not to any theory about natural rights of man.

Church lands on the whole were more intelligently and efficiently managed than lay lands, but the oft-repeated statement that the condition of serfs on Church lands was less onerous and their treatment more humane is not borne out by the facts. Since all historical writers were clerks until the thirteenth century—and most of them so even then—

their statements must be used with caution, for naturally the writers would not bear adverse witness against themselves, or their order. But ecclesiastical professions of humanitarianism and altruism must be taken with reservation. No one who knows intimately the sources of the twelfth century can believe the benign utterance of Peter the Venerable (died 1156), abbot of Cluny, that the monks of Cluniac houses "regarded male and female serfs as brothers and sisters." For Cluny was a notoriously aristocratic and exclusive monastic order, no one not of noble blood being permitted to become a member of it. A close scrutiny of the cartularies of the monasteries shows that serfs on church lands were not better off than those on lay lands. There is ground even to believe that as a whole their lot was worse. The *Miracula* of St. Benoît show frightful poverty and suffering, although this may have been an extreme case. The fact that the Church exercised an empire over souls proves nothing as to the economic condition of the peasantry upon the church lands. The Church was the most conservative member of society in the matter of enfranchisement of slaves and manumission of serfs. Almost all cases of general enfranchisement are by lay, not by ecclesiastical lords. There is no example of emancipation of serfs in numbers by monasteries. Indeed, emancipation of slave or serf, unless compensation was made for the loss entailed thereby, was forbidden by canon law. When Smaragdus in the ninth century advocated the emancipation of serfs on the ground of the equality of all men, the utterance was a mere rhetorical gesture. On the whole, the Church was opposed to emancipation and did its best to protract serfdom. Every medievalist capable of independent and detached thought must concur with the verdict of the late Professor Achille Luchaire, than whom no higher historical authority can be quoted. His opinion is all the more trustworthy for the reason that in the earlier stage of his career as a scholar he believed the old tale, and only changed his mind when later, deeper, and prolonged examination of the sources so compelled him. He has written this careful paragraph which embodies his mature conclusion:

The clerics of the Middle Ages showed almost as much cruelty to the peasants and burghers as did the men of the sword. In fact, the feudal conception prevailed in the Church, which consisted of the priesthood. The sentiments and the acts of the privileged religious aristocracy dominated. This aristocracy, proprietor of considerable lands and enormous numbers of serfs, both male and female, was an integral part of the feudal system. It sought to preserve its rights and revenues; it defended them with jealous harshness and succeeded all the better because the lands were inalienable. It harshly exploited the lower classes. No one has yet been able to demonstrate that the serfs of the Church were better off than those of the lay lords, and it is absolutely certain that the bondage of the Church endured for a much longer time than that of the nobles and the king. There were even found some clerics who upheld serfdom not only as necessary and legitimate, but as a divinely ordained institution.[10]

Similarly, Pollock and Maitland's severe verdict upon the Church and especially the monks, as landlords may hardly be gainsaid, for no two scholars are more cautious and more scientific than they:

There is plenty of evidence that of all landlords the religious houses were the most severe—not the most oppressive, but the most tenacious of their rights; they were bent on the maintenance of pure villein tenure and personal villeinage. The immortal, but soulless corporation with her wealth of accurate records would yield no inch, would enfranchise no serf, would enfranchise no tenement. In practice, the secular lord was more humane, because he was more human, because he was careless, because he wanted ready money, because he would die. . . . We find that it is against them (the monks) that the peasants make their loudest complaints.[11]

The Belgian historian Vanderkindere in an extended study of the condition of serfs on Church lands in Belgium has come to the conclusion that the condition of ecclesiastical serfs was inferior to that of serfs on lay lands.

To the honor of the Cistercian Order, it refused to accept serfs as gifts of endowment. Even when this rule was abrogated, and the Cistercians, too, become possessors of bondmen and bondwomen, some reminiscence of the former humanitarianism in their original conduct is found in their adherence to the principle that no serf of a Cistercian monastery should ever be given in exchange to any other lord, and that families should not be broken up. As to this latter practice, intelligent and just-minded medieval churchmen recognized that the Church's legislation was less humane than that of Roman Law. Thus Regino of Prüm bluntly says: "Roman law certainly seems to lay down a far better precept in this matter." So great was the oppression of its serfs by the chapter of Notre Dame de Paris in the reign of St. Louis that Queen Blanche remonstrated "in all humility," whereto the monks replied that "they might starve their serfs as they pleased." But Blanche was a woman of spirit, forced the gates of the abbey, and liberated the imprisoned serfs.

Peasant insurrections against the excessive fiscal exactions of the Church were not uncommon in the thirteenth century. In 1207 and 1222 the bishop of Orleans had to resort to use of arms to compel payment. In 1216 the villagers of Nieuport killed the collectors of the abbey of Ste. Walburge when they sought to collect the tithe. The abbots seem to have been more addicted to extreme measures than the bishops. In 1220

[10] Luchaire, *Social France at the time of Philip Augustus.*
[11] Pollock and Maitland, *History of English Law*, I, 378 (2d ed.).

the serfs of Saint Père de Chartres rebelled; in 1246, those of St. Germain des Près; in 1250, those of Mont St. Michel. On the other hand, peasant insurrections against harsh treatment and brutal exaction by lay proprietors are rare in the thirteenth century. The driving force behind the Pastoureaux movement, the peasant insurrection in France in 1251, was religious emotionalism born of the Crusades, mingled with hostility toward the clergy, especially the monks, in which even the Franciscans did not escape, because of excessive ecclesiastical exactions. The excitement was popular as long as it inveighed against the clergy. The towns along the route fed the mob and passed it along. The host spread over whole provinces. Some visited Amiens, Rouen, Orleans. Rioting and street fighting ensued. Blanche of Castile at first was not disinclined toward them, for her own resentment against the clergy was great.

One of the grievances which the servile peasantry on monastery lands resented most was the requirement to have all their grain ground in the abbot's mill. In 1274 the English peasantry on the lands of the abbot of St. Albans refused longer to submit to this exaction of villein service, and began to use handmills of their own. The abbot Roger of Norton sought to coerce them. The town was in an uproar owing to the tumult stirred up by the rebellious villeins, while in the monastery the great bell was rung as an alarm and processions of monks filed before the high altar in the chapel chanting the seven penitential psalms and invoking the help of God and St. Alban. The king's intervention in favor of the abbey temporarily crushed the movement. But in 1314 the struggle was renewed. The villagers resorted to great violence and swore they would even kill the monks, gruesomely erecting a scaffold in the market-place. It was well that the abbey walls were strong, for it was subjected to a regular siege. The king again interfered, but relief from the abbot's onerous exactions did not come until long after.

As it was with the agricultural peasantry upon the glebe lands of the Church, so was it with the serfs employed as artisans and craftsmen in the great shops of the churches and monasteries, as carpenters, woodturners, wool-carders, dyers, weavers, metal workers, cobblers, saddlers, harness makers. Long after the lay world had perceived that serfdom was economically unprofitable and wasteful, and that a free farming peasantry and a free industrial peasantry laboring for daily cash wages was more profitable than service labor, the Church obdurately clung to the old order of things. The Church was opposed to the liberation of industry and to the formation of independent associations of craftsmen. Hence the anticlerical tinge which characterizes the attitude of the industrial classes in the thirteenth century. Moreover, the free gilds resented the competition of the Church's shops of servile workmen. For the practice of the abbots and the bishops, especially the former, was to sell the surplus of their manufactured wares upon the local market, where naturally they could undersell free production owing to the fact that they paid low wages and were exempt from taxation, market dues, etc. An economic source of the Reformation is to be found in this condition.

Radical as the Church was in some particulars, it was singularly conservative in others. The result was that peasant rebellion, when it occurred in the twelfth and thirteenth centuries, was almost always and everywhere upon church lands, against ecclesiastical manorialism, and tinged with anticlericalism. The same was true of the burgher movement in the towns when it arose. Bishops and abbots, far more than secular feudatories. were hostile to it and labored to suppress it.

This is not the place to consider the rise and spread of the town movement. It is sufficient to note the fact that the old Roman cities (*civitates*) had naturally become the seats of the bishops, and that around monastery walls dense clusters of peasantry were gathered, who labored as serfs upon the glebe lands of the abbeys. When the social and economic awakening of Europe began in the eleventh century these groups were stirred as never before. A spirit which had lain dormant for nearly a thousand years began to be active in their midst. These populations, on the rejection of their demand for charters not merely abating abuses of which they complained, but granting fixed rights of self-government like that of levying their own taxes and administering their own courts, rebelled against the overlord, whether bishop or abbot, and formed a commune. The word became a detested one in the ears of the clergy. *"Communio autem novum ac pessimum nomen*—new and most outrageous word," exclaims Abbot Guibert de Nogent of the rebellion of the people of Laon against the feudal authority of their bishop.

The most consistent attitude taken against the towns was that of the clergy, and it was almost universally hostile. The dignitaries of the Church were often barons dressed in the cloth and saw in the new institution subversion of their rights. The words of Guibert of Nogent are echoed by Bernard of Clairvaux and Ives of Chartres. More than one pope demanded the abolition of a commune: Innocent II ordered the abolition of Rheims; Eugene III, that of Soissons. The ecclesiastical writers of the time seem to have been utterly incapable of understanding the town movement. Richard of Devizes called it a *"tumor plebis, tumor regni, tepor sacerdoti."* But of all the invectives against the communes none is so bitter as that of Jacques de Vitry against Beauvais.

Feeling sometimes ran so high against the local clergy that the incensed populace would indulge in anticlerical mockery and horseplay. At St. Valéry, in ridicule of the clergy, the crowd marched around the building, attired in ecclesiastical robes, pretending to scatter holy water. It burned down the doors of the church and threw the images of the Virgin and John the Baptist into the fire; and later, a child having died, two of their number performed the funeral ceremony. At St. Riquier, where the monks were accustomed to carry the relics of St. Riquier and those of St. Vigor in an annual procession, the people of the town, with a great show of solemnity, carried a dead cat and the bone of a horse and, having wrought a miracle with the relics, deposited them in the sanctuary of St. Riquier.

And yet the Church had had, unwittingly, a large influence in promoting this very communal movement which it tried to suppress. For the Hildebrandine programme by seeking to emancipate the altar everywhere, whether cathedral, abbey, priory, or parish church, from secular control, had thereby both relaxed the power of the ruling authority in the community and given the members of that community an example of new freedom. The communal spirit and aspirations of democracy were powerfully stimulated during the War of Investiture. The most striking instance of this is, of course, the papal advocacy of the Saxon peasantry and the Patarian party in Milan. In the issue, the Gregorian reforms raised a social and political spirit which the Church could not exorcise and which ultimately rebelled against the Church's temporal prerogatives.

Democratic, yet aristocratic; charitable, yet exploitive; generous, yet mercenary; humanitarian, yet cruel; indulgent yet severely repressive of some things; progressive, yet reactionary; radical, yet conservative—all these are qualities which characterize the conduct of the Church in the Middle Ages. Nevertheless, such contradictions were not as singular as they may seem. For it must ever be kept in mind that the Church was not one thing but many things, a complex, cosmopolitan institution, and still an intensely local institution, exercising both spiritual and temporal power, an intricate economic and social polity. It was so intimate and personal in its relation that it touched every man, woman, and child, yet high and far removed and idealistic. Under such conditions it is no wonder that the Church was a bundle of complexities and contradictions. While the highest offices of the Church were always open to men of lowly birth, the Church as an institution was both aristocratic and autocratic. Even the leaven of the Cistercian Order, which was more democratic both in spirit and in organization than the old Benedictine and Cluniac orders, and the broad and sincere democracy of the Franciscan and Dominican orders, failed to democratize the Church. To the end of the Middle Ages it remained politically and spiritually autocratic, socially and economically aristocratic.

The charity of the medieval Church was not wholly disinterested. One may readily admit its large activities in poor relief, the social service afforded by its hospitals and orphanages. But its own practices of economic exploitation often induced the poverty which it was called upon to relieve, and it is questionable whether in proportion to its enormous resources the Church actually contributed as much as lay society to poor relief. It was not infrequently more inclined to petition and even to compel the laity to contribute to poor relief than to dispense its own resources. One gets a painful impression of the mercenary attitude of many churchmen in the *Life of St. Eloi,* who lived in the seventh century. There a good Christian is pictured as one who presents the oblation, who consecrates a part of the fruits of his industry to God, who offers presents and tithes—this was before the tithe was imposed by law—to the clergy. The Church placated criticism and silenced complaint by temporary doles made in extreme exigency, but was not always genuinely humanitarian. The Church's charity sometimes seemed an anodyne to social discontent; palliative, but not effectively remedial. Much that was given to the Church for alms was in the form of permanent endowment.

The medieval Church was a poor political economist, but exercised an ingenuity approaching genius in revenue and fiscal matters, as in domanial exploitation, market management, and mint rights. The mechanism of Church administration was converted into an elaborate machine for raising money. This is truer of the secular than of the regular clergy, for the reason that the bishops were the Church's authorized administrative agents, while the monks were not, and because the bishops more than the abbots had affinities with feudal courts and the political world in general. Even early in the twelfth century it was notorious that "money talked" in church affairs. The abbot Guibert of Nogent tells how, when Pascal II was in France in 1111, knowing that the cardinals in the papal train "had great hopes of money," he came to the papal court "stuffed with money, I and my fellow-abbot Adalberon of St. Vincent, each of us carrying twenty pounds of money with which the wide gap of their expectations was filled." We have already seen how intensely economic and fiscal were the factors involved in the War of Investiture. The long drawn out conflict with the Byzantine Empire to establish religious unity once more after the separation in 1054 has been intelligibly interpreted in terms of economic motive. Among those who most severely criticized the Church for its corruptions, and who were most unsparing in their denunciations of the character of the clergy were some of the most saintly, as well as some of the most thoughtful sons of the Church—men like St. Bernard, Peter Damieni, Peter Cantor, Hildebert of Le Mans, Peter of Blois, and Robert Grosseteste.

The ever-widening jurisdiction of Rome opened the door to fiscal abuses and corrupt influence. Churchmen of vision like St. Bernard and John of Salisbury, as early as the middle of the twelfth century looked with misgiving and alarm upon the growing menace to the papacy's spiritual nature liable to arise from the enormous mass and complexity of administrative duties thrown upon the popes by the concentration of so much church business in their hands, and the danger of corruption owing to excessive fiscality. "Could I but see," deplored St. Bernard in a letter to Eugene III, his close friend, "before my death the Church of God as she was in ancient days when the apostles cast their nets to capture not gold or silver, but souls!" He condemned the *dominium temporale* of the papacy and the political position of the bishops everywhere. A few years later we discover John of Salisbury complaining of the immense burden of the papal office and fearing, as well he might, for the health of his friend Hadrian IV. The killing nature of the office a century before this had excited the curiosity of Peter Damieni, and he gave the popes not over four or five years as their limit of life. And indeed the only medieval pope of long pontificate is Alexander III (1159–81). The notoriously unsanitary nature of medieval Rome undoubtedly largely accounts for the mortality of the popes, but the immense burden of administration must have been a factor in their swift breakdown, although, too, it should be remembered that most of them were not young when elected. Yet even youthful popes like Innocent III did not live to advanced age.

We have detailed accounts of various sources of papal revenue . . . in the *Liber Censuum* drawn up under the direction of the camerarius Cencius, afterwards Pope Honorius III, in the year 1192. Besides the revenue from the papal domain proper, a census was received: (1) from monasteries which had placed themselves under the papal "protection," and who in the course of the twelfth century gained exemption from the spiritual as well as the temporal control of their diocesans; (2) from some lay rulers and nobles, who put themselves under papal "protection," or, like the kings of Aragon and the Norman rulers of South Italy and Sicily, recognized papal overlordship; (3) in the form of Peter's Pence, from England since Anglo-Saxon times, and, in the twelfth century from Norway, Sweden, and some other countries as well.[12]

New sources of revenue were found in veneration of relics, miracles, private masses. In the latter part of the ninth century a new penitential system of Irish origin came in which sanctioned a whole series of tariffs which the Frankish Church had once rejected.

The Crusades, especially through the disposal of indulgences, proved a mighty money-maker for the Church.

In 1184 those who cannot themselves take the cross are bidden to give alms to support the Crusade, and, in return for these contributions and for a threefold repetition of the Paternoster, are promised a partial indulgence. In 1195 Celestine III writes to Hubert of Canterbury as his English legate that "those who send of their goods in aid of the Holy Land shall receive

[12] *Cambridge Medieval History,* V, xi.

pardon of their sins from their bishop on the terms he shall prescribe." In 1215 the Fourth Lateran Council goes a step farther and promises a plenary indulgence to those who shall contribute to the crusading funds in proportion to their means. With that step the downward path was begun.[13]

Yet it would be unjust to hold the Church wholly responsible for this degradation. The barbarian codes had substituted a scale of graduated fines for offenses to such a vast degree that the abstract moral nature of misdeeds was obliterated in the popular mind, and the penalty was regarded not as a fine but as a quittance. The psychology of medieval Europe must be understood if one is to be just to the medieval Church. It is literally true that in the Middle Ages everything had its price—offices of Church and State, "presents" to judges, advantageous marriages and marriage settlements, wardship, etc. Fees were attached to all such administration. With the prevalent thinking so concrete, it was unavoidable that the penitential system should reflect such psychology. As far back as the fifth century Salvian mournfully complained that "excepting a very few saints, men have thought to atone for their crimes with a piece of money."

The doctrine of a treasury of merit due to the supererogatory works of Christ, the martyrs, and the saints, in the popular thought too often was construed into belief that good works or money might compensate for delinquencies, and the important condition attached thereto by church teaching, that sincere repentance must precede indulgence was lost sight of or lowered to a great degree. The theory and the practice alike of indulgences, indeed, may be theologically justified, but nevertheless the system of indulgences was probably the most widespread form of raising church revenue and the one most liable to abuse.

But there was a better and brighter side to the system of indulgences. They were a remarkable social factor in the development of medieval civilization. The tens of thousands of indulgences that were granted for charitable works had an immense influence upon social and economic conditions. So, too, churches, schools, hospitals, bridges, road and harbor improvements, the redemption of marshes and fens, or making forest clearings, gilds and confraternities organized for works of mercy and relief, loan associations such as the *"Montes Pietatis,"* were started and sustained by the sale of indulgences. Money was thus raised for material improvements, and community enterprises thus swung which otherwise could not have been carried through with success.

The hundreds of incidents and anecdotes told of the corruption of the clergy in the thirteenth century, even after allowance for exaggeration, leave a painful impression and vividly picture the avarice of too

[13] *Ibid.,* 323.

many high churchmen of the time. Corrupt ecclesiastical government ultimately led to corrupt practice in administration of the sacraments—the barter and sale of spiritual values, the debauching of sacerdotal prerogative and authority to mercenary ends. In a measure the charge may be made that the Church capitalized its spiritual authority for revenue purposes. Although the Church, of course, never officially approved of such a course, there is abundant evidence in ecclesiastical legislation that such abuse widely prevailed. Unscrupulous priests refused to perform the sacraments of marriage, baptism, and even extreme unction and burial unless a fee were paid, thereby converting "voluntary offerings" into fixed charges. In 990 the bishop of Puy in a proclamation to the clergy of his diocese declared: "No priest shall take money for baptism, for it is the gift of the Holy Spirit."

Count Robert of Robertstone complained to the local archdeacon that the latter was impoverishing the peasants of his manors by the excessive number of "ransoms for sin" which he imposed upon them, and denounced him as an "exacter of crimes and lover of transgressions." The anecdote is told of a simple knight who naïvely said: "I thought that priests performed masses for the offerings' sake." Another knight thought that the priest had invented the mass as a magical formula for the sake of the offerings. It is told of a rich man in Provence that when he died he left a large sum of money to a neighboring abbey. His son complained that the abbot had said nothing for his father's soul except "*Requiescat in pace*," but the abbot showed him that those words outweighed the money.

Legacy-hunting on the part of the clergy became a scandal, even in the twelfth century. Alexander III in 1170 decreed that no one could make a valid will except in the presence of a priest, and notaries who drew wills were liable to excommunication. An English church council decreed that when a man made a will he must dispose of part of his property to the Church for the good of his soul, and that a priest must be present when the will was made. The gallant William Marshall, a famous jouster and hero of tournaments in his prime, when on his deathbed was importuned by a priest by his bedside to leave all his rich prizes to the Church. In 1234 the council of Arles decreed that wills not made in the presence of a priest were invalid. If so made the testator was deprived of burial in consecrated ground and the notary who drew the will was liable to excommunication. To die intestate was regarded as robbing the Church.

Even the heretical movements of the twelfth and thirteenth centuries had important roots in economic and social conditions. Leutard of Châlons, who founded a short-lived sect in the diocese of Châlons, got a following among the "rustics" by preaching that the exaction of tithes was not authorized in the New Testament and was an abuse of the clergy. Waldo of Lyons and the Waldensians, or "Poor Men of Lyons," represented a reaction against the riches and worldliness of churchmen in high places, and endeavored to restore apostolic poverty and simplicity once more. Arnold of Brescia tried to employ the communal revolution in northern Italy to the same end by persuading the burgher governments of the cities to secularize the local wealth of the clergy. In the first quarter of the twelfth century a notorious and popular heretic in Flanders was one Tanchelm, whose following of peasantry and rustics was enormous; he preached the abolition of tithes and the manorial dues exacted by the clergy, together with other radical religious and social doctrines. When he perished a blacksmith named Manasses attempted to preserve the movement he had inspired and formed a fraternity called, significantly, a "gilda." It is significant, in the south of France where the great Albigensian heresy held sway for many years, that so many of the culprits dragged before the courts of the Inquisition were poor weavers, and that the very word for weaver (*tisserand*) became a synonym for heretic. In lower Germany the Stedinger movement was closely associated with peasant protest against the hardening of the manorial régime and the burden of the tithes. The heresies were often vehicles for the expression of a vast and complex social unrest and the instrument of rebellion against prevalent economic grievances and abuses.

Unfortunately, instead of remedying the corruption within its own system, which in the thirteenth century was largely the provocative cause of the prevalence of heresy, the Church hardened and sharpened its policy toward heresy. It confounded with heresy political and economic teaching at variance with its own material interest, and involved all dissidents, of whatsoever sort, in a common condemnation and a common ruin. The Church became as sensitive to popular attacks upon the freedom and property of the clergy as to criticism of its dogmas. Both the attempt of city magistrates to impose taxes upon church property, which it must be remembered was of enormous value and entirely exempt from taxation, and the rebellion of the rural peasantry against exorbitant tithes, were branded as outrageous heresy. Finally the Church resorted, in the south of France, to methods of extermination and organized the infamous Albigensian "Crusade."

The basest of economic motives were appealed to in this Crusade. The property of heretics was promised to informers. Feudal nobles and city magistrates enriched themselves by this means of spoliation. Delatorism became a profession. The confiscation of property and the burning of heretics became a species of economic aggrandizement and enrichment by avaricious clergy and covetous nobles and officials. "Persecution became almost as much a financial speculation as a matter of faith." Lucius III in 1184 endeavored to make the Church the sole beneficiary of all property confiscated from condemned heretics, but could not enforce it. The Church had to divide the spoil. In the first and most fanatical stage of the Albigensian movement all property was swept away. In 1237 Gregory IX declared that the dowers of catholic wives of heretics were not to be confiscated "except in certain circumstances." Ten years later Innocent IV formally excluded dowries of catholic wives from forfeiture. In Italy usually one-third of the property of a condemned heretic went to the informer, one-third to the Inquisitors, one-third to the local magistrates. The bishop of Rodez boasted that he had made 100,000 *sols* in a single "drive" on the heretics in his diocese. The bishop of Albi did a rushing business in selling commutations of confiscation to condemned heretics who repented. Persecution of heretics often was a lucrative form of extortion and enrichment.

At the end of an extended inquiry into the subject of "Confiscations for Heresy" the late Henry C. Lea summarized the economic and social effects of the Church's persecution of heretics in the thirteenth century, especially the Cathari or Albigensians, in these words:

It is easy to see how prosperous cities were reduced to poverty, how industry languished, and how the independence of the municipalities was broken. . . . Some inventories have been preserved of the goods and chattels sequestrated, as when in December, 1290, and January, 1300, twenty-five or thirty of the wealthiest citizens of Albi were suddenly seized and condemned. . . . That of Raymond Calverie, a notary, gives us every detail of the plenishing of a well-to-do burgher's household—every pillow, sheet, and coverlet is enumerated, every article of kitchen gear, the salted provisions and grain, and even his wife's little trinkets. We have a similar insight into the stock of goods of Jean Baudier, a rich merchant. Every fragment of stuff is duly measured off—cloths of Ghent, Ypres, Amiens, Cambrai, St. Omer, Rouen, Montcornet, etc. His town house and farm were inventoried with the same conscientious care. . . . In addition to the misery inflicted by these wholesale confiscations on the thousands of innocent women and children thus stripped of everything, it would be almost impossible to exaggerate the evil which they entailed upon all classes in the business of daily life. All safeguards were withdrawn from every transaction. No creditor or purchaser could be sure of the orthodoxy of him with whom he was dealing; and even more than the principle that ownership was forfeited as soon as heresy had been committed by the living, the practice of proceeding against the memory of the dead, after an interval virtually unlimited, rendered it impossible for any man to feel secure in the possession of property, whether it had descended in his family for generations, or had been acquired within an ordinary lifetime. . . . Persecution of the dead by the inquisitorial process was a mockery in which virtually defense was impossible and confiscation inevitable. . . . Not only were all alienations made by heretics set aside and the property wrested from the purchasers, but all debts contracted by them and all hypothecations and liens given to secure loans were void. . . . As no man could be certain of the orthodoxy of another it will be evident how much distrust must have been thrown upon every bargain and every sale in the commonest transactions of life. The blighting influence of this upon the development of commerce and industry can readily be perceived, coming as it did at a time when the commercial and industrial movement of Europe was beginning to usher in the dawn of modern culture. . . . It was this, among other incidents of persecution, which arrested the promising civilization of the south of France and transferred to England and the Netherlands, where the Inquisition was comparatively unknown, the predominance in commerce and industry.[14]

As pontifical authority waxed and the papal monarchy rose high over all Europe both in Church and in State, the revenues of the pope kept pace with the enlargement of his prerogative. When the papacy wrested lay investiture from the hands of the kings and princes the popes exacted a prodigious fee from every new bishop, which rose progressively until in the form of annates it became the entire revenue of the diocese during the first year of the new bishop's incumbency. What this may have amounted to in actual money may be appreciated when it is said that the revenue of alien clerics alone, chiefly Italians and Savoyards, in England in 1252 was three times as great as the income of the king. The income of the Lateran in the thirteenth century must have exceeded the combined revenue of all the sovereigns of Europe at that time. Annates, or "first fruits," fees arising from appellate causes carried up from episcopal courts to the pope sitting *in curia,* dispensations, pluralities (permission by dispensation for a cleric to hold more than one office, and often many offices simultaneously), and its opposite, the practice of pyramiding several merely nominal incumbents (for a fee) upon one office—these, and many other administrative devices of the papacy provided resources that by the thirteenth century staggered Europe. The papacy was the greatest banker in Christendom. Its fiscal agents, the detested "Lombards" and "Cahorsians" were spread like a net over the continent.

Inasmuch as most of the weight of these new forms of taxation and exploitation fell upon the people at large, for the. clergy naturally passed on the burden imposed upon them from above to their parishioners, one may judge of the magnitude of the ecclesiastical taxation imposed upon Europe. Some of the roots of the Reformation are to be found in the luxury and profligacy of the clergy and the burden borne by the masses from the thirteenth century onward until the storm broke in the sixteenth century. It is true that Europe in the thirteenth century was far richer than formerly, but it may be questioned whether the material weight of the ecclesiastical system borne by Europe was

[14] *English Historical Review,* II, 235–36.

not at the same time greater than it had been in earlier centuries, in spite of Europe's greater wealth and increased population.

To all these forms of ecclesiastical taxation must be added the enormous expenditure made for erection of the great cathedrals and minsters when that building enthusiasm which gave rise to the Romanesque and later Gothic architecture swept over Europe. The cost of building the great cathedrals and minsters which so charm the traveler in Europe today, and the maintenance of their daily services and altars entailed extensive annual revenues imposed upon the industry and savings of the people. The taxation and diversion of capital and labor to such an immense number of church edifices and for the celebration of an unnecessary number of services must have been very heavy. Figures show that the ratio of increase in number of churches far exceeded the ratio of increase of Europe's population. In the three centuries between 1100 and 1400 the population of England increased about 700,000, or about ten per cent in each century. Yet in the whole of England during the 150 years between 1066 and 1216 the number of *monasteries alone* erected—to say nothing of parish churches and the great cathedrals— was 476 abbeys and priories, and 87 alien priories.

The loftiness of the motive must not deceive us as to the burden of these sacrifices by or compulsory charges upon the people. "While these structures were in some degree the expression of ardent faith, yet more were the manifestation of the pride of the prelates who erected them. . . . We must not lose sight of the supreme effort which they cost." And they had not the excuse of being public improvements like many secular buildings. The contemporary literature of protest against these exactions is too positive for us naïvely to think that all these beautiful cathedrals, abbeys, and minsters were the result of pure and intense religious passion. It speaks volumes for the great material advancement of Europe during the eleventh, twelfth, and thirteenth centuries, and is striking evidence that the population must have rapidly increased, that society was able to bear the immense burden of such expenditures and still raise the standard of living and the physical comfort of the people.

The Church's economic practices failed to keep abreast of changes in economic condition. It was, as we have seen, the greatest land-owner of the Middle Ages. In the days when Europe was almost wholly agricultural and almost all material wealth was in terms of land and the by-products of an agrarian society, like hides, leather, sheep, wool, and raw materials in general, the Church was very rich. But the economic revolution of the eleventh and twelfth centuries due to the rise of commerce and industry began to produce new forms of wealth like commercial commodities and articles of manufacture which competed with the older forms of wealth and attracted the peasantry from the fields to the towns. The result was that the Church had increasing difficulty in finding farm labor. The Church became "long" on unprofitable land and "short" on labor; in other words it began to get "land-poor."

Moreover, the economic revolution entailed a rise in prices and an increase in the cost of living for which the Church was unprepared, because it did not understand nor anticipate the profound changes which were taking place, or was unwilling to accommodate itself to them. The once ample stipends of bishops and abbots now failed adequately to support them. Ecclesiastical revenues all over Europe showed alarming shrinkage so that not only salaries and maintenance became increasingly difficult to meet, but even the expenses of worship became an anxiety. In this critical position the Church, as we have seen, recouped itself by capitalizing its authority, and by means of indulgences, dispensations, fees, and annates refilled its coffers. But this expedient was at the price of forfeiting much of the respect of Europe, and at the same time becoming flagrantly corrupt and notoriously avaricious. "The Church," it has been well said, "was the least flexible member of society . . . and had not the means of entering into the new conditions."

The demand made by churchmen of vision that there be "fewer churches, fewer altars in them, fewer persons ordained, and more care in their selection as well in the higher as in the lower orders" was not popular among the clergy. In a remarkable book entitled *Gemma Ecclesiastica* a bishop of the late twelfth century described some of these evils in the Church and pointed out the remedy. But his words fell on deaf ears. Alluding to the fact that under the old law there was but one temple and one altar he writes: "In imitation therefore of the one temple there ought to be in every town but one church; or, if the city be very populous, a few only, and these subject to the great church. The multiplication of chapels has given occasion to unlawful gifts and many other monstrous and disorderly practices. It would be far better that the churches be fewer in number and divine service performed in them less frequently."

Instead of meeting the increased cost of living and the rise in prices by measures of constructive economic reform, the Church shortsightedly tried to make both ends meet by multiplying the number and kind of tithes exacted, by increasing the manorial dues imposed upon its peasantry, by inventing a multiplicity of ecclesiastical fees, in addition to other expedients, in order to augment its income. It increased the number of chapels in the cathedrals and great churches in order to attract gifts of money for their erection and the endowment of the altars in them; two, three, four, and even more masses were celebrated consecutively and on the same day and fees exacted for the celebration

of masses and obits. Unscrupulous bishops multiplied fees and condoned
the extortionate methods of their officials. In one instance a bishop,
having consecrated a new church, immediately suspended divine service in it because his fee was not sufficiently large. In another an archbishop justified this simoniacal practice by arguing: "I do not sell the
church. I only sell my favor. Why should any one have my favor who
has done nothing to deserve it?" The practice among bishops of be-
stowing church benefices upon nephews while mere children, that under
pretext of wardship they might longer pocket the profits was a great
abuse. Church endowments and nominal offices were frequently bestowed upon relatives who were ne'er-do-wells in order to provide for
them. Church benefices were bestowed in reversion. Church offices were
multiplied and sold to rich aspirants for clerical honor or clerical privilege for a large sum of money while a poor priest actually performed
the duties of the office; or, in many a case, no duties were attached to
the office. "A wickedness exists beyond that of the priests of Baal,"
records a bold and indignant critic of the twelfth century, "for the
bishops exact an oath of their inferior clergy that they will carry all
causes out of which money can be made into the bishop's court in order
to extort fees and fines."

With the pontificate of Innocent IV (1243–54) "the greatest power
on earth was in the hands of a consummate man of business," and an
incomparable lawyer, who brought to bear upon the resources of the
papal office the astuteness of one born and brought up in the rich and
intensely mercantile city of Genoa. His fiscal operations constituted a
turning-point in the history of the medieval papacy when, so far as
one can judge from the evidence of over 20,000 documents, the head
of the Church prostituted his spiritual prerogatives for power and riches.
To the *plenitudo potestatis* which Innocent IV possessed and effectively
used (as in 1246, when by skilful distribution of dispensations he broke
up a combination of French nobles against him), he added the temporal
power of the States of the Church. Dante does not mention Innocent
IV by name among the papal denizens of Hell, as.he does his successors, Nicholas III and Boniface VIII, whom he "is never weary of
branding with the name of infamy"; but modern research has conclusively shown that it was with Innocent IV that the fiscal prostitution
and debauching of the papacy began. Nicholas III, who was of the
Orsini family, was described as "a Bear too eager to advance the cubs"
—a biting allusion to his nepotism—and one who "put vast wealth into
his own purse."

In the light of facts like these one understands more clearly than
ever the mission of St. Francis of Assisi in his idealization of poverty
and his condemnation of clerical worldliness and temporal magnificence.
More than any other man he and the movement he inspired saved the

Church from extinction through corruption. Clear-headed and deeply religious leaders like St. Francis and St. Dominic scathingly condemned the corruption of the Church, its worldliness, hardness of heart, mercenary character, social arrogance. The latter said that the bishops had ceased to be shepherds of their flocks and had become wolves. When the pope showed the austere saint the treasure of the Lateran Palace with the remark that the successor of St. Peter was not compelled to say like Peter, "Silver and gold have I none," Dominic dryly replied: "Yes, neither can Peter's successor say, 'Take up thy bed and walk.'" The Begging Friars, or Franciscans, and the Preaching Friars, or Dominicans, alike laid emphasis on practical charity and on popular preaching in the vernacular language in order to bring the gospel home to the people. They preached in the open air in the streets, market-places, at fairs, along the road as fellow travelers with the swarms of pilgrims bound for holy places like the tomb of Becket at Canterbury, St. James of Compostella, Mont St. Michel, and Rome. Until the thirteenth century preaching was little part of the office of the parish priests. That was a duty and a right of the bishops only, who usually were too much engrossed in ecclesiastical adminstration or politics to give attention to it. This weak point in the system of the Church the heresies took advantage of, and thereby gained popularity with and control of the masses. In self-defense—and prompted by the success of the friars—the Church adopted the method of its adversaries, and made preaching in the vernacular the duty of every priest. In spite of its aristocratic leanings and its hierarchic character, the Church had to be responsive to the new democratic spirit and condition of the thirteenth century, when serfdom was waning, towns had arisen, trade and commerce, eminently the means of livelihood of the common people, had developed. Only by popularizing its methods could the Church keep its popularity and retain its hold upon society.

While many individual churchmen in the Middle Ages displayed unusual capacity as practical administrators, and some of them, notably Gregory VII, large economic vision, the Church as a whole was a poor political economist. The roots of the Church's economic theory are to be found in the radical social democratic ideas of early Christianity recorded in the New Testament.

The teaching of the Gospel as to worldly goods had been unmistakable. It had repeatedly warned men against the pursuit of wealth, which would alienate them from the service of God and choke the good seed. It had in one striking instance associated spiritual perfection with the selling of all that a man had, that he might give it to the poor. It had declared the poor and hungry blessed, and had prophesied woes to the rich. Instead of anxious thought for the food and raiment of the morrow, it had taught trust in God; instead of selfish appropriation of whatever a man could obtain, a charity which gave freely to all who asked. And in the members of the earliest Christian Church it presented an example of men who gave up their individual possessions, and had all things in common. We cannot wonder that, with such lessons before them, a salutary reaction from the self-seeking of the pagan world should have led the early Christian Fathers to totally condemn the pursuit of gain. It took them further—to the denial to the individual of the right to do what he liked with his own, even to enjoy in luxury the wealth he possessed. . . .

If, however, to seek to enrich one's self was sinful, was trade itself justifiable? This was a question which troubled many consciences during the Middle Ages. On the one hand the benefits which trade conferred on society could not be altogether overlooked, nor the fact that with many traders the object was only to obtain what sufficed for their own maintenance. On the other hand they saw that trade was usually carried on by men who had enough already, and whose chief object was their own gain: "If covetousness is removed," argues Tertullian, "there is no reason for gain, and, if there is no reason for gain, there is no need of trade." Moreover, as the trader did not seem himself to add to the value of his wares, if he gained more for them than he had paid, his gain, said St. Jerome, must be another's loss; and, in any case, trade was dangerous to the soul, since it was scarcely possible for a merchant not sometimes to act deceitfully. To all these reasons was added, by many of the more saintly churchmen, yet another, which, had it been listened to, would have put an end to secular activity altogether. The thought of the supreme importance of saving the individual soul, and of communion with God, drove thousands into the hermit life of the wilderness, or into monasteries; and it led even such a man as Augustine to say that "business" was in itself an evil, for "it turns men from seeking true rest, which is God." [15]

In the earlier centuries of the Middle Ages these doctrines were not a great economic hardship and provoked little protest. For commerce was at a low ebb from the fifth to the eleventh century; both public and private economy was almost wholly of an agricultural nature, and economic "self-sufficiency" in primary staple productions the prevailing condition of things.

But in the eleventh century began a great moving of the stagnant waters. The growth of towns, the formation of merchant bodies, the establishment of markets—even if they did no more than furnish the peasant and the lord of the manor with a market for their surplus produce, brought men face to face with one another as buyer and seller in a way they had not been before. But they did more; they prepared the way for the growth of a new class, a class of craftsmen, who could exist only on condition that they were able to sell their manufactures. At the same time, new needs for money appeared both in the Crusades and in the passion for church-building, which the religious revival of the tenth century brought with

[15] Ashley, *Introduction to Economic History*, 126.

it. Hence economic questions, especially such as concerned the relations of seller and buyer, of creditor and debtor, became of the first importance. With these new dangers before them, churchmen began once more to turn their attention to economic matters, and to meet what they regarded as the evil tendencies of the Roman law, "the principle of the world," by a fresh application of Christian principles. On two doctrines especially did they insist—that wares should be sold at a "just price," and that the taking of interest was sinful. They enforced them from the pulpit, in the confessional, in the ecclesiastical courts.[16]

The "just price" was estimated upon the cost of production and the degree of need without regard to competition, which was held to be sinful. The Church endeavored to sustain this "just price" by force of law, ignoring the elements of supply and demand, and competition. St. Thomas Aquinas recognized the new necessity of commerce, but tried to save the economic theory of the Church by making allowance for the *motive* with which commerce was conducted, and made this the criterion of legitimacy. "There are two ways," he says—I borrow the translation of Miss Davison, *Forerunners of St. Francis,* pp. 341–342—

in which it is possible to increase the prosperity of a commonwealth. The more worthy is the production of an abundance of necessities by virtue of the fertility of the land; the other is by means of commerce by which what is necessary is brought to a common market from different places. The former is the more desirable condition, since it is better that a state should possess an abundance of riches from its own soil, for when merchants are necessary to maintain the people, injury may result to them in time of war when communications are checked. Also the coming of foreigners is apt to corrupt the morals of any people. If the citizens devote themselves to commerce, there is opportunity for many vices. For when merchants desire to increase their gains, the others also are filled with cupidity. The calling of a merchant is widely different from that of a soldier. The former abstains from manual labor, enjoys the good things of life and becomes soft in body and flabby in mind. For this reason a state should restrict its commercial pursuits.

In the matter of wages and rent scholastic thinking was also as far removed from the actual operation of economic laws. Today it is recognized that the wages of the artisan shall increase with an increase in the market price of what he has labored to produce. The scholastic, however, regarded labor as a commodity to be bought and sold like wares, of which wages were the price. The remuneration of the worker was measured not by the value of his product, but by the extent of his needs—a doctrine which if effective would have kept wages permanently low and reduced the artisan classes to an industrial proletariat.

[16] *Economic Journal,* XXXI, 233.

As to rent, the scholastics regarded it as a species of partnership in which the owner of the land contributed one factor of production, the laborer the other. It was recognized that land might vary in value according to fertility, improvement, location, etc., but since there was not opportunity for modern free dealing in land in a feudal society, rents tended to remain fixed, or customary. Thus it will be seen that in general the doctrine of the "just price" hurt the merchant, the doctrine of wages hurt the artisan, but that the doctrine of rent was favorable to the lower class and operated against the welfare of the land-owning class.

Maximum and sumptuary laws, the "just price," became the order of the day. Here the Church and the secular courts parted company, however. The Church discouraged—or at least professed to discourage trade as worldly and sinful—while the State frankly sought to promote it. The secular courts followed the line of practical wisdom and experience. The Church's ordinances embodied an economic ideal which was both unpractical and impracticable, and, moreover, was regarded by the workaday world of merchants and artisans as grossly unjust and calculated to enforce perpetual poverty. The Church's concept of "value" was something absolute and apart from value in use and value in exchange, something independent of supply and demand, something intrinsic and fixed; its theory, derived from Aristotle, that "money is sterile," that the gospel phrase "Lend, hoping for nothing again," must be taken literally and practised universally; its prohibition of the taking of interest as both opposed to Christian teaching and unethical, since it was exploitation of something free to all and common to all, namely, *time* (for to charge interest was, as it were, to sell a thing and then charge for the use of it) ; its denial in theory and in practice of the mobility of capital (indeed, its doctrine that capital itself was worldly and the possession of it sinful) ; its denial of the principle and practice of credit—all these economic doctrines which were advocated by the scholastics and enforced by civil and canon law, had a detrimental influence upon the material welfare of medieval society.

By the twelfth century, when commerce and industry had become awakened and immensely active, these theories became issues of practical importance which no longer interested only theologians and doctrinaires, but interested princes, governors, legists, merchants, tradesmen and the common people. The economic practice of the people refused to follow the teachings. The decrees of the Church were either ignored or, what was more common, surreptitiously evaded. The business ingenuity of the times invented "indirect exceptions" of many sorts.

CHAPTER XXVI

FEUDALISM AND THE FEUDAL CLASSES

THE medieval state was a loose agglomeration of territories with "rights of property and sovereignty everywhere shading into one another." The several states were very much alike in political and social institutions; they professed the same religion and the governing classes had identical interests everywhere. Each was feudal in form of government, in institutions, in social structure.

Medieval political theory was based upon a tripod: the Roman law, the teachings of the Fathers, and Germanic legal traditions and social institutions. Antiquity believed the State to be real, supreme, immutable, permanent, above all, and not responsible to its subjects. Christianity, through St. Augustine, taught that civil society, *i.e.,* the State, being derived from sinful man (Nimrod was its founder), was *ex origine* evil; that the Church was the perfect form of organized society, and the State at best was only to be tolerated within and subordinate to the Church. With the primitive Germans, on the other hand, even when the inchoate State began to be formed among them, the emphasis was laid upon the rights of the individual. All three of these antithetic conceptions entered into the fabric of the medieval State.

The Frankish Empire was essentially feudal in theory and practice. With its rupture this feudal character was communicated to the several states which were formed out of its decomposition. But this process of political decomposition was not arrested with the formation of the six several kingdoms into which the Frankish monarchy was split. The kingdoms themselves tended to subdivide into semi-independent principalities, so that each realm became a loose agglomeration of feudal fiefs. Under these conditions power became more and more personal. It was impossible to separate the principle of rule from the person of the ruler, and the bond which held society together was the mutual relation of lordship and homage. The relation of the lord and the vassal was a contractual one; and the theory of contract was pushed upward to include the king. The State, instead of being, as in the past, a compact political entity, was converted into a loose contractual social organism.

The beginning and the end of the Carolingian house (752–887)— for after the latter date the king was a mere seignior, the crown elective, and each king dependent upon the support of a handful of great nobles—

were the poles of a single process, to wit; the rise and triumph of feudalism. The Carolingians were brought to power and sustained in it for a century by a potential feudalism, or rather vassalage. But the Carolingians were strong only so long as they retained their proprietary predominance. In the ninth century, however, the system became one of reverse action. The vassals grew stronger and made themselves greater proprietors than the kings. They left the kings the husks of royalty and seized the corn for themselves. Their fidelity became a fiction, their service a gesture. But the process of dissolution did not stop with the destruction of the Frankish Empire. For the same particularistic forces which had detached the grandees of the crown and the great provinces in the ninth century from royal control, in the tenth century wrought to divide and subdivide the provinces into quasi-independent fiefs. The high nobles became the victims of the same psychology and the same forces which they had employed against the monarchy.

The remote roots of feudalism are to be found in the former Roman patrimonial proprietorship, which the Church and the Germans imitated and continued, and in the old Germanic concept of personal loyalty of all the members of the primitive *comitatus,* or war-band, to its chief. Thus Rome contributed the property relation, the Germans the personal relation. Their fusion together formed the essential nature of feudalism. The two institutions became the obverse and the reverse side of the same thing. The union of the Carolingian benefice (or grant of land subject to fixed services) with vassalage—itself a compound of ancient Celtic clientage with German loyalty—created the fief of the landed noble, which he held of some superior noble. The link in the long chain of phases by which this result was achieved was commendation, or the promise of fidelity by the vassal to the overlord, or suzerain. The remote ancestors of the nobility of the Middle Ages were the armed domestics (*antrustions,* or men in the *trust* of the king) of the barbarian kingdoms, who at first were personal vassals bound by an oath of commendation; these later, in the time of the Carolingians, became vassals owning property in the form of benefices or fiefs. The obligation became both a personal and a property one, *fidelitas* representing the moral side, homage the material side of the relation, and the ceremony of commendation uniting the two into a single institution. Historians are divided in opinion as to which of these two separate sources was earlier in point of time, or greater in point of influence—the personal or the property relation. It really makes little matter and is a point for antiquaries. But it is important to know that this system as a form of government and a structure of society grew up out of the disruption of the Frankish Empire in the ninth century, and incorporated much of the debris of that state into its organism.

An additional contributing factor to the formation of feudal society was the invasions of the Norsemen and the crying need, felt especially by the lower classes, for protection and security. The freeman of the ninth and tenth centuries in these adverse conditions had three options: to become a vassal of a landed proprietor more powerful than himself, in which case he, too, became a noble of inferior degree to his suzerain; to enter the Church; or to become a serf. Naturally the last was the fate of the largest part of the free population. For only the man possessed of considerable land could interest another in helping to protect his property, and this the suzerain would do only upon condition of the performance of stipulated services to him by the vassal.

It must not be supposed that this development was always made in an orderly way. As a matter of fact there was much wantonness and spoliation of the weak by the strong, much injustice, much brutality. The negative nature of some of these early promises—*not* to injure or to hurt—is instructive. Nevertheless, in spite of its often violent and sinister character, there can be no doubt that feudalism as a whole was a phenomenon of social progress, of social integration, and not one of decay. If we take the long view we can see how constructive and how original and how great a civilization that of the feudal age was. The period of transition, the ninth and tenth centuries, it cannot be denied, was hard upon mankind, but when that period of transformation was overpassed and the new social institutions which were in process of formation had at last taken form, then a better era was ushered in. The new feudal régime found itself in new institutions of a political, social, and economic nature which were in harmony with and expressed the new society that had come into being. One may sympathize with the men of the ninth and tenth centuries in the "revel of barbarism" which then prevailed, who looked back wistfully to the age of Charlemagne as a Golden Age, when Europe dwelt together in unity. Yet those violent centuries possessed the germs, the promise, and the potency of a new and greater civilization than that which had vanished away. By fixing society to the soil feudalism brought an end to the fluctuations that had characterized the barbaric life of the sixth, seventh, and eighth centuries. Europe became more stabilized. The principles upon which feudalism rested were different and of higher morality than the autocracy and slavocracy of the later Roman Empire. Feudalism reduced the earlier excessive and barbaric individualism to obedience to law and order, crystallized in institutions of suzerainty, vassalage, fidelity, service, the rights and the duties of contract. In its finest form it produced a new civilization. Feudalism was not, an eminent historian has written, a bridge cast across the gulf between barbarism and civilization—it was itself a civilization, a high culture which reached its apogée between 1150 and 1250.

If the rights and obligations, the duties as well as the liberties, of this society had not early (by the beginning of the eleventh century) become thus defined and regularized, its customs socialized and their force given the sanction of law by political or church authority, the civilization of the feudal age would never have been born, and Europe would have sunk into a storm of anarchy compared with which the violence of the ninth and tenth centuries was but a tempest in a teapot. For these first lords of the land, these ferocious warriors, formed "the freest population that ever existed," whose sense of liberty frequently extended into license. This anarchy would have been incompatible with the very survival of society if these same men had not voluntarily combined themselves together by conventions and contracts which custom and tradition gradually hardened into law and which honor compelled them to obey. The necessity of defense against itself forced the feudality to hierarchize itself, so that every proprietor, great or small, was bound to another lord above him, who could at the same time give him protection and exact obedience to the law.

The necessity of purchasing fidelity—for the lesser nobles drove shrewd bargains with those above them—was an important cause of the disappearance of movable wealth in the tenth century. It could not be spent, since there was nothing to purchase beyond what was furnished by the soil, and the products of the soil were theirs already. Hence it was hoarded. Accordingly, services more and more tended to be paid for in land, and as roads were bad, security slight, and all traffic beset with tolls, the circulation of commodities became intensely localized. Hence almost all produce was consumed upon the domain, no surplus was left for sale, and therefore the feudal age was one without capital. The only capital was land, and it was fixed, not mobile, a fact deeply responsible for the static condition and fixity of social structure in feudal society.

It is sentimental to regret the decline of ancient civilization or disappearance of the ancient free German village community and the degradation of thousands of small freemen in this process. One may argue the question as to which is a preferable form of government. But the fundamental function of all government is to protect life and property, and, given the time, the elements, and the conditions, no other form of government and no other form of society was possible in Europe, than feudalism. We must deal with historical conditions as we find them, and not indulge in theories and doctrinaire opinions.

In theory the feudal system was probably the most ideal form of government the brain and heart of man has ever devised. The master of English historians has observed:

It would have been a very excellent device if it could have been administered by archangels. . . . The essence of the system was mutual fidelity, and its proper consequence the creation of a corporate unity, and the recognition of it by every member, from the king to the villein. The bond was not a voluntary one, to be taken up and put aside at pleasure; the principle of cohesion was uniform throughout the mass. If then, on the one hand, the maladministration of the system forced the different constituents of the nation into a physical union of interests, the essential character, which no maladministration could neutralize, supplied the very elements which were wanting for moral strength. Self-reliance was proved not to be incompatible with order, mutual faith, and regard to law; and these are indispensable for national strength and national spirit.[1]

When the period of anarchic transition had passed and Europe began to settle down under the feudal régime, it was not a reign of anarchy but a reign of law, despite the many infractions of law. In its best days feudalism probably enforced the law about as effectively and as honestly as modern society does. Because the ideas and the practices of the Middle Ages were very different from those of today, we must not be deceived into thinking that the civilization of the past was necessarily inferior to our own. The feudal system has gone the way of history, but its fundamental principle, that the possession of property entails public duty, and that great private wealth owes something to society, is of the essence of good government and just social relations.

It is easy for one imbued with current ideas of political and social democracy to condemn the aristocratic nature of the feudal régime. But, as the best members of that aristocracy were actuated by a sense of responsibility to one another, both to those above and to those below themselves, so they were possessed by a sense of responsibility and social obligation to the whole society around them, of which they were members. This aristocracy was a landed aristocracy, its wealth was in land. The medieval concept of government was that wealth and social influence conferred the right to govern. The relation between administrative service and the possession of land was close. Landed wealth determined politics. But this medieval concept also held that property entailed the performance of duties to society and involved responsibility together with privilege. "Medieval liberty," wrote Lord Acton, "differs from modern liberty in this, that it depended on property." To the same effect Maitland has said: "In the Middle Ages liberty and property are closely connected ideas."

The diversity of kinds of law in those days may have found stimulus in their very variety, while with us there may lurk enervation and monotony in uniformity. Whatever prejudices we may have for present conditions, when feudalism finally found itself it was a noble form of government and contributed to the creation of a splendid civilization.

[1] Stubbs, *Introductions to the Rolls Series,* 109.

The interdependence of vassal and suzerain, the actual rights of the former to the lands he theoretically held as a gift, the power to transmit these lands to his descendants, these principles and others, which gradually developed and adjusted the framework of medieval society, had been generally recognized by the middle of the tenth century. . . . When firmly fixed they prepared the way for a new conception of humanity. The generation which was first wholly fashioned by them could drop the century-long debate over matters of administration. Relieved of the discussion of methods of government it could devote itself to its social and intellectual welfare. . . . The activity of decades was consumed in the strife, but the end justified the effort.[2]

As early as 988 not merely the Church but secular princes could dream, as a result of the reduction of private war, of the idea of universal peace and actually sketch the plan of a federation of the states of Europe for that purpose.

One need not imbue with the tinge of romance some of the social teachings of feudalism in order to admire them. In actual practice they were high and noble, and though many of them, as in all society, were often more honored in the breach than in the observance. The idea of personal honor and loyalty was a vivid moral force even in the most violent times. One has only to read the little *Manual of Dhuoda,* written in the depth of the ninth century, to realize this, and to discover that the injunctions therein were not mere empty precepts. The most infamous crime in the feudal calendar was murder of one's overlord, and it is the rarest crime to be met with in the Middle Ages. There is no instance of the murder of a sovereign by a vassal or subject in the centuries of feudalism. King-killing was a political recourse of the generations of the Renaissance and Reformation. In the chanson *Girart de Roussillon,* which reflects the hardest age of feudalism, we find a remarkable example of the high moral value attached to the relation of a vassal bound by oath of fidelity to his suzerain. In the story Girart, having taken refuge in a forest, finds shelter for the night with an old hermit to whom he tells his plot to assassinate his overlord. The hermit is deeply shocked and exclaims:

Thou wouldst kill thy suzerain! Neither clerk nor saint, not bishop nor the pope would ever consent to grant thee the Church's forgiveness. Theology and Holy Writ declare what should be done to a traitor. He shall be torn asunder by horses, his body burned, his ashes scattered to the winds, the place of his execution shall be infamous, neither grass nor herb shall grow upon it.

When Guibert of Nogent inveighs against the treason of Bishop Ascelin

[2] Warren, in *Proceedings Modern Language Assoc.,* N. S. XVII, p. LI.

of Laon in the tenth century, the shocking thing to him is not that a bishop could so do, but that one who had taken an oath of fealty to his lord could go so far as to break it and to plot against him.

No more intensely personal form of government was ever conceived than that of feudalism, and the cardinal principle of it was mutual responsibility. The State was a loose contractual social organism. The teaching of the Church imparted a religious character, it is true, to the State; but at bottom the sanctions were more feudal than religious. Even the political thinking of the bishops ran in a feudal groove.

The Church, as the interpreter and ordainer of the will of God among men, substantiated the theory of its ascendancy in actual practice by deposing Louis the Pious and Charles the Fat. Since justice was an attribute of God, and the Church was of divine foundation, the Church claimed the authority to determine what was right and just and what was not, in the conduct of kings.

In order to make it more certain that the king would reign justly, the king was required to subscribe to a *promissio,* or coronation oath, in which the contractual, feudal nature of the king's authority is clearly manifested. It was the duty of the king to do justice and himself to obey the law. If he failed so to do the contract could be abolished; his subjects had the right to repudiate the contract. In feudal law a vassal had the right to war upon his suzerain, even the king, if denied justice. He could repudiate his homage and challenge his overlord. The converse was also true; the lord might repudiate his suzerainty and challenge the vassal.

It is a vulgar impression that the Middle Ages were a period of irresponsible and arbitrary violence and force. Violent the period was, but it was not one without law. Indeed, paradoxical as it may seem, the very sensitiveness for law was oftentimes the reason for the violence. Bishop Stubbs has shown this in one of the most illuminating passages penned by any modern historian.

Medieval history is a history of rights and wrongs. . . . The idea of right or rights was the leading idea of the Middle Ages—right or rights, because, whilst in the greatest men of the period there was a conscious attempt to exalt law and a willingness to abide by it, there was in the inferior actors, in the worse men, a disposition to maintain their own rights within recognized limits, and, when they attacked the possessions or infringed the apparently equal rights of their opponents, to do it on the ground of legal pleas. . . . The Middle Ages . . . were ages of legal growth, ages in which the idea of right, as embodied in law, was the leading idea of statesmen, and the idea of rights justified or justifiable by the letter of law, was a profound influence with politicians. . . . There was no fear of shedding blood, but there was great fear of destroying right . . . something that may be justified by law, not merely by the logic of the strong hand. . . . Medieval wars are, as a rule, wars of rights: they are seldom wars of unprovoked, never wars of absolutely unjustifiable, aggression. . . . There was war in abundance, public and private war. . . . What was meant was not that men loved law, but that they did so far respect it as to wish to seem to have it always on their side. They did not attack their neighbors because they wanted glory, or because they could not bear rivalry, or because their neighbors' armies were too strong for their safety, or because their neighbors' armies were so ill equipped that they might be an easy conquest; but they alleged a legal claim or a legal grievance; and in the majority of cases really legal claims and really legal grievances. . . . Men went to law to avenge their wrongs and to vindicate their right, and, when they could not get law that was strong enough to enforce itself, they went to war.[3]

The very sensitiveness (one might almost say supersensitiveness) of the men of the feudal age to questions of justice is proof of this mental attitude. The idea of justice was never less a theory and never more actual than in the feudal age. But justice implies a sanction, and this sanction must be law. Now law, for the medieval man, was the product of experience and tradition. It was custom, the accretion of generations in the past, and silently accepted by the men of the present. Even the prince could not contravene this customary law. Customary law was the supreme law, and any modification of it had to be accepted by all, or at least, if the community were too large and too widely dispersed to make approval or disapproval impossible, then it had to be accepted by the governing class, by the *major* or *sanior pars*. The king himself was not above the law, for he was of the noble class and contributed to the formation of the law of his kind. He, too, was subject to the customary law of the land. His authority was very far from being that of a despot. The maxim of St. Augustine that an unjust law was not law reënforced this doctrine of "natural rights," which were distinguished from positive law. The ancient German principle that the State was subordinate to law was at odds with the classical tradition that law was made by the State.

We see this new and positive ideal reflected in the historiography of the eleventh century. At this same time too, the student of medieval law begins to detect elements in it which are neither of Roman nor of ecclesiastical nor of German origin, but which may be described as feudal. It is evident that some new and constructive ideas were beginning to leaven feudal society. The day of anarchy and sheer brute force, of unrestrained violence and brutality such as characterized so much of the history of the tenth century, was beginning to pass away, and a new epoch was dawning in which the mutuality of rights and duties, of privileges and obligations was better understood and more regarded.

[3] Stubbs, *Seventeen Lectures on Medieval and Modern History*, 241-53.

Socially speaking, feudal society was aristocratic. We have some illuminating literature with reference to social attitudes. The conception of a tripartite society of three "estates"—the clergy to pray, to praise God, and to minister spiritually to mankind; the nobles to preserve order, exercise police power, and protect the country against invasion; the people to labor for the support of these two privileged classes—appears early in medieval history.

We find the two upper classes already distinguished and characterized as to social function in a letter of Pope Zachary to Pepin the Short and the prelates and grandees of the Frankish state in 747. Fifty years later Alcuin, writing of England, deplores the "secular vanities" of the clergy, and the "avarice" and "injustice" of the nobles (*bellatores*). The term "three orders" (*tres ordines*) appears in an address of the Frankish bishops to Louis the Pious in 821, and "each order" (*uterque ordo*), meaning clergy and nobility, is found in a capitulary of 828. By the end of the ninth century the three orders are fully distinguished in the *Miracles of St. Bertin*. A little later we find the relations of the second and third classes of feudal society, the nobles and peasantry, defined by Odo of Cluny in terms of protection by the former and work by the latter. Again, writing about the year 1000, Adalberon, bishop of Laon, addressing King Robert the Pious of France, says:

> Triplex ergo Dei domus est quae creditur una:
> Nunc orant, alii pugnant aliique laborant.

Jacques de Vitry said that the clergy were the eyes, for they saw and pointed out to men the road to safety; the nobles were the hands and arms, whose duty was to protect society, to enforce justice, and to war for defense of the realm; the common people (*minores*) were as the lower parts of the body, to sustain and bear the upper parts of the body politic.

These ideas of privilege and caste permeated the whole of medieval society in all countries where feudalism prevailed, and that means all of central and western Europe. We find the idea of tripartite society in Anglo-Saxon England, in a manuscript attributed to Ælfric: "Every just throne stands on three props, that stands perfectly right. One is *oratores,* another is *laboratores,* the third is *bellatores.* The *oratores* are the men of prayer, who shall serve God and by day and night intercede for the whole nation. The *laboratores* are those who work." The Norman conquest of England confirmed and hardened this social attitude of Anglo-Frenchmen. Thus in the twelfth century John of Salisbury, using the old Pauline figure of the body and its members, declaims as follows:

I call the feet of the State those who, exercising the humble crafts, contribute to the material progress of the State and its members. These are the laborers permanently bound to the glebe, and the artisans who work in wool or wood, iron or brass, those who are charged with the care of maintaining us, those who make the thousands of objects necessary to life. It is the duty of those who are inferior to respect those who are superior; but these in their turn must aid those beneath them, and provide for their needs.

Among German, Italian, and Spanish writers of the feudal age we find identity of thought and expression in defining the social attitude of the two ruling classes toward the ruled. In medieval wills one not infrequently finds instances of a serf "and all his brood" (*sequela*), a phrase used to describe a litter of puppies or kittens, being disposed of.

Far more than the clerical hierarchy, the military hierarchy tended to make itself a closed class in which every member was a noble of some distinction or other. Whosoever was not "born" into the class, had little hope of entering it. In Germany feudal ranks were called "shields": (1) the king; (2) ecclesiastical princes as vassals of the crown; (3) the great dukes and margraves and later the counts palatine, or palgraves; (4) lay princes who held of the Church; (5) counts and barons who were vassals of greater lay princes; (6) free knights, vassals of counts or barons; (7) *ministeriales,* or men of servile origin who by virtue of performing military service and prowess might rise out of serfdom into the status of semi-knighthood. These might hold of true knights or others, but not of one another. In France the gradations were at once looser and more aristocratic. Strict separation of rank, though, early ceased to have significance. One count might hold of another (even the king was once a vassal of the abbot of St. Denis) and even men of low scale be accepted as of highest rank, like the viscount of Limoges, who was more powerful and of higher dignity than many counts, and the sieur de Coucy, whose boast was: "I am neither duke nor count. I am the sieur de Coucy." On the other hand no man not noble born could hope to attain nobility. Such an invasion of the noble class from below as the *ministeriales* in Germany was impossible in France. The highest rank a simple freeman could attain was knighthood, and even then his prowess had to be clearly proved.

Every vassal was the follower of a baron of rank higher than his own. The lowest rank in the feudal hierarchy was that of knight. The landless knight was known only in Germany and originally he was not of noble blood but a serf doing military service. Elsewhere knighthood pertained solely to the aristocracy, and a knight was a person of estate. Knights were without castles usually, but formed part of the entourage of a great baron. They were the baron's constabulary in time of peace and his personal guard in time of war. But there was another variety of knights employed not in field service, but in less active tasks, especially castle-guard. These were called *vavassors*. "They were stay-at-homes, fixed quantities, who tilled their land without the distractions or temptations of the knights proper. They form a link with the lower vassals, who in their turn introduce us to the peasant class."

In spite of the fact that social distinctions seem to have been clear-cut in the feudal age, actually the gradations in each class were blurred, and the classes blended into one another. Were the *minores, minocres, mediocres,* the very lowest grades of the noblesse, so low that they were mere petty squires? Or were they a peculiar form of freemen, higher than ordinary freemen? If so, how? Or were they the remnant of such alodial [4] proprietors as the pressure of feudalism had spared? As nobles shaded off into freemen, so freemen shaded off into various degrees of the unfree. As freemen might rise to knighthood, so in Germany talented or fortunate serfs might rise to be *ministeriales*.

In Germany social distinctions were not so sharply defined as elsewhere. Lords used their unfree servants (such as were fitted) as mounted messengers, followers on journey, bodyguard and as soldiers in their petty feuds, and even let them swell the host of free retainers when joining the army. The *minsterialis,* the house-slave, the bodyservant, armed and mounted, figured largely in the retinues of the lords, and for such service received equipment and endowment of land so as to be always ready. These *ministeriales* came to form a special class of armed retainers, of inferior rank but with great opportunities for preferment in important and responsible positions, and with ultimate equality with free-born soldiers and knights. They had charge of castles, bridges, trading posts, tolling places. Highest in honor were the imperial *ministeriales,* but those belonging to bishops or princes were likewise made bailiffs and administrators of towns and districts. Their position was so advantageous that the knighthood class was invaded by these upstarts, and thus was created a subordinate equestrian order, *ordo militaris,* divided into major and minor, the *ministeriales* being the *milites minores.*

The extent of the persistence or survival of freeholders in the midst of and through the intensest period of feudalism is a subject as important as it is difficult to resolve. We know that in Saxony, Tuscany, and part of Languedoc considerable masses of such freeholders persisted until late and never were wholly worked into the feudal régime

---

[4] The word *alod* was compounded from the German particle *an* and *lot* or *lod, i.e.,* "lands obtained by lot," and is reminiscent of the way the lands of the Romans were divided during the Germanic conquests in the fifth century. It was a freehold. (See Chapter IV.) The word *feodum* (whence "fief") was compounded from the word *lot, lod, od,* meaning "estate or real property," and *feo,* signifying "money" or "wages." Thus a fief originally was a stipendiary grant.

either politically or socially. The courage of men of this class in resisting the pressure put upon them by feudal neighbors to compel them to accept vassalage, the persistence with which they withstood violence and attempts at subjection without the protection of a suzerain is remarkable. The eleventh century seems to have been the time when the feudalization of alods was strongest. In Languedoc in the twelfth century some freeholders formed a league of defense. We do not know its fate. It probably disappeared in the devastation of the Midi as the result of the Albigensian Crusades.

In the chapter upon the manor we shall see that the medieval baron as a proprietor enjoyed certain incomes derived from monopolies which he possessed in his manors, such as court fees, the bake-oven, the brewery, and the mill. But independently of these manorial revenues he had other incomes derived from his "rights" as a feudal lord, which historically represented localized vestiges of the former sovereignty of the central government. Among these were the right of judicature ("high" or "mean" justice) according to his rank, coinage, market, tolls, *péages*, etc. Few nobles were elevated by any sense of public spirit in exercsing these prerogatives. When Odo of Tours in the eleventh century built a bridge over the Loire and permitted free crossing of it, his conduct created astonishment.

Before the twelfth century, when there was great increase of money owing to the Crusades and awakening of trade, to pay in coin was a sign of great wealth. The nobles jealously guarded this right of coinage, for it was a lucrative one. The right of coinage was part of the domain of the prince. Carolingian money was pure silver, the oldest baronial money likewise. Little by little the coin was debased, the metal alloyed, the weight diminished. "The alteration is legal, persistent, progressive." What was the reason for issuance of a coinage economically bad?

Probably the chief reason for the constant alteration of moneys is to be found in the nature of the right of coinage which the lord considered as one of the chief sources of revenue of his domain. He benefited himself in deriving the maximum profit from possession of the prerogative. Money became the element of a manorial *redevance*. The seigniorage was converted into a proportional tax upon all purchase and sale. It had the convenience of being a tax easy to apply, cheap in cost of administration, and made no vexatious distinction between classes or persons. This is shown by the constant temptation to which the great proprietors yielded, both to adulterate the metal, and to cancel old issues and institute new ones. This was one of the greatest grievances of the epoch, for it impoverished or ruined many. Moreover, the wide variety of coins was a serious bar to the conduct of any but the most local trade.

Other revenues arose from the prerogative of the lord as a suzerain.

Under feudal law an overlord was the guardian of the children of a deceased vassal during their minority, and the custodian of the property which had been left to them. It frequently happened that in this capacity the overlord wasted or absorbed the entire estate. An immense amount of the litigation which crowded feudal courts, and many a petty war, thus arose, when the relatives of the wronged heir appealed to the courts or the sword for redress. Similarly an overlord possessed jurisdiction over the widow of his deceased vassal. Since his primary interest was to have a redoubtable and robust vassal to serve the fief of which he was suzerain, he usually compelled the widow again to marry, and often imposed upon her a husband of his own selection, without the faintest regard for the feelings of the lady. Medieval marital relations, far from being the sentimental attachments which romance depicts, were very often marriages of convenience and were brutally enforced. Young and tender girls were compelled to marry rough, and often lecherous, husbands. Proverbial "May and January" matches were common. From this tyranny the young virgin and the young widow had practically only one recourse, to enter a convent and take the veil. Many a nun was a broken-hearted widow or young girl. A rich widow, like Penelope, had many inconvenient suitors, who often resorted to violent methods of pressing their suits, like besieging the lady's château, or kidnaping her. When Eleanor of Aquitaine was divorced from Louis VII of France and was returning to Bordeaux she was pursued by five aspirants, each of whom was desperately determined to capture her, for she was the richest heiress in Europe. One may believe that her haste in marrying Henry Plantagenet was partly due to the necessity of having a husband able to protect her lands against seizure. For a rich widow resolved still to live in the world had the world against her.

Marriage was often a contract entered into to make an advantageous alliance, to escape escheat of a fief, to keep a particular piece of land in the family, to acquire new lands. On few occasions do we find the consent of the maid or her mother recorded as having been solicited. An incident like the following is rare. "The lord of Arden and his wife were very agreeable to the proposal of the count of Guisnes, and showed their pleasure openly, and spoke to their daughter to ask if she would consent. The girl was not displeased but seemed glad and of a good sort, so that by her face she proved her willingness, and in such fashion her eyes shone at the words of her father and mother that it was evident that she never would have chosen anything more agreeable."

The Medieval Age, no less than our own time, had its woman question, and with it as with us, it was one chiefly of occupation. Then as now the proportion of women was in excess of that of men, and in a warlike and strikingly masculine form of society the problem of finding a place for women in it probably was greater than today. Bücher has expressed the opinion that women were not excluded from any industry in the Middle Ages of which they were capable. For some the convent was a refuge, for others the thirteenth century created *béguinages, same-nungen*—"settlements," we would call them—where women of culture but of small means were able to find a home. Taken all in all, one may say that the Middle Ages were as successful as modern times in dealing with the woman question. For every age acts according to its lights.

Something has been said in the chapter dealing with the Church about the evils of private warfare in the Middle Ages and the efforts of the Church through the Peace of God and the Truce of God to regulate or to suppress it. It has also been shown in the present chapter that much medieval war was a "struggle for rights," an endeavor of the wronged person to defend and sustain his "right" with the sword in the weakness or absence of courts of law, or the injustice of an overlord.

It is now pertinent to seek the economic motives and the economic results of private war. But before doing so a word of caution may be said. When not actual brigandage, like waylaying merchants and travelers, and not perpetrated by robber barons, from which it must be clearly distinguished, private war was mostly of a very petty and very local sort. Moreover, its prevalence has been grossly exaggerated. A medieval chronicler was not unlike a modern newspaper reporter. He recorded the exceptional, the extraordinary, the unusual. Our own civilization would largely seem to be one of battle, murder, and sudden death if the estimate of it were based solely upon the columns of the newspapers. A bad deed usually shines farther than a good deed in the world. The silence of the chroniclers as to thousands of good and true men who tried to lead honest lives, who were careful of the lot of the serfs upon their lands, who did not molest their neighbors, does not prove that none such existed in those times. If we had fuller evidence it would show undoubtedly that at all times and in many places the everyday life of castle and manor pursued its customary routine with little to derange it. It is well to remember that history, as set forth in a modern journal, is "little more than the register of the crimes, follies, and misfortunes of mankind," which Gibbon cynically thought to be the chief content of history after all.

The roots of much medieval war were inseparable from the economic soil from which it sprang.

The manorial system with its interlocking claims of lord and tenants, and its complication of common and individual rights, was intensely provocative of disputes. The chances of dispute also were multiplied by the prevailing custom of landed families holding estates, often in very small parcels, widely scattered over the country. . . . Instead of an effort to concentrate their interests in any particular section of the country, it was rather the manifest desire of every great family to extend its claims into every nook and corner: so that it was necessary for a landlord nearly as much as a merchant to be forever on the road, traveling on horseback or by river barge from one country seat to another.

Militarily speaking, feudalism was

the system in which a standing army, quartered on the tillers of the soil was entrusted with the defense and administration of the country. War and government were both private undertakings. For a purely agricultural population, with a natural economy, there was no other solution of the problem. The peasants, scattered and occupied on the land, could not be utilized for war; nor could soldiers or officials be paid except by grants of land. . . . Land being the only source of wealth, the only form of business enterprise was to acquire more land. To do this, there were only two means—marriage and war. Both were, therefore, pursued as systematically as any form of industrial enterprise is today. . . . War enriched the feudal lords through lands and serfs; it enriched their knights and retainers through booty and ransom. . . . It was this vested interest of the nobility in the continuance of war that for centuries defeated every attempt to abolish private war. They had sublet their estates for the purpose of providing troops until the land could not support so many non-producers and war was the only business in which they could be employed.[5]

In Normandy the exhaustion of the resources of the baronage in intestine feuds before 1066 made them eager to back William the Conqueror in the invasion of England. The Crusades, as we have seen, are another similar instance upon a large scale.

The structure of feudal revenues also offers partial explanation of this phenomenon of chronic and petty warfare. No process of accumulation was possible with perishable wealth like farm produce, and in the depth of the feudal age, except for jewels and plate, no baron had any other sort of riches. To possess the land which produced this form of riches and the labor of the serfs upon it, was the sole means of enrichment open to a covetous baron, and the readiest means of acquisition was war. The plan everywhere was, "First destroy the land, then one's foe." But this practice entailed constant repetition.

The gradual cessation of the evil of private warfare was not wholly due to the repressive measures of the Church and the kings, when at last centralized monarchy emerged triumphant over localized feudalism. Part of the explanation is economic. In such struggles the weaker went to the wall; the great only were left and thus the number of contestants was diminished. At the same time the improvement of agriculture, the growth of population, increased the revenues derived from the manorial system so that the volume of output was greater, and hence at least one important provocative cause of private war was diminished, even if not eliminated. That point was reached by the middle of the eleventh cen-

[5] *Political Science Quarterly*, XV, 599–600.

tury, and then the militant energies of the baronage found an outlet in Crusades in Spain and the Holy Land.

This tendency to substitute external war for internal strife was intensified by the gradual change wrought in the law of inheritance. Ancient German law provided for equal division of the land between the sons of the family. But in the feudal age the theory of indivisibility of baronies and *fiefs de haubert* (military fiefs) gradually came into general acceptation (except in Germany), which in turn led to the establishment of the law of primogeniture, or the succession of the eldest son to the entire patrimony of the father, and thus threw the younger sons upon the world to make their fortune elsewhere by the sword. If primogeniture had not been adopted the feudal world would have remained indefinitely a chaos of jarring states, some of them of atomic dimension. For otherwise all the labor of a noble in building up the landed power of his house would have gone by the board when he died and the lands were dissipated once more. The ruin of the house of Vermandois is a case in point. In the tenth century Herbert of Vermandois spent a long life in getting into his hands the counties of Vermandois, Champagne, Troyes, and Meaux, together with the advowson over numerous abbeys and bishoprics. When he died in 948 they were divided among his four sons and the great state he had labored so hard to create was reduced to shreds.

Much has been written of the sufferings which the medieval peasantry endured owing to the practice of "private war" among the baronage, when the Peace of God and the Truce of God were instituted to restrain it in the tenth and eleventh centuries. Without intending to minimize the extent of the evils which the peasants suffered from the violence of the times, one must make careful distinction between private warfare and mere brigandage. The former at least possessed a principle, however much that principle has become obsolete today. Moreover, first the Church and then the kings soon stepped in to regulate, if not to suppress it. Much that is chronicled by historians of these violent episodes has been mistaken for private warfare when actually it was mere highway robbery, and as such crime, and nothing else. The distinction is not always clear, it is true, but it is always incumbent upon the historian to endeavor to distinguish between these two forms of violence. From a careful reading of the annals of the ninth, tenth, and eleventh centuries, I am sure that brigandage and not private warfare was the greater evil. During the one hundred and fifty years elapsing between 850—the epoch of the ruin of the Carolingian Empire—and the year 1000, at which date we may say that feudalism at last had become established as a form of government and a social and economic system, it is juster to say that brigandage much more than "feudal anarchy" was the gross evil. "Private war" did not enter into the category until the "rights" of feudalism emerged and the principles of feudal law gave room for the assertion of those "rights" which were at the root of private war.

Brigand associations were common in the ninth and tenth centuries, less so in the eleventh as government became more settled. The later Carolingian capitularies abound with allusions to *latrones* and *deprœda-tores;* a letter of Lupus, abbot of Ferrières, mentions an association of brigands in 856; the *Annals of St. Bertin,* another such in 870. Flodo-ard's *History of the Church of Rheims* thrice mentions such groups in the tenth century. More than a hundred years before the institution of the Peace of God we find the Church attempting to restrain these marauders by threat of excommunication. It may be doubted, though, whether ordinary life did not go on as uniformly, taken all in all, in the feudal age as now, except in case of actual invasion from without. The automobile bandit today is comparable to the armed rider of the Middle Ages, and terrorizes rural America probably as much as the similar medieval type terrorized the rural population of France and Italy. For example, Illinois has the unenviable record of having had more country bank robberies than any other state in the Union. In the year 1924 there were seventy-three bandit raids on rural state banks. Between January and June there were twenty-one bank hold-ups. If one were to estimate American civilization from the newpapers our society would probably seem as violent to an historian of the year 2500 as the society of the tenth and eleventh century seems to us.

It is often difficult to distinguish these bands of brigands from hireling troops, of which we find occasional mention in the tenth and eleventh centuries, and whose employment on a large scale by great feudatories and even kings in the twelfth century gave rise to prodigious suffering on the part of the peasantry. The times naturally bred a riffraff born of the women who followed the feudal hosts, men without family or home, who took to a life of rapine. The frontier regions of Europe, in France the "marches" of Brittany, Brabant, and Lorraine, the Spanish Mark between Christian and Mohammedan Spain, Apulia in southern Italy, and the Slavonic marks along the eastern border of the German kingdom were breeding places of this class. Hence they were often called *coterelli* (border men) or *marchiones,* or Brabançons (from Brabant in the Low Countries or in the south Catalans (from Catalonia) or *routiers,* meaning "roadmen" who infested the highways. The earliest allusion to these *routiers* occurs in a chronicler of Rheims in 992. The feudal limitation of military service of vassals to forty days, which appears as early as 948, led to increased use of these mercenaries. These ruffians, much more than private warfare, were responsible for violence and brigandage. The raids of rival barons were relatively limited in area, confined to devastation only of the lands of each other. Sometimes these bandits held up entire villages to ransom. The interest of the local baron was as great as that of his peasantry in suppressing these marauders. His material interest here worked in accord with his instinct as a ruler, for his whole fortune was represented in his crops and the labor of his villagers. In this sense every baron was a sort of rural constable.

Medieval chronicles abound with allusions to and often picturesque description of such forays. Of a village thus attacked in 1138 we read: "It so happened that the farmers were threshing the grain in the open street of the hamlet, and great heaps of straw and chaff lay scattered in front of the cottages, so that food for the flames was easily found. The whole village was burned." When such an attack befell, if there were time, the cattle were loosed in the woods to shift for themselves. The swine of course ran at large in the woods. They were thin, razor-backed beasts, very fleet of foot; the old boars with their huge tushes were really formidable animals, almost as much as the real wild boar, and unless attacked by wolves in pack, hogs were generally able to take care of themselves. But it was quite different with sheep. Naturally timorous and given to flocking together, they were slaughtered "like sheep" or driven off.

Sometimes the peasants had a natural place of retreat where they took refuge in time of danger. An interesting example of such is the Kuhstall near Schandau in Saxony. It is a great archway of rock accessible on one side only, and so named because the Saxon peasantry in time of peril drove their cattle up there for safety. Often the village church, especially if it were built of stone, became an asylum, into which all the cattle were driven and the household possessions of the villagers carried.

The brigandage and private warfare of the Middle Ages have been much exaggerated by historians of the high feudal age, both contemporaries and modern interpreters, for the reasons which we have seen. The "grand" wars of the thirteenth century and later when the combatants were kings fighting with large resources and along long lines, were far more destructive than the local warfare of a quarrelsome baronage, chronic as their petty feuds may have been, and, as said, the professional mercenaries employed by them were a scourge.

And yet we must guard against regarding later centuries as more "civilized" than the feudal age in the matter of war. One of the most competent of modern scholars has written that "feudal warfare was probably, by its very nature, less horrible than the warfare of later centuries, when society had lost its military character and was as yet unprotected by international conventions. It is impossible to believe that Normandy or Touraine suffered in John's reign as France suffered during the Hundred Years' War, or Germany before the peace of Westphalia." [6]

[6] Powicke, *The Loss of Normandy*, 357.

Medieval war was not without some regulatory practices.

In spite of many changes, feudal society at the end of the twelfth century was regulated by principles which applied to war no less than peace. Law in a feudal society was inseparable from force, but was not obscured by it; they were combined in the theory of contract which informed all feudal relations. . . . Force was never absent, yet was never uncontrolled. In civil procedure we find the elements of war, such as the duel and the hue and cry; and in war we find constant applications of legal theory. War was a great lawsuit. The truce was very like an essoin; a treaty was drawn up on the very lines of a final concord, the hostage was a surety, service in the field was the counterpart of suit of court.

Some attempt was made to regard the rights of the non-combatant population and to provide compensation for those who had suffered great loss.

To some extent equity and charity were more active in time of war. The payment of dues was officially remitted on lands wasted in war, preparations were made for the reception of fugitives from threatened towns, compensation was sometimes secured for the destruction of ecclesiastical property, and alms were more freely given to the poor. But such measures as these offered no relief to the man who was forced by the hardness of the times to sell his lands or to leave the country. They could not cope with the widespread effects of famine or with the passions of mercenary troops. We can only guess at the amount of beggary, prostitution, and starvation produced by feudal warfare. All we can say with certainty is that those who suffered must have been very numerous.[7]

Yet surely it is not for our age to cast stones at the feudal age.

The worst evil of the Middle Ages was its cruelty to enemies, captives, criminals, and heretics. And here the traditions of the Roman law of war and the criminal law were largely responsible. However, one must be cautious not to confound cruelty with brutality. The former is the product of ingenious devisement. The latter often proceeds from lack of sensibility and imagination. The hard and materialistic life of the Middle Ages—at least until very late, when greater refinement began to have its influence—and the social prejudices arising from the caste structure of society, accentuated this indifference. The medieval man, whether noble or peasant, was of tougher fibre than the modern man; his nerves were neither so tender nor so close to the surface. His was a lustier and more red-blooded life. Modern society may have been the loser by the disappearance of some of these sturdier qualities.

A man in the Middle Ages did not live so long as a man in modern times. The average longevity was much less. But he got into a man's game earlier in life and lived more strenuously. Old age is a compara-

[7] These two quotations are from the same author, p. 356.

tively modern achievement of the human race. From an exhaustive study of 1500 medieval skeletons a distinguished scientist has computed that the "peak" of the death rate occurred at the age of forty-two in the Middle Ages, whereas today it is at seventy-two. Modern hygiene and modern medicine have more than neutralized the decline in the birth rate. Although, proportionally speaking, modern families are smaller than medieval ones, a greater number of children survive and there are many more families. The potential duration of human life undoubtedly remains stationary through the ages, but the actual prolongation of many more lives than formerly is an important historical fact. It is interesting to contemplate some biographies. Compared with modern rulers and statesmen, the life of medieval men in similar positions was short. The average length of life of the German kings between 918 and 1250 was forty-six years; that of the French between 987 and 1270, fifty-five years; that of the English between 1066 and 1272, fifty-four years. Only six out of the fourteen German kings lived to be over fifty. Frederick II died at fifty-six, yet his career had been so great that he has been called the "Wonder of the World." Philip II (Augustus) died at fifty-eight, yet he doubled the size of France in that time; Louis IX died at fifty-six, and had doubled again what his grandfather had doubled. Richard Coeur de Lion died at forty-two, and William Rufus at forty-four—both of wounds, it is true, and not disease. But then war-risk was part of the everyday life of a medieval king. William the Conqueror lived to be sixty only. Lothar II and Frederick Barbarossa were the only kings of the feudal age who reached seventy.

It must be remembered that these persons who died in the prime of life represent the élite of medieval society. The more sheltered life of churchmen may have given them a little greater longevity. But what shall we say of the mortality of the peasant and burgher class? No modern insurance actuary would consider any man of the Middle Ages —possibility of death in battle aside—as a good risk.

The mortality among children of all classes was certainly high. Probably not more than three or four out of a dozen or more lived to maturity. The *Chronicle of Ardres,* which is rich in family particulars and covers three generations, shows that 36 families had 71 boys and 55 girls, an average of 3.5 per family. In thirteen cases the women had second husbands; second and third marriages were frequent.

Life in a medieval castle was not the thing depicted by romantic novelists and poets. The age was a hard one and imposed hard conditions of living. When the castle first appeared in the ninth century it was a mere blockhouse built upon a hill or the edge of a cliff, or in the loop of a river, or if in a flat country, upon an artificial mound made by heaping up the earth dug out of the ditch or moat which encircled it. These early castles were built wholly of timber. Stone castles do not appear before the late eleventh century, and even then for many years in most instances the upper work was timber. Only the great "keep" was wholly of stone. In them comfort was sacrificed for security. Windows were mere slits in thick walls; rooms were dark and damp; stairs were steep. As the building art was developed, the castle was enlarged and improved. Architecturally a medieval castle was a walled and sometimes moated courtyard in which a strong and high tower was the important edifice. Historically it was the old-fashioned farmstead fortified. In the plain around the château were spread the farms of the peasantry, and often the village was huddled at the foot of the castle hill. Castrametation was applied to other buildings besides castles. Churches, monasteries, bridges, city gates, even cemeteries were fortified. Every fief was a complex, interlocking arrangement of such fortifications. Even cathedrals partook of this military aspect. Durham cathedral has been aptly described as "half house of God, half fortress 'gainst the Scot." The buttresses of Albi cathedral are veritable bastions, and the porch is approached by a ramp, while the roof is battlemented. Because castles sometimes became the rendezvous of robber barons it has been too hastily inferred that the medieval castle was a social abuse and tolerated for so many centuries only because the people were unable to dispossess the occupants. The truth is otherwise. A castle was erected for purpose of defense, not offense; it was a protection often for many leagues around it, a bulwark against outside invaders, a suppresser of violence and brigandage. The great castle of Carcassonne secured peace and tranquillity in the large circle of territory round about for nearly three hundred years.

A castle rarely stood in isolation, but was generally a part of a definite system of fortifications. . . . The castle, from a military no less than from a financial standpoint, was inseparable from the surrounding or dependent area. The *castellaria* or *châtellenie* comprised castle, lands, feudal duties, and fiscal arrangements; it was an artificial bundle of property and services, designed for the maintenance of the fortress and the profit of the lord. The body of relations of which a castle was the centre was intricate and complex. The administration was like a net overspreading the fief and including all within its texture from the highest noble to the lowest serf and the hermit in the forest.

The activities of merchants and the bustle of fairs and markets had their place in the scheme. Monasteries were supported by the tithes of distant bailiwicks. . . . A hundred points of law and custom depended upon the existence of a great keep. . . . Its chapel was served by a little church or religious house beneath the cliff. Its maintenance was largely due to the labors and bargains of men who had built up the little town under its protection. The royal (or baronial) revenues supported hospitals and lazarhouses outside the gates or in some desolate spot. In the castle hall the bailiff did justice over the countryside for miles around and protected the Jews, who were allowed to transact their useful but dangerous business with a safety that they could buy nowhere else. All kinds of men, each with his peculiar writ or safe-conduct or errand, met in the streets of the town and jostled each other in the great gate. . . . Justices, recognitors, claimants, knights with the king's prisoners, servants with treasure, falconers and dog-keepers with their precious charges, men with wine, fish, building-stone, or bundles of shafts and pikes, merchants, pilgrims, monks on the business of their house, wine-sellers, peasants.[8]

Of course not all a lord's manor-houses were converted into such imposing structures. While the manor-house was sometimes palisaded or hedged and sometimes moated, in time of war the lord relied upon his château if his fief was invaded. Great nobles had many castles but many nobles had few castles. A châtelain was lord of a single castle. A large castle contained a considerable population: the lord's family and visiting friends, and domestic servants of many sorts; and on the outside of the lord's dwelling but inside the walls, dwelling in adjacent structures connected with the main edifice by courtyards, arcades, or bridges, hostlers, grooms, gardeners, guardsmen, many of them with their families. The odor of the stable and the cow barns, mingled with that of wet or reeking leather, permeated the place. Fowls had the run of the establishment, even my lady's chamber unless watched. Sometimes a garden and an orchard were within the enclosure where the ladies sat in pleasant weather, busied with embroidery or music, or playing games while the lord was off hunting, for hunting was a privilege and a passion of the medieval noble, and there was no closed season for such sport.

But daily life in a medieval castle was pretty dull except in war time, especially for the women, who did not see so much of the outer world as the men. Before the literary awakening of the twelfth century few of the laity could read or write; hence books were not to be found. The lord's wife and daughters had their separate routine tasks of supervision and administration of the household, but beyond these time hung heavy on their hands. Consequently the blowing of his horn by the watchman on a tower to notify of the approach of a stranger was a welcome event, unless mayhap it was that of an enemy. Be he who he might, bishop or monk, baron, pilgrim, traveling merchant, vagabond, minstrel, strolling player, or acrobat with a dancing bear, one and all were welcomed and given hospitality according to their rank.

Food was plentiful but of limited variety, and plain cooking prevailed until the Crusades brought in spices and condiments from the Levant. The esculent vegetables were cabbages, turnips, carrots; the only plenti-

8 Powicke, *English Historical Review*, XXII, 27.

ful fruits were apples and pears. Meat was a staple article of diet and heavy eating was universal. Cooking was over charcoal or on a spit and with pots in the fireplace. The furniture was scant and primitive, plank tables on trestles, plank forms or settees, few chairs, but rather stools, and many chests around the walls harboring clothing and bedding. Until the Crusades introduced rugs and tapestries floors and walls were bare and chilly. Rushes or willow wands or straw covered the floor in winter until it became so noisome from the filth of hunting dogs and the bones cast to them at meal time that the litter was removed. Woolen garments were universal, summer and winter; indeed, the interior of these castles was so drafty and so chilly that heavy clothing was necessary even in summer. Under garments were introduced during the thirteenth century, again owing to the introduction of silk and cotton goods during the Crusades. But such material was expensive. Night garments were unknown. The highest lords and ladies slept naked in bed, and the bed was high above the floor and hung with curtains to prevent drafts. Kings and queens were no better off in this particular than the richest of their subjects. When the ship on which St. Louis was returning from the Holy Land caught fire, the queen of France appeared on deck stark naked. Nevertheless modesty was observed. The wife usually retired first and was in bed when her husband undressed. In the morning the husband dressed first, and the curtains around the bed protected the proprieties. It is a popular error to believe that the upper classes were indifferent to cleanliness. The famous description of medieval civilization as "a thousand years without a bath" is untrue. Every castle courtyard had a well and if possible running water was often introduced. Lead piping was used in the Middle Ages. As there were bath tubs so there were latrines in the better castles and monasteries. In the precincts of Kirkstall have been found twelfth century arrangements for the periodical flushing of the drains. In Lewes Priory each of 120 monks had his private and separate convenience. At Westminster the filtering cistern of the abbey has been recently discovered.

The lighter, more romantic, more idealistic side of nobility was expressed in chivalry. Chivalry was far from being a mere fashion. It was an institution. Intimations of it appear about 1100, but it was not until a century later that its principles and practices became formulated and the institution acquired full-fledged form. As an ideal it may be studied in the statutes of the knightly orders, in the high-flown manuals of knightly conduct and above all in the romances of chivalry. Of high illustrative value are the pictorial remains to be found in the miniatures which adorn this class of sources. The roots of chivalry are to be found in the comminglement of German and Christian traditions in the feudal age, but Saracenic civilization influenced chivalry in some degree, especially in the institution of heraldry. In the thirteenth century the knight had his coat of arms, insignia consisting of colored shield with a helmet, which was not transferable. Like the cleric, he was free from taxes and was distinguished from his inferiors by his costume and his *cingulum militare* which consisted of girdle and sword. In 834, when Louis the Pious was humiliated at Attigny, he took off his sword and belt and laid them at the foot of the altar, and abstained from resuming his sword until he was again belted by the hand of a bishop. The knight belonged to a certain class which again had its subclasses according to the rule that whosoever is another's vassal is not his equal, although both are knights. The reason of this change is not far to seek. In early feudal times when baronial war was common, a noble had need of a great number of armed retainers and was able to support them out of the profits of his campaigns. But with the growing pacification of Europe, thanks to the peace movement of the Church and the increase of royal authority, the baron's need of knights to follow him and his means to support them diminished. Then the order of knighthood began to harden into a close, aristocratic corporation, entrance into which was jealously guarded. This policy of exclusion is manifest in the latter half of the twelfth century, and by the thirteenth century knighthood was almost a closed circle everywhere in feudal Europe, except in Germany.

The Christian ingredient in chivalry naturally came through the Church. When the Church became feudalized and bishops and abbots performed military service, a revolution began in Christian ideals. While the church had nominally deplored all war as sinful, it justified war against pagans and infidels. But even then it deprecated the participation of churchmen in campaigns. But practice was stronger than principle. Fulbert of Chartres early in the eleventh century told King Robert the Pious that no occasion justified a bishop in taking the field. But his son Henry I bluntly told the pope that the bishops and abbots could not attend the council of Rheims because he needed them to crush a feudal rebellion. Abbo of Fleury (died 1004) discourses at length *de militantibus clericis et corum stipendiis.*

In yielding to the exigency of circumstances, the Church, however, found comfort in the New Testament reflection that every Christian was a "soldier of the cross" and the Pauline teaching to "put on the whole armor of God." Moreover, it discovered a principle, and distinguished between "wrong" and "right" wars. This distinction had been implicit in the Truce of God and the Peace of God and was finally worked out logically in chivalry and the Crusades. At first designed to suppress brigandage and private warfare, to protect clerical persons and property and the defenseless portion of the population, as women and children, the peasant and merchant, the justification of war rose to a height in the adventurous expeditions of French knights against the Mohammedans of Spain, whence it was another stride to similar expeditions for the recovery of the Holy Sepulchre and Christian conquest of the Holy Land from the Infidel.

The influence of Cluny upon this revolution in ideals was very great. It was Cluny which promoted the Truce of God; it was Cluny above all that preached the Spanish Crusades. It was from Cluny that the Templars and Hospitallers, and chivalry as a whole, derived its ideal that the perfect knight should be celibate, and even tonsured, like the Templars; the sacramental nature of the knight's oath and the sacrosanct nature of the initiation ceremony. The satire of Bishop Adalberon of Laon, relating how a Cluniac monk, having been sent upon an errand, "returned in the evening mounted on a foaming steed," was a slap at Cluny's bellicose ideals. The bishop could scarcely recognize him and asked: "Are you my monk whom I sent out?" He answered: "Sometime monk, but now a knight. I here offer military service at the command of my sovereign, who is King Odilo of Cluny."

St. Bernard has recorded his dismay when, in the inception of the Second Crusade, he was chosen as leader of the expedition. "Who am I," he exclaimed, "that I should have charge of a camp and go out before the faces of armed men? Is there anything more inconsistent with my profession?" But even St. Bernard overcame his scruples, and if he did not formally participate in war he preached both the Second Crusade and the German Crusade against the heathen Wends as just expeditions. Theology was made to fortify the new attitude. "Just" wars were represented as a means of expiation for the conscience laden with sense of sin, since its sufferings, wounds, and dangers no less than its power of arousing enthusiasm and performing wonders of endurance, courage, and self-sacrifice might stir up an otherwise dull and slothful nature. To Christianize war, since war was demanded for the extension of the faith, to reduce its terrors, keep ferocious instincts in abeyance and make the fighting propensities of humanity subject to rules of conduct without which battle was little more than carnage—these things the Church tried, and to some extent succeeded, in establishing. The founding of a class of professional soldiers who learned, as it were, the art of war and were admonished not to war against their fellow believers but only against the heathen and unfaithful, to protect the defenseless and support the law, was her aim.

The great Orders of Chivalry were international institutions, whose members, having consecrated themselves a military priesthood, had no longer any country of their own, and could therefore be subject to no one save the Emperor and the Pope. For knighthood was constructed on the analogy of priesthood, and knights were conceived as being to the world in its secular aspect exactly what priests, and more especially the monastic orders, were to it in its religious aspect; to the one body was given the sword of the flesh, to the other the sword of the spirit; each was universal, each had its autocratic head. Singularly, too, were these notions brought into harmony with the feudal polity.[9]

The idea that a knight could not break his word of honor without degrading himself was not original with the Church, but she further impressed upon his mind the sanctity of the pledge so that the knight could not break his oath without risking his salvation. The moral discipline of chivalry was largely due to the influence of the Church, as its military discipline was derived from feudalism.

Like so many other institutions, in its prime, chivalry had its uses. And like so many institutions it outgrew its time and became either ridiculous or an abuse. When Crusades abroad were over and ended, and at home strong national and municipal governments had become established upon the ruins of provincial feudalism, and the small feudal courts which had been the nurseries of knights were shrunken or gone, chivalry had outlived its day of usefulness. The knight had become an anachronism. Then the knight of chivalry degenerated into a highway robber, a road agent, or into a carpet knight. In the former, adventure was translated into robbery, pride into arrogance, protection into extortion and blackmail. To live in the saddle and the stirrup and by the sword came to be to live as a robber. He preyed upon unprotected peasants, obstinate townsfolk, and scurvy traders. He was particularly cruel toward peasants and detached burghers on the smallest pretext. Towns were forced to build themselves walls and towers against these "foes to all, who called themselves friends of God and women." In some parts they were so feared that the peasants dug themselves caves wherein they hid with their cattle to escape raids. Less objectionable, but vastly more ridiculous, were knights who roamed the land in search of combat in honor of their chosen lady. One of these knights-errant was famous as serving two ladies, and being little valued by each. Tristan was his model and his dame must therefore be an Isolde. Every wish of his lady was a command which he unflinchingly obeyed. For her sake he chopped off a finger that she might believe he was in earnest. Others traveled as absurd Lohengrins, and on the way measured their arms with numerous knights, being conquered by none. As King Arthur they journeyed through the country performing other acts of gallantry.

Heraldry, like knighthood and chivalry, although mocked at today by sophisticated writers, had its uses in the feudal age, and certain social implications, while its influence upon art was very great. The remote root of heraldry is probably to be found in the ancient tribal totemism of the Celts. In certain old Irish manuscripts even the evangelists are portrayed in the guise of animals, which savors of fetishism.

But real heraldry originated when the closed helmet came into vogue.

[9] Bryce, *Holy Roman Empire.*

This was not until the tenth century. The earliest instance occurs in 923, the case of Count Robert of Paris, who before going into the battle of Soissons, in order that he might be identified by his men, drew his long gray beard through the throat-latch and let it stream over his breastplate. When the helmet became universal among the feudality, it was impossible to tell friend from foe without some distinguishing device. Geoffrey Plantagenet wore a sprig of broom corn (*planta genesta*) in his helmet, and the custom gave rise to the surname of the dynasty. At first such devices were simple, homely emblems, but the Crusades introduced elaborate and strange devices like lions, leopards, and unicorns besides strange and brilliant colors, while arms and castles contributed a quota of castles, portcullises, etc.

In time the loose and almost riotous practices concerning devices and colors became subjected to rigid formality, giving rise to those queer and exquisitely beautiful forms and colors we associate with heraldry. Proper usage of both forms of expression became an exaction of polite society, and contributed to decorum as chivalry influenced courtesy and manners, while good taste and artistic cultivation was promoted by heraldic design and color combinations. Implications of chivalry, too, are to be found in the heraldic mottoes, in which honor, truth, courage so often recur as sentiments. In all these ways heraldry was of social significance and social influence.

CHAPTER XXVII

THE key to the understanding of the economic and social history of the Middle Ages is in the nature and extent of the manorial system. Medieval economic life was primarily a matter of natural economy and landholding, and the obligations of the peasantry pertaining thereto. The manorial system was at once a form of government, a structure of society, an economic régime prevalent over all that part of central and western Europe conterminous with Latin and German Christendom.

The evolution of medieval society starts from the predominance of landed aristocracy and the private estate. A complete synthesis of all the elements which entered into the composition of the manorial régime is quite impossible, for below the superficial uniformity which it seems to possess, we find almost infinite variety, both quantitative and qualitative. Historical tradition, local custom, natural conditions, like relief of the soil and many other factors, so entered into the formation of the manorial system that no simple explanation suffices. As an expression of intensely organic life, the manorial system was one of constant change. These transformations reflect the general transformation of European civilization from century to century, so much so that the economic and social equation of Europe is largely to be found in the equation of the manorial system.

The manorial system was the lower side of feudalism. It was the relation of the landed proprietary class to the servile, villein, and slave dependents dwelling as farm laborers upon the estates of that class, or the relation of the noble to the non-noble class in medieval society. In point of time it was already solidly established when feudalism was yet in process of formation. While the roots of each system go deep down into the past, broadly speaking it may be said that manorialism became fixed by the end of the ninth century, while feudalism did not acquire form and fixity before the eleventh. The Romans in Gaul had practised the system of *villæ*, great farms with their dependencies, centres of grand domains upon which dwelt a numerous tenantry, grouped or scattered, who, under the name of slaves or colons, were directly dependent upon the proprietor. These *villæ* had survived under the Frankish monarchy; there existed a great number of them in the time of Charlemagne. The classic tableau distinguishes, on the one hand, the habi-

* MAP. Shepherd, *Historical Atlas,* 104 (a manor).

tation of the lord and the lands subject to his direct exploitation (*indominicatum*) ; on the other, the land occupied by a tenantry of various conditions ; and finally the vaguer parts—forests, pasturage, marsh, serving for the common use of all the cultivators of the domain.

The life of the common people in the Middle Ages was almost wholly rural and agrarian. There was little modification of it until the eleventh century, when commerce and industry began to develop, chiefly owing to increasingly intimate contact with the Mediterranean lands and the East. Compared with modern economic and social conditions a far larger proportion of the population of Europe dwelt in the country than today. The towns were few and small and the majority of the people in them were not free, but servile workmen and craftsmen. Relatively speaking, rural villages in medieval Europe were more numerous than now, in spite of the great increase of population in modern times. Within every fief and dotted over its surface were a number of villages the inhabitants of which, with few exceptions, were unfree or servile peasants whose whole occupation was farming. In the legal sense each of these villages was a villa or manor. It was the lowest administrative unit, the simplest social organism above the family, which of course was a purely private group. The "manor" does not appear in historical sources before the late Merovingian epoch, and did not become current until the Carolingian period But the organism as an economic and social entity was as old as the later Roman Empire.

The manor has been variously defined as "the unit of land management" in the Middle Ages ; as "an estate forming both a possessory and an administrative unit" ; as "the main and normal constitutive cell in the social structure." The physical properties and mechanical working of the manor are fairly clear. But unfortunately the origin of the medieval manor is among the thorniest problems of medieval institutions.

Were these manorial communities of which the noble living in his castle was landlord and governor (seignior) descended from the servile and slave communities of the later Roman world? Is the medieval manor or villa to be traced back to the ancient Roman patrimony? Was the lord of the manor the medieval successor of the Roman patrimonial proprietor? Or were these medieval village communities descended from ancient German village communities (the *Mark*), whose once free inhabitants had become reduced to serfdom? Are *villa* and manor identical? How far did Roman and German forms of village life, social institutions, agricultural practices, fuse together? Was the originally free German class depressed to serfdom by pressure from above? or was it dragged down by force of social gravitation, so to speak, exerted by the weight of the great mass of slaves and serfs with whom the free Germans came in contact when they settled within the Roman Empire? Or did the mass of the German people start in serfdom and rise out of it, as some scholars contend? Did the manor grow out of the village community? or the village community grow out of the manor? Did the manor gradually disappear at the end of the Middle Ages, leaving the village community as a legacy to modern times? Was the "open field" system the "shell" of serfdom? Did re-allotment of arable shares ever obtain in the open field system? Did any freemen survive during the feudal age? Was there any freehold land in feudal Europe? or were all non-noble landholdings reduced to tenures, *i. e.*, conditional ownership? What gave rise to the variety of social classes—serf, colonus, collibertus, villein, etc.—among the lower population? What was the relation of land occupation or land ownership to the differentiation of these classes? How did land come to determine social status? What is the origin of the local taxes imposed by the lord upon these manorial peasants? Were they derived from Roman proprietary practice? Did they have a legal origin? or did they arise from usurpation of royal prerogative, in the ninth century? Was there a legal limit to their imposition either in written or in customary law?

These and many other questions arise when one attacks the problem of the origin of the medieval manor, analyzes the elements in its structure and attempts to trace their historical genesis and development. In the words of Professor Pollock, "the truth seems to be that in institutions, as in language, there has been widespread and complex interaction. In many cases the contact of more or less similar Germanic and Roman ideas has led either to a complete fusion, producing something different from either of the originals, or to what the philologists call 'contamination.'"[1]

That the medieval manor in its social ingredients and its agricultural practices represented a fusion of Roman and German institutions— sometimes commingled with elements of earlier and especially Celtic racial customs—is now hardly denied. In the mighty march of the races of history across Europe "the migration of one of these peoples may have served to stamp the features of their system upon a land which had originally borne the features of another." There is evidence of the persistence of German law, custom, and psychology in far southern Romance lands like lower Italy and Spain as late as the twelfth century. Extreme determinism one way or another is unhistorical in spirit in any endeavor to determine either the proportion of the elements of composition or the degree of fusion of them.

The problem of interpretation is made the greater because of the fact that the documentary material available is very scant and the meaning of it is often obscure. The technical difficulties in the way of understanding the little which we have to read are great. Unfortunately for the

[1] *English Historical Review,* XVI, 750.

early centuries, the sources are sparse and not explicit enough for us to get a clear idea of the economic life of the time. Moreover these sources are almost all of ecclesiastical origin, and we do not get a corresponding view of secular economic conditions. So far as German sources are concerned, some assistance may be derived from the study of later Teutonic law, notably that of the Norse and Danes. But perhaps the greatest help has come from the study of modern survivals of medieval rural practices. By a process of inverse reasoning much new understanding of old ways has been achieved. Peasant folk as a class are proverbially conservative and tenacious of ancient custom. Europe even today abounds with medieval agricultural survivals in many rural areas, especially where modern industrialism and commercialism have not invaded, and where the people still are customarily and habitually a farming community, which has preserved its almost primitive simplicity. Not only the continuity of these habits, but the tenacity with which the peasantry of Europe has clung to the ancestral soil, in spite of all the changes and vicissitudes experienced since the Middle Ages terminated, has been recently strikingly shown. A German historian discovered a family near Osnabrück, which was still living on the "old farm," the farm in this instance being over six hundred years old. Some time ago the French government announced that it would decorate with the Order of Agricultural Merit all those who could produce documentary evidence that their families had farmed the same land continuously for at least three hundred years. This brought forth nearly 750 such families, the record being held by a family of Coutie near Molières which had dwelt on the same land since the eighth century. Seebohm has described the

picture of open field husbandry as one still gets it from the height above the old Roman town of Andernach, looking down upon the flat plain bounded by the wide sweep of the Rhine and stretching away into the far distance like a great map. Or going farther into the heart of central Europe the same may be said of the view from the tower of Ulm cathedral (minster) over the rich Bavarian corn-fields. . . . Over a large part of continental Europe in French, German, and Slavonic countries it is still more or less a living system. . . . The system has in many places left indelible marks on the ground which will remain for centuries longer, and perhaps forever, to tell of its existence in the past.[2]

Nothing exactly similar to the manor is to be found in the tribal arrangements of the Celts. The medieval manor was of mixed Romano-German origin with perhaps vestigial remains of earlier agricultural and village practices occasionally woven in. A consideration of the Roman villa, accordingly, is our first interest.

[2] *Customary Acres, 3.*

The Roman villa was a great farm owned by a rich landed proprietor, on which were villages of both slaves and servile dependents (*coloni*) who worked the fields for him and got little more than subsistence for their labor. The slave was a chattel. The serf was a former freeman sunk to economic dependence and bound to the glebe from generation to generation by arrear of rent which while theoretically acquitable, never was acquitted since it accumulated with every day and the day's work merely discharged the current rent and subsistence given him for the support of himself and his family. He was a prisoner for debt, working off but never canceling the obligation by his daily toil in the open air upon the lord's lands. His holding was called a tenure (from Latin *tenere,* "to hold"), but in law the tenure held the serf, not the serf the tenure. It fixed his status legally as a bondman, and socially as a dependent. The portion of the villa, which the lord continued to farm directly by slaves [3] was known as the lord's demesne. But as slavery in Europe—but not the slave trade—declined, it came to pass that the demesne also in course of time was farmed by the serfs, labor for a certain number of days in the season upon the demesne being required of each serf in addition to that labor exacted of his own tenure.

"The Roman villa presents all the chief features of the medieval manor. The lord's demesne acted as a centre round which the coloni clustered; cultivators who did not divide their tenancies because they did not own them." [4] The village (*vicus*) had no political identity, being merely an agglomeration of houses within the area of the town (*municipium* or *civitas*) until the collapse of the Roman provincial administration released the patrimonial proprietor from that superior political control. Then, and then only, may one say that the Roman manor became "both a possessory and an administrative unit." It may be doubted, however, whether the pure type of Roman manor existed anywhere in Europe outside of Italy and southern Gaul. Rome never was actuated by a mania to enforce perfect uniformity and was tolerant of local customs and conditions. Earlier traditions and survivals lingered obstinately. "It would not have been possible for the Romans even if they had wished, to change the whole character of the cultivation, and override all the natural tendencies of the northern cultivation." [5]

In the provinces of the Rhine and the Danube German agricultural practice naturally tended to fuse with Roman ways. How prevalent the Roman system was in these regions is difficult to determine. The *Notitia dignitatum,* compiled in the fourth century, shows that Roman sway once extended to a distance of eighty leagues beyond the Rhine,

---

[3] When we find slaves in the high manorial period, they are usually household servants, not farm laborers.
[4] Vinogradoff, *Origin of the Manor,* 33.
[5] *Economic Review,* XV, 395.

so that it must have reached almost to Fulda, and we know that this régime endured there over 250 years. One must be cautious in forming too exclusive a judgment either in favor of Roman continuity within the zone of early Barbarian occupation, or in favor of the supremacy of German village institutions and farming practices. There is evidence that Roman methods of farming and customary habits survived in northern Europe even when the imperial organism had wasted away and dissolved. Roman patrimonial proprietors continued to farm their acres after the Barbarian invasions had spent their force, and the Church, the greatest land-owner and the most Roman institution in both organization and spirit, not only survived intact but actually increased in power in the fifth, sixth, and seventh centuries. The communal system of the Germans (if it ever was communal) tended to give way to the more profitable rural economy known to the Romans and practised by the Church. The result may have been economically advantageous, but it was at the cost of personal freedom.

What did the Germans bring in and add in the way of village life and agriculture? The Germans were tribes of nobles and freemen—they had some slaves but nothing approaching the proportion found in the Roman Empire, and translated to Roman soil the ancient free (so one says) German village community, which became a servile village community after the German conquests in the fifth and sixth centuries. If this supposition is true, then the free village community—the German *Mark*—must later have sunk to serfdom, unless, as is contended by other scholars, the Germans in the mass were not free but dependent even in their homeland, and merely transferred the German servile village and villagers to Roman soil. We have already seen when this process of degradation appeared and seen the nature of the "forces at work capable of transmuting a village full of free landholders into a manor full of villeins." The great factors were the civil wars of the Merovingian epoch, the heavy weight of compulsory military service in the time of Charlemagne, the wars, anarchy, invasion, feudal violence in the ninth century when small freemen were compelled to seek the protection of the great proprietors even at the price of loss of freedom, or as often happened, were deprived of liberty and reduced to serfdom on their own acres by a land-hungry baronage. Thus the serf of Roman origin found a fellow in misery of German origin in the ninth century and the two classes and the two conditions were blended into one, dwelling together in a social unit called a manor (*mansus*),[6] itself an institution blended out of Roman and German ingredients. The Roman villa and the enserfed German village community have not merely an analogy; the two separate and different forms tended to blur and to blend into a single composite economic and social group. The history of the Ger-

6 The word *mansus*, from Latin *manere*, first appears in the seventh century.

manic origin of the manorial system begins with a more or less free and lordless village community which by a process somewhat complex yet now fairly clear, was, in slow and perhaps disconnected stages of depression, converted into a wholly dependent manorial group between the sixth and ninth centuries. If the co-villagers of the *Mark* were free before this process overcame them, then the reduction of this class to the condition of a servile tenantry must have entailed a profound economic and social revolution.

From this sphere of interesting but perplexing theory we may now pass to things which are of a more concrete nature in medieval village economy. If the reader will carefully examine the map of a representative medieval manor,[7] and then in imagination take his stand in the heart of a typical medieval village, he will find himself in the roadway running across the manor in the midst of an agglomeration of thatched cottages huddled closely together, the "nucleated" village, yet with space enough around the houses for a patch of vegetables, a chicken yard, a cow byre or stable, a hayrick. A stream rising from a spring in the woods runs through the village transversely to the road and terminates in a pond with marshy edges, which is the village duck-pond. From the marsh extends the meadow, perhaps a natural one, perhaps redeemed from the marsh by drainage. Across the road lies the lord's demesne, the best farm land in the village, and on a knoll above it, the fairest site in the village, stands the lord's castle, if the manor be a large one; or a less imposing manor-house, if it be a small manor, with a barn and cattle shed adjacent. Hard by it is the little church with a tiny burying ground and the house of the priest. But where are the fields of the villagers? One observes that there are lanes or cart roads spreading fanwise from the village, and following one of these for a distance of half a mile, it may be, or more, one finds the fields. Exclusive of the lord's demesne, all the arable land of the village is comprised in three separate great blocks, the spring planting ground, the autumn planting ground and the fallow. This is the "three-field system." If the hay has been gathered the cattle are feeding in the meadow. If not, stones or stakes indicate each villager's portion in the hay lot. These "lot meadows" persisted until late in many parts of Europe. At any rate the cattle are pretty sure to be grazing on the young grass of the fallow, and if the harvest is gathered, they may be grazing on the stubble. If it is early autumn the men will be plowing for the winter wheat.

The two-field system had been the Roman practice and was universal among the Germans. But at some unknown time, probably in the eighth century (the earliest evidence which we possess upon the origin of the three-field system is in the year 771), a revolutionary change began to

---

[7] The best example may be found in Shepherd's *Historical Atlas*, p. 104; this is an indispensable book for every student of history.

come to pass. This was the transition from the two-field to the three-field system. Its early prevalence in High Germany and spread over the Rhinelands and northern and eastern Gaul and its adoption upon the lands of the Church and the Carolingian fisc would seem vaguely

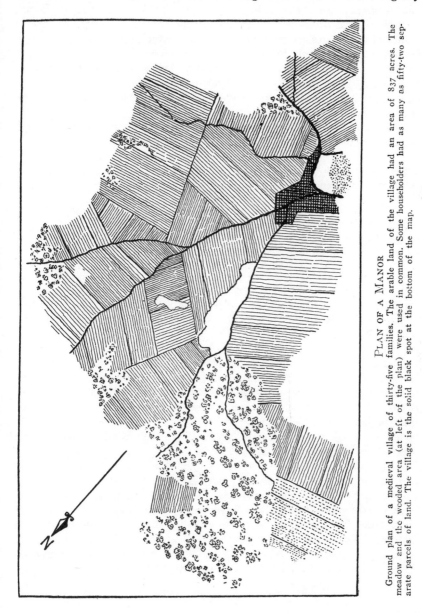

PLAN OF A MANOR

Ground plan of a medieval village of thirty-five families. The arable land of the village had an area of 837 acres. The meadow and the wooded area (at left of the plan) were used in common. Some householders had as many as fifty-two separate parcels of land. The village is the solid black spot at the bottom of the map.

to point to the Bonifacian monasteries in Hesse, like Fulda and Hersfeld, as the probable place of origin. We know that St. Boniface was instrumental in instituting the tithe in the Frankish Church, and that the heavy burden of it created great distress and complaint even before Charlemagne's time. It is a keen suggestion of Meitzen that the introduction of the three-field system was due "to the pressure of heavy manorial and ecclesiastical rents and tithes, which required that a large amount of grain should be raised." But, abandoning conjecture for facts, we can have no doubt of the enormous economic advancement implicit in this change. The discovery that wheat or rye might be sown in autumn as well as in spring, thus giving two yields where one had been had before, is undoubtedly one of the most beneficial discoveries in the progress of man. Professor Gras,[8] has strikingly shown the superiority of the three-field system over the two-field system.

Let us compare [he says] the two systems on a manor containing 1800 acres of arable land. In the two-field system we would have:

900 acres (arable plowed once)................	900
900 " (fallow " twice)	1800
Total acres of plowing	2700

In the three-field system we would have:

600 acres (winter grain plowed once)...........	600
600 " (spring " " ")	600
600 " (fallow " " twice)	1200
Total acres of plowing	2400

Thus in the two-field system we get only 900 acres of crops for 2700 acres of plowing, whilst in the three-field system we get 1200 acres of crops for 2400 acres of plowing.

The alternation was now spring planting, autumn planting, fallow, in three separate arable areas, or a rotation of two crops and a fallow. It is certain that this new practice does not reflect tribal usages, and may not be said to be either of Roman or of German origin, but was rather the development out of agricultural experience and observation. While never universal, for the older practice still was followed, the new system was widely adopted in the Middle Ages.

Although seldom noticed in works upon medieval civilization, unless of a specifically economic nature, there is no doubt that the introduction of the three-field system constitutes one of the greatest medieval advances over antiquity and is a very valuable and unique contribution to civilization. The first tract was planted with wheat or rye in the autumn and harvested in the ensuing summer; the second tract was planted with oats, barley, and pease in the spring and was harvested also in the following summer. The third was left fallow. Thus two-thirds was made prof-

[8] *History of Agriculture*, 48.

itable each year and one-third allowed to rest and utilized for pasture in supplement to the meadow after the hay had been gathered in. Barley, it may be said, was the "drink" grain used for making beer, and many a manor had a local brew-house.

Far more remarkable, however, than the three-field system, interesting as that is, is the way in which the arable area was divided in strips among the villagers, and the combination of individual ownership with coöperative (or collective?) labor.[9]

Whether this arrangement was of communal origin, or was at first a peculiar form of coöperative (or collective?) village enterprise combined with ownership in severalty, from any point of view the open-field system possessed a distinctive character not found in the farming habits of Roman or Celt or Slav. And it is all the more amazing when one reflects upon the persistence of this form of farm in scattered strips around a village. For it still survives in parts of continental Europe. An English observer has written:

At the present day the country, viewed from the rising ground to the south of St. Omer, presents the appearance of an irregularly checkered board; the various crops are cultivated often in—to English eyes—incredibly small areas. . . . The *maire* (mayor) of Eperlecques at the present time (1913) works a farm of about 92 "measures"; it is in 45 to 50 pieces, and the most distant piece is 3½ kilometres from his house.[10]

Decomposition of the manor seems to have been aggravated by those same forces of disintegration which prevailed in the feudal world. Just as the Carolingian Empire in the ninth century was broken into kingdoms, the kingdoms into duchies, counties, viscounties, chatellanies, etc., so the forces which wrought the destruction of the State percolated downwards and decomposed the manor, the lowest cell in the social structure. The break-up of the great manors into small manors in the ninth century and the tendency toward splitting of tenures were part of the process of decomposition of the Frankish Empire. Military necessity already in Charlemagne's time had compelled the fractioning of freeholds. The process was intensified during the ninth century, so much so that Charles the Bald in 864 forbade, but unavailingly, further subdivision.

[9] The existence of much strictly private ownership of property in land among the early Germans is not denied by competent students from Tacitus downward. The question is whether ever, and if so to what degree, communal ownership in land existed among the early Germans. Under the early Carolingians it is indisputable that there was private property in the hide lands everywhere. There is no necessary connection between common fields and joint-plowing. Coaration never universally obtained, and where it is found the practice seems to have been due to peculiar local conditions. (See Kovalevsky, I, p. 267.)

[10] Coopland, *The Abbey of St. Bertin.*

Fractional holdings of many degrees, halves, quarters, eighths, six-teenths, are common, even usual in the high manorial age.

In the surface and lineal measurements of the plowlands of the medieval manor we find the historical origin of our system of land survey. The man who follows the plow or who sows grain naturally treads out the measurement of his acres. He measures by his tread the length of the furrow or the amount of seed he scatters. His double-tread will average five feet; two or three double-treads made a rod. In Bavaria the rod was ten feet, in England, fifteen; in Normandy the acre was twice the size of an English acre; a Bavarian acre was two-thirds of an English acre; a quarter-acre was called a rood, but a rood in Normandy was equal to a half-acre in England. A virgate or yardland was one-quarter of a plowland, or thirty acres. The acre was the unit of cul-tivation, the unit of a day's work with the plow, and its long and narrow shape, 4 rods wide and 40 rods long, was determined by the actual convenience of the implement employed. Since plowing was done in long furrows, when the plowman had turned the "stubborn glebe" for 40 rods, or one furlong (*i.e.* one furrow-long), he turned and went back. Long experience showed that an average morning's labor could plow a piece of land measuring 4 by 40 rods, and hence the acre or *morgen-land, i.e.,* one morning's land. At the rate of 72 furrows to the acre a team would normally cover nine miles in a day's work. Plowing was fin-ished at noon, for in the afternoon the oxen had to be sent to pasture.

These medieval village measurements naturally passed into units of survey. As Seebohm has said:

> When the villagers came out to play on the stubbles, it was easy for them to choose an acre-strip to throw their ball across from balk to balk. The exact width of the statute acre, 22 yards, is now the cricket pitch. For practice with the long bow Henry VIII decreed that the shortest butts should be a furlong, eleven score, or exactly the acre's length. The stade was a furrow before it was a footrace, and the length of the furrow and back again still survives with us as a standard race in the quarter-mile.

Under manorial conditions, the village preserved its ancient practices, although of course its doings were subject to the lord's regulation. There is a remarkable example preserved in a document of the year 957 in which the serfs of the abbey of St. Mihiel functioning as a village com-munity, without interference on the part of the abbot, laid out the arable area of the village according to the three-field system, apportioned the lots in the hay meadow, located the village site, marked off the demesne of the lord-abbot, built a market hall, set the boundaries of the common waste and woods, etc. The very existence of evidence like this shows that even under serfdom some degree of liberty and local self-government might remain, although of course the exercise of it was by grace of the lord and could not be exacted as a right.

In contrast with this remarkably kindly and intelligent abbot, we may cite the atrocious reduction of the free peasantry of the village of Wolen in what is now the Swiss canton of Soleure in 1038. The peasants of this region were still largely free in the eleventh century. But feeling the need of protection the villagers of Wolen appealed to a neighboring lord named Guntran, who betrayed the trust reposed in him by promptly reducing them to serfdom. When Henry III of Germany visited this corner of his Empire these poor people in vain sought to get a hearing. They could not get through the crowd of nobles and officials around him, and their uncouth dialect and countrified manners offended the aristocratic pride of the king's entourage. The domain thus created by violence and fraud passed in 1106 to the abbey of Muri, in which an honest monk found the documents of this incident.

Whether the manor was a village of formerly free peasants who had been reduced to serfdom, or a servile community from the beginning—although some free persons were nevertheless to be found in the system in spite of the prevalence of subordination—there were two agrarian elements fused together in the composition of a manor; viz., the village community and "the home estate of the lord tacked on to this settlement." For before the lord became a village proprietor he was already a domanial proprietor with some hereditary serfs to work his fields. This explains why in every manor of the high feudal period the lord's demesne —sometimes called "inland"—was sharply set off from the tenures, and perhaps why also the lord possessed slices of demesne intermixed with the strips of the villagers. These slices of demesne separate from the body of the demesne may have been "a vestige of original tribute imposed by the lord." The fully realized manor, therefore, was the union of a manorial estate (villa) with an enserfed village community (mark). The former free peasantry was converted into a servile one; the lord's court supplanted the ancient mark moot; the enterprises of the villagers, as in time past, still persisted because the fundamental economic functioning of the village had not been altered by depression from freedom to serfdom; but these activities were now compulsory services imposed by the lord. The organic interlocking of peasant village and lord's demesne made the manor. There is evidence of the prefeudality of many manorial institutions. Predial services, a wide variety of rights in common, the distinction between demesne land and land in service, the free tenant, all are to be found in the eighth century. Base tenants who were not personal slaves appear long before the feudal age, being increased from above by commendation of freemen, and from below by emancipation.

The distinction between the demesne of the lord and the tenures of the serfs appears as early as the Allemannic and Bavarian codes, and is manifest for Austrasia in the Frankish capitularies. The *corvée,* or forced labor, is found in the German codes. Evidently we here have a clue to the approximate time of formation of the manorial system, whose slow extension and fixation continued from the sixth to the ninth century, and by 900 had become coextensive with central and western Europe. The crying need of protection during the ninth century, when Norsemen, Magyars, and Arab pirates ravaged Europe and the breakdown of the Frankish Empire made the establishment of strong local authority necessary, gave the manorial régime its fixity and crystallized its institutions. The walled manor-house or castle with the village huddled close beneath it then became typical and emblematic of the time.

There were actually seven different kinds of land in a typical manor, as a study of the map will show: (1) the lord's demesne, which was strictly his own and was farmed partly by special serfs of the demesne and partly by the serfs of the village, whose service was exacted; (2) the lord's *close,* which was a portion of the demesne rented out to villein or tenant farmers; (3) the *tenures* of the serfs of the manor, scattered in strips of virgate or yardland over the three areas of arable land; (4) the hay meadow; (5) the woods; (6) the waste; (7) the domain of the parish priest, or "God's piece" as it was sometimes called. Such glebe land might be either in a single area or in strips amid the village plowlands, like the demesne strips of the lord. It, too, was worked by the peasantry for the priest.

The buildings belonging to the lord consisted of a manor-house and a grange. The manor-house contained at least three principal rooms: the hall, the dormitory, and the solar or parlor or logia. We have a lengthy description of a wooden manor-house built by Arnold II of Ardres for his wife Gertrude.

There were three stories so that like the sun it appeared to be suspended in the air. The cellar was a spacious place where were great woven baskets, wide-mouthed jars, and barrels, and other domestic utensils. The first floor contained a great living-room, with a huge fireplace, pantries, cupboards, the bedchamber of the lord and his wife, near to which was a lavatory and servants' rooms, and a room or dormitory for the boys. The reception hall, which was called a logia, where visitors were received, was also used as an oratory or chapel. The kitchens were on two levels; on the lower, pigs were roasted, geese, capons, and other birds killed and prepared for eating. On the other floor of the kitchen other provisions were cooked, and here were prepared most delicious viands for the lord, by means of many cooking vessels, and by laborious scraping and paring prepared for eating.

On the upper floors were various rooms connected by passages or halls.

The furniture of the manor-house was scanty. Glass windows were rare; a table put on trestles, a few forms and stools or a long bench stuffed with straw or wool, with one or two chairs and a chest or two of linen, formed the hall furniture. A brass pot or two for boiling and two or three brass dishes; a few wooden platters and trenchers or more rarely of pewter, an iron or leather candlestick, a kitchen knife or two, a box or bowl for salt, and a brass ewer or basin, formed the moveables of the house. . . . The dormitory contained a rude bed and but rarely sheets and blankets, for the gown of the day was generally the coverlet at night.[11]

No estimate can be made of the size of a manor. We have not sufficient data to determine the "average." The system was neatest and best in abbatial lands. But the admirable cartularies of the abbeys show that no uniformity of size existed and that areas varied greatly. A manor had no fixed or customary extent. It was neither more nor less irregular in this particular than an American farm. It must have been much greater, though, than the average modern farm. A manorial village with less than ten families is almost inconceivable. In statistics gathered from Domesday we find 14 manors with 32 households, 14 others with 14 households, and a third group of 14 with 11 households. At such a rate and with each tenure forming thirty acres, the smallest manor would have had 350 to 550 acres at the least, without including meadow, woods, and waste, and the lord's demesne. There must have been many manors much larger than this. Generally they were fairly compact in arrangement. But in cases where old Celtic tribal survivals may have been incorporated, or in which the manor had been formed by the agglomeration of fragments of a broken Roman villa, the manor may have had a somewhat loose arrangement and have seemed to sprawl awkwardly over the land. The village bounds of many a European hamlet today quite accurately correspond to the extent of the former medieval manor from which the village has sprung, and very few such hamlets are less than a thousand acres in area. As the maxim of feudalism was "No lord without land, no land without lord," a lord with but one manor must have been of the lowest rank in the feudal hierarchy. The great nobles —dukes, counts, and even viscounts—were possessed of hundreds of manors, while churches and monasteries numbered them by thousands.

The "domain" of a noble (not to be confused with "demesne") was the whole body of manors which he possessed, whether many or few, large or small. In the case of the king these domains were called crown lands and collectively known as the fisc. They were not always, perhaps not usually, contiguous, but scattered over an entire province or fief, the lord's vassals sometimes possessing manors intermingled with those of their suzerain. Many of the land transfers of the Middle Ages were

[11] Thorold Rogers, *Work and Wages.*

made as the result of effort upon the part of nobles, bishops, abbots to acquire contiguous manors by purchase or exchange. Cases of knights and small nobles possessing but a single manor must not have been rare. Thus Tancred of Hauteville, the sire of the famous family of that name, was a knight owning only a single manor near Coutances in Normandy.

Custom, which in this case was nothing but necessity hardened into tradition, required simultaneous and often coöperative work in the common tasks of the manor. The peasants plowed at the same time, sowed at the same time, reaped at the same time. But coaration applied only to the lord's demesne, not to the peasants' own lands. It was not always done in the same way. On some manors the whole demesne was plowed by the full team of all the oxen of the peasants; on others a part of the demesne was allotted to each peasant to plow. Grain was cut with a sickle, a slow and back-breaking process. We hear much complaint of the peasant who filched his neighbor's grain in harvest time by surreptitiously reaching across the line and seizing a handful in the parallel strip belonging to his neighbor; or of one who stole a breadth from his neighbor's field by secret use of the spade; or who moved the stones or stakes used as landmarks to get a few inches more of hay. A common and significant village regulation was that no one might go to the field in harvest time before sunrise, or after sunset, whether with or without a cart. Threshing was done either by treading out the grain with oxen as described in Scripture, or by beating it with flails and winnowing it in the wind—a task often performed by the women and children.

There never was any question as to the prior rights of the lord's demesne. It had always to be plowed first, sowed first, and reaped first. Frequently the peasants must have had to desert their own fields when they needed attention most, because the lord demanded their services. If a storm came up and the crop was endangered it was the lord's crop that was saved. The same "right of way" was enjoyed by the lord when selling his produce. His grain, his wine, his stock went to market first. When the serf died the lord was entitled to the best ox and the best sheep which he left and which he took as a *heriot,* or inheritance tax.

The meadow had a dignity unknown to us today, for the reason that it was the only source of hay production. Grass-seeding and the introduction of the various clovers was not known until the seventeenth century. Until the discovery that grass-seed could be gathered and that the great trefoils were of nutritive value to the soil, meadow hay was the only hay there was. Naturally the supply was limited, for only the low-lying moist land belonging to the village could produce it. Moreover, since there was no rotation of crops in the meadow, the soil gradually became exhausted. The influence of hay on history is a very positive one, though its importance has been but slightly perceived by historians of agriculture. It has been statistically proved that in the Middle Ages meadow land, in comparison with arable land, was five times as valuable as it is today. Nowadays a farmer grows hay where he wishes, and grows as much or as little as he chooses. In medieval times the quantity of hay was seriously limited in every village community, and the quality of it, owing to the law of diminishing returns, tended to deteriorate.

The staple grains were wheat (but rye in Germany), oats, barley. Flax was raised in certain regions where water conditions favored it, and hemp was sometimes cultivated. Spelt was a cereal intermediate between wheat and barley. Common vegetables were turnips, beans, peas, onions, cabbage, kohlrabi, parsley, garlic, sage, celery. Among fruits we find apples, pears, quinces, plums, cherries. Berries do not seem to have been cultivated, but wild ones were picked. The walnut tree was common and in the south of Europe the vine and olive were universal. The grape, however, was widely grown and ranged much farther north in the Middle Ages than today. Vine culture represented the highest and most differentiated form of agriculture. Domestic animals and fowls were as those we know except for the turkey. The hog was the commonest farm animal. Pigeons were bred by the lords, but forbidden to the peasantry. Bees were raised everywhere. In fact, the economic dignity of the bee was very great in medieval times. It supplied the only form of sweetening except fruit syrup; the consumption of wax for seals and candles in the churches was enormous. Beehives were often specifically disposed of by will and even enfeoffed—a fact which speaks volumes for the value put upon bees. Oxen were far more used on the farm than horses. They were cheaper to keep and less liable to disease, besides providing beef when they got old. The cattle, however, were light and scrubby and weighed much less than draught oxen of later centuries. Unless in milk the cows grazed in the waste and along the forest edge. The hogs ran wild. Both of these animals could fairly well fend for themselves, but sheep, owing to their timidity and habit of "milling" together, were an easy prey to wolf and marauder. With the little hay produced, the difficulty of wintering stock was great. It was fed almost wholly on straw and tree loppings, and cattle were often so thin in the spring that they could not walk and had to be carried out into the meadow. It was the common practice at the beginning of winter to kill and salt all save those needed for draught purposes and breeding. As to milk, there was precious little of it. Even in the thirteenth century, when farming methods had improved, Walter of Henley, an English farmsteward who wrote a famous agricultural treatise, expected only three and one-half pounds of butter per week from three cows. Most milk was used to make cheese. The customary farm implements were: the plow, a cumbrous affair without iron save at the point; the harrow, often a thorn tree weighted down with a log upon it; spades, shovels, mattocks, picks, scythes, sickles, flails, beetles for breaking clods, crowbars, axes, augers, adzes, etc.

The life of the villagers was the hard, monotonous life of a farmer unrelieved by modern machinery. The hard and sometimes brutal conditions under which the peasantry lived dulled and deadened their sensibilities in a way which would shock us today. Even the most essential amenities of modern life were ignored. When the weather was very hot men often worked stark naked side by side with women in the fields. Philip of Harvengt tells how in summer he "saw most of the peasants on market day walking about in the streets and on the square of the village without a vestige of clothing on, not even trousers, in order to keep cool. Thus naked they attended to their business. When some monks who were shocked at the sight indignantly protested, they roughly answered: 'What business is it of yours?' "

The cottages of the peasantry were all of wood or wattle with thatched roofs and without chimneys, so that it was impossible for each cottager to bake his own bread in the house. Cooking in summer was chiefly done out-of-doors at the door-front, and in winter on the earth floor of the cottage, the smoke getting out of the door, when opened, or a hole in the roof, and always blinding the wretched occupants of the house. The medieval peasant had no artificial light in his one-room shack with a clay floor. Fagots as torches were dangerous, for the thatch might catch fire; candles he could not afford. Moreover, he had nothing to do after dark. He could not work. He could not read, for he had no books and did not know how to read, even if he had had a book. Consequently he and his wife and children went to bed at sunset. But what a bed! It was merely a heap of straw in the corner, alive with vermin and often damp. He slept in his clothes. Yet we are tempted to exaggerate the hardships on the medieval peasant, as we shall see later on.

The industrial life of a normal manor (for although infinite variety of customary practices prevailed, the variations were generally differences of degree rather than of kind) has been described by Karl Buecher as follows:

Under this system the small land-owner supervises in person, the large land-owner through an overseer. The demesne land lying immediately about the manor-house is cultivated by serfs permanently attached to it, who there find food and lodging, and are employed in agricultural and industrial production, household duties, and the personal service of the lord, under a many-sided division of labor. The demesne land is intermixed with the holdings of a larger or smaller number of unfree peasants, each of whom tills his "hide" of land independently, while all share with the lord the use of pasture, wood, and water. At the same time, however, every peasant-holding binds its occupant to perform certain services and to furnish certain dues in natural products to the estate. These services consist of labor reck-oned at first according to requirement, later according to time, whether given in the fields at seed-time or harvest, on the pasture-land, in the vineyard, garden, or forest, or in the manorial workshops or the women's building where the daughters of the serfs are spinning, weaving, sewing, baking, brewing beer, etc. On the 'days devoted to manorial service the unfree la-borers receive their meals at the manor-house just as do the manor-folk themselves. They are further bound to keep in repair the enclosures about the manor-house and its fields, to keep watch over the house, and to under-take the carrying of messages and the transport of goods. The dues in kind to be paid to the estate are partly agricultural products, such as grain of all kinds, wool, flax, honey, wax, wine, cattle, hogs, fowl, or eggs; partly wood cut in the forests of the mark and made ready for use, such as fire-wood, timber, vine-stakes, torch-wood, shingles, staves and hoops; partly the products of industry, such as woolen and linen cloth, stockings, shoes, bread, beer, casks, plates, dishes, goblets, iron, pots and knives. This pre-supposes a certain specialization of industry in supplying commodities. Intermediate between service and rent are duties of various kinds, such as hauling manure from the peasant's farm to the fields of the lord, keeping cattle over winter, providing entertainment for the guests of the manor. On the other hand the lord renders economic assistance to the peasant by keeping breeding-stock, by establishing ferries, mills, and ovens for general use, by securing protection from violence and injustice to all, and by giving succor from his stores, in accordance with his pledge, when crops fail or other need arises.[12]

We thus have here a small economic organism fairly sufficient in it-self, which avoids the rigid concentration of the ancient Roman slave estates; which is able to secure to each peasant a separate cottage and fields for his own family needs, and therewith a certain personal in-dependence.

The self-sufficiency of the manor, while never whole and complete, for salt, iron, and millstones especially had to be brought in from the outside, was a real actuality in the depth of the feudal age. The idea that the great estates employed "negotiators" to purchase outside com-modities and to market the surplus of the manor is not tenable. Every manor produced and manufactured its own staple necessities. There was little local market for wheat and other cereals except in time of famine, or for wine, beer, wool, linen, leather, furs, etc. These things were made upon the manor and consumed upon the manor.

The character of the occupations of the medieval peasantry and their seasonal nature has been preserved for us in many a quaint illustration found in medieval calendars, the ancestors of our modern farmer's almanac, and may be read by every observant tourist in the carvings of many a cathedral, as in the great doorway of Amiens cathedral which

[12] Buecher, *Industrial Evolution*, pp. 103–105.

so manifestly was erected amid an agricultural community. Millet's picture, the Angelus, illustrates the part the village evening bell played in every hamlet. The speech of the medieval peasant was racy with figures derived from his daily life. There is sometimes interesting psychology in these expressions. The English peasant called his field his "plowland" or his "furrows." The German peasant called it *Morgen-land,* or *Tag-werk,* (day's-work), in both terms the element of time being the factor rather than the work itself, or *Gewende* (from *wenden,* "to turn"), in allusion to the plow-turns. The end of the plowland where the team was turned in the furrow was always the last part plowed, and was sometimes called a "headland." It marked the term of the day's work. "So this last work of the jaded plowman and worn-out oxen at the end of the season became the familiar symbol of the last struggle at the end of a life of toil. The Breton peasant nearing his end with labored breath is said to be 'plowing his headlands.' "

We are not to think of the social structure of a manor as consisting of a series of superimposed "layers," one over another. The word "texture" better describes the condition, for the classes were intricately interwoven one with another and formed a compact social group, although of variegated pattern. The meanest class were slaves. But slavery so rapidly declined in medieval Europe after the eighth century that by the year 1000 it was practically negligible as an institution. The few slaves which are found are not field laborers but household servants. The practices of manorial economy were repugnant to the perpetuation of slavery in Europe. Of the total dependent population upon the crown lands of England when the Domesday survey was made (1086) only nine per cent was slave. Slavery gradually declined in medieval Europe not because of humanitarian feeling, or a new conscience, but because its prevalence was incompatible with the economic condition and social structure of the time. Even southern Europe gradually reduced slavery and went over to serfdom instead, substituting "the Germanic code which was the outgrowth of serf economy for the classic law of Rome that was the product of slavery. . . . By the twelfth century Roman jurisprudence and the books of Justinian had fallen into oblivion in Italy and the code of the Lombards held full sway." The later revival of the Roman law was due to wholly new and different economic conditions.

Status and tenure were so interwoven in lower medieval society that it is impossible to consider social texture apart from the nature of the tenure. Broadly speaking the body of the folk upon a medieval manor was composed of serfs and villeins. These two classes of dependents differed in historical origin, in social status, and in economic condition. The original body of serfs was descended historically from the Roman *colonus* and the German *litus, i.e.,* the two classes of servile farming tenantry familiar to the later Roman Empire. The fiction of the law—which technically regarded him—was that the serf was personally free but economically a bondman. But during the Carolingian epoch the old servile class was clearly increased by the depression of many freemen to a state of serfdom, which thus included not only those without property but also those whose property was too small for support of themselves and their families. Every freeman living on seigniorial land sank to inferior condition. These "poor freemen" (*pauperes liberi*) differed little from actual serfs and ultimately were blended with them. Not theories of law, but kind of tenure and services exacted, conditioned status. A cartulary of the ninth century shows us three sorts of serfs, a *colonus,* a *litus,* and a servile freeman, dwelling upon the same manor.

Superficially it may seem that the lot of the serf hardly differed from that of the slave. But this is not true. The slave was a chattel and could be bought and sold like cattle. The serf could not be sold off the land; if the manor were sold he went with it to a new manorial lord. Thus the serf possessed a patrimony, or rather it possessed him, for he was an inseparable portion of it. Moreover, the serf enjoyed a family relation unknown to slavery; his wife and children are frequently mentioned in documents. It is true, however, that until relatively late in the Middle Ages he could not marry without his lord's consent, nor marry a woman outside of the manorial community without permission, and that he had to pay a fee when he so married (*formariage*). The earliest instance of the prohibition of *formariage* is in the letters of Gregory I. Mixed marriages were at first rigorously forbidden, for they tended to break the social integrity and diminish the economic efficiency of the manor. But this rule could not be enforced. Natural and social inclinations were against it, and the Church's opposition to the rupture of the family by distributing the issue of mixed marriages between the manors of the lord of the husband and the lord of the wife finally secured the abolition of *formariage*.

At first glance it seems as though the establishment of feudalism aggravated the lot of the peasantry and made their condition worse than before. But there was a partial compensation for the economic exploitation which the peasantry suffered in the increased security which they had upon the manor, where it was to the interest of the lord to protect them and their property, and where the castle afforded some kind of shelter in case of violence from without. In the ninth and tenth centuries protection was more desirable than freedom. The rights which the fallen freeman lost were dear and empty rights by the time of Charlemagne, for they cost more than they were worth. So numerous were the emperor's wars, and all of them fought upon remote frontiers, that the burden of military service upon the freeman became more than he could sustain. By sinking to serfdom he was exempt from military service and could stay home, and the new manorial exactions which he bore were no greater than, if as great as, the burden of military service and the loss of time and produce he was liable to suffer owing to prolonged absence in spring and summer months, when his fields were to be plowed and seeded, and harvests garnered. The peasant's lot may even have been better in the ninth century under the new régime than under the older system. The cartularies show labor and toil, but they do not disclose dire hardship or poverty. An anecdote recorded by the Monk of St. Gall, who wrote about 884, shows that there were peasant plowmen then who sang to their oxen as they trod the furrow, as they still later did under more adverse conditions.

Serfdom and villeinage are often regarded as identical and often confused. Truth to tell, the distinction between the two classes is frequently difficult to establish. There were degrees of villeins, as there were of serfs; and the villein's status, like the serf's, was conditioned by the sort of tenure which he held. Tenures in rent were considered free tenures; tenures by work, servile tenures. The villein has been described as "the meanest of freemen." He might, too, be described as the most fortunate of serfs. We find a reflection of the difference between him and the serf in the English law which protected his life by a 200-shilling fine, while the serf's life was estimated at only 60 shillings. Historically the villein class is of later origin than the serf class. The latter, as has been said, reverts to Roman times. The villein, on the other hand, was a product of early feudal times when feudalism was inchoate and still in process of evolution. In England the villein first appeared during the transition from tribalism to feudalism before the Norman Conquest; on the Continent he was the victim of the dissolution of the Frankish monarchy and especially of the immunity, that institution which gave the rural domain its independence and autonomy, and which so weakened the power of the crown and so enlarged the essential traits of the manorial régime. The villeins were originally recruited from that group of very small free land-owners whose possessions were not large enough to make the great *fideles* seek their alliance as vassals, who were not strong enough in the anarchy of transition to maintain their lands without protection. They were of that class of small land-owners for whom Charlemagne had relaxed the burden of military service by providing that of two men having two manors each, one should equip the other, or of three men each of whom had a manor, two should equip the third, or five half-manor men should equip a sixth, etc. In a word, the villein was a former small free farmer above the condition of the inhabitant of a free village community, who under stress of circumstances surrendered ownership of his acres to some powerful landed neighbor. The latter annexed the little property to his own great manor (villa) and the former owner thereof sank to dependence and was fused socially with the servile village community, although he retained some vestige or reminiscence of his former position. "To have free land was all very well, but sometimes a feudal lord was a protection in troublous times."

Serfs might be made so *en masse* by reduction of an entire free village; villeins were made so individually by economic and social adversity. Tradition and custom protected the "free" villein from the worst abuses of serfdom. The very words sometimes used to describe them—*homines consuetudinarii*, men of the custumals—are indicative of this fact. The villein was not *taillable à merci*, that is to say, he could not be taxed without limit or beyond a fixed rate or amount; he could leave his personal property to his children; the terms of his tenure, however hard the conditions of its holding, were fixed by customary contract, not written, yet having the force of law; his labor could not be indiscriminately and almost boundlessly exploited like that of the serf. The villein was a perpetual tenant, but not in person bound to the glebe like the serf; his condition so to speak, was less *personal* than *real;* not because his father was a villein before him but because he held a villein tenure (land *in vilenagio*) was he a villein. The enfranchisement of the serfs, as we shall see, will go along the line of relief indicated by the status of the villein. For the tangency and even fusion of the two classes had the effect of adjusting things according to the higher rather than according to the lower condition. The villein pulled the serf up to his status and both together ultimately emerged into freedom. In the twelfth and thirteenth centuries many serfs became villeins by enfranchisement.

Villein tenure, while it seems analogous to the fief, must be sharply distinguished from it. The manorial world was the lower side of the feudal world. Politically a fief was a territory ruled by a noble who held it in vassalage under a superior noble. Economically a fief was an aggregation of "domains," and a domain was an aggregation of "manors." Every manor was a unit in a domain, and every domain was an entity in a fief. The lord was a noble of some degree, lower or higher; his tenantry on each and every manor were serfs and villeins. Their holdings were called *tenures*. As the peasants were non-noble, so their tenures were non-noble, whether servile or villein in nature and origin. In a single document of 1251 we find upon the same area three possessors holding under different titles: the suzerain, the vassal-in-chief, and the villein tenant.

When the free villein had performed his services and paid the taxes (*redevances*) imposed upon his tenure he had the full and entire disposal of it; theoretically he could alienate it, subject to payment of a fee to the lord, though in practice this rarely happened, for villein tenure inclined to be a perpetual relation and condition; moreover, the burdens were generally so heavy as to prevent a villein from getting ahead far enough to be so economically independent.

Another degree of villeinage comprised those unfortunate petty landowners who were unable to live an independent life, or whose alods were too small to support them, and who therefore surrendered the title to some proprietor—often a monastery—but continued to occupy them, paying quit rent (*cens, Zins*) therefor. These obligated themselves to the performance of certain manorial services, sank to inferior condition, became unfree villeins, and were blurred with serfs. A third class of villeins were those who rented land. For it not infrequently occurred that a noble having more land than he could work profitably with serf and unfree villein labor, would rent a tract of his land under contract to an industrious peasant. The terms of such holding were fixed with precision. The sources are silent on the villein's services, but he probably helped in spring and autumn plowing and in harvest time on the lord's demesne.

It is obvious that the free villein was a late evolution of manorial society, of emergence in the late twelfth and thirteenth century. Much still remains to be studied in the history of villeinage—its origins, its obligations, and above all the germs of freedom it contained. The legists of the thirteenth century wrote learnedly of the villein, but his legal status and his actual, historical condition by that time were widely different things.

Serfs and villeins were the two broadest and most numerous classes of manorial society. But, besides these two classes, we find many other classes of the peasantry which, all told, made a confusing variety of gradations; inferior dwellers having lots in the village of even less dimension than yardlands. Such were *colliberti*, borderers, crofters, cotters. The *collibertus* is one of the greatest puzzles in medieval history. The derivation of the word, from *cum* and *libertus*, conveys no suggestion and every opinion as to his origin and status is conjecture. He certainly had no relation to the *collibertus* of Roman times. Was he halfway between serfdom and villeinage? or between villeinage and freedom? Was he a superior type of serf? or a superior type of villein? Whatever opinion is held, it seems certain that he was in a condition to be envied by others below him and possessed of rights which he could maintain in a court of law. The famous process of the colliberts of St. Aubin d'Angers shows this much—even when we do not discover what the collibert was. Borderers were so called from their small holdings which bordered upon, but were not part of, the open fields. They were recruited probably from newcomers, men broken away from their former moorings owing to many adverse causes, war, abuse, famine, disaster like flood—the "wandering men" or *homines migrantes* of the codes—who drifted into the manor and were given leave to stay as *hospites* and permitted to break a new holding out of the waste on the edge of the manor. *Cottarii* and *bordarii* did not have "splinters of holdings" among the open fields, as, some historians have thought, but pieces of land along the margin of the manor, and probably were so poor that they were compelled to borrow a yoke of oxen from their neighbors or from the lord to do their plowing. Obviously such a small holding could not have supported them wholly, so that they eked out by outside work done for the lord or the richer peasants of the village. Crofters were men without any tenure at all, but possessed of a cottage with a tiny yard around it; cotters were wretchedly poor men who had merely a cottage—usually but a shack or shanty. These two classes worked as hired hands on the strips of the richer villeins, or did "chores" for the lord of the manor.

In all these various social degrees of the unfree, legal status was traversed by economic condition; the form of the tenure more than birth or previous condition determined the unfree man's position in the society of the manor and his daily manner of living. The mass of these intermediate social elements was sometimes denominated boors (*buri*). But the existence of these intermediate degrees which formed a heterogeneous blur is important, "and must tend to raise our estimate both of the legal freedom and of the economic welfare of the great mass of peasants."

Manorial life was not necessarily or always a wholly deadening life. The manor may not be regarded as a phenomenon of social decay. It had promise and potency in its make-up. A society never dissolves, nor does it utterly disappear. It does not die; it changes, it adjusts itself to meet new conditions, it is organic, it lives, it grows.

In spite of the fact that serfdom was an hereditary condition, that marriage of a freeman with a serf woman caused him to forfeit his freedom, that occupation of a servile tenure for a year and a day entailed loss of freedom by the free tenant, that warfare, punishment for crime, and spoliation often reduced poor freemen to servile condition, nevertheless a steady amelioration of servile conditions is observable straight through the feudal age. By the eleventh century serfs were giving way to tenants holding by lease. The rapid increase of Europe's population in the eleventh and twelfth centuries would have been impossible if the manorial system had been always and everywhere what it is often reputed to have been. Serfdom was rapidly on the wane in Europe after 1100. Predial serfdom could not survive the economic and social revolution which Europe by that time was experiencing. The word "serf" continued in use, but the condition of serfdom was one of steady amelioration even to disappearance. One gets the impression of general agrarian progress in Europe in the twelfth century. Doubtless the peasant's daily life was an arduous one, his social status a low one, and he was heavily taxed. But on the other hand he could not be wrested away from his home lot; and customary law, independently of written prescription, inclined more and more to protect him. The lord could not demand unlimited or impossible services. The peasant was bound to fixed requirements and to definite exactions, which were paid as rent.

We are in danger of underestimating the effect of custom in protecting the serf. An example will illustrate. It occurred as early as 905. The serfs of the monastery of St. Ambrose complained to the archbishop that the abbot subjected them to new and unusual *corvées*. The archbishop replied that as serfs they were required to pay what was imposed upon them. The serfs did not deny their servile condition, but continued to argue that the abbot had no right to impose new and unusual obligations. The archbishop made investigation and, finding things as the serfs alleged, ruled that the abbot must not go beyond custom and tradition in his exactions. There are examples of just and humane lords as of unjust and inhumane lords. There are instances of serfs refusing emancipation.

Fifty years ago the great French scholar Léopold Delisle protested against the false and sentimental representations of the romantic school of history with reference to the peasantry of the Middle Ages, and the researches of more modern scholars like Lamprecht, Henri Sée, and Vinogradoff go far to sustain Delisle's contention. The fact that the medieval peasant was without things we deem necessary to comfort does not prove that he was miserable. He knew no better comfort. As the late Sir William Ashley has written:

Doubtless the yardlings and cotters and craftsmen sometimes suffered from famines; doubtless their surroundings were often unsanitary. Still there was a standard of comfort which general opinion recognized as suitable for them and which prices were regulated to maintain. But now we are content that wages should be determined by the standard of comfort which a class can manage to maintain, left to itself, or rather, exposed to the competition of machinery and immigrant foreign labor.[13]

Serfdom had its advantages to the serf in the form of protection and support.

The lord was responsible for the fines of his serf; he might be called upon to pay his debts, and it was to his interest to see that his rural tenants were in good material condition. The dues of the serf when fixed were generally lower than those of freemen, their land was practically hereditary, divided as a matter of course amongst the male children. . . . Above all, the theory of serfdom was something very different from the practice. . . . There were many so-called questaux who were in a far better position than the study of servile reconnaissances would lead one to expect.[14]

[13] *Introduction to Economic History*, I, 139.
[14] Lodge, *The Estates of St. André de Bordeaux*, 96–97.

In his admirable study of the serfs of St. Bertin, Mr. Coopland observes:

How far was serfdom above slavery or below freedom? It is probably safer on the whole to deny the existence of any permanent level than to describe one which existed at a given moment and infer that it held good for centuries. There was in all likelihood no permanence from the ninth century onwards and the danger of the classic or standard descriptions is that they imply always some state which was permanent and uniform. . . . Nowhere is this danger greater than in that part of the standard description which states that the serf could be bought and sold, could be given or bequeathed, or enfranchised. What we may term the extreme view is that the serf, given or sold, was in the same position exactly as the modern tenant-farmer who changes masters. He has paid his rent to one; he now pays to another. This view has been ridiculed; it is not the whole truth, but contains at least part of the truth for which we are seeking.

Free tenants rapidly increased in the eleventh and twelfth centuries, when the proprietary class discovered it was more convenient and more profitable to allot holdings in rental than to exact fixed services or charges. The altered condition relieved them of the responsibility and vexation of supervising. The rent at first was paid in kind, but in the twelfth century, when a money economy began to prevail, payment often was in coin. Many of this new tenant class were recruited not from serfs who had passed into the renting class, but from the former alodial peasantry who had lost their ancestral holdings under pressure of war or economic adversity and so became a renting class instead of an owning class of small farmers.

Did any freehold or alodial owners survive in and through the manorial age? Yes, and in considerable masses in certain parts of Europe. In Saxony the free peasantry were not reduced to serfdom until the end of the eleventh century. In Tuscany, the mountainous or hilly nature of the country preserved very much of the local population from manorialization. Many freemen, too, survived in the mountainous parts of France, especially in Auvergne. The feudo-manorial régime was preëminently based upon an agricultural society, and where agricultural conditions were most favorable, there feudo-manorialism most obtained. Accordingly we find freemen also existing in considerable numbers in the marshes of Frisia and Ditmarsch. Naturally the manorial pressure upon such free groups was very great and most of the alodial class succumbed to it. Alodial owners were free from all feudal services, but with slight other protection than their own resources in case of war or usurpation. In Languedoc, in the south of France, we have an interesting record in the twelfth century of an alliance of freeholders to protect themselves and their lands against feudalization. This "society" is unique in medieval history. At least we have record of no other of similar nature. Broadly speaking, except for isolated places and cases, it may be said that the freeman class greatly diminished during the ninth and tenth centuries. The enormous growth of villeinage in this period points this way. An abbatial survey made in 812 enumerates 2080 colons, 220 serfs, 35 *liti,* and only 8 freemen. These figures are interesting as statistics. But the descriptive terminology of these classes is also of other interest. It shows that the peasantry, at least in Romance countries, was chiefly descended from Roman *coloni ingenui* (Roman freemen reduced to economic bondage) and not from the Roman slave class, and that the German *litus* of the later Roman Empire also contributed a portion. The villein is not yet apparent. Just as there were different degrees of serfs and villeins, so there were also social gradations among the free class. The *accolæ* and *hospites* were the "very dust of the free population." Where they survived "the lands of the simple freemen tended to be much smaller than those of the nobles. . . . A great quantity of them were tiny holdings, sometimes consisting of a few strips of arable land, a row or two of vines, or simply a house and garden, or a portion of one." But not even in the depth of the feudal age was the freeman wholly extinguished, and where he survived he was the freest of men. His land was non-noble, but it was also non-servile. His only obligation was to pay the *cens,* in this case not a quit rent but a local tax, to the neighboring lord as political ruler, not as manorial proprietor, over him.

So far in this chapter much has been said of the peasantry of the manor and of farming, but little has been said of the lord of the manor, who was both ruler and proprietor of a manorial community. It is this local political jurisdiction which must now be considered. He possessed both taxing and judicial power over his serfs and villeins. These prerogatives, too, constituted part of the lord's domain, which was composed of both corporeal and incorporeal possessions.

What was the source of these local prerogatives? The answer to this question is a controverted one. The historian of legalistic mind is inclined to discover their origin in former public law, the prerogatives and functions of which were usurped by the feudality. Others, who are more disposed toward economic and social interpretation, find the source not in the dismemberment of the State and usurpation of public power by the seignior, but in the economic and social constitution of the domain, a natural and direct effect of great landed proprietorship in a milieu in which the very idea of the State had vanished. *Banalités, taille, péages, corvées,* every sort of service or exaction, it is argued, was an emanation of domanial rights and validated by the confusion of public law and private right which was of the very essence of feudalism. Whatever the truth of these two contentions may be, it is at least certain that many of these prerogatives were not due to sheer brutal usurpation, but fell to the lord of the manor as of necessary exercise in the ruin of an anterior state of things.

Properly speaking, public taxation did not exist in the depth of the feudal age. Even the kings "lived on their own," that is to say, upon the revenues of the royal manors, and not upon revenues raised by taxation. The author of the *Dialogue on the Exchequer,* an Anglo-Norman document written in the twelfth century, writes:

As it had been handed down to us by our forefathers, in the early state of the kingdom after the Conquest the kings received from their manors not sums of gold or silver, but only payments in kind [*victualia*] . . . and the officials appointed for the business knew how much was due from each manor. . . . I have myself seen people who have seen provisions brought up to the court at appointed times from the king's manors.

The intimate relation that might exist between a lord and his tenantry is portrayed in the same document where it is said of Henry II of England—but of his Norman and Angevin manors, not those in England—that "there often poured into the King's court a complaining crowd of husbandmen, or, what was more disagreeable to him, they often met him as he passed by, holding up their plowshares as a sign," sometimes to complain about an unjust steward, sometimes protesting over the decay of agriculture, whether due to weather, war, or taxes.

Local custom varied greatly in the number and kind of manorial taxes, and the names employed to describe them are almost infinite. In Du Cange's *Glossarium* of medieval Latin the list of them fills twenty-seven quarto columns. One universal fact in regard to them is that they were all direct taxes. Indirect taxation is of late medieval and early modern origin and does not appear until commerce and trade has become of large importance. Various categories may be made of them, but the simplest classification is that depending upon their form. Thus they may be distinguished into (1) *redevances,* or renders, (2) *prestations,* and (3) *corvées.*

Redevances were payable either in money or in produce. Among the most important of these were the *capitatio,* the *cens* (German *Zins*), the *taille* or *questa,* the *champart,* the *péage,* and the *banalités.* The *capitatio* was a head tax imposed upon serfs, and not upon villeins or freemen. None but serfs and others of the lowest social gradation in the manorial world, like Jews, paid it. It was regarded early as odious, for it symbolized serfdom. Vexatious offspring of it were the lord's right to tax marriage among his serfs and to exact a super-marriage tax of any serf who married outside of the manor (*formariage*).

The *taille* (from *tallagium,* a notch cut in a stick, whence "tally," a method of keeping accounts in the Middle Ages; in German it was called *Bede, i.e.,* that which was bidden or demanded) was the most typical and most widespread manorial tax. It was levied on serf, villein, and freeman, one or more times a year and was more commonly paid in produce than in coin. The term first appears in the eleventh century, but existed anteriorly. It was levied upon the family as a group. No medieval tax more strikingly illustrates the complicated conditions arising out of the confusion of proprietorship with sovereignty than the *taille*. Was it of legal origin? Or was it an arbitrary imposition? By some writers it is regarded as a variation or emanation from the servile capitation tax. But if so, how did it come to be applied to villeins and freemen? There are those who contend and those who deny that it was legally descended from Roman times. There are those who contend and those who deny a continuity between Carolingian exactions and the *taille* of the feudal age. Was it a personal or a real tax? There are times when it seems one, and again the other. Sometimes it is difficult to distinguish it from the *cens* or *censive,* which was certainly a form of quit rent. However it may be, the *taille* became so general that it often covered all of the *redevances*. There was great difference in its enforcement, though. The serf was taxable to any degree—in the euphemistic phrase of the age, he was *taillable à merci,* that is to the limit of the lord's mercy— while with villein and freeman the *taille* became a fixed, customary sum. Its fixation even for serfs in the thirteenth century marks a true advance in servile status, and a step toward freedom. The arbitrariness of the *taille* made it a most vexatious tax. In course of time it came to be imposed upon almost everything, sheaves of grain, hay, vintage, stock, chickens, bees-wax. As a tax on agriculture it was sometimes known as a *champart*. But each particular object taxed gave a name to a kind of tax. It is no wonder that the demand for fixation of the *taille* was strong and finally prevailed. As administered by an unscrupulous lord it became a bundle of exactions.

The *cens (census)* was a species of rent sometimes payable in produce, but usually a money imposition. It was not paid by serfs, but by villeins and freemen. It is the one manorial tax apparently derived from the ancient Roman land tax, which was appropriated and dispersed during the Carolingian and feudal epochs. Yet some historians contend that the *cens,* too, was of servile extraction. Variant names for the *cens,* arising from the fact that it was a house tax, are *focagium* or *fumagium* (hearth tax), *masuragium* or *masnagium* (house tax). Failure to pay the *cens* entailed loss of his tenure by the delinquent. In the case of a freeman the *cens,* of course, was not a rent but a straight land tax.

The *banalités* were the incomes which the manorial lord derived from monopolistic control of certain necessary economic activities of the community. He owned the mill, the brewery, the bake-oven, the wine-press, the village bull, sometimes even the village well. The advocates of primitive German communalism regard these monopolies as manorialized survivals of once free village institutions. Others look upon them as examples of selfish exploitation by the lord. Are they German or domanial in origin? Certain other historians ascribe the origin of *banalités* to the military conditions imposed by castle life. It is a pleasant although erroneous theory of some sentimentalists, that these enterprises were instituted by the manorial lord as philanthropic measures for the welfare of the community, but unfortunately for the truth of this amiable theory, the facts disclose that the lord was always actuated by motives of gain. He capitalized his local prerogative and used it to squeeze his tenantry.

Prestations were less onerous, more casual but not less vexatious forms of taxation. They were chiefly enforced hospitality. The lord in his travels from manor to manor, when he stayed only a few days in one place, had the right to billet himself and his retinue upon the villagers, who were compelled to furnish him, his followers, and their animals with provisions; even to feed his hunting dogs. It was susceptible of great abuse and early became regularized into a customary obligation enforceable only thrice yearly, when it did not become obsolete. The historical origin of the practice may be traced back as far as the Roman post system (*cursus publicus*) whereby subjects were required to give lodgment and food to government couriers and other officials. The German kings converted this law into an obligation upon their subjects to sustain them and their courts when traveling, from whom the feudal nobles borrowed the practice and applied it to their own immediate benefit.

Corvées (the word is derived from the Roman law term *corrogata,* signifying requirements of forced labor) were a whole body of compulsory services exacted of the peasantry by the lord of the manor, such as road and bridge work, building dams, furnishing horses and carts for hauling, carrying produce to market; other *corvées* were a certain number of working days or series of chores which the lord exacted without compensation for his own demesne and manor-house. Castleguard and watch-and-ward of the premises were *corvées*. Strictly speaking they were not military service at all, but manorial *servitia*. The word *corvée* is found in the Barbarian codes and the form of exaction was one of the oldest of manorial obligations. Most *corvées* were seasonal exactions naturally, imposed in spring, harvest time, and late autumn.

There is no denying either the weight or the arbitrariness of many of these servile exactions, and sometimes the brutality with which they were collected. At the same time the worst of them gradually became obsolete and the others tended to become fixed and customary or else were commuted into money payments, which alleviated much of their arbitrary and brutal nature. It must also be remembered that the collection of them was usually in the hands of bailiffs or stewards, often serfs themselves converted into *ministeriales,* who either were hard taskmasters in order to impress the lord with their efficiency, or else magnified or abused their authority as small-bore men are prone to do. Frequently the lord was unfamiliar with onerous or abusive conditions until he happened to visit such a manor, or found it out first through an insurrection of his peasantry. It has been well and wisely observed that "unpopularity in medieval administration often went hand in hand with efficiency, and violence was merely a perversion of energy." The real responsibility for manorial oppression may perhaps be better attributed to the oppressive practices of bailiffs and stewards than to wilful abuse by the lord of the manor. Then, too, it is always to be remembered that complaint against taxation is an old, old trait of human nature. There is suggestion in the anecdote told of Count Geoffrey of Anjou, who once met one of his own serfs who did not know him by sight, along the road and fell in with him. To the count's question the serf highly praised his lord, but complained bitterly of the conduct of his manorial agents and the injustice of their exactions. Broad generalizations either of approval or of condemnation of the manorial régime are to be avoided. There were good lords who were considerate of their tenantry; there were bad lords who abused their tenantry. Certainly it is impossible to believe that the majority of lords were so outrageously cruel as the notorious Thomas de Marne, or that manorial injustice and abuse was a universal evil.

No consideration of medieval economic history may omit notice of the important part which the forest played in medieval life. The forests of Europe were then far more extensive than now. From time immemorial the forest had been a place of free supply for the peasant. Thence he got his firewood, there his swine and cattle browsed, for the meadow grass was for winter fodder. The value of a forest tract was estimated by its capacity to support swine; an acre of beech was usually regarded as sufficient for ten hogs. Before the nobles began to appropriate the forests any member of the village was at liberty to make a clearing and till a patch of ground. Assarting diminished the danger of want by increasing the arable area around the village, and tended to protect the flocks and herds from predacious animals. It was also a reduction of the danger of forest fires. About the sole limitation was upon cutting the hardwoods, or trees like oak, beech, and chestnut, on whose mast the swine fed. These clearing were called *aprisiones* (from *prehendere,* to take or occupy), *bifangs,* German *bifænge* (from *bifahen,* to enclose with a hedge).

As feudalism spread its net ever more widely and the manorial régime tightened its grasp upon the peasantry more and more, sturdier spirits sought relief by penetrating deeper and deeper into the forests, making a clearing there and sowing their wheat and spelt between the stumps as the American pioneer centuries later was to do in the Blue Ridge and the Alleghenies. Little use was made of fire in forming these clearings, for the danger was too great. The work was done with axe and bar and spade. *"Die Axt is das eigentliche Werkzeug des Neubruchs,"* was a proverb in Germany. Such forest settlement, however, required more collective enterprise in the Middle Ages than here in America. The medieval man was much more dependent upon group association than the modern man. His implements were few, crude of workmanship, expensive to get, and too heavy to be used easily. The work of felling even a single tree required the services of several men working together. We have only casual information in regard to medieval lumbering, but that there was some technique in the business is curiously shown in Willibald's *Life of Boniface* (763), where there is a particular account of the saint felling the sacred *Robor Jovis* (the Latin rendering of the *Tree of Thor,* the sacred tree of the heathen Hessians). The first or lower notch was cut to the centre of the tree on the side toward which it was intended it should fall, and a second upper or "fore" notch was cut on the side opposite.

Place names indicative of forest clearings abound all over Europe from the eleventh century onwards. Examples in English are the place-suffixes *-holt, -hurst, -hart, -chart, -royd, -haw, -weald, -wold;* in German, *-reut, -rode, -wald, -hain, -holz, -hagen, -schlag, -brand, -brenn.* Of these, *-chart, -brenn, -brand* recall the use of fire, which charred or burnt the trees down; *-haw* and *-hagen* signify "hewn"; *-royd, -rode* imply that the place was "rid" of trees. The word "field," when used as a suffix, usually does not mean a field, but a place where trees have been "felled."

The oldest forest grant of which we have record is of the year 559. Forest villages begin as early as the seventh century. The earliest claim that the forest pertained to the royal fisc is in 697. Charlemagne at first imposed no restraint upon forest clearing—*ubicumque inveniunt utiles homines detur silva ad stirpandum*—but in 810 began to restrict the practice, either in order to prevent freemen oppressed with military service from escaping it, or to preserve the forests as hunting parks. Probably both motives influenced his legislation. Increasing perception of the value of the forests is observable through the tenth and eleventh centuries, not merely as places for hunting. The brutality of the game laws undoubtedly was great, but the greater grievance of the peasantry was over the enclosure of the forests by the feudal nobles, who appointed foresters and exacted licenses to fell wood, to fish, to hunt, to pasture swine in them. As private control was extended more and more over the forests the first settlers retreated farther in, so that we find the former squatter clearings peopled by a second wave of incomers. The latter class, however, was not possessed of the hardier spirit of the first settlers. They were rather of the lower grades of the manorial peasantry, borderers, cotters, crofters, marginal men who sought to better themselves by getting a larger holding than a tiny yardland or toft. So great was the exodus from the manors to the forests in some places that we actually find complaint of abandoned farms in the Moselle lands in 1114. Cæsarius of Prüm, writing in 1222, but looking backward into the twelfth century, summed up this long and interesting history of forest colonization in a sentence. He writes: "During this long space of time many forests were felled, villages founded, mills erected, taxes ordained, vines planted, and an infinite amount of land reduced to agriculture."

What is true of the forests is true also of the marshes and swamps. The redemption of these aqueous areas to cultivation all over Europe is an astounding evidence of the increase of population and the indefatigable industry of the people. We find it in Flanders, Frisia, and Holland, in the network of rivers in western France where spread the marshes of Poitou and La Sèvre, in the bottom lands of the Weser, the Elbe, the Oder in Germany, in Lombardy and Apulia. Again the suffixes—*au* ("meadow"), *-ried*, ("swamp"), in German; *-fen*, *-moor* and *-mere* in English; *-marais* in French, tell the tale. A notable example in Germany is the *Goldene Aue*, or Golden Meadows, near Nordhausen, and in France the *Marais de Dol*, a fertile plain which was inundated by the sea in 709 and reclaimed in the twelfth century and protected by a dike twenty-two miles in length. Engineering operations like these requiring so much labor, redeeming so much land, indicate a great increase of population in the eleventh and twelfth centuries. Forest and marsh afforded an outlet for the surplus population. Division and subdivision of tenures no longer sufficed for support. The equilibrium between land and population was passed in the eleventh century. The overflow found homes in newly made lands, or drifted into the towns and lived by craftsmanship and trade. For the upset of the ancient ratio between agriculture and population gave room for new species of employment.

The competition between manorial proprietors to retain their serfs and villeins, or to increase the number of those whom they had, broke down the ancient fugitive serf law entirely. An enterprising lord coaxed his neighbor's peasants away. "Every page of the documents testifies to frequent migrations from the manors in opposition to the expressed will of the lord." The great turn toward the emancipation of the serf came when the fund of available land diminished in proportion to increase of population and even forest clearing and marsh redemption failed to keep pace with it. In order to keep their tenants the lords had to moderate the terms of serfdom; in order to clear forest or swamp the lords held out advantageous terms of settlement. These *hospites* or incomers became a new social and economic class in the eleventh century, a privileged type of villein approximating the freeman in status and often more advantageously situated. It was from this class of leaseholders who held their land for a term of years or for life or for a series of lives that the word "farmer" comes. For they paid a "ferm" (medieval Latin *firma*), or "farm," for the use of the land for a certain period. Originally the word was not necessarily connected with agriculture but was applied to any real property leased for a fixed term. Gradually it lost this broader meaning and came to be exclusively applied to land leases. The evolution is interesting as showing the origin and relatively late appearance of the free farmer.

The medieval farmer was far more the victim of untoward conditions than the modern farmer. With his crude implements, his limited agricultural knowledge, the peril from warfare and wolves, his margin of living at best was a narrow one. Weather conditions, which to a modern farmer might be inconvenient, to him might be a positive disaster. This accounts for the immense number of observations upon the weather which one finds in medieval chronicles—allusions and even extended descriptions of the effects of drought, heavy rains, unusual cold, high water, murrain, plagues of grasshoppers, locusts, and caterpillars. Rats were a plague. The farmers' buildings were all made of wood or thatch, and rats could not be kept out. One could write an interesting article upon the rat in the Middle Ages. It had the importance of an historical personage. Wolves also were a pest. The forests were many and large. In regions devastated by war wolves increased enormously. Great cold would often drive them out of the forest into the open country, where their depredations on cattle and sheep wrought frightful damage. There are numbers of instances of wolves even endangering people of the towns. Worms in the twelfth century was terrorized one winter by a big wolf which haunted the region outside the walls. In the winter of 1418–19 a huge wolf filled Paris with dismay; it even invaded the streets of the city in daylight. What then must have been the position of the rural peasantry?

Against insect plague the medieval farmer had next to no protection. If he tried to use fire he endangered his vines and his crops. Insecticides he had none. As he was intensely superstitious he generally had recourse to the aid of the Church. The priests of the countryside were often almost as ignorant and quite as superstitious as he. Consequently we find resort to the anathema of the Church in order to exterminate insect pests. Here is an example of such a malediction:

In the name of God, Amen. Complaint having been made by the inhabitants of Villenoce in the diocese of Troyes against the locusts and caterpillars and other such animals that have laid waste the vineyards of that place for several years and continue to do so, to the great detriment of the inhabitants of that and neighboring localities; and their request having been considered that the aforesaid animals should be warned by us [the bishop of Troyes] and compelled by threats of ecclesiastical punishment to depart from the territory of the said town,

Now, therefore, we, by the authority which we exercise in this diocese, warn the aforesaid locusts, caterpillars, and other animals, under whatsoever name known, by these presents, under the threat of curses and malediction, to depart from the vineyards and lands of the said town of Villenoce by virtue of this sentence, within six days from the publication of this warning, and to do no further damage either there or elsewhere in the diocese of Troyes. But, if the above mentioned animals do not implicitly obey this our warning within the specified time, then at the expiration of the six days, by virtue of our said authority we will maledict them through this document, and curse them by the same.

In 1120 the bishop of Laon also solemnly issued a malediction against caterpillars and grasshoppers.

Superstition and belief in witchcraft were universal in the Middle Ages. Hundreds of examples of weird, cabalistic formulas, rigmarole verses, meaningless doggerel, have come down to us for casting out "spells," driving away disease, and curing cattle. Some of them are as old as the ancient Romans and may be found solemnly recommended by Cato in his treatise on farming. Others are descended from our Germanic ancestors. Children's doggerel yet preserves much of it. How impressive sounds the "Daries, Dardaries, Astaries, Disunapiter!" which is Cato's charm against sprains! How mysterious the medieval Latin charm, "Alau, tahalaui, fugau!" to call back strayed hogs! Here is a typical exorcism:

> Aius, sanctus,
> Cardia cardiani!
> Mouse and she-mouse,
> Hamster, mole,
> Marmot, cony,
> Young and old
> Leave the land,
> I command.
> You are banned!
> Up above and down below
> From the fields get you hence,
>   Pestilence!
> Go with you, where'er you go,
> Afrias, aestrias, palamiasit!

"Servi qui non timent, tument—serfs who aren't afraid, will rebel." These words were written by Ekkehard of St. Gall, one of the most

famous of medieval chroniclers, about the year 1000. They may be taken for a text upon which to hang some account of peasant revolts during the feudal age. Until the researches of economic and social historians modified prevalent belief, it was the almost universal disposition of nineteenth century writers, imbued with the vague idea of popular right given birth by the French Revolution, to regard the condition of the serf in the feudal age as one of abject fear and gross abuse. But, as we have seen, the serf was a civil person and not always willing to accept injury for fear of worse to come. There are not a few instances of serfs daring to resist the lord and defending their cause in court. The case of the colliberts of St. André d'Angers has been noted.

Two important observations may be made in regard to serf rebellions in the feudal age: they may be geographically differentiated and distinguished also in time. Before the thirteenth century, when the Crusades and other conditions had familiarized the peasantry with large-scale examples of turbulence, the "zone" of peasant rebellion was the northern coast of Europe, extending from lower Saxony through Flanders and Normandy to Brittany. As to time-limits, almost all such movements fall in the ninth and tenth centuries. The few of which we have record in the eleventh and twelfth centuries are local and transitory in their nature, while the Pastoureaux and kindred movements in the thirteenth century were not revolts, but turbulent popular demonstrations against alleged evils as much imaginary as actual, and tinged with religious fervor.

Nineteenth century historians were wont to attribute fantastic attachments to these peasant movements, to find in them a union of the associative impulse and brotherly love of the primitive Church with the early German gild formation; or see in them "the memory of primitive [German] communism. . . . The continual peasant revolts of the Middle Ages . . . always had in the background the ideal, vague though it may have been, of ancient [German] freedom." These theories are too romantic to be given weight. The facts belie them. One and all—the rebellion of the Frisians in 821, of the Saxon Stellinga in 842–43, of the peasantry of western Normandy in 997, of the Bretons in 1024—were violent protests against the excesses and abuses of the manorial régime. Reminiscences of former Germanic freedom may have played a part, probably did so, in the Frisian and Stellinga movements, but there was not a vestige of Germanic communalism in them; in the case of the Norman and Breton peasantry it is clear that the abuses were the thing against which protest was made. There is evidence of the survival in all northern France of the debris of Carolingian institutions which the drift toward feudalism and manorialism tended to destroy; of this the historian Freeman was unaware, but his conjecture was a shrewd one when, in writing of the peasant rebellion in Normandy in 997 he said that "we can hardly doubt that it had a groundwork in local institutions . . . and that the so-called rebels were simply defending the inheritance of their forefathers." This heritage of Carolingian institutions is what the Norman peasants struggled to preserve in 997. Wace, writing nearly two hundred years later of this rebellion, reflects his own time instead.

Between 1000 and 1200, there were no formidable peasant revolts except in Saxony in 1075, where, as we have seen in a former chapter, the conditions were exceptional, giving the Saxon rebellion a unique but local significance. The reason for the general absence of tumult in these two centuries is to be found in the fact that they actually were years of increasing prosperity for the peasant and melioration of serfdom. The geographical area or zone of peasant rebellion is explained, not by the fact that serfdom was lighter in the south of Europe than in the north, but by the fact that along the whole seaboard of the North Sea and the Channel dwelt peoples like the Low Saxons and the Frisians whose immunity from feudalism had long been protected by the marshes and fens in which they lived, but whose ancient liberties began to be jeopardized as feudalism became a more settled form of government and land became more valuable, by the invasion of these marshy tracts by the manorial class, whose purpose was to reduce the free peasantry there to serfdom. In other terms, the greater of these peasant rebellions were less revolts of serfs for freedom than revolts of freemen against the menace of serfdom. Finally it is important to observe that almost all, if not all other such movements in the twelfth and thirteenth centuries, occurred on the lands of the Church. The reason of this appears in the chapter upon the Church and feudal society.

It is rash to generalize too broadly in regard to the evil condition of the peasantry in the Middle Ages. There were good lords and bad lords. There are plenty of instances of bad barons who abused their serfs. But on the other hand there are examples of wise and just lords who were intelligent and even generous in the treatment of their serfs, charitable toward them in time of sickness or privation, and not overburdening them with exactions. The average medieval lord was not a brute in the treatment of his dependents ; neither was he a sentimentalist. The general theory of the upper classes in the Middle Ages was that the peasant was made for toil. "God forbid," says a chronicler, "that the peasants, whose proper lot is daily toil, should abandon themselves to sloth and indolently spend their time in laughter and idle merriment."

Beyond all doubt the worst privation of the medieval peasant was famine. This, if of a widespread and general nature, was almost always due to adverse weather conditions. War was responsible for numerous local famines, but few general ones. A notorious example of the latter is the terrible devastation of southern France in the Albigensian Crusades, which wasted whole provinces. There is a curious periodicity and also often a curious regionalism about many famines. Central Europe suffered greatly in the time of Charlemagne between the years 790 and 793 and again between 805 and 809; France suffered in 842–43 and the distress actually had an influence upon the treaty of Verdun; in the tenth century there was relative relief. But the eleventh century was a time of terrible and widely prevalent famine which indubitably was responsible for the remarkable restlessness of the population, group movements and religious exaltation extending sometimes to sheer mania. Lorraine and eastern France suffered for three years together twice in this century —1003 to 1006 and again between 1031 and 1033. Of the latter Ralph Glaber, a monk of Burgundy, has preserved a fearful account, including cannibalism. Western and southern Germany during the reign of Henry IV was visited nine times by famine, twice in cycles of three years (1060–62 and 1092–94) while northern Germany suffered four successive crop failures in the years 1066–72. The influence of these adversities upon the turbulence of Germany in Henry IV's reign—the rebellion of the Saxons and of the feudality, the violence of the War of Investiture—is certain. The twelfth century opened with three years of famine in South Germany and in 1125 famine was general throughout Germany and Flanders. The middle of the century (1145–47) saw famine all over Europe. The Wendish Crusade and the Second Crusade, both in 1147, must have felt something of the recoil of this widespread suffering. As the twelfth century opened, so it closed, with general famine (1195–98). In the thirteenth century the years 1224–26, 1269–73, 1280–82 were hard years. The first quarter of the fourteenth saw famine or semi-famine years in 1310–17. Invariably these visitations were associated with hard, cold, long winters or drought in summer. A summary shows four general famines in the ninth century, two in the eleventh, five in the twelfth, and one in the thirteenth. Local study of Germany and the Low Countries shows that between the ninth and the thirteenth centuries Belgium had 11, the Rhinelands 8, Southwest Germany 12, Bavaria 13, Saxony 13, Austria 7, Bohemia 4. No competent survey has yet been made for other countries of Europe. Counting together general and local famines, Belgium had 18 famines in four centuries, the Rhinelands 18, Southwest Germany 22, Bavaria 19, Saxony 22, Austria 11, and Bohemia 6. The result of further study undoubtedly would throw much light upon our understanding of medieval economic' and social conditions—increase of serfdom and, per contra, escape from serfdom, movements of population, deserted hamlets and abandoned farms, sometimes the flight of whole villages, colonization and settlement of new regions, the decline of agriculture owing to the necessity of slaughtering the working oxen, the depravation of morals, like brigandage, vagabondage and vagrancy, the pest of wolves which came out of forests to feed on dead bodies. The chronicles abound with tragic and curious information on all these matters. "Many were compelled to leave their native country and to emigrate to other lands," writes Hugh of Flavigny of the great hunger of 858. In the famine of 1043 the bishop of Liège distributed pence every fortnight among his serfs, "lest under stress of hunger they sell or slay their oxen and so the land be left unplowed." Of the famine in Bavaria in 1053 we read that "therefore the serfs fled and very many villages were deserted." In the great famine of 1196, "many were compelled to emigrate. . . . Packs of wolves infested the roads and even entered the villages without fear."

It is true that except in the case of widespread general famines, local failure of crops might have been relieved if there had been good roads. But conditions were aggravated by the exploitive policy of the feudality (Charlemagne once punished a bishop for corn-mongering), who refused to abate tolls and *péages* and even cornered grain in time of scarcity in order to get higher prices later on. "Cornering" and "forestalling" were common medieval practices in spite of secular and ecclesiastical legislation against them.

CHAPTER XXVIII

THE RISE OF THE TOWNS AND FORMATION OF THE GILDS

In certain chapters which have gone before we have seen various examples of the new collectivistic sense, or associative impulse which was manifested in Europe in the eleventh and twelfth centuries. Important as many of these movements were, no one of them was of such lasting significance as the rise of the towns. More than any other medieval movement the town movement marks the passing of the Middle Ages and the beginning of modern Europe. Schmoller, one of the greatest of modern scholars, has declared that

this movement was an economic revolution which I consider more important than any later revolution, even than that of the Renaissance, with the invention of printing and the discovery of the compass, or than that of the nineteenth century and all the revolution in industry which flowed from it. For both these later revolutions are but secondary consequences of the great economic and social transformation of the twelfth and thirteenth centuries.[1]

In the rise of the towns we have written, for the first time in European history, it has been finely said, "the biography of the people." A new social group, unknown before, appeared, the burgher class or bourgeoisie. A new means of production of wealth began to prevail, a commerce and industry destined to enrich Europe far beyond what peasant organization and agriculture had been able to produce. "Naturally the newly rising or risen towns were the seats of these markets. Some towns, because they were walled, became centres of trade. On the other hand the reverse was true; it was the interest of places which became foci of trade to be fortified. Traders began to build booths round the market-place."[2]

The towns were something new in the world, and one of the earliest expressions of modern life. The town movement was not a national movement. It was a social and economic phenomenon which appeared in every country and among every people of central and western Europe, independently of race, language, or frontiers. But

---

[1] Schmoller, *Strassburgs Blüte und die Volkswirtschaftleiche Revolution in XIII Jahrhundert* (1875), p. 16.
[2] Maitland, *Domesday and Beyond*, 193.

while the movement was one, naturally the type in each country differed, according to differences in historic tradition, environment, material and moral civilization, and local political conditions. The greatest influence, however, which conditioned the life of a medieval town was the geographic factor. Location and surrounding natural resources, above all, gave a town economic identity and importance.

General causes for the emergence of the towns are to be found in the economic and social changes described in former chapters, which took place in the twelfth century, and whose influence ran on into the thirteenth, when they were consummated—the increase of population, the development of group consciousness among the masses, decline of serfdom, the rise of commerce and industry, with a corresponding growth in importance of a money economy which tended to displace the older "natural economy," increase of public order, improvement of roads and construction of bridges, etc. It is not always easy to distinguish between cause and effect in these phenomena, but the general results are incontestable. But in searching for town origins one may not rest satisfied with such general explanations as these, or be content with that vague impulse which has been called "the principle of association." Intelligent understanding of the movement demands more concrete historical realities. Unfortunately the documents are widely scattered and very fragmentary. There are no sustained accounts of town history before the fourteenth century, and the few narrations which have come down to us are of episodes or critical incidents only, as of Cambrai in 997 and Laon in 1111–12. The only large knowledge of the town movement before the thirteenth century which we have is in the case of the Lombard cities in their struggle against Frederick Barbarossa (1162–83). A survey of historial sources both as to place and time would reveal enormous lacunæ in our information. Immense areas of Europe and long sequences of years are veiled as with a curtain of darkness. When the curtain rises the towns are already formed. But how, under what conditions, and when were they formed? From the seventh to the eleventh century there is hardly a document, and in all probability the enormous hiatus will never be bridged.

Like every other great and complex historical manifestation, the roots of the towns go far back into the past, and all towns did not have the same root. The multiple origins of the town movement and the variety of sources are baffling. Nevertheless, in spite of the difficulty, an endeavor must be made to understand. Leaving aside the old theory that the germ plasm of the towns is to be found in the mutilated survival of the ancient Roman *municipia*—a theory which no historian believes today—we still have historical hypotheses, each of more or less plausibility or actuality:

(1) The theory that the medieval town developed out of the ancient

free German village community, or *Mark*. For a century this has been a favorite explanation among German historians, and it is still widely advocated in Germany, although many modern historians consider the theory to be as dead as the Roman municipal theory. For whether the ancient German village community originally was ever free, and whether, if so, it preserved its freedom through the depth of the feudal age except in isolated regions like mountainous Switzerland and marshy Frisia are mooted questions.

(2) The theory that the medieval town emerged out of the manor by the conversion of manorial institutions into town institutions and that the community was of servile, not free, origin. The dependent petty administrative officials (*ministeriales*) and skilled artisans of the manor, it is argued, were the nucleus of the later town community, and from them the administrative officials were first chosen when town government emerged. In support of this theory great significance is attached to the world *métier* or craft, which is most certainly derived from the old manorial term, *ministerium*. But how could a town of such origin become a jurisdictional unit, a district which had its own court? As Maitland has said:

No mere accumulation of economic facts will enable us to answer that question. We are in search of a legal principle. . . . The village often had a manorial court. The lord grants a charter and lightens the pressure of seigniorial power. Thus the village might grow into a burghal community. But this process and this explanation will not suffice for all instances. . . . If there are still any among us who would start from village courts as from primitive data, they can indeed, afford to disregard a great deal of . . . controversy, but I cannot think that in other respects their lot is enviable.[3]

(3) The market-law theory, according to which the "peace" which presided over markets created a protected area detached from local feudal tribunals, and thus gave rise to a protected group, principally of artisans and merchants. The market cross in the case of clerically controlled markets, and the "Roland" or *Weichbild,* a statue of Roland, the paladin of Charlemagne, in markets under secular jurisdiction, were the emblems of this authority. The nucleus of the future town group thus was these early merchants and artisans, and out of the administrative system of the market (*Marktrecht*) grew the administration of the town. This theory is popular in Germany, where the numerous so-called "Ottonian privileges" are pointed to in evidence. But even in Germany there is skepticism concerning this explanation, and elsewhere it is regarded as "a beautiful dogma." The market was not the origin of the

[3] *English Historical Review,* XI, 14.

town community, nor market-law the source of urban law. The importance of the Ottonian privileges and the *Marktrecht* theory is discounted when we reflect that these early medieval markets in the ninth and tenth centuries were annual or seasonal affairs, and therefore in the nature of things could not induce any permanent augmentation of the local population. Moreover, very many such markets pertained to the clergy of the cathedral towns, and were not an actual municipal institution; and their foundation and organization were anterior to the rise of the towns. It is not tenable that markets were the generative cause of the towns. These markets were owned by the bishops or the canons of the church, who derived large profits from them, and for this reason they were timed to fall on popular saints' days, when many pilgrims and visitors might be expected. The conversion of many of these annual markets into monthly or fortnightly markets in the twelfth century owing to great increase of population does not help the argument that the source of town origins is to be found in the market. For the legal nature of the market could not be altered merely by increasing the frequency of the institution. That there is a close connection between the "town" when it appeared and the special peace which prevailed in it is undeniable. But what the nexus was, is not easy to determine. Whence did this special peace emanate? And how did this originally temporary peace become permanent and continuous? It is difficult to follow those who contend that the *Marktrecht* was the primitive source of burghal law, and those who so argue seem to be putting effect for cause.

(4) The immunity theory. This is advocated especially of episcopal towns, and again is a German theory, for it was in medieval Germany that the bishops enjoyed to the largest degree exemption or immunity from all other jurisdiction save that of the king. This immunity, it is argued, extended over not merely the group of people within the walls of the bishop's *civitas,* but also over neighboring villages, and thus a borough was constituted, whose inhabitants finally cast off the bishop's authority and established self-government. Naturally such a place, even when its inhabitants were still of serf condition, attracted merchants and craftsmen, who in time became fused with the original population. But this theory, like the market-law theory, is a tenuous one. The area of "immunity" was much greater than the circle of a mere market, and the franchise of immunity was a far different thing from a market franchise. Within an immunity there was no need for special *Marktrecht,* for it was implied in the grant of immunity. But immunity was not implied in a market franchise. Neither theory can be reconciled with the other, and each sounds too dogmatic to be historically acceptable. The immunity theory predicates too much. For such a place was not always a *locus* of economic production. "Its inhabitants lived off the labor of

peasants in surrounding estates; its court, its mint, its market were supported by outsiders." [4]

(5) The garrison theory. This is a favorite thesis in Germany and to some extent in England. In the former country the numerous *Burgwärde* [5] or fortified and garrisoned points erected by Henry the Fowler (919–36) in Thuringia and Saxony as protection against the raids of the Hungarians, and in England the Five Burgs (Leicester, Lincoln, Nottingham, Stamford, and Derby), erected by Edward the Elder to guard the Midlands against the ravages of the Danes, are pointed to in order to sustain this theory. In France the nearest approach to such erections were the *castella* which Charles the Bald erected to protect the basin of the Seine from the Norsemen, in which we find "watch and ward" instituted, a custom already referred to as *"antiqua consuetudo"* in a capitulary of 864. It is argued that the members of these garrisons had holdings round about the burg, that burghal colonization flowed into these protected places, bringing trade and industry in its wake, and so the nucleus of a future town was formed there, which historically had been free for centuries from feudal authority. The weakness of this hypothesis is that it is too local and too military. At most it will account for only a small category of towns.

(6) The theory that the Carolingian local civil administration survived in a mutilated and obscure form, and that out of the persistence of the ancient *échevins*, or Frankish officials of the "hundred" or township, sprang later the civil magistrates of the towns, when at last the towns emerged. This theory finds remarkable confirmation in Noyon, east of Paris, which seems to have enjoyed an almost cloistral peace through the feudal age under its bishop, and where as late as 1237 the electoral regulations preserved the identical formulas of the Carolingian capitularies. But this case would seem to be almost a unique survival, though traces of local persistence of the *échevinage* can be discovered in northeastern France and Belgium as late as the twelfth century.

(7) Another school of historians seeks to find the source of the towns in the ancient Germanic gilds, or fellowship and drinking associations—for there is no thought that the ancient Roman *collegia* survived.

---

[4] Stephenson, *American Historical Review*, XXXII, p. 11.

[5] The old German word *Burg* originally meant simply a stronghold, and did not necessarily imply a clustered population, or even any civil population at all. It is a singular fact, that although the word is incontestably German, the first examples of the word *burgus* occur in northern France (in Anjou), whence it spread to Flanders and through Lorraine into Germany. But in France *burgus* never meant a fortress, as in Germany, but signified merely a group protected by a palisade. These burgs were walled communities. The wall became one of the universal characteristics of every town, and distinguished the urban group from the masses in the country. Hence the name of one entire class of the population (*burgenses*) came from that class which dwelt in a fortified enclosure.

But no connection has ever been satisfactorily proved between these crude associations and the later industrial and commercial gilds. We find evidences of these *geldioniæ* (notice that the word "gild" is of Germanic origin) in the legislation of Charlemagne. Both government and Church attempted to suppress them, for they were too heathenish and too riotous to be tolerated. But all mention of them disappears after the ninth century. The medieval gild was post-communal, not ante-communal. In England, in the most important towns such as London, Bristol, York, Exeter, Yarmouth, the gild merchant either never existed at all or very soon disappeared. Similarly, in the most important Flemish towns, as Bruges, Ghent, Ypres, no gild form of commune was entered into.

Even on the estates of the largest monasteries where there were undoubtedly large groups of handicraftsmen, we may question whether any gild-like organization may be discovered. That in many crafts helpers were needed who were likely to be in a subordinate position to the masters of the craft was certain; many trades could not be carried on by an individual without help; but the existence of *"magistri artium"* no more points to an organization of the masters of a single craft than the presence of a butler points to the existence of a gild of butlers. . . . When the needs of their household have been fully satisfied, the servile craftsmen are supposed to have had leave to dispose of their handiwork to their own advantage; their free labor made them able to secure independence and when independent they made effective use, through their autonomous gilds, of the power of union which they had been taught in servitude. Text after text that might be taken to point to gild-like unions on the early monastic or rural estates is quoted by Keutgen, and the baselessness of the interpretation demonstrated.[6]

If the gild theory were valid, then we ought to find many towns springing up on monastic sites. For the great monasteries by their economic importance, by the industrial and commercial activities in which they engaged, by the attraction which celebrated relics exercised in bringing masses of people together, ought to have grown into prominent urban centres. But as a matter of fact, while a few monasteries developed into towns when the servile community around revolted, as St. Vaast in Arras and St. Gall in Switzerland, most of the great abbeys lost their population by emigration to the towns and so sank into poverty and desuetude. Neither Cluny nor Clairvaux nor Fécamp nor Corbie nor Hersfeld, grew into a town; instead, all degenerated into half-deserted rural communities.

As for the theory of early nineteenth century romanticism, that the origin of the medieval towns is to be found in so vague a thing as "the human principle of association" or "the principle of free association"

[6] *English Historical Review*, XIX, 762.

or mere revolution, one need not take space to refute it. The revolt of the *cives* of Cambrai against the bishop between 959 and 962 was not a communal rising, but merely an insurrection of the inhabitants against an unpopular lord-bishop. We find an analogous rising about the same time in Liège. The people of Europe were not yet politically self-conscious enough in the tenth century to dream of forming an independent town government. The word *cives* at this time simply signified the populace in general and did not mean burghers.

We can discern the chief factors in the origin of the towns, but are unable to determine the relative weight and importance of each one of them, or even their relation to each other. But beyond doubt no single germ and no single explanation is sufficient for all cases. The weakness of much historical scholarship hitherto has been that each writer has emphasized his own theory too exclusively, and sometimes national prejudice has warped judgment. According to the way in which these new institutions were formed, various systems had been proposed; each author attaches them to a preceding different institution; but all are conjectures established upon generalization from certain cases. What is true for Germany may not apply in equal degree to Flanders and France and Italy. Local conditions, geographical and historical, must always be given due weight. The elements of town life in Europe differed greatly, both in degree and in kind. Prof. Keutgen has well said: "Any deduction of these theories as to the origin of the institutions of one country should be preceded by a study of the facts of the corresponding part of the history of kindred nations." [7] In the face of so many divergent theories it would seem that this wide difference of opinion represents a real variation in the history of different towns. It is vain to seek to derive the towns from this or that principle of either Roman or German law. The medieval town was the product of economic and social forces.

The people of the early towns were the merchantmen of the Middle Ages, who either sold the products of others—as wine, grain, merchandise of other countries—or, being artisans, sold the products of their own handiwork. Who were those men who sold? Were they outsiders established in the new centre, or were they the former workmen of the *familia* of the feudal lord? This question is much discussed. In France artisans were called by a name which points to the former serfs of a feudal lord; their activities were called *ministeria,* whence the French word *métier.* In any case, however, they had ceased to work for the feudal lord; they were, above all, sellers. In the northern countries *mercatores* were synonymous with *burgenses* and included at the same time artisans and merchants. They sold either in their own houses *super fenestras* (over the windowsill), or in the market-place.

[7] *English Historical Review,* VIII, 120.

It is certain that in the beginning of the town movement a great number of artisans in person brought to the market the articles which they had made and that no distinctions had yet developed between producers and merchants. This brings us to the most satisfactory explanation yet advanced in regard to town origins, the "mercatorial" theory. The true clue to medieval town origins seems to be in the terms *mercatores, burg* and *burgenses.*

But this burg, whence the medieval town was derived, was not the old garrisoned burg, like the erections of Henry I in Thuringia. It was a *new* burg, a palisaded or walled enclosure formed outside of the feudal castle, or, in the case of an ancient Roman *municipium* outside of the old *castrum;* in reality it was a *faubourg* or *Pfahlburg.*

It is neither an old free (*altfreie*) community which slowly becomes an urban group, nor yet a servile or semi-servile group which gradually struggles into liberty and civic life; but a new community which from the first had been a community of *mercatores* and from the first had enjoyed a kind of land tenure such as was not found in the rustic world. . . . The *mercatores* make their settlement close to the walls of some castle or abbey so that hard by the tract that they occupy there will be homesteads and cottages of the count's or abbot's villeins and serfs, who are living under a *droit domanial* or *Hofrecht.* At a later time, if this new "mercatorial" community is successful it will extend its local limits; it will engulf and absorb the *vieux bourg.*[8]

A striking instance is Bruges, where after 962 Count Baldwin Iron-Arm built a castle in a loop of the little river Lys, outside of which soon arose a new *burg* or *faubourg* inhabited by traders, artisans, and tavern-keepers. The record reads:

After this castle was built, certain traders began to flock to the place in front of the gate to the bridge of the castle [i.e., the bridge over the river], that is, merchants, tavern-keepers, then other outsiders (*hospitarii*) drifted in for the sake of the food and shelter of those who might have business transactions with the count, who often came there. Houses and inns were erected for their accommodation, since there was not room for them within the château. These habitations increased so rapidly that soon a large ville came into being which is called Brugghe by the people from the word for bridge.

The stones for this castle had had to be brought from the ruins of an ancient Roman town miles away, for around Bruges there was no building stone procurable. The palisade around this new *burg* or faubourg was a wooden palisade until the middle of the twelfth century.

[8] Maitland, "Landholding in Medieval Towns," *English Historical Review,* April, 1890.

Before 1195 the *burg* which had grown up around the old castle of Eu near the Channel coast on the frontier between Normandy and Flanders was still unenclosed. One gate of the ancient town still stands and is known as the Porte d'Empire, a most curious corruption. For it was originally called the *Porta emporii,* or Gate of the Market.[9]

What happened at Bruges is typical of what happened all over Europe in the ninth and tenth centuries. In the far south, in southern France and Italy where Mohammedan corsairs continually threatened, we find these burgs erected outside the *castrum* of old Roman *municipia,* or medieval castles.

Towns grew up on the Continent where, and only where, trade conditions were favorable. Many Roman cities again became rich and populous, as commerce once more flowed along its ancient channels, but besides them were a host of new centres of distribution developed by new routes. The nucleus of such a town was frequently the mercantile colony that grew up around a princely stronghold. The new burg quickly became *the* burg; and by the end of the eleventh century *burgenses* meant neither soldiers nor servitors of a castle, but burghers. Yet there were always cities, as there were always castles, which remained untouched by the new economic currents and which the thirteenth century found much as they had been in the tenth. For one monastery that became the germ of a town, there were a dozen that did not; nor did every village market give birth to a metropolis.[10]

The origin of the town, therefore, is to be found in a "new" burg, inhabited by merchants and artisans, and not in the *castrum.* The latter was occupied by count or bishop where he dwelt surrounded by guardsmen, knights, *ministeriales* and tenurial serfs. In the eleventh century when commerce began to waken we discover many instances of itinerant merchants and strangers (*advenæ*) settled in a faubourg which in course of time came to be surrounded with walls. The true town was therefore the "new" burg, which was not born before the eleventh century, and not the "old" burg or castle.

This faubourg, or *suburbium,* in numerous instances, was not coeval with the emergence of the merchant group. Examples are to be met with in the ninth and tenth centuries, and even in the eighth. Of twenty-three towns in France whose faubourgs are attested, one of the texts cited is of the eleventh century, four are of the tenth, the rest of the ninth and eighth. It is evident that we have to deal with an ancient thing. As a fact, the faubourg goes back as far as the later Roman Empire, to be specific, to the invasions and brigandage of the third century when the breakdown of military and police power and the decline of popula-

---

[9] Stapleton, *Rotuli Normaniæ,* I, introd. lxxxiii.
[10] Stephenson, in *American Historical Review,* XXXII, p. 15.

tion made it impossible for a municipality adequately to defend the long line of walls around, so that, instead, within a corner of the city a citadel or *castrum* was erected out of the dismantled old walls and towers. This *castrum* or "old" *burg* was the seat of some local official, while on the outside, the civilian population formed a "new" *burg* or *faubourg,* also walled with the remains of ancient and abandoned municipal edifices. With the restoration of security by the Carolingians these areas became unnecessary, and the local population dwelt more widely scattered. But in the invasions and anarchy of the ninth century the ancient practice was revived, and the old *burg* and *faubourg* acquired new use. Thus in many places two distinct groups dwelt side by side, although sometimes a considerable distance separated them, as at Autun, where we find the ancient Roman *castrum,* or "old" *burg,* and at some distance away the walled *faubourg* (or *forum,* or *emporium,* or *portus,* for all these terms occur),[11] both erections built out of the stones of the ruined Roman city, and a row of wretched houses amid the quarried ruins straggling between the two points and vaguely uniting them. Thus the ancient Roman *faubourg* was sometimes the anterior germ of the later medieval *faubourg.* But the latter had commercial importance, the former had not.

The beginnings of this fecund social process go back to the period of the Norse invasions and the anarchy of the tenth century. The deeper we penetrate into the details of the history of these two centuries the

[11] The word *forum,* being Latin, is common in Romance countries. The word *portus,* however, was current in northern Europe, especially in the Low Countries, where density of population and historical geography conspired to the enormous development of commerce. It was once thought that the word was derived from *porta,* by which was meant the gate of the *castrum,* or citadel, before which the colony of primitive merchants was settled. But this explanation is true neither to philology nor to history. Medieval Latin transferred the word *portus* from the (classical) fourth declension to the second declension, and commonly used the word in the locative sense, "at the port." (Compare the case cited of Bruges.) This usage gives the historical clue to the meaning of the word. The *tonlieu,* or toll, being necessarily collected by the lord in the *portus* or *emporium,* this place naturally became the seat of the first merchants. But the fiscal nature of the *portus* disappeared in its more important mercantile significance. In time the word *portus* (or *poort*) in Flanders and the Netherlands came also to signify the town itself, whose citizens, *i. e.,* those who had burgess rights, were called *poorters.* "These facts," it has been pointedly observed, "are so much more significant in that we find no trace of the *mercatus* in Flemish towns, where the markets which were established there are of relatively recent date and subsequent to the formation of municipal institutions."—Pirenne, "Villes, marchés et marchands," *Revue Historique,* LXVII, 63. "The mediaeval town sprang from a merchant group localized before or near some castle or castrum, in a burg, or forum or emporium or portus (for all these terms occur). We must distinguish two foci, one old and military—the castrum, the other newer and economic and social—the burg. In the end the latter swallowed the former and the two became conjoined into one community."—*English Historical Review,* XVI, 555.

more we discover that this epoch was fertile in social origins, in the adjustment of society to new conditions, in the evolution of new institutions. In the eleventh century a new population given to commerce came to be settled side by side with the old domanial population of servile condition, and in course of time the commercial *faubourg* absorbed the old group and gave the joint population new forms of land title and new customs. The germ plasm of the town is to be found in clusters of merchants, who settled down under the shelter of castle or monastery, and whose protection was gradually extended over the local dependent population, whom they ultimately raised to their own level.

Apparently the Westphalian cities, the Rhenish and Danubian cities, that is to say, most of the German cities situated upon the two chief arteries of commerce, the cities in Flanders and northeastern France, and the cluster of cities in Lombardy and Tuscany owed their origin to groups of *mercatores* who had established themselves under the walls of castle or *civitas*. Municipal life first evolved outside of the walls of the primitive *castrum,* in the *faubourg* or "new" burg, where as early as the tenth century we discover immigrants, or *advenæ,* seeking the shelter of the *castrum* and living not on agriculture but upon the sale of imported or locally manufactured products.

There is a risk, of course, in stressing this mercatorial theory of the origin of the towns too much, but there can hardly be any doubt that the medieval town was primarily an economic and social phenomenon due to the necessity of the promoters of commerce to be protected, in spite of examples of some urban communities apparently existing before local merchant groups are found there. It is a certainty that gild constitutions never were the origin of urban constitutions, but that charters given to merchant groups often were.

And yet although this theory answers to more known facts than any other theory—and in truth is so historically established that it is not an hypothesis—one must not make it too general or too schematic, and must at least give room for the play of other elements. We have practically no evidence as to what the state of the towns was before the appearance of the commune. But one fact stands fast; namely, that the rise of the medieval town was the work of the people. Beyond all doubt the primary forces which gave birth to the towns were of an economic nature. Differences of detail are many, but it is important to observe that "families" of towns are distinguishable, and that these similarities or identities are indifferent to national and linguistic boundaries, and were not ordained by ethnographic or political conditions, which goes to show that the real origins of the towns are to be found in economic and social conditions. Thus Cologne, Mainz, and Worms are closely similar to Rheims, Cambrai, Noyon, and Laon; Lille and Arras, whose population was Romance, are related to Ghent and Bruges, which were Flemish

(German). It is historically wrong to attempt to establish national categories of towns. This renaissance of the twelfth century was not national. In the two extremities of Europe the urban movement manifested itself; in the maritime republics of Italy and the maritime republics along the Baltic and the North Sea.

In the Lombard plain of northern Italy the commercial development was slower than in the maritime cities of Venice, Pisa, and Genoa. With allowance for differences in detail the history of the rise of the Lombard cities is part of the general history of the development of urban life throughout Europe in the tenth, eleventh, and twelfth centuries. The growth of town life in Europe, in this epoch, presents certain analogies, whether the locality be northern Italy or northern France, Flanders, or Germany, and is intimately connected with the economic development of city life. In the south of Europe, as in the north, the three elements of medieval town life, trade, burghers, and town government, are closely identified. Everywhere the gradual conquest by the bourgeois of the rights of local public authority dispossessed the older feudal jurisdictions. The functions of the consuls of the Lombard cities hardly differ from those of the magistrates of cities in the north. Everywhere three successive forms of organization develop—the community of the citizens (*universilas civium*), special and temporary administrative commissions, and finally a permanent organization (*collegium*), always political and at the same time representative and administrative: consulate, *échevinage*, or council. The legal capacity of the *boni homines* was always the point of departure of their attributes, the juridical basis of future municipal independence, since everywhere the urban community did not govern itself, but was directed, in opposition to the rural community, not by a single magistrate, but by a corporation which tended to perpetuate itself in an increasingly exclusive and oligarchic form.

The fundamental common principle is that these urban centres were derived from the same generative and active principle, namely, trade. The maritime relations with Byzantium and the Levant, in the case of the cities of Italy, played the same part that the wool trade did in the cities of the Low Countries, like Ghent, or as the Rhine commerce and Hanseatic trade did in the cases of Bruges, Cologne, and Lübeck. The primitive rôle which the *boni homines* had in the economic interests of the cities everywhere justifies us in comparing the urban communities of the south with those of Flanders and Germany, many of which acquired control of a large zone of territory round about the city, of common land, forest, and pasturage. In the hands of this group the city government was vested: bourgeoisie and town are equivalent terms. The origin of this bourgeoisie is the same. In the maritime cities of the south, or in the industrial communities of the north, it was a group of merchants or former merchants become landed possessors. There were no more servile tenures; each owner was free. Wealth determined the burgher class and gave status. As with the birth, so also with the development of the city, its erection into an autonomous community, the enlargement of the powers of the bourgeois, the formation of an urban law, all proceeded from the growth of the wealth of the community.

This theory that the majority of medieval towns owed their origin as municipalities to local colonies of merchants squares with more of the known facts than any other theory, although opponents of it strenuously deny the existence of a class of men living exclusively on commerce before the end of the twelfth century.

Suppose [writes one critic of this mercatorial theory] that a story of this sort, a story of immigrant merchants, can be proved for this, that, and the other town, dare we make it typical? . . . Without denying the existence of homeless traders who traveled in caravans, we may gravely doubt whether such persons were strong enough in numbers and wealth to obtain land from bishops and counts on peculiarly favorable terms and to found sedentary local communities of a new kind and an abnormally free kind. . . . Still it is an interesting theory, this theory of mercantile colonies.[12]

The words *mercator* and *negotiator,* in the eyes of these critics do not indicate a separate merchant class, but merely vendors of any sort of movable property which they might possess. But this interpretation is too narrow. Doubtless there were many who were vendors on occasion only, and as such may have been called *mercatores* and *negotiatorcs,* as in comparatively backward and undeveloped towns like Frankfort, which still preserved a semi-agricultural life. But in the case of the important towns the evidence is too ample and too conclusive in the other direction. In the Lombard towns, in Cambrai, Dinant, Cologne, and other places, years before the Crusades, we find men who were merchants pure and simple, and several of these are even named in the chronicles. It is significant, too, that the profession of the merchant is distinguished (*qui de mercimoniis suis vivunt cujuscumque officii*) in a charter of Dinant (1096) ; Alpert, an eleventh century writer, distinguishes merchants "from others of the community (*ab aliis vicinis*)."

Burgfriede, not *Marktfriede,* town peace, not market-peace, was the first town law. Almost from the first mention of them, these *burgs* were "places of peace," but the peace which prevailed there was very different from that which the texts reveal when the towns finally emerged. For the market-peace was sanctioned by charter derived from a grant by some superior public authority, and infraction of it was punished by a heavy fine, while infraction of "burgher peace" entailed corporal punishment. The latter peace could not have proceeded from the former and possessed this quality. If *Stadtfriede* was identical with *Burgfriede,*

---

[12] Powicke, in *History,* Jan., 1926 (a review of Pirenne's *Belgian Democracy*).

if from the point of view of penal law the dweller in the *suburbium* was identical with the inhabitant of the *burg,* then we ought to find the word *burgensis* in early medieval times. But this is what we do not find. The documents call them *cives, castrenses, civitatenses, castellani,* but never *burgenses* until late, and then *burgenses* and *mercatores* occur as interchangeable terms. In the charter of St. Omer in 1127 the *burgenses* are sharply opposed to the *milites castrenses.* At St. Omer in 1127 the commercial interest and influence was paramount and the privileges accorded were almost wholly of a commercial nature. In this case the gild of merchants and artisans—for they were not yet separated—seems to have been completely assimilated with the commune. The association is called a *gilda,* it has its *gild-halla,* and the officers of the gild seem also to have been *échevins* of the town. But it is important to observe that the gildhall belonged to the count of Flanders, and that the court of the count also convened in this gildhall. What seems to have happened in 1127 is that a de facto régime was legalized and erected into the local government of St. Omer, the count, however, preserving a reserved authority over the doings of the commune.

An analysis of kinds of property holding in these early towns sheds further light. We find mixed ownership of real property in the towns at the time of their birth. The *cens seigneurial* was a servile quit rent owed by serfs of the lord within the town, who still remained his serfs even after some or most of the population of the former domain had become free and acquired burgher status; they were vestiges of that manorial past out of whch the town arose. On the other hand, the *cens foncier* was a direct tax on real property with no tenurial conditions attached thereto. The latter was the form of holding held by merchants. They were subject to the count's political authority, but not to his manorial jurisdiction. The qualification for senatorial rank in an Italian town during the eleventh century was the possession of real property, which entitled the owner to a voice in the government of the city. We find in this distinction the genesis of urban real property (town lots) as distinguished from domanial tenures.

By the twelfth century, then, merchants appear as a separate class almost everywhere in Europe. There were two kinds of these. One class was composed of more or less local merchants who were stationary, while the other was made up of Italian merchants from the great marts of Venice, Genoa, Siena, and Milan, who were "birds of passage" who came through in the spring and summer with oriental luxuries and returned home again in the autumn.

But merchants and artisans did not form the sole population; there were also agriculturalists, who cultivated the fields surrounding the town; this condition was general, even in Italy. Even in the large towns there were pastures, granaries, regulations for the feeding of swine, etc.

There was no opposition between the *mercator* and the free cultivator, but there was such between the *burgenses* and the *villani*. It was a difference not of occupations, but of condition.

Was there a landed proprietary class living within the town? There were certainly some of this class by the thirteenth century. Were they the sons of merchants who had become rich, or of former proprietors rich enough to let their lands to farm? The reply is doubtful with reference to the northern countries; but in Italy and the southern countries there were certainly some knightly proprietors (*milites*). There was, therefore, a great diversity in the social composition of the towns.

For although essentially composed of merchants and artisans, the town naturally drew to it some knights and some proprietors. These people of various origins had no unity in manner of life, but acquired a unity of legal condition (franchise). Thus a society was formed of a variety of freemen who were not isolated but grouped together, and had somewhat the character of modern society. These classes were politically equal, but not necessarily all equal in a social sense. They were not equal except before the law. From the very beginning there were individuals of a superior condition in the town. In the Italian cities in the thirteenth century there was an aristocracy of wealth, composed of merchants and proprietors, above the artisans. It was a new nobility, a burgher nobility, which gradually absorbed power in the city.

The rise of the towns was evolutionary in process, but revolutionary in result. Long association together and common interests and common experience at last bred in the inhabitants a strong community sense which found expression either in a peaceful demand of the lord, whether baron, bishop, or abbot, for recognition as a self-governing community; or, if refused, in violent rebellion against feudal authority and demand for chartered liberties. For after all

the commune was only a form necessary, perhaps, as a safeguard against a too powerful lord, but not needed by towns placed in happier circumstances. It may, indeed, be said, that all those medieval cities which attained the greatest and the most lasting independence found that that independence was the better the less its growth was confined within bounds which could not easily be relaxed, though they might have been useful at first as securing the coöperation of those who might otherwise have been its enemies.[13]

Politically speaking, this demand for recognized urban rights and privileges was a demand upon the part of the newly formed bourgeoisie that the principle of contract, for many centuries valid in the feudal world, should be extended to the non-feudal world. The common people

[13] Keutgen, *op. cit.*, 124.

also demanded "rights" and "liberties" to administer their own justice, taxation, coinage, market regulation, etc., as the feudal princes did in their territories, and refused longer to submit to feudal authority in these intimate affairs of local interest. They demanded a place in, and not under, the feudal régime. They did not wholly repudiate the lord's authority and were willing to continue to owe services and to pay taxes, but the nature and degree of these exactions were to be strictly measured and defined. The town would levy them, not the lord. It was to have its own magistrates, its corporate seal, its town hall, its belfry. These were the symbols of its independence. Thus

the town constitution has a double source, a public and a communal. The public source consists in such ordinances as the government of the land shall have appointed for the towns under its jurisdiction. The communal source consists in the customs of, and the by-laws passed by, the organs of the town community.[14]

History shows that the townsmen would go to any length of violence in order to secure the "rights" which they demanded, one of the keenest demands being for the abolition of the manorial *cens*. Their motto was, "Peaceably if we may, forcibly if we must." In some places the insurgent people formed a sworn association (*conjuratio, communio*); they took an oath to stand together in order to obtain a change of condition. Some such examples, though very rare, are known to us by narrative accounts, as in the cases of Laon, Cambrai, later Vézelay, and the episcopal cities of the Rhine. The case of Laon is notorious. Here was

"a populace always ready for a fight; bishops always encroaching on the royal rights on the one hand and the liberties of the commune on the other; a great and bloody insurrection, a bloodier revenge of the nobles; a great conflagration; a great massacre—such in abridgment are the annals of Laon. Gaudri, bishop of Laon, bad successor of a line of bad bishops, who swore to observe the charter which he had sold dear to the citizens, violated it as soon as he could, and in every way possible, and was slaughtered for his reward."

When at last secured, the charter was a valuable document. It was kept in the archives of the town hall under three locks and keys. Sometimes even it was graven on the wall of the town hall or upon that of a church. The "Privileges of Speyer," which Henry V granted in 1111, were set in gold letters in the great door of the cathedral. The same was done at Mainz in 1135 with the charter granted by Archbishop Adalbert.

14 Keutgen, *op. cit.*, 121.

At Montélimar the charter of 1198 was graven upon the town wall. The inhabitants thus became free burghers, whence the term "franchise." By the thirteenth century practically every townsman was a freeman. "Town air makes free," ran the saying of the time.

The rapid development of the towns led to amelioration in the condition of the peasant. Labor became so much in demand in the towns that there was every inducement to flight if the serf were badly treated. Once in the town he got his freedom after a year's stay. In Italy the Guelf cities promoted emancipation, in some cases even providing the peasants with money to purchase their freedom, a practice which the Ghibelline cities could not prevent. The new urban law invariably repudiated antiquated and hateful old feudal processes of law, sometimes in the preamble stigmatizing them as "odious," "unnamable," "bad customs." The warlike attitude of the inhabitants often is shown in legislation forbidding them to fight among themselves. And yet at the same time an almost passionate wish for peace was expressed. The preamble of the charter of Valenciennes contains a veritable hymn in glorification of peace.

The town as a free, self-governing community of burghers was a new political and social organism in medieval Europe, for which the earlier feudal centuries had had no precedent. Yet, important as the town movement was, it is astonishing to see how little early contemporary observers understood it, and all of them, being of the privileged classes, naturally condemned it. The writer of the *History of the Bishops of Cambrai,* writing in the eleventh century, uses the cant phrases of literary tradition derived from the Old Testament, the Greeks and the Romans. In the twelfth century, however, with the teachings of Arnold of Brescia, we find a new and positive burgher political philosophy, a philosophy taught with the passionate earnestness that characterized the teaching of the "rights of man" in the eighteenth century, or social democracy today. Otto of Freising, the deepest historical thinker of that century, although he was hostile to the town movement, nevertheless was capable of looking at it with level eyes. It would tax a modern writer to describe the rise of the Lombard cities better than he has done. Jacques de Vitry, the great French preacher, about 1200, paid a remarkable tribute to the civic spirit prevailing in the cities of Italy. "The citizens," he said, "are prudent in counsel, diligent and studious in public affairs, refusing to be subject to others and defending their liberty against all. They make their own laws and obey them." Sometimes a town would send a commission to other towns to study their government. In 1187 two towns sent a commission to Soissons. Tournai studied the charters and local workings of six different towns. Augsburg in 1386 and Cologne in 1396 sent a commission to visit Basel, Constance, Mainz, Worms, Speyer, Ulm, and Strassburg. Ghent's famous "thirty-nine" commissioners are found at Hamburg, Bremen, Magdeburg, Speyer, and Lübeck. It was this practice which in part accounts for municipal similarities or identities.

In course of time the feudality not only became tolerant of the town movement, but even grew to promote it, not from democratic or proletarian sympathies, but from interest. As commerce and trade increased the nobles discovered that it was profitable to have a commercial centre in their lands; that one way to keep from losing their serfs to other places was to establish towns in which former serfs could earn a livelihood as craftsmen and tradesmen instead of farming; that under the new money economy which was supplanting the old natural economy, it was easier to collect taxes in money than in kind, and to have the towns raise these than to raise the taxes themselves. Emancipation of communities en bloc became profitable. So the lords established *villes neuves*—new towns, sometimes known as *"bastides"*—upon their estates and offered attractive inducements in the form of light and regular taxation, liberal justice, local improvements like roads and bridges "all in," cottage sites, gardens, and market booths. Certain of such liberal charters became so popular that we find them widely imitated. The Laws of Beaumont and the Customs of Breteuil were so famous that more than three hundred examples of each are found. William of Champagne, archbishop of Rheims, and uncle of Philip Augustus, in 1182 gave to the inhabitants of Beaumont a famous charter which had many imitations. The servile class in northeastern France owed much of its liberation to this famous law, which spread, not by force of arms, but by peaceful agreement, and stimulated agriculture, industry, and commerce. The establishment of a "new town" was perpetuated in one of two forms—in a written instrument, or by the erection of a symbolic cross in the place. The latter way was common in northeastern France, where the *Franche Croix* was often to be seen in the little towns. It is also found in Lorraine, Luxemburg, and even in Alsace.

These new towns presented a far different appearance from that of the old towns which had grown up higgledy-piggledy, by agglomeration, with crooked, narrow streets and alleys and often wretched houses without even rudimentary sanitation. Instead they were laid out in geometric form, in squares, hexagons, octagons, with rectangular streets running across them from gate to gate. Everywhere in France we find this new town type, but especially in Languedoc, where the destructive effect of the Albigensian Crusades reduced the land to a *tabula rasa* and made possible the erection of absolutely new towns. So in the colonial lands of Germany east of the Elbe we find towns with straight streets and municipal sanitation. Lübeck had a water system in the thirteenth century, although most towns depended upon wells.

The whole problem of devising administrative institutions and improvising a government faced these rude burghers. It is no wonder that they made many mistakes, that there was much tumult within the towns. When we remember that it took feudalsm one hundred and fifty years, in the rough, to work its institutions into a just and effectively working government, we must be charitable of the errors and the violence of these burghers, with whom self-government was a new thing. There was little precedent to be found in feudalism, for the town movement was anti-feudal in its nature.

The modern city is the offspring of the medieval city, and perhaps nothing in medieval civilization was of greater social importance to humanity. Not merely did the tangled mass of moribund survivals have to be unraveled; nascent growths had to be developed and a vast amount of fruitless experimentation had to be done. There were tangles of origin, tangles of class, church tangles which found expression in the new parish organization, industrial and commercial rivalries crystallizing in gild groups of craftsmen and merchants, all of which had to be unravelled and the place and function of each established. Among the dwellers in these places, according to varied conditions, various ties were formed which differed from those which had bound them to the lord. These were ties of caste. Those of knightly rank—if there were such—and the richer bourgeois united against the lower-class population.[15] Capitalistic influence worked along the line of social selection; the *boni homines* displayed an increasing tendency to form an urban aristocracy which governed the affairs of the city, so that the end was a city patriciate resting upon economic power. Thus the city organization often, even usually, terminated in an oligarchic plutocracy.

The local power was organized for the administration of the town. We find executive officers, a legislative body, a court, and lesser civil officials to govern the town. The system is found under very various forms, for it proceeded from an agreement expressed or implied between two powers, the noble and the body of the people, and it resulted from an equilibrium, or agreement between the two.

Every town had administrative institutions which looked to the necessities of public defense and of public order: a militia, a tax, a treasury, a court, a council, etc. There is a great variety of detail and a great number of agents and representatives. The commonest political phenomenon is annual change of magistrates. But it is safe to say that the burghers in the course of a hundred years or more exhausted every governmental device and invented almost every imaginable combination, such as single and plural executive, direct and indirect election, electoral qualification and universal suffrage, class representation, pro-

[15] In Le Mans we find *cujusdam regionis proceres;* in St. Quentin (between 1045 and 1080), *bourgeois, chevaliers, et clers* swore fealty to the commune. Evidently *clerici, milites,* and *mercatores* formed three classes of a single population.

portional representation, long term and short term in office, rotation of offices. The composition of town councils ran the gamut from extreme aristocratic domination by the rich (*otiosi*) to ineligibility or disfranchisement and even exile of the upper classes and complete domination by the masses. The local machinery sometimes became so intricate that the machine jammed and revolution or anarchy ensued, for party feeling ran high in medieval towns. In Avignon, Vienne, and Montpellier the complication once became so great that the magistrates were selected by throwing names in a bag and drawing lots. At Ghent an ingenious system was adopted—a council of the "39" formed three groups of thirteen persons, those actually in charge, those in office the preceding year, and those to be in office the next year.

The highest examples of medieval towns were those free cities which exercised sovereign rights, especially in Italy and in Germany, where we have the episcopal *freie Städte* and the *freie Reichstädte* on the domain of the king. Power rested in the body of notables (*consilium, Rath, credenzia*), which became little by little a sovereign body. It ordained regulations, made law, made war, made peace. In this way were formed the true republics of the Middle Ages, some of which maintained their independence for centuries, as Venice, Florence, Genoa, the Free Cities of Germany and Switzerland. The executive power was entrusted to magistrates called *Bürgermeister, maire, podestà,* the last word designating an Italian official which began to appear in the second half of the twelfth century, the *podestà* generally being a foreigner imported for the government of the city for six months.

A régime analogous in fact but different in law had its origin in some towns which had a lord who left all the power to a group in the town. This was the system that prevailed in France and Flanders, and we find it also applied in some seigniorial towns of Germany. These towns had elective officers, chosen from the bourgeois and the patriciate. They were called consuls in the south of France, *échevins* in the north, and peers or *jurats* in the west. Their number was variable. There were eight consuls at Avignon, twelve in Marseilles, and twenty-four at Toulouse; there were fifty *jurats* at Bordeaux. These officials formed a council of administration controlling the town militia, appointing police, laying taxes, etc. This council was formed of rich burgesses of two classes; proprietors (*otiosi*), whose wealth was in their rents, and merchants (*ditores* or *boni homines*). The dignity was without a doubt hereditary. In spite of opposition the great families retained control of the council. Ordinarily, also, there was a council of notables, perhaps a general assembly of the inhabitants, which probably was without real power and convened only in order to approve the acts of the corporation. Under these two similar forms the magistrates who represented the body of the people had all the power: they declared war, commanded the militia, were guardians of the town ramparts and town gates; they authorized and levied taxes; they kept the treasury; they rendered justice and established ordinances; in a certain sense we may say that such a body of magistrates was a collective noble, for it possessed all the rights of the former feudal lord as much in the towns of the south as in the communes of Picardy.

In many towns the lord still retained rule over a portion of the town, and his agent, called a bailiff or a provost, exercised a certain authority. This is particularly the case in the towns of West France and in England. This agent of the lord presided over the local court, commanded the militia, and defended the city. Another variation, illustrating the numerous degrees of municipal liberty, was that whereby the noble gave the bourgeois only the freedom and the right to be judged according to their *coûtumes;* they had no power to establish a government of their own; the chief official was the agent of the lord, who exercised all the rights, issued judgments, levied taxes. This form was typical in France. The French kings favored the communal movement in the interior of the great fiefs in order to abridge the power of the high feudatories. But they were intolerant of it within their own domains. However, they made concessions to the rising bourgeois class by granting a great many limited charters of exemption like the famous Customs of Lorris, which curtailed the powers of the royal provosts. They also permitted the provost of Paris and the *échevins* of the city to judge causes in which the issue was of a commercial nature and concerned the Parisian hanse, so that the bourgeois gradually came to have a hand in the government of the city. Thus in the interior of the communes as well as in the *prévôtal* villages a third estate developed which in the fourteenth century acquired a significance of national proportions.

Physically speaking, a medieval town was composed of three parts: (1) the town proper, which was included within the walls; (2) the *faubourgs,* or suburbs outside the walls; and (3) the *banlieue,* or outer zone, so named from the ban-league, *i.e.,* the belt of territory a league wide under the town's law or ban (*bannaleuga*), which might be studded with tiny hamlets under the town's jurisdiction.

The wall conditioned the actual life of the people more than any other object, for it was the town's chief protection. Watch and ward and upkeep and repair of the wall were perpetual. The town sometimes derived an income from renting spaces on the wall or in the moat for gardens and even cottages. The great towers were used for granaries, storehouses, and stables. As population increased, the value of house lots and houses within the walls rose so that the owners of such property, usually the richer merchants of the town, became a wealthy rent-collecting class; and as rents rose the feeling of the lower classes against the rich intensified. The wall also had the effect of superinducing congestion of population, a condition which was met by building the houses very high, at times five and six stories, and also extending the upper stories out over the streets so that the street was converted into a covered arcade. This practice, by cutting off sunlight, often made the streets dark and noisome, so that we find "skyscraper" ordinances limiting the height of buildings and prohibition against building over the streets.

Skyscrapers are not a modern evil. The walled cities of the Middle Ages rendered land valuable for building, and, to secure proper returns, capitalists were forced to erect high structures. On the other hand, the legal authorities were obliged to enact building laws to prevent these buildings being so lofty as to endanger the public safety. The islands on which Venice was built were limited in area and property was very valuable— so much so, in fact, that the council was compelled to pass a building law limiting the height of buildings to 70 feet. In Florence, so long as the city was confined by walls, the limit was 100 feet, in Paris, 60, and in Toledo, 75 feet. Rheims had a curious building law forbidding any structure for residence purposes to be erected higher than the eaves of the cathedral, and it is recorded that whenever a building was going up the archdeacon was enjoined to look out daily from the portholes in the eaves and see that the walls of no structure rose higher than the level of his eyes. The burghers of Amsterdam probably borrowed the idea from the council of Rheims and ordered that no tenement or residence should be higher than the third story of the Rathhaus, this building being the pride of the city, being thus jealously preserved in its preëminence over all others.

The lower classes dwelt outside the walls in the faubourgs, and if they did not labor in their cottages, as many did at "piece work" and "cottage industry," came into the town when the gates were opened at sunrise and went out again at sundown. Gardens and orchards were often found within the town, and the rural hamlets in the *banlieue* supplied the residue of foodstuffs necessary.

We can measure the growth of the medieval city by the successive walls. For between the twelfth and the fourteenth century many a town dismantled its old wall, filled up the old moat and built a new wall which took in the faubourgs. A century later the same thing would be done again, for new faubourgs arose and a new wall was erected to include them. "Pisa already had her new walls by 1081, Piacenza before 1158; Florence was building her Second Circle in 1172–74, Modena in 1188, and Padua in 1195; and the fact implies the existence of important suburbs outside the old walls for some time previously." Careful examination of the ground plan of such old cities will often disclose the fact that there is a ring of streets within the city, a circumstance arising from the fact that they have been laid out upon the sites of the medieval walls. The inner boulevard system of Paris is a striking and clear example. The town tax (*firmitas*) for maintenance of the walls was a heavy and unpopular one, and because of the difficulty of collecting it in direct form it was frequently converted into an indirect tax, usually upon comestibles. In this form it is still preserved as the local *octroi* in France, Italy, and Germany. A medieval town sometimes owned forest land: Liège sold its valuable timber off to defray the cost of its wall. Towns also rented mill rights and water rights, hunting and fishing rights in the *banlieue*.

No exact figures are possible until relatively late with reference to the growth of cities in the Middle Ages, either the number of them, their population, or their revenues. But there is reason to believe that the number of corporate cities increased tenfold between 1100 and 1300 and that their population sometimes doubled and trebled. A corresponding increase of revenue, of course, followed. Genoa certainly doubled its revenue between 1214 and 1293, and had doubled it again by 1395. During William the Conqueror's last illness, the noise of Rouen becoming insupportable to the sufferer, the king gave orders that he should be conveyed out of the city to the church of St. Gervais standing on a hill to the west. The public square was naturally the centre of the town. Sometimes it was a market square, sometimes the broad area in front of the principal church, sometimes that in front of the town hall. In Italy it was called *piazza*, in Germany, *Platz*, in France, *place*. But in every case the word is derived from the ancient Latin word *platea*. In Narbonne and Nimes those who owned houses or shops on the public square were known as *"gens de platea," "platerii,"* or *"platearii."*

Before the thirteenth century public improvements, except in Italian towns, were not much advanced. Paris was without a paved thoroughfare until Philip Augustus paved the roadway in front of the Louvre in 1184. In 1131 a son of Louis VI, riding down the Rue St. Jacques in the Latin Quarter, was killed, when a hog which was rooting in the offal in the street charged between his horse's legs and threw him. In the thirteenth century, however, progressive towns like Cologne and Lübeck paved the market-place and adjacent streets. We find instances of expropriation and eminent domain being exercised in order to make improvements. Most towns depended, at the risk of typhoid fever, upon wells. But large and progressive cities had some water supply through conduits. In 1187, at the siege of Alençon, the water supply from the Sarthe River was cut off by cutting the conduit. In 1256 some workmen engaged in cleaning an old sewer in London were overcome by the foul gas in the pipe. Sewers, not merely surface drainage, and latrines are mentioned in the twelfth century in some towns. The former were made of brick or barrels fastened end to end and buried in a ditch. The only street lighting known was an occasional lamp burning before some shrine, except upon festival occasions, when the burghers used to put candles in the windows. The hazard of fire was great in a medieval city owing to the large number of wooden houses, so that the rich built stone houses and even the lower classes in some towns were required by law to have tile roofs instead of thatch. By 1400 medieval towns were very largely built of stone or of timber and cement-work. Houses inside the walls, as said, were high. But the houses of the poor in the faubourgs were small and squalid cottages. Congestion was great in the heart of a town owing to lack of space and high rents, as many as ten to sixteen living in three rooms. Sometimes we find a large house coöperatively owned, each owner possessing a floor or more often a few rooms in it, the title being fractions of the whole, as a quarter, an eighth, a sixteenth, and even a thirty-second portion of the fee and the building.

Like the town, the gilds of the Middle Ages had a complex origin, which is much in dispute. Various theories are current. The theory popular early in the nineteenth century that the gilds were derived from the Roman *collegia* and *sodalitates* has few advocates today, for the reason that the survival and continuity of those ancient associations is no more demonstrable than the survival of Roman municipal institutions.

Another theory, a favorite among the same German historians who seek to derive the town from the old German *Mark,* finds the origin of the gilds in one of several primitive Germanic associations, as the ancient German drinking clubs (*convivia*) or kindred-and-clan groups organized for self-protection (*frith-gilds*).

A third class of historians, in whose thought economic and social forces are of greater importance than racial institutions, finds "in the economic microcosm of the manor the embryo of the gild." This class is divided, however, into two groups. One group seeks the origin of the gild in the crafts of the manor, in the unfree artisans of the manor who, it is contended, gradually split up into groups composed of workers of the same type, as cobblers, saddlers, wood-turners, weavers, fullers, and iron-workers. The allocation of these craftsmen in quarters upon great manors, like St. Riquier, is pointed to as proof of this argument. The second group considers that the gilds emanated from the officialdom of the manor (*magisterium*)—that is to say, from the "masters" or "super-intendents" of the artisans and craftsmen of the manor, who, though themselves of servile condition, yet formed a higher and better trained class of workmen, and who also possessed experience and qualifications for management and control of industry.

But no one of these theories solves the important question whether these workers were gilded when still in serfdom; or whether the gild was formed after they came up out of serfdom. Even if we admit any one of them, it remains yet to prove that the primitive association—the nucleus of the gild—was gilded when the members of the association were still serfs. Every one of these theories seems to cover too much, or not to cover enough, or else to strain the evidence which we have. They are too narrow or too broad and do not make sufficient allowance for local deviations or variations due to racial group survivals, difference of historical tradition, influence of local economic or social conditions. Moreover, are merchant gilds as referable to any one of these sources as craft gilds? It is comparatively easy to understand how pressure of population and development of technique gradually brought about a division of labor in the crafts, and also how the skilled artisan might become a peddler of the products of his handicraft in market or fair or town, and thus a class of *negotiatores* distinct from craftsmen might arise. But in contravention of this hypothesis that both craft and merchant gilds originated in the trades of the manor (many lords finding it necessary to make some of their men traders in order to supply home needs), we find evidence of quite another class of merchants (*mercatores*), who seem never to have been unfree *negotiatores* ministering to the outside wants of abbey and manor, but always to have been merchants. Not all merchants in a burg were former "men" of the lord. Were these latter those itinerant or caravan merchants who first settled the burg of the towns? Or were those earliest "burghers" manorial serfs engaged in merchandising, who finally became wholly detached from the manor? Were the traders of the manor gilded when still incompletely differentiated from craftsmen? or were they gilded after they became full-fledged merchants? And when were the caravan merchants gilded? Could a gild be legally self-organized? or were both merchant and craft gilds created in virtue of a legal act by some political authority, as a market was established by law? There is no clear answer to these questions. But it would seem that chartered rights of the gilds, like the charters of the towns, were either formal grants of political authority, or confirmation by the reigning lord of rules and regulations formulated by the group and presented to the lord for confirmation.

Another group of historians would find the origin of the gild in the various kinds of parish confraternities or brotherhoods of the Church, which existed as charity associations for the relief of the poor, the care of the sick, and the burial of the dead. But this theory lacks substantial support. The argument advanced that all gilds invariably had patron saints is inept for the reason that it has been shown that the practice of the gilds in adopting patron saints was late, and not early in their history. Moreover, the names of these patron saints are different from those of the confraternities, being names like St. Crispin, the martyr-cobbler, and St. Nicholas, the martyr-merchant, etc. Finally, a very few writers have thought to discover the germ of the gild in those local associations created by the Peace of God or the Truce of God, but this theory, too, is unsubstantial.

There is a double hazard in this search for gild origins: first, of using the term in a sense much wider than is warranted by historical evidence; and second, of too rigidly insisting upon exact definition of the term and so losing sight of the motives lying behind the institution. Without reposing confidence in so vague a concept as "the principle of association," we may freely admit that the lowly society of the early medieval world everywhere felt the necessity of some sort of combination into groups. We may concur with Keutgen's cautious judgment:

The one fact . . . is that the spirit of free association and organization for a lasting, practical, and reasonable object was rife among our forefathers at an early age, and for this no further derivation need be sought. It needed no foreign example, but arose as soon as the general state of their civilization allowed and required it, and took very various shapes, such as the frith gild, the religious gild, the gild merchant, the *summum convivium*, the commune, according to the circumstances and the end in view. . . . The towns were peopled to a great extent by immigrants from the country round. Those people were by their change of abode separated from their kindred, and therefore from those who were legally bound to act with them in the law courts and who were their natural support in the manifold contingencies of life. It was their kindred's place which the gild in some measure undertook to supply.[16]

The historical importance of the gilds is not in their political, but in their commercial and industrial activities. They were the medieval solution of the problem of business and labor in that time. They controlled capital and regulated labor; they governed production and distribution; they fixed prices and wages. But there was a social influence in their formation, too. The purpose was partly social and partly for mutual protection. Merchant gilds were almost, if not quite as early as craft gilds. Mutual protection and guaranties, at home and abroad, was a large factor in the purpose of their organization. The gilds, especially those of the crafts, were distinctly democratic in spirit in the beginning; the path from apprenticeship to mastership was open to all who fulfilled the requirements. But later, in the thirteenth and fourteenth centuries, the gilds became as oligarchic in organization as the towns. The same exclusive phenomenon is reflected in each.

The gild was a corporation. As such all the members lived in the same quarter in the town. All independent labor was eliminated. Everybody who plied his art had to belong to a special gild. They judged and fined the members of the corporation. Within the corporation there existed the "hierarchy of the workshop," the gradual rise from apprentice to "companion," to master. The relation between the master and the apprentice was patriarchal. The apprentice was treated as a member of the master's family and his moral education was looked to as well as his

[16] *English Historical Review*, VIII, p. 125.

technical. He might not be married, might not sleep outside of the master's home. The apprentice paid a fee in money and received board and clothes, but no wages. Apprenticeship lasted from two to five or even to seven years. The journeyman, or "companion," worked for small wages. The master was a craftsman of superior excellence, who had produced his *chef d'œuvre*. The instruction of the workman was always verbal or by example. For this reason very little is known of the inner workings of gild education. From the whole Middle Ages there is but one written document of this nature, the *Album* of Villard de Honnecourt.

From their inception the gilds manifested great eagerness to acquire privileges and to establish monopolies. While jealous of internal competition and savagely repressive of it, they encouraged their members to kill outside competition and "to sell in the foreign," which might be the next county or town or parish, at what price they could get.

In the gilds, which were at first democratic within, a cleavage soon developed, which, by the end of the thirteenth century, became fixed. The masters grew into an aristocracy within the membership of the gild, and later shut out the common working class, thus converting the gild into a close, capitalistic corporation, membership in which passed from father to son among the rich families which now formed the gild. Thus the conflict between capital and labor was staged in the later Middle Ages. The ordinary workman became like a factory hand—although there were no factories—the workman procuring raw material from the gild master and working it up in his home; he became a wage-worker, "striking" against a reduction in wages, or for higher wages, subject to the hazard of unemployment and "hard times," derided as a "blue-nail" by the *"otiosi"* or rich employers, who profited by their possession of the hoard of the gild and their manipulation of prices and wages, and who added to these gains the rents derived from owning property in the town.

The working classes formed an unorganized industrial rabble in which the only cleavage was one of technique, as carders, weavers, fullers, tanners, dyers, and saddlers; while the employers were grouped together in great mercantile or craft companies. More often, however, the criterion of distinction was not of kind of business, but of capital at command of the various gilds. Thus, in Florence we find the *arti maggiori,* or greater gilds, and the *arti minori* or lesser gilds. The number of the former was seven, and at their head stood the richest citizens in the chief lines of business in the city. Between these two classes, the master workmen who were superintendents or "bosses," had an intermediate rank. The men who did the heavy work labored by the week and dwelt in miserable faubourgs, in unsanitary lodgings; their hours of labor were fixed; they were ruled by the town clock, and their working day was very long. They lived from hand to mouth and their situation was analogous to that of lower-class workmen today. They were subjected to the patrons or employers, who appointed inspectors to supervise their work and to fix the rate of wages. As to the lowest stratum of the laboring population, the raw worker without training who had nothing but his brawn, we know nothing. History is silent regarding the ungilded, casual labor class known as "tensers."

In Florence the great gilds were: (1) notaries, because of their knowledge of the law; (2) the Calimala, whose business was importing foreign cloths and dyeing and dressing them anew into richer forms; (3) bankers and money-changers; (4) drapers—the woolen gild was the richest in Florence, and the manufacture of woolen cloth the staple industry; (5) doctors and druggists; (6) mercers, or silk merchants; (7) furriers. The usual number of Florentine minor gilds was sixteen: butchers, shoemakers, iron workers, leather workers, stone masons, wine dealers, bakers, oil dealers, pork butchers (a specialty apart from general butchering), linen drapers, locksmiths, armorers, harness makers and saddlers, carpenters, innkeepers.

This list may be regarded as a representative one, though, of course, variation in number and kind of gilds is to be found from city to city. The difference would be due to local economic conditions: for instance, to the large, readily available supply of some raw material, as iron; or, say, to the commercial advantage of a special geographical situation, as in the cases of Venice, Genoa, Cologne, Bruges.

Thus it will be perceived that in the thirteenth century both an economic and a social revolution had taken place in the gilds, and in the towns too. Everywhere the wealthy classes controlled the local town government and local trade and industry, and passed statutes in support of their interests, like privileges and monopolies, or expressive of their contempt for the masses. Thus, in Bruges in 1241 the law associated counterfeiters, thieves, and artisans together. Strikes and riots in the densely populated industrial regions of Europe, as Lombardy, Tuscany, and Flanders, are common from the middle of the thirteenth century onward. In 1244 there was a riot of the workingmen in Douai; in 1248 revolt broke out in a general fashion in Bruges, Ypres, Ghent, and Douai. The violence of rural life in the heyday of private war was matched by the violence and brutality in the towns in the thirteenth, fourteenth, and fifteenth centuries. History shows no improvement in manners and morals in this matter. The violence simply shifted from country to town. So far was coercion carried that we find legislation to extradite fugitive workmen, just as we find legislation in the manorial age to return runaway serfs.

This state of things led to a new form of association—namely, leagues of the great gildsmen in all the cities of a province or region

—and to attempts on the part of the working classes to form unions in their own midst and even to knit together such combinations in adjacent towns. But all such efforts were abortive in the Middle Ages, except in Florence, and then only successful for a short season. The trade union is of modern origin; it was not a medieval institution.

Thus, to sum up: the settlement of the old economic and social problems of the eleventh and twelfth centuries by the gradual revolution which then took place, settled nothing absolutely. For the new conditions, however much they may have been an improvement or amelioration of the past, gave rise to new problems as acute as the former ones, to new grievances, to new injustices. Until about 1200 the social-economic problems of Europe were in the country. After that time they were in the towns, where the very congestion of population made them more acute than they had been before. Under the manorial régime the peasant, whatever he may have suffered from, did not suffer from unemployment; he usually had enough to eat, the wherewithal to clothe himself, and firewood to keep himself warm; he did not suffer from crowded conditions of living; his income, though meagre, was not subject to the constant fluctuation of the wages of the workingman, and after customary services were commuted into fixed money payments, the peasant prospered greatly owing to the fact that foodstuffs, which he supplied, increased in price, while neither his rent nor his taxes were increased in the same proportion. The purchasing power of money declined and prices rose, but neither movement hit the peasant heavily.

On the other hand, in the towns, the lower working classes paid high rents; they lived in mean cottages and under congested conditions in the faubourgs, the most unimproved and least sanitary quarters of the town; their wages were subject to a sliding scale depending partly upon the market, partly upon the action of the employers; they suffered from long spells of unemployment; they might hunger for lack of money to purchase food when the market stalls were heaped with it; they might lack pence to buy fuel in winter. In a word, the later Middle Ages—from 1300 onward—created the problem of the proletariat, the problem of poverty, the problem of housing conditions, the problem of capital and labor. It will not do for the modern student of the history of society to throw stones at the feudal age, for he is living in a glass house.

CHAPTER XXIX

THE CLOSE OF THE MIDDLE AGES

THE profound difference which separates the civilization of the tenth and eleventh centuries from that of the twelfth and thirteenth must be emphasized. For the thirteenth century saw a revolutionary change in Europe. Partly owing to the Crusades, partly owing to forces independent of them, a New Europe had come into being, a Europe still preserving much that was medieval, but also characterized by much that was modern in its nature. So true is this that if the thirteenth century may be called the end of the Middle Ages, it was no less the forecourt of Modern Times.

One of the most apparent changes which transpired was the breakdown of feudal government. Kings took advantage of the absence of their vassals in the East to strengthen themselves in many ways. The nobility was weakened. Towns bought their independence of their feudal lords who wished to go on a Crusade. Fiefs were consolidated, bringing vassals into closer connection with their overlords; serfs became free farmers or artisans in the towns; the old military and financial system was revolutionized; feudal law began to give way to the revived Roman law. Government incomes from feudal incidents and accidents were supplanted by fixed revenues derived from land taxes, and taxes upon commerce. New methods of assessment and new forms of collection obtained. The gradually growing practice of commuting military service into money payments (*scutage*) is a striking evidence of this change. The Saladin Tithe of Henry II, the procedure instituted for the collection of the ransom of Richard I, and that later for the release of St. Louis, when taken captive in Egypt, are other reflections of this change, and established administrative precedents. The extraordinary revenues of government vastly increased the volume of resources available. Indirect taxes became more common because they were more lucrative. The growth of an industrious population—for the great progress in public security made in the thirteenth century is notable—in town and country, multiplied these incomes. "If rents were inelastic, loans, tallages, and fines were capable of vast extension."

This new life transformed the practical conditions of government. Since it put more money into circulation, it enabled the sovereigns to hire mercenary armies; and hence it created the permanent necessity for money which is characteristic of the modern state, conditions which have grown to such enormous extent in our modern standing armies and our modern public debts. Finally, the new régime, by creating new wealth and new tastes, multiplied the number and the kind of taxes.

The cessation of internal destructive wars, and the emergence of capable government, both central and local, furthered production. Society was at once more stable and more fluid. Communication was easier than in time past. The competition between the new money economy and the older natural economy, prosperity and good prices, stimulated both forms of production.

The double prosperity of Europe was without setback, except locally (and notably in Languedoc), from the inception of the twelfth century to the beginning of the fourteenth. In England it dates from the Norman Conquest (1066), in France and Flanders from the beginning of the Crusades (1095), in Germany from the middle of Henry IV's reign (ca. 1085), in northern Italy from about 1000, in southern Italy and Sicily from the Norman Conquest there (1016–90). In the Christian states of Spain this term did not arrive until the union of Castile and Leon in 1230 and the reigns of Alfonso the Wise of Castile (1236–84) and James I of Aragon (1213–76).

The new condition of Europe, as universal as it was variegated, was attended everywhere by the fall of the old feudal government, old economy, old society. The tradition of the fief, the manor, the parish decayed. The old permanent links and associations, the old mutualism of interest, old behaviorism, old neighborhood fellowships, old local relations of person and of property gave way before a rapid succession of new changes, new contacts, new conditions, a new state of mind.

Every age, if not every people, has its own ideas with reference to person, property, and conduct. Such conventions are largely the effect of conditions. Change the conditions and the conventions change. This is what happened in the thirteenth century. Medieval serfdom declined rapidly and broadly, even if it did not wholly disappear; medieval government and forms of economy faded, even if they did not wholly vanish away; the texture of medieval society was transformed, so to speak, by insertion of new threads woven according to a different pattern; the immobile capital formerly locked up in landed wealth was displaced by the mobile capital of trade and commerce; that capitalistic enterprise which had maintained itself across the centuries in Byzantium was carried into the West during the Crusades by the Italian cities, notably by Venice and Genoa, where it combined with that new wealth created in the West independently of the influence of the Crusades; money economy and the cash nexus began to prevail where a natural economy had reigned for centuries. It was a revolution both of person and of property. New kinds of property came into being, new changes ensued in the form and the degree of possession. A new class of possessors was developed.

These alterations in social and economic condition were so manifold and so complex in their relation, one to another, that they worked a profound transformation, and induced what may be described as molecular social and economic changes. These changes were accelerated by the influence of the Crusades, but many of them were not originated by them, and would have developed independently of the Crusades. Like all such forces, they were intricately interwoven, and cannot be dissociated historically, although logically they are distinguishable.

One of the foremost of the factors was the increase of population in Europe during the feudal age. We know little of the early Middle Ages with reference to mass or density of population, the weight of taxation, the amount of revenues of governments and the Church, of the incomes from domains, beyond general expressions. But from the twelfth century onward we have evidence which, though far from being full, is nevertheless capable of some positive interpretation, even if it is not "statistics" in the modern acceptance of that term.

The population of Europe began to decline in the second century of the Roman Empire, and seems steadily to have fallen until the eighth. There may have been a slight increment in the time of Charlemagne, but it was arrested by the civil wars and invasions from without of the ninth and tenth centuries. There is a perceptible increase later in the tenth century, notably in Germany. From 1000 onward until 1349, when the Black Death scourged Europe, the increment of population was steady and large, so much so that it more than canceled the drain made by the Crusades. Fortunately, during these centuries, the increase of means of subsistence kept pace with this increase of population. The most thorough study of the increment of population during the feudal period is that made by the German historian Lamprecht. It applies only to the valley of the Moselle, but perhaps may be taken as a fair index of the growth in many places in Europe. The figures are as follows:

Year	Villages	Population	Year	Villages	Population
800	100	20,000	1150	810	140,000
900	250	60,000	1200	990	220,000
1000	350	80,000	1237	1180	250,000
1100	590	100,000			

This increase of population is manifested in the progress made in public improvements, like diking rivers and seaboards, draining marshes, leveling forests; in the enormous numbers of new and better edifices, religious and secular, erected in these centuries, for the previous generations could not have endured the cost of them or provided the labor for them; in the constant overflow of surplus populations into more sparsely populated regions—the northern French and Flemings over-

flowing into England, the southern French into Spain, the Germans into the Slav lands beyond the Elbe, and all Europe during the Crusades into the Levant; in the growth of towns, and the drift of the rural population into them; in the more intensive cultivation of the fields, the break-up of ancient commons, the enclosure of heaths and waste, the clearing of forest tracts, the conversion of pasture lands into villages, and the increase in number of villages.

In the feudal age, that is to say, before the rise of the towns, perhaps 90 to 95 per cent of the population of Europe dwelt in the country, as against 40 to 50 per cent in modern Europe, except in England, where the town population is proportionally even greater. Certain regions of Europe, notably Lombardy, the Moselle valley, and Flanders, by 1100 show high density alike in the economic and in the geographic sense,[1] and it is by data from these regions that we can estimate what was taking place elsewhere. As early as 1127 Flanders is described as *terra valde populosa*, a densely populated land. In the Moselle land the population nearly doubled between 900 and 1000; by 1250 it had quadrupled. The result was an increase in land values, especially around the towns, due to the necessity of feeding denser population in them. It has been held by many economists that the primary source of human improvement is to be found in increase of population and increasing pressure upon subsistence, and it would seem that the history of the eleventh and twelfth centuries bears out the statement. It certainly seems that the many and intricate phenomena of change which mark this period may be ultimately referable to this fact.

The landed proprietary class became deeply compromised by the changes which ensued. For centuries feudal government, feudal society, had rested upon landed monopoly. Landed possession conferred wealth, determined aristocratic status, supported government, maintained serfdom. As far back as the fifth century the Burgundian Code forbade the sale of land to persons who did not already possess land. By abridging right of ownership to land, by forbidding access to cheap land by removal or emigration, in a word by maintaining serfdom, by putting a high value upon land beyond what the laborer could pay for its purchase, the feudal aristocracy had managed to keep its supremacy.

But the steady increase of population first relaxed and then broke this grip. The boldest element among the servile population, as pressure upon subsistence increased, refused longer to be bound by servile ties, and emigrated to new parts. When the towns began to rise the

---

[1] In considering any question of population, distinction must be made between "economic density" and "geographic density." By the former is meant the pressure of population upon subsistence measured by the production of foodstuffs and natural resources; by the latter, the numerical relationship between population and area of occupation.

rural population drifted into them. The result was that the least progressive element of the working population was left upon the manors; hence the economic efficiency of the manor declined. In order to prevent further depopulation of their lands, the lords were forced to hold out inducements to the peasants to make them stay, in amelioration of conditions, commutation of services into fixed payments, and finally even emancipation. It is evident that from late in the twelfth century onward into the fourteenth, the landed proprietor in medieval Europe found difficulty in securing sufficient heavy labor to work his lands. Some writers have rashly assumed, without sufficient knowledge of conditions, that wars at home and abroad, combined with a mortality far greater than today, reduced the numbers of the working population, and accordingly, with so much land available, the lord was compelled to hold out inducements in order to keep his serfs. But this explanation is belied by the facts, for the evidence is overwhelming that population greatly increased in Europe in these centuries. The economic embarassment of the proprietary class was due to quite different conditions.

This economic distress of the nobles is perhaps one of the chief reasons why so many of them at first multiplied the manorial impositions like the *cens* and the *champart*. In these days a land-owner can augment the productive capacity of his land by developing a higher technique, by introducing farm machinery, by adopting more intensive methods of farming, by varying his crops. But in the Middle Ages he was too much bound by prevailing economic conditions. Even yet farming conditions are the last and the least to be reformed. And so when the expedient of coercion of the tenantry failed, the lords, if they possessed the right to coin money, resorted to the practice of manipulating and even debasing the coinage, profiting by the seigniorage derived from each successive new issue. They capitalized their prerogative, much as the Church capitalized its authority. The popular distress and inconvenience to trade arising from such practice was a factor in the decline of the baronage and the growth of the power of the king, who gradually supplanted local and provincial feudal authority by royal government and suppressed local circulation of money in favor of the royal currency.

When this expedient failed, the proprietors began to emancipate their serfs, to promote free villein tenures, to introduce *hospites,* cotters, crofters (free but low laborers) in the effort to provide themselves with a sufficient and stable labor. And when even this resort failed of entire success owing to the fact that the cost of living mounted faster than revenues increased, the proprietors went frankly over to a rental system. The fall of feudal economy was inherent in this transition from services to rents, whose rapid growth is a feature of the twelfth century.

The former villein services and "renders," having failed to supply an adequate income to the lord even before the introduction of the rent system, the lord took care to have the rent made adequate when this transition came. Dues were insensibly transmuted into fixed rent charges. As payments formerly made in kind became transmuted into money payments and the nature and extent of both servile and villein services became fixed and customary, the condition was eased. But in virtue of the immense weight attached to tradition, when once established, these rates remained unalterable. Once taxes and rents were fixed, it was not customary to change them. A property might be sold a dozen times, but neither the assessment nor the rent of the land could be changed. The only change was in the rent of the house and the tax on the dwelling. The terms of these conditions usually were preserved by tradition from generation to generation. A well-known document, alluding to the "husbandmen now worn out with years, whose memory on these matters is hoary," says they "have learned from their fathers and know perfectly well how much they are bound to pay." It is significant of this change that the word *coustumier* by the thirteenth century is commonly employed to describe this new class of peasantry. These "customs" might be more or less onerous, but the fixity of their form and the unalterable nature of their incidence were in themselves guarantees of a better condition of things. The peasant was protected against new taxes or increase of the old. And it is an established principle of economists that the best taxes are those which have long been familiar to the people, and which are collectible without difficulty or protest. To understand the great advance made in taxation of the peasantry and the value of fixed custom as over against arbitrary imposition, we have only to contrast this condition with the grievances of the Irish peasantry so late as the last century against the evils of "rack-rent." Nothing so abominable as that practice existed in any but the most backward parts of Europe by the end of the thirteenth century.

By 1300 the serfs, or at least several millions of them, had ascended to freedom, or if they still were called serfs, it was a legal fiction owing to the attachment of certain old conditions to certain lands which they might own or rent. *Cens, lots,* and other obsolete terms which once had meant real services and real burdens were now become simple words, vestigial survivals of empty prerogatives like the curious conditions one sometimes sees attached to property today, which revert for their origin to some remote testator. If the peasants had not become freeholders, at least they were a free tenantry. The former manorial village had become a village of free farmers and a sort of rustic magistracy had taken the place of the government of the former lord of the manor.

The economic revolution in Europe had forced emancipation. It is absurd to think that a sentiment of humanitarianism played any large part in this process. If idealism had motivated the movement, Church serfs ought to have been the first to be emancipated, whereas they were the last. The clergy lagged behind secular proprietors in this. The charitable formulas, "for the love of God," "for the welfare of my soul," etc., are conventional, stereotyped phrases.

But the lord had made the mistake of permitting the term of rent to be a long one, following the precedent of manorial custom in which the amount and kind of services, once agreed upon, remained fixed. He failed to read the future and to reckon upon the steady rise in prices, the steady increase of cost of living, which mounted from the middle of the twelfth century to the end of the thirteenth. The result was that in course of time, as the cost of living went up and rents remained fixed, the lord still found himself in economic distress.

In reality the peasant gained much more than the lord. Just because money-rents displaced the plowings and reapings very gradually, they assumed the most important characteristic of the latter—their customary uniformity; tradition kept them at a certain level which it was very difficult to disturb, even when the interests of the lord and the conditions of the time had altered a great deal. Prices fluctuate and rise gradually, the buying strength of money gets lowered little by little, but customary rents remain much the same as they were before. Thus in process of time the balance gets altered for the benefit of the rentpayer. . . . [In England] one of the chief reasons for holding the Glastonbury inquest of 1189 was the wish to ascertain whether the rents actually corresponded to the value of the plots, and to make the necessary modifications. But such assessments were very rare, it was difficult to carry them into practice, and the general tendency was distinctly towards a stability of customary rents.[2]

The Church, as the heaviest land-owner, and notably the monasteries were hit especially hard by these changes. For the monasteries were eminently rural foundations, while the seats of the bishops were in the towns.

The landed aristocracy, when it did not disappear, was reduced, both in numbers and in influence. In creating new species of wealth the revolution created new elements in society. In addition to the bourgeoisie of the towns, a new parvenu noblesse sprang up whose titles were derived from royal favor instead of birth, whose wealth was in the form of government stipends, pensions, and offices, instead of land. The old feudal families survived as an antiquated, proud, but often poor aristocracy.

We have some curious illustrations of this growing penury of the old feudality. For example, since the cost of becoming a knight was very great—for the new knight had to be provided with a charger and re-

[2] Vinogradoff, *Villeinage in England*, 181–182.

serve horse, armor, gay attire, varlets, to which the expense of the initiation ceremony and festive entertainment must be added—one observes a tendency to defer *adoubement*. In the early days of chivalry one might be made a knight at fifteen years of age; then it was delayed until the eighteenth year; later still, to the twenty-first. If the would-be knight were a scion of a conspicuous family, it was considered a social disgrace for at least the eldest son not to be knighted when he reached his majority. The result was that many a family fell into the clutches of Jew money-lenders in the endeavor to keep up their social prestige on falling revenues. The same phenomenon also is found with reference to dowries. The marriage of the daughters was delayed, and if the eldest daughter got married, her sisters were practically certain to have to wait until the family could recoup its fortune by a lucky stroke, or by careful saving.

As rents did not rise in proportion to the rise in the cost of living, the nobles grew more and more impoverished. They were compelled to mortgage their estates, and when the interest was defaulted, the mortgage was foreclosed and their lands were lost to them. Twelfth century Europe experienced in less acute degree what the world has experienced since 1918; namely, the distress of those living upon fixed income. The income of the merchant, the artisan, the free farmer, was flexible and, if he was industrious, likely to increase rather than decrease. But not so was the case of the landlord living on fixed rents drawn in terms of long leases. He got poorer year by year as the cost of living mounted. This process of decay of the feudal aristocracy was most marked in Italy, but prevailed everywhere in greater or less degree. In 1250 the last of the lords of Tintinnano, one of the high nobles of Tuscany, thus had lost his ancestral lands and died a beggar in the streets of Siena, dependent upon charity.

But if poorer, the old nobility had better manners than their forbears. The days of the earlier, brutal feudal society, when the greatest of barons were ignorant and illiterate, were past in the thirteenth century. Yet this new refinement had its dross. The pride of the aristocracy—and French pride especially was proverbial—too often hardened into arrogance. While the Crusades were influential in spreading the ideas of chivalry, those ideas lost their earlier humane quality and class ideals. Chivalry became an international corporation, an international caste. The rough brutality of the eleventh and twelfth centuries was succeeded by a refined cruelty, which was worse. The result was that one discerns in the literature of the thirteenth century an ominous note of prejudice against the bourgeoisie and the free peasantry and free villeins, and an unwholesome scorn of these classes by some, though not all, of the aristocracy.

Of course it must not be assumed that all feudal nobles were unfortunate. Those who were wise enough to retain some portion of their lands in their own hands, not to put it out to rent but to farm it themselves, hiring labor when needed, and dismissing it when the work was over, managed to pull through. If the nobles and the proprietary class had worked their own lands as the peasantry did, their situation would have been different. But this they would not and could not do, nor could they afford to pay the new scale of wages which free farm labor exacted. The noble found difficulty in working his acres, for the peasants would either quit him for the town, or demand too high wages. But as a whole, the nobles had little aptitude for business and little or nothing in the traditions and practices of the manorial régime had educated them to understand the new conditions. Land had become a commercial asset, an object of purchase and sale, a commodity—a thing unheard of in the feudal age. The truth is that the proprietary class between 1150 and 1250 was caught between shrinkage of income, whether due to inability to work their lands profitably or due to the impossibility of raising rents, and the increase in the cost of living and high prices. For the period was marked by a price and wages revolution.

An exact history of prices for the Middle Ages is not possible on account of the variety of money current, its fluctuations, and especially the impossibility of ascertaining what the purchasing power was at any given time and in any given country or province. But, speaking broadly, there is no doubt that there was a great rise in prices and wages in the late feudal period. The rise in wages, since it kept a rough parity with the increase in prices, compensated the workingman and the farmer who produced food supplies; but the man who lived upon rents and investments suffered. In other words, the nobility and the Church suffered most. But the latter could always make up the difference by petitioning gifts, and, as we have seen, capitalized its spiritual authority to vast fiscal advantage, while the nobility could make no such appeal nor adopt such practices.

The influence of the towns, in which urban rents were increasingly devoted to the promotion of commerce, upon the passing of feudal economy, and their relation to the disappearance of manorialism and the formation of a free peasantry, is another feature of the revolution of the thirteenth century. Certainly a primary factor in the betterment of the peasantry was the activity of the towns that were large enough to carry on an external trade.

It was the interest of these towns to advocate freedom in order that they might get access to raw material. Then the growth of capital in the towns led to the wish on the part of the citizens to invest capital in land. The feudal system with its serfs bound to the soil on an hereditary tenure was a hindrance to the free investment of land, and was another cause why the towns were hostile to serfdom. Hence the towns of central Italy initiated the freeing of serfs en masse, not in order to give the land to the peasants, but in order that the towns might be able to invest in land when it became a marketable commodity.

Especially in Tuscany and Lombardy is this rôle of the towns in breaking up the old manorial system of cultivation of striking effect, by which both personal status and form of land tenure were altered.

In Brescia in 1303 there was a special post created to assist the enclosing of land and the abolition of common fields. Indeed, there soon arose a considerable market for land, and there was a considerable demand for it in the thirteenth century in Italy. Much the same revolution was in fact going on in Italy in the fourteenth and fifteenth centuries as occurred in England in the sixteenth; namely, the substitution of the town bourgeoisie for the nobles as land-owners, the substitution of the short lease and share system for hereditary tenure, the division of land into compact holdings, the rise of the wage-earning agricultural laborer, and a great improvement in the methods of agriculture.[3]

The new nobility and rich bourgeois were the chief purchasers of land. Even many former serfs, now become freemen, who were ambitious to own their own farms, also bought land in the thirteenth century. Land values around towns, where increased population made truck-farming profitable, or where wealthy merchants wished to possess country seats, increased most.

The rise in the standard of living and high prices hit the upper classes more heavily than the lower classes. For, as Adam Smith long ago pointed out, "the prices of necessaries do not rise as wealth increases in a country, or falls as it diminishes, as the prices of superfluities do." The relation is a variable one, not a constant one, and the advantage of the market is on the side of the common man. Or, as one has expressed it: "It was the desire for superfluities, merging into the desire for money, which acted as the solvent that ended the old and produced a new order of things . . . and villeinage disappeared from the face of the earth."[4]

By 1300 the old manorial régime in Europe was reduced to a mere framework, a shell, a skeleton of what it once was. New economic and social forces had worn away the substance of it as the forces of the atmosphere weather away a building. Where the manor persisted, it was a new and different economic unit, having a new and different economy, a new and different social texture.

The medieval peasant, by 1300, had traveled a long way from his condition in 850, although, of course, there were still backward regions.

[3] These two citations are from the *Economic Journal*, XXI, 438 (a review of Kovalevsky).

[4] Carlile, *History of Money*, 257.

The truth is, European society had been in a constant state of flux and change since the ninth century. "Serfdom existed in 1300 and in 1100, but a great gulf lies between the meanings of the term at the earlier and the later date. . . . Time is on the side of the serf." [5]

The oft alleged lateness of the appearance of a money economy in medieval Europe is an economic inference based on too superficial inspection of evidence. Exactly when was the medieval manor a self-sufficing unit, which needed and knew no money economy? Such generalizations need scrutiny. As far as ministerial accounts are concerned, we find no trace in the thirteenth century of that specific revolution which substituted a money for a natural economy in the manor. The rise of a money economy was apparent before the Crusades began. Much evidence points to the early appearance of a money economy in medieval Europe, although, in the words of the late Professor Vinogradoff, "the struggle between natural husbandry and cash nexus in medieval times cannot be circumscribed by exact chronological distinction."

One may say of many other questions of medieval economic history that they do not admit of fixed dates or simple solution. Purchasing power of money, prices of staple products, amount of wages and salaries, weight of taxation, are very difficult matters to determine in terms of such things today. The purchasing power of money, of course, was greater in the Middle Ages than now. But how much? If, for purposes of comparison, we let one represent the purchasing power of money in 1914 (before the Great War), then the purchasing power *may* have been nine times as great in 850, and four and one-half times as great in 1200. But the really important matter is the *then* relation of purchasing power to price of standard commodities. It is certain that there was a steady fall in the value of money from the ninth century forward to 1300.

The Levantine countries would take nothing but gold in payment of their importations, except in the case of a few commodities like cloth: consequently what gold western Europe had was constantly drawn off. On the other hand, when the Crusades began, immense quantities of hoarded silver were thrown on the West, in addition to which much silver plate and ingot metal was melted down and coined into money. Richard I's ransom was mainly obtained from the plate of the religious houses. The result was a glut of silver in the West, the ratio of which to gold constantly fluctuated and slowly declined. In the time of the First Crusade this unstable relation between gold and silver is manifest, and repeated alteration of the coinage is to be found. Thus in 1103 an old chronicle records: *"In hoc anno fuit magna tribulatio et nummi argentei pro auris mutati et facti sunt*—In this year there was great tribulation and silver money was changed in its relation to gold

[5] Coopland, *The Abbey of St. Bertin*, 95, 147.

and made over." Nine years later, in 1112, we read, *"Iterum nummi mutati sunt et cum granis alii facti*—Again the coins were changed and others made of new grain," *i.e.,* of new relation to gold. And for a third time, in 1120, is the record: *"Mense Novembre mutati sunt nummi*—In the month of November the money was changed." Thus in the course of seventeen years there were three different depreciations. Mean rulers like Philip I of France tried to indemnify themselves by cheating the people by alloying their silver coinage with copper, "so that through this practice" writes Guibert of Nogent, "many were reduced to poverty and the ruin of many hastened." [6]

The remedy lay, of course, in the establishing of the gold standard in the West. But this was impracticable before the latter half of the thirteenth century, when Norman Italy, Venice, Genoa, Florence, and then France introduced a gold coinage. The intricacies of new finance, the subtle operations of credit, the problem of new forms of taxation, were perplexing to those generations, and European governments had yet to learn the elementary principles thereof.

The burden of depreciated silver, the immense amount of it in circulation in the West, and the immense amount required, when exigency demanded, to pay an obligation in silver whose value was estimated in gold, is illustrated by the ransom of St. Louis in 1250, after his capture at the battle of Mansurah. "There was sent to him as much money in talents, sterling coin, and approved money of Cologne [not

---

[6] "The currency employed was that of the silver penny, and the pound was a term of account meaning 240 of these pennies. The reckoning was based on weight, what we now call troy weight; 20 pennyweights make an ounce; 12 ounces make a pound. But in money the values of the intermediate stages, as they became finally settled, were inverted, so that in the twelfth century, as now, 12 pennies make a shilling and 20 shillings make a pound. But the idea of weight was not forgotten. . . . 8 ounces make a "mark." But there were no coins corresponding to any of these denominations [*i.e.,* neither mark, shilling, nor pound]. . . . The ratio of gold to silver . . . being 9:1 [in the twelfth century], the ounce of gold equaled 15 shillings and the mark of gold 6 pounds. But neither the pound nor the mark nor the ounce was a coin. . . . The Norman name for the English silver penny was 'esterlin.' It is found as early as about 1100. It was necessary to use a distinctive term because the English penny was worth two pennies of Le Mans and four pennies of Rouen, Angers, and Tours. The meaning of the name is unknown, but it certainly has nothing to do with the Easterlings or German merchants, as most books tell us. The word appears in Latin as 'sterlingus' or 'sterlingo' and down to the latter part of the thirteenth century meant an English penny. . . . The obolus was a half-penny. . . . Occasionally a foreign gold coin, the bezant, was used. . . . The bezant (or aureus) is generally said to be the Byzantine 'solidus' brought into the West through the dealings of merchants. It was sometimes called rhetorically a talent. But it is possible that the word indicates also the ducat, which was first coined by Roger II of Sicily in 1140 and derived its name from the legend on it, which read 'dux Apuliæ.' "—Stanley Lane-Poole, *The Exchequer in the Twelfth Century,* p. 83.

the *base* money of the Parisians or of Tours] as eleven wagons could be loaded with, to each of which were four strong horses, by which it was carried to the seacoast, where it was received on board a Genoese ship to be transported to the king. Each wagon carried two large iron hooped casks prepared for the purpose and filled with the aforesaid money." When this great volume of money arrived at Damietta, the French king apologized for it, saying, "We of the West do not so much abound in gold as you people of the East."

The difference between the old and the new condition of medieval Europe is reflected in the difference in land values. When we compare the value of freehold or rent-land on long leases with manorial land, we find the latter worth much less than the former. Some figures for Germany seem to indicate that this depreciation was as much as 33 per cent in the twelfth century, and twice that in the thirteenth century; or, to put it the other way, freehold or rent-land was worth from 33 to 66 per cent more than manorial land.

The mobility of rural labor in the thirteenth century strikingly contrasts with the fixed condition of the tenth and eleventh centuries. The constant movement of knights and nobles, pilgrims and Crusaders, wandering peddlers and groups of merchants had long been a familiar sight. But it was new to see bands of free peasants in harvest time traveling from manor to manor, and paid by the day and even "striking" for higher wages in the midst of the harvest time, taking advantage of the necessity of the land-owner to get his crop in when it was ripe at almost any cost, or losing much of it. Most astonishing of all, we find town laborers going into the country in harvest time.

While this improvement in the condition of the rural classes was due to the influence of many economic and social forces—the fall of the old feudal economy, fixed rents and other changes, a rising market for farm produce owing to increase of population and the prosperity of the new bourgeoisie which formed a large consumer class—it must not be lost sight of that the improvement of agriculture did not keep pace with improvement in other activities, and that the farmer's profits were derived more from high prices than from better farming methods. Yet it would be an error to think that there was no improvement in farming methods. The use of cattle dung and marl as fertilizers increased—on the seashore rotted seaweed was used—bare fallowing was more and more abandoned, the three-field system was extended and the two-field system less and less obtained, rotation of crops was more general, consolidation of holdings slowly began to displace the old manorial condition of scattered properties. Least progress was made in new and better tools. But this remained true until the modern age. As to soil exhaustion, it is an allegation which cannot be proved. The indirect evidence available—direct comparative evidence fails us—will not sustain the proposition of progressive soil exhaustion. "If men found it harder to get food because of the exhaustion of the soil, how can we explain the expansion of industries and commerce which did not increase the food supply? And why did wages rise?" And how explain the steady growth of population if agricultural conditions were so adverse?

The profound transformations and changes through which Europe went in the twelfth and thirteenth centuries could not fail to interest thinking men, and it is interesting to observe that the ablest writers, like Guibert of Nogent, Otto of Freising, William of Newburgh in the twelfth century, and Roger Bacon, St. Thomas Aquinas, and Robert Grosseteste in the thirteenth, were aware of them. Even speculative philosophy took cognizance of them. There is an obvious decline of interest in Augustinian philosophy and obsolete theological theories, and a desire for a more practical and concrete thinking. Men had become impatient of the eschatological point of view and the apocalyptic motif, and demanded something more practical and concrete, something more capable of terrestrial application. Live thinkers were interested in society and the changes taking place in it. We find evidence of an increasing boldness of criticism of government, of protest against privilege in economics, authority in religion, and in thought. Just as there is a close affiliation to be found between logic and the experimental sciences in the thirteenth century, so an affiliation is to be found between philosophy and the social organism. Even St. Thomas Aquinas, magnificent metaphysician though he was and harmonizer of Augustinian theology with Aristotelian philosophy, yet was observant enough of the rise of the towns to comment upon the proper site for a town and the relative advantages of agriculture and commerce as sources of municipal wealth. Hugo of St. Victor, reckoned the supreme mystic of the twelfth century, formulated a theory of the progressive evolution of humanity not only spiritually, but in material civilization, and emphasized economics, government, and history in his teaching. Living in the time when the free artisan, the free craftsman, was coming up out of serfdom, when gilds were forming, these new activities and associations interested him exceedingly and he went so far as to classify the mechanical arts after the manner of the seven liberal arts, the *trivium* and *quadrivium* of the schools. Thus he distinguishes earth-culture, food-science, and medicine in the former, and costuming, armor-making, architecture, and— mark the significance of it—business (*mercatura*) in the second. If we pause to reflect, such social thinking in and for its time is as intelligent and as cogent as modern thought in its time.

The roots of modern society run deep down into medieval history.

Medieval history is the heritage of the modern age. It ought not to be alien to us. Its civilization in many ways has entered into our civilization. It is as Goethe has said:

> What you the spirit of the ages call
> Is nothing but the spirit of you all
> Wherein the ages are reflected.

BIBLIOGRAPHIES *

INTRODUCTION

Suggestive reading on the content and value of medieval civilization:

THOMPSON, JAMES WESTFALL, *Reference Studies in Medieval History*, pt. i, introd. (University of Chicago Press, 1923); ADAMS, G. B., *Civilization during the Middle Ages*, chs. i–ii; STUBBS, W., *Seventeen Lectures on Medieval and Modern History*, chs. ix–x; TAYLOR, H. O., *The Medieval Mind*, I, ch. 1; KER, W. P., *The Dark Ages*, introd.; SHOTWELL, J. T., "Middle Ages," *Encyclopædia Britannica*, 11th ed.; HEARNSHAW, F. J. C., *Medieval Contributions to Modern Civilization;* EUCKEN, RUDOLPH, *Main Currents of Modern Thought*, pp. 331–344; TOUT, T. F., "The Place of the Middle Ages in Teaching," *History*, new ser., IV; BURR, G. L., "Anent the Middle Ages," *American Historical Review*, XVII, 714, XX, 813; KEUTGEN, "On the Necessity in America of the Study of the Early History of Modern European Nations," *Annual Report of American Historical Assoc.*, 1904, 94; THORNDIKE, E. L., *Short History of Civilization*, bk. vi; BLOCH, "La Société du haut moyen-âge," *Journal des Savants*, Nov., 1926; WOLFF, G., "Ueber den Zusammenhang römischer und frühmittelalterlicher Kultur' im Mainlande" (*Einzelforschungen über Kunst- und Altertumsgegenstände zu Frankfort*, vol. I, 1908); *Archiv für kulturgeschichte*, XVI (1925) (a symposium).

CHAPTER I

THE ROMAN EMPIRE

Classified bibliography of literature in English in

THOMPSON, JAMES WESTFALL, *Reference Studies in Medieval History*, pt. i, 1–8 (University of Chicago Press, 1923).

General Works

* ROSTOVTZEFF, M., *Social and Economic History of the Roman Empire* (Oxford, 1926); GIBBON, EDWARD, *The Decline and Fall of the Roman Empire*, ed. J. B. BURY, London, 1900, vols. I–IV (Bury's notes and appendices are very valuable); NILSSON, MARTIN, *Imperial Rome;* DURUY, VICTOR, *History of the Romans*, vols. IV–VIII (English transl.); HODGKIN, THOMAS, *Italy and Her Invaders*, vols. I–II; FRANK, TENNEY, *Roman Imperialism;* JONES, H. STUART, *The Roman Empire;* E. S. BOUCHIER is the author of various works (*Life and Letters in Roman Africa; Spain*

* Unless published before 1900 dates are not usually given.

under the Roman Empire; Syria as a Roman Province); MILNE, J. G., *Egypt under Roman Rule;* GRAHAM, A., *Roman Africa* (an outline of the Roman occupation of North Africa).

Lives of the Emperors

GARDHAUSEN, *Augustus;* TARVER, *Tiberius;* WILLRICH, *Caligula;* HEN-DERSON, B. W., *Nero;* DE LA BERGE, C., *Trajan;* GREGOROVIUS, F., *Hadrian;* LACOUR GAYET, G., *Antonin le Pieux;* WATSON, P. B., *Marcus Aurelius;* PLATNAUER, M., *Septimius Severus;* HOPKINS, R. V. N., *Alexander Severus;* CREES, J. H. E., *Probus;* HOMO, L., *Aurélien;* PREUSS, *Kaiser Diocletian;* FIRTH, J. B., *Constantine;* GARDNER, B. M., *Julian, Philosopher and Emperor;* NEGRI, G., *Julian the Apostate.*

Commerce

* MOMMSEN, THEODOR, *Roman Provinces,* 2 vols. (English transl.); * CHARLESWORTH, M. P., *Trade Routes and Commerce of the Roman Empire* (1924); MARQUARDT, J., *Organisation des römischen Reichs,* (1881); MARQUARDT, J.; "Finanz" and "Militarwesen" (both of these in MOMMSEN AND MARQUARDT, *Handbuch der römischen Alterthümer* (1884); there is a French translation of this monumental work in 17 vols.; vols. IX–X are a survey of the provinces); ARNOLD, W. T., *Roman Provincial Administration;* SANDYS, J. E., *Companion to Latin Studies,* secs. 644–48, 659–71; BESNIER, "Le Commerce romain," *Journal des Savants* (1920).

On the commerce of Rome with the Orient, see:

* HIRTH, F., *China and the Roman Orient,* (1885); * RAWLINSON, H. G., *Intercourse between India and the Western World from the Earliest Times to the Fall of Rome,* chs. vi–viii; * SCHOFF, W. H., *The Periplus of the Erythrean Sea;* BURY, in Gibbon's *Decline and Fall of the Roman Empire,* IV 534–35; SOOTHILL, *China and the West;* WILLIAMS, E. T., *China Yesterday and Today,* ch. xvi; PARKER, E. W., *History of China,* pp. 41–50; SCHOFF, W. H., *The Parthian Stations of Isidore of Charax;* HAIG, M. R., *The Indus Delta,* pp. 25–33; CLARK, W. E., *Classical Philology,* XV (1920), 11–22; WARMINGTON, E. H. *The commerce between the Roman Empire and India* (1927); COUYAT, *Les ports Greco-Romains de la Mer Rouge, Comptes-rendus de l'Academie des Inscriptions* (1910), 525 *ff.*

Industry and the Collegia

* WALTZING, J. P., *Les Corporations professionales chez les Romains* (1896), 2 vols., * WESTERMANN, W. L., "Trades of Antiquity," *American Historical Review,* XXIII, 102; * BROWN, W. A., "State Control of Industry in the Fourth Century," *Political Science Quarterly,* II, 494; HOPKINS, R. V. N., *Alexander Severus,* 151–53; DILL, S., *Roman Society from Nero to Aurelius,* bk. ii, ch. iii; DAREMBOURG AND SALIO, *Dictionnaire des Antiquités,* article "Corporation"; ABBOTT, F. F., *The Common People of Ancient Rome,* 205–33; RENAN, E., *The Apostles,* 268–74; DURUY, V., *History of the Romans,* VIII, 32–37.

Agriculture

* HEITLAND, W. E., *Agricola*, pp. 336–459; * JONES, H. STUART, "Land Problems in Ancient Rome," *Edinburgh Review*, ccxxiv, 60; HUNTINGTON, ELLSWORTH, "Climatic Change and Agricultural Exhaustion as Elements in the Fall of Rome," *Quarterly Journal of Economics*, Feb., 1917; FRANK, TENNEY, *Economic History of Rome*, chs. vi and xvi; SIMKHOVITCH, V. G., "Rome's Fall Reconsidered," *Political Science Quarterly*, XXXI, 201; JONES, H. STUART, *Companion to Roman History*, pp. 304–15; WESTERMANN, W. L., "An Egyptian Farmer," *Univ. of Wisconsin Studies in Language and Literature*, no. III.

Colonate

* PELHAM, HENRY, *The Imperial Domains and the Colonate;* * ROSTOVTZEFF, *Studien zur Geschichte des römischen Kolonates*, (Leipzig, 1910); * FUSTEL DE COULANGES, "Le Colonat romain" (in *Recherches sur quelques problèmes d'histoire*, 1885); * VINOGRADOFF, P., *Growth of the Manor*, bk. i; * SEECK, O., "Kolonat," in Pauly-Wissowa, *Real-Encyklopaedie;* * ROSTOVTZEFF, "Kolonat," in *Handwörterbuch der Staatswissenschaft*, 3d ed.; * BEAUDOUIN, E., *Les Grands Domaines dans l'Empire Romain*, (1889); HEISTERBERG, B., *Die Entstehung des Colonats*, (Leipzig, 1876); HARDY, E. G., *The Roman Colonate;* SEGRE, G., "Studio sull' origine e sullo sviluppo storico del colonato romano," in *Archivio giuridico*, 1889–91; SCHULTEN, *Die römischen Grundherrschaften* (cf. *Historische Zeitschrift*, XLII); MISPOULET, "Le Colonat romain," *Journal des Savants*, May, 1911; GUMMERUS, *Die Fronen der Kolonen*, Helsingfors, 1906–07; MOMMSEN, T., in *Hermes*, XIX (1884); KOVALEVSKY, M., *Die oekonomische Entwicklung Europas*, vol. I (1905).

Imperial Domains

* HIS, *Die Domänen der römischen Kaiserzeit*, (1896); * PELHAM, H., *The Imperial Domains and the Colonate;* HOMO, L., "Le Domaine impériale à Rome, ses origines et ses développements," *Mélanges d'archeologie et d'histoire*, (1898); HIRSCHFELD, *Beiträge zur alten Geschichte*, 1902; FOURNIER, *Revue Historique*, (1882).

The Roman Landed Aristocracy

In addition to the works cited under Agriculture, the Colonate, and the Imperial Domains, see:

* BEAUDOUIN, "Étude sur les origines du régime feodal: La Recommendation et la justice seigneuriale," *Annales de l'énseignement supérieur de Grenoble*, vol. I, no. i (1889); * BEAUDOUIN, "Les Grands Domaines dans l'Empire Romain," *Nouvelle Revue historique de Droit*, 1897, pp. 543 ff. (with valuable bibliography), 1898; * FUSTEL DE COULANGES, *L'Alleu et le domaine rural* (espec. 1–97); * ZULUETA, F. DE, "Patronage in the Later Roman Empire," in *Oxford Studies in Social and Legal History*, I (1909), essay ii; FLACH, J., *Les Origines de l'ancienne France*, vol. I; LECRIVAIN, C., *Le Sénat romain depuis Dioclétien*, (1888); RODBERTUS, "Die agra-

rische Entwickelung Roms unter den Kaisern," *Hildebrands Jahrbücher*, II, 206, 293.

Municipia

* REID, J. S., *The Municipalities of the Roman Empire*, espec. chs. xiii–xiv; * DILL, S., *Roman Society from Nero to Aurelius*, bk. ii, ch. ii; WARDE-FOWLER, W., *The City State of the Greeks and Romans;* SANDYS, J. E., *Companion to Latin Studies*, secs. 542–563; *Cambridge Medieval History*, I, 553–557; DURUY, V., *History of the Romans*, VI, ch. lxxxiii.

Taxation

SANDYS, J. E., *Companion to Latin Studies*, secs. 498–519, 556–63; ARNOLD, W. T., *Roman Provincial Administration*, ch. vi; VINOGRADOFF, P., *Growth of the Manor*, 52–83, 104–113; *Cambridge Medieval History*, I, 38–44.

Oriental Influence in Roman Empire

CUMONT, F., *Oriental Religions in Roman Paganism;* DILL, S., *Roman Society from Nero to Aurelius*, bk. iv, chs. v–vi; DILL, S., *Last Century of the Western Empire*, 3–26, 74–112; LECKY, W. E. H., *History of European Morals*, I, ch. ii; HAY, J. S., *The Amazing Emperor Heliogabalus*, ch. vii; HOPKINS, R. V. N., *Life of Alexander Severus*, chs. i–ii; LEGGE, F., *Forerunners and Rivals of Christianity*, 2 vols.; PLATNAUER, M., *Life of the Emperor Septimius Severus*, ch. ix.

Diocletian's Price Edict

* MOMMSEN, *Berichte d. königl.-sächsischen Gesellschaft d. Wissenschaft, phil.-hist. Klasse*, 1851; WADDINGTON, *Séances et travaux de l'Académie des sciences morales et politiques*, XXXVIII; LORING, *Journal of Hellenic Studies*, II (1890); HULTSCH, *Neue Jahrb. f. Philologie und Pädagogik*, vol. CXXI (1880).

Causes of the Decline of the Roman Empire

* SEECK, O., *Geschichte des Untergangs der antiken Welt*, 3 vols., Berlin, 1895–1909, 2d ed., I–II and 2 supplements, 1898–1911 (the ablest inquiry into the whole subject; for reviews of this work see *Historische Zeitschrift*, LVIII and LXXXIV; *Vierteljahrschrift f. Sozial und Wirtschaftgesch.*, XVI; *Byzantinische Zeitschrift*, XXIII; *English Hist. Rev.*, IV.). * ROSTOVTZEFF, M., *Social and Economic History of the Roman Empire;* * ROSTOVTZEFF, M., "Foundations of Social and Economic Life in Egypt in Hellenistic Times," *Journal of Egyptian Archæology*, VI, 161; BELL, H. IDRIS, "The Decay of Civilization," *ibid.*, 1924, 207 ff.; * VINOGRADOFF, P., in *Cambridge Medieval History*, I, ch. xix; * WESTERMANN, W. L., "The Economic Basis of the Decline of Ancient Culture," *American Historical Review*, XX, 723; * HEITLAND, W. E., *The Roman Fate, an essay of interpretation;* * BELL, H. IDRIS, "The Byzantine Servile State in Egypt," *Journal Egyptian Archæology*, IV, 86; * FRANK, TENNEY, "Race Mixture in the Roman Empire," *American Historical Review*, XXI, 689; SIMKHO-

VITCH, "Rome's Fall Reconsidered," *Political Science Quarterly*, XXXI, 201; DURUY, V., *History of the Romans*, VIII, 364–82; BURY, J. B., *Later Roman Empire*, I, bk. i, chs. iii–iv; * DILL, S., *Roman Society in Last Century of Western Empire*, espec. bk. iii; HODGKIN, T., *Italy and Her Invaders*, vol. I, espec. pt. ii; MARVIN, F. S., *Western Races and the World*, ch. iv (by H. S. Jones); LECKY, W. E. H., *History of European Morals*, I, ch. ii; MURRAY, GILBERT, *Four Stages of Greek Religion*, ch. iii; TAYLOR, H. O., *Ancient Ideals*, II, 1–96; HODGKIN, T., "The Fall of Rome," *Contemporary Review*, LXXIII, (1898), 59–70; SALVIOLI, *Sullo stato e la popolazione d'Italia prima e dopo le invasioni barbariche*, Palermo, 1900. PIRENNE, J., *Revue de l'Université de Bruxelles*, XVII, 555 (a remarkable synthetic survey of various theories in explanation); KEISELBACH, W., *Der Gang des Welthandels und die Entwickelung des europäischen Völkerlebens im Mittelalter*, (Stuttgart, 1860).

CHAPTER II

THE CHURCH IN THE ROMAN EMPIRE

Extended bibliography in

Cambridge Medieval History, I, 624–43 (London, 1911).

Classified bibliography of literature in English in

THOMPSON, JAMES WESTFALL, *Reference Studies in Medieval History*, pt. i, 9–20.

Only a brief list of the enormous literature is possible here:

* HARNACK, A., *Mission and Expansion of Christianity*, 2 vols; * RAMSAY, W., *The Church in the Roman Empire;* * HATCH, EDWIN, *Organization of the Early Christian Church;* * *Cambridge Medieval History*, I, chs. iv–vi; * DILL, S., *Roman Society in Last Century of Western Empire*, bk. i, chs. i–iv, bk. ii, ch. i; *·CUMONT, F., *Oriental Religions in Roman Paganism*, espec. ch. viii; DU CHESNE, L., *Early History of the Christian Church*, 3 vols.; HARDY, E. G., *Christianity and the Roman Government;* CARR, A., *The Church and the Roman Empire;* GLOVER, T. R., *Conflict of Religions in the Roman Empire;* HUTTMAN, M. A., "Establishment of Christianity," in *Columbia University Studies*, LX; COLEMAN, C. B., "Constantine and Christianity," *ibid.*, LX; BOYD, W. K., "Ecclesiastical Edicts of Theodosian Code," *ibid.*, 1905; FIRTH, J. B., *Constantine;* BURY, J. B., *Later Roman Empire from Theodosius to Justinian;* WOODWARD, E. L., *Christianity and Nationalism in the Later Roman Empire*. HAVET, "Julien," in *Revue Historique*, VI (1878).

CHAPTER III

THE BARBARIAN WORLD. THE GREAT MIGRATIONS

Extended bibliography in

Cambridge Medieval History, I, 649–53; LAMPRECHT, *Deutsche Geschichte*, XII, 86–95.

Classified bibliography of literature in English in

THOMPSON, JAMES WESTFALL, *Reference Studies in Medieval History*, pt. i, 21–29.

Factors influencing the migrations:

* PETRIE, W. FLINDERS, "Migrations," *Journal Anthropological Institute*, XXXVI (1906), 189 (with remarkable maps); * WIETERSHEIM, *Geschichte der Völkerwanderung*, new ed. by Dahn, 2 vols., 1880–81; * PALLMANN. R., *Geschichte der Völkerwanderung*, 1863; * LAMPRECHT, K., "Frankische Ansiedelungen und Wanderungen im Rheinland," *Westdeutsche Zeitschrift*, I (1882), 123; * FUSTEL DE COULANGES, *L'Invasion germanique;* DOPSCH, A., *Wirtschaftliche und soziale Grundlagen der europäischen Kulturentwicklung*, 2 vols. 1918; ARNOLD, W., *Deutsche Urzeit*, 3d. ed., 1881; BETHMANN-HOLLWEG, M. A. von, *Ueber die Germanen der Völkerwanderung*, 1850; GAUPP, E. T., *Die germanischen Ansiedelungen und Landtheilungen*, Breslau, 1844; WACKERNAGEL. "Handel und Schiffahrt der Germanen," *Ztschft. f. d. Alterthumskunde*, XXI (1853), 553; RICHTER, H., *Das weströmische Reich besonders unter den Kaisern Gratianus, Valentinianus II und Maximus*, 1865; SCHMIDT, L., *Geschichte der deutschen Stämme bis zum Ausgang der Völkerwanderung*, 1902; HAYES, C. H. C., *Sources relating to the Germanic Migrations*, Columbia University Press; HODGKIN, T., "The Barrier of the Roman Empire Between Rhine and Danube," *Archæol. Aeliana*, New Series, IX (1882), 73.

Early Germanic Institutions:

For a critical examination of the modern literature on this subject see:

* ASHLEY, W. J., *Surveys, Historical and Economic*, pp. 115–36, 161–66; FUSTEL DE COULANGES, *The Origin of Property in Land*, trans. by Mrs. Ashley; SEEBOHM, F., *The English Village Community*, espec. ch. ix; LAPSLEY, G., "The Origin of Property in Land," *American Historical Review*, VIII, 426–46; The controversy between the "Roman" and the "German" schools may be best understood from a reading of the literature upon Coulanges. See: JENKS, *English Historical Review*, XII, 209; FISHER, HERBERT, *ibid.*, V, 7; ELTON, *ibid.*, I, 427; DARESTE, *Journal des Savants*, Oct., 1886; IMBART DE LA TOUR, *Le Correspondent*. Mar. 25, 1905; MONOD, *Revue Historique*, LXI; ARBOIS DE JUBAINVILLE, *Deux manières d'écrire l'histoire* (adverse); VINOGRADOFF, P., *Growth of the Manor*, pp. 114 ff.;

GUIRAUD, *Fustel de Coulanges*, 1896, and his article in *Séances et travaux de l'Acad. des Sciences Morales et Politiques*, CLXVI (1896), 287. KEHR, *Historische Zeitschrift*, LXXI (unjust); GOOCH, G. P., *History and Historians in the Nineteenth Century*, pp. 208–213.

Character of the invasions:

* DILL, S., *Roman Society in the Last Century of the Western Empire*, bk. iv; * FUSTEL DE COULANGES, *L'Invasion germanique;* * LÉOTARD, E., *Essai sur la condition des barbares établis dans l'Empire Romain au quatrième siècle*, 1873; MUNRO AND SELLERY, *Medieval Civilization*, pp. 50–59; LAVISSE, E., *Histoire de France*, II, pt. i, 61–67; HAYES, C. H. C., *Introduction to . . . Germanic Invasions*, chs. vii–viii; ASHLEY, W. J., *Surveys, Economic and Historical*, pp. 137–43 (review of literature); SEEBOHM, F., *English Village Community*, pp. 272–88, 316–66; HODGKIN, T., *Italy and Her Invaders*, vols. II–III (diffuse); OPITZ, *Die Germanen in römischen Imperium*, 1867; STACKEL, *Die Germanen im römischen Dienste*, 1880; GAUPP, *Die germanischen Ansiedelungen und Landtheilungen in den Provinzen des römischen Reiches*, 1844; M. BLOCH, "La société du haut moyen-age et ses origines," *Journal des Savants*, Nov. 1926; K. SCHUMACHER, *Siedelungs-und Kulturgesch. des Rheinlandevon der Urzeit bis in das Mittelalter*, 2 vols., 1921, 1925; G. WOLFF, *Ueber den Zusammenhang roemischer und frühmittelalterlicher Kultur im Mainlande* (1908).

CHAPTER IV

THE GERMAN KINGDOMS

General bibliographies in:

Cambridge Medieval History, I, 654–55, 658–59, 671–75; THOMPSON, JAMES WESTFALL, *Reference Studies in Medieval History*, pt. i, 25–31; LAVISSE AND RAMBAUD, *Histoire générale*, I, 92, 95, 158, 272.

General works:

DAHN, F., *Die Könige der Germanen*, I–II (1861), III–IV (1866–71), V–X (1894–1907); MARTROYE, F., *L'Occident à l'époque byzantine: Goths et Vandales*, 1904; LAVISSE AND RAMBAUD, *Histoire générale*, I, chs. ii–iii, v; HODGKIN, T., *Italy and Her Invaders*, 8 vols.; GIBBON, E., *Decline and Fall of Roman Empire*, I–II; BURY, J. B., *Later Roman Empire*, I; WIRTH, MAX, *Deutsche Geschichte im Zeitalter germanischer Staatenbildung*, 1862 (there is a French translation of this work by Crombrugghe, under the title *Histoire de la fondation des états germaniques*, 2 vols., Paris, 1873).

Visigoths in Spain:

* HODGKIN, T., *English Historical Review*, II, 209; * SHAW, R. D., *ibid.*, XXI, 209; * DAHN, "Ueber Handel und Handelsrecht der Westgothen," *Ztschft. f. Handelsrecht*, XVI (1871), 387; *Cambridge Medieval History*, II, ch. vi; FREEMAN, E. A., *Western Europe in Fifth Century*, pp. 171–287; GAUPP, E. T., *Die germanischen Ansiedelungen und Landtheilungen*, pp. 372–

414; YVER, G., "Euric, roi des Wisigoths," in *Etudes Monod* (1896); 11–46.

Vandals in Africa:

*SCHMIDT, L., *Geschichte der Vandalen,* 1901; HODGKIN, T., *Italy and Her Invaders,* II, 241–90; LECLERCQ, H., *L'Afrique chrétienne,* II, 143–213; FERRÈRE, *La Situation religieuse de l'Afrique romaine depuis la fin du IV* siècle jusqu'à l'invasion des Vandales;* NATHUSIUS, *Zur Characteristik der Circumcellionen* (Greifswald, 1900).

Huns and Attila:

Cambridge Medieval History, I, ch. iii (remarkable); HODGKIN, T., *Italy and Her Invaders,* II, bk. ii. PARKER, E. H., *A Thousand Years of the Tartar,* bk. i; WYLIE, "Relation of Ancient Huns with China," *Journal Anthropological Institute,* V, 452, VI, 41, IX, 53, X, 20.

On the theory of the desiccation of central Asia as a factor in the invasion by the Huns and Chinese relations with them, see: HUNTINGTON, E., *The Pulse of Asia;* also "Climate and History," *American Historical Review,* XVIII, 34.

Theodoric the Ostrogoth:

*HODGKIN, T., *Italy and Her Invaders,* III; *HODGKIN, T., *Theodoric the Ostrogoth;* *LECRIVAIN, C., *Le Senat romain depuis Dioclétien;* BURY, J. B., *Later Roman Empire,* I, bk. iv.; FREEMAN, E. A., "The Goths at Ravenna," in *Historical Essays,* ser. III; GREGOROVIUS, F., *Rome in Middle Ages,* I, 253–333; DUMOULIN, M., *Revue Historique,* 1902.

Lombards:

*HARTMANN, L. M., *Geschichte Italiens,* vol. II; *ROMANO, G., *Le Dominazioni barbariche in Italia,* bk. iii (Milan, 1910); *Cambridge Medieval History,* II, ch. vii; HODGKIN, T., *Italy and Her Invaders,* vols. V–VI; BURY, J. B., *Later Roman Empire,* II, bk. v, ch. viii.

Byzantine Italy. Gregory the Great and the formation of the papal patrimony:

*DUDDEN, F. H., *Gregory the Great,* I, 295–320; *DUCHESNE, L., *Beginnings of the Temporal Power of the Popes;* *DIEHL, C., *Études sur l'administration byzantine dans l'exarchat de Ravenne;* *MOMMSEN, T., "Die Bewirtschaftung der Kirchengüter unter Gregor I," in *Ztschft. f. sozial und wirtschaftsgeschichte,* I (1893), 43–59; *EWALD, P., "Studien zur Ausgabe des Registers Gregors II," in *Neues Archiv der Gesellschaft für altere deutsche Geschichtskunde,* III (1878), 433–625 (summary in Hodgkin, V, 333–43); *FABRE, "Les colons de l'église romaine au VI° siècle," *Revue d'histoire et de lit. religeuse,* I (1896), pp. 73–91; VINOGRADOFF, *Growth of the manor,* 104, 111; Beadouin, "Le patrimoine de église romaine sous Gregoire I," *Nouvelle revue historique de droit* (1898), pp. 201–219; *GRISAR, H., in *Ztschft. f. katholische Theologie,* I (1877), 321–60, 526–63; HODGKIN, T., *Italy and Her Invaders,* V, 309–322, VI, 446–

49; GREGOROVIUS, F., *Rome in Middle Ages*, I, 178, II, 59–61, 194, 247, 251–58, 359–69; SPEARING, E., *The Patrimony of the Roman Church in the Time of Gregory the Great;* SUTCLIFFE, E. F., *Irish Ecclesiastical Record*, July, 1921; *Cambridge 'Medieval History*, II, 231–35; HARTMANN, *Geschichte Italiens*, II–III; COHN, I., *Die Stellung der byzantinischen Statthalter in Ober- und Mittel-Italien.*

CHAPTER V

MONASTICISM

Extensive bibliography in

Cambridge Medieval History, I, 683–87.

Classified bibliography in English in

THOMPSON, JAMES WESTFALL, *Reference Studies in Medieval History*, pt. i, 45–50.

Egyptian monasticism:

* DUCHESNE, L., *Early History of the Church*, II, ch. xiv; * *Cambridge Medieval History*, I, ch. xviii; BUTLER, E. C., *The Lausiac History of Palladius*, Cambridge, 1898–1904; LECLERCQ, H., Article "Cénobitisme" in *Dictionnaire d'Archéologie chrétienne* (1910); WATSON, "Palladius and Egyptian Monasticism," *Church Quarterly Review*, Apr., 1907; MACKEAN, W. H., *Christian Monasticism in Egypt to the Close of the Fourth Century.*

St. Basil and Early Greek Monasticism:

CLARKE, W., *St. Basil;* GARDNER, ALICE, *Theodore of Studium;* LAKE, K., *Early Days of Monasticism on Mount Athos;* TOZER, H. F., "A Visit to Mount Athos," *Church Quarterly Review*, 1912; "Provincial Life in the Days of Basil," *Church Quarterly Review*, CLXXXVI, 420.

St. Martin of Tours and Early Gallican Monasticism:

BAS, H., *St. Martin de Tours;* CAZENOVE, J. C., *St. Hilary of Poitiers and St. Martin of Tours;* COOPER-MARSDEN, A. C., *Cæsar, Bishop of Arles;* COOPER-MARSDEN, A. C., *History of the Islands of the Lérins;* HOLMES, T. S., *History of the Christian Church in Gaul.*

Irish Monasticism:

* BURY, J. B., *Life of St. Patrick* (supersedes all former biographies); * ZIMMER, H., *The Irish Element in Medieval Cutlure;* * PFLUGK-HARTTUNG, "The Old Irish on the Continent," *Trans. Royal Historical Society,* new ser., V., 75; MCNEILL, J. T., *The Celtic Penitentials;* MEYER, KUNO, *Learning in Ireland;* WATTENBACH, W., "Irish Monasteries in Germany," *Ulster Journal of Archæology*, VIII, 227 *ff.*, 295 *ff.;* HADDAN, A. W., "Irish Missions on the Continent," in his *Remains*, p. 258; SLOVER,

C. H., "Early Literary Channels between Britain and Ireland," *Univ. of Texas Studies in English,* No. vi (1926).

St. Benedict and the spread of the Benedictine Order:

CARTER, J. B., *Religious Life of Ancient Rome,* ch. vii; HODGKIN, T., *Italy and Her Invaders,* IV, bk. v, ch. xvi; DUDDEN, F. H., *Gregory the Great,* I, 109–115; II, 160–73; TOSTI, L., *San Benedetto,* transl. W. R. Woods, London, 1896.

Economic and Social Influence of Monasticism:

* MARIGNAN, A., *Études sur la civilisation française,* vol. I, "La Société mérovingienne," vol. II, "Le Culte des Saints sous les Mérovingiens"; DUDDEN, F., *Gregory the Great,* I, 296-320; II, 173-201; BREWER, J. S., *Introduction to Opera of Giraldus Cambrensis,* IV (Rolls Series); MUNRO AND SELLERY, *Medieval Civilization,* pp. 114–28; CUNNINGHAM, W., *Western Civilization in its Economic Aspects, Ancient and Medieval,* sec. 82; CUNNINGHAM, W., *English Industry and Commerce,* I, sec. 33.

CHAPTER VI

EASTERN ROMAN EMPIRE, 395–802: JUSTINIAN

Extended bibliography in

Cambridge Medieval History, II, 720–27, 747–57, 766–69.

Classified bibliography in English in

THOMPSON, JAMES WESTFALL, *Reference Studies in Medieval History,* pt. i, 33–36, 58–60.

Commerce and industry, taxation and finance:

* DIEHL, C., *Justinien et la civilisation byzantine au VI⁰ siècle;* * HEYD, *Histoire du commerce du Levant* (1886), I, 1–24; * BURY, J. B., *Later Roman Empire,* I, 472 ff.; * BURY, J. B., *Eastern Roman Empire from Theodosius to Irene,* I, 441–47, II, 316–33; HOLMES, W. G., *Age of Justinian and Theodora,* I, chs. i–ii, II, chs. ix, xii; GIBBON, E., *Decline and Fall of Roman Empire,* ed. J. B. Bury, IV, ch. xl; *Quarterly Review,* LXXIII, 346–76.

Europe and the Far East, China, and India:

* HIRTH, F., *China and the Roman Orient;* GIBBON, *Decline and Fall of the Roman Empire,* IV, 230–35, 534–35; SOOTHILL, *China and the West;* CHAPOT, *La Frontière de l'Euphrate de Pompée à la conquête arabe,* 1907; DILLMAN, A., "Zur Geschichte des axumitischen Reiches vom iv bis vi Jahrhundert," *Königl. preuss. Akad. d. Wiss.,* 1880.

Social structure and conditions:

  * Bury, J. B., *Later Roman Empire*, II, bk. iii, ch. i, bk. vi, ch. vi; * Diehl, C., *Justinien et la civilisation byzantine au vi° siècle;* Diehl, C., *A History of the Byzantine Empire;* Grehier, P., *L'Empire Byzantin: son evolution sociale et politique*, 2 vols., 1904; Hessling, *Essai sur la civilisation byzantine;* Baynes, N. H., *The Byzantine Empire.*

Slavonic Settlements in the Balkans:

  * *Cambridge Medieval History*, II, ch. xiv; * Bury, J. B., "Early History of the Slavonic Settlements in Dalmatia, Croatia and Serbia" (*Proceedings* of the British Academy); * Bury, J. B., *Later Roman Empire*, II, 114–44, 274–80, 331–38, 450–58, 470–76; * Bury, J. B., *Eastern Roman Empire from Theodosius to Irene*, II, 292–315; Bury, J. B., "The Treaties De administrando imperio," *Byzantinische Ztschft.*, XV, 517–77; Gibbon, E., *Decline and Fall of Roman Empire*, ed. Bury, VI, 543–51; Beazley, C. R., *Dawn of Modern Geography*, II, 467–514; Schevill, F., *History of the Balkan Peninsula*, chs. v–vi.

Egypt under Byzantine rule:

  * Bell, H. I., "The Byzantine Servile State in Egypt," *Journal Egyptian Archæology*, Apr., 1917; Milne, *Egypt under Roman Rule;* Rouillard, G., *L'Administration civile de l'Egypte-byzantine*, Paris, 1922.

Leo the Isaurian and the Iconoclasts:

  * Bury, J. B., *Later Roman Empire*, II, 318–38, 460–69, 494–98.
  * Harnack, A., *History of Dogma*, V, 304–329; Gardner, A., *Theodore of Studium;* Brooks, E. W., "The Emperor Zenon and the Isaurians," *English Historical Review*, VIII (Apr., 1890); Lea, H. C., *Studies in Church History*, pp. 25–31.

CHAPTER VII

MOHAMMED AND THE RISE OF ISLAM

Extended bibliography in

  Cambridge Medieval History, II, 760–65.

Classified bibliography of literature in English in

  Thompson, James Westfall, *Reference Studies in Medieval History*, pt. i, 52–57.

Arabia before Mohammed:

  * Arnold, T. W., *The Preaching of Islam*, ch. i; * Hogarth, D. G., *Arabia;* * Hogarth, *The Penetration of Arabia;* * Houtsma, M. T., article "Arabia," in *Encyclopedia of Islam*, 1913; Hughes, T. P., article "Arabia," in *Dictionary of Islam;* Barton, *Semitic Origins*, index under "clan," "oasis," "palm," etc.; Goldzieher, *Mythology among the Hebrews,*

pp. 79–89; WELLHAUSEN, J., *Skizzen und Vorarbeiten*, IV (1889) (Medina before Mohammed).

Expansion of Islam:

*ARNOLD, T. W., *The Preaching of Islam*, chs. ii–vii (best work in any language) ; *MARGOLIOUTH, D. S., *Islamic Civilization; *Cambridge Medieval History*, II, chs. x–xii; GOLDZIEHER, *Mohammed and Islam;* HELMHOLT, *History of the World*, II, 270–342, 694–711, III, 255–69, 298–347; BERCHEM, MAX VAN, *La Propriété territoriale et l'impôt foncier sous les premiers Califes*, (Geneva, 1886) ; GIBBON, E., *Decline and Fall of Roman Empire*, ed. Bury, V, ch. li, VI, ch. lii; KISMER, A. L., *A Study in Tolerance as practiced by Mohammed and his immediate successors*, Columbia Univ. Press, 1927.

Persia, Syria and Egypt: North Africa, Spain, Sicily:

*BURY, J. B., *Later Roman Empire*, II, 261–73, 510–17; * BUTLER, A. J., *Arab Conquest of Egypt; *DIEHL, C., *L'Afrique byzantine;* SYKES, P., *History of Persia*, II, 261–73, 510–17; GUEST, A. R., "The Foundation of Fustat," *Journal Royal Archæol. Society*, Jan., 1907; BROOKS, E. W., "Conquest of Egypt by the Saracens," *Byzantinische Ztschft.* (1895), p. 435; "The Arabs in Asia Minor," *Journal Hellenic Studies*, XVIII, 182; LANE-POOLE, S., *Egypt in the Middle Ages;* CAUDEL, M., *Les Premières invasions Arabes dans l'Afrique du Nord;* FOURNEL, H., *Les Berbers: Étude sur la conquête de l'Afrique du Nord par les Arabes*, 2 vols.; DOZY, R., *Spanish Islam;* AMARI, M., *Storia dei Musulmani di Sicilia.*

Saracenic civilization, commerce, trade, industry, social and economic conditions:

*MARGOLIOUTH, D. S., *Islamic Civilization; *KREMER, A. VON, *Culturgeschichte des Orients unter den Califen*, 2 vols.; *HEYD, *Histoire du commerce du Levant*, I, 24–74; *LE BON, G., *La Civilisation des Arabes*, 1884; LANE-POOLE, S., *Arabian Society in the Middle Ages;* HUART, C., *Arabic Literature;* PALMER, E. H., *Life of Haran-al-Rashid;* LE STRANGE, G., *Lands of the Eastern Caliphate;* BEAZLEY, C. R., *Dawn of Modern Geography*, I, 392–425 ; SPRENGER, in *Journal Royal Asiatic Society*, XIV (1844), pt. ii, 519; JACOBS, *Story of Geographical Discovery*, III; NYS, E., *Researches in the History of Economics* (1899), ch. i; OSBORN, "Mohammedan law, its Growth and Character," *Contemporary Review*, XXIX, 1092–1111, XXX, 55–71.

CHAPTER VIII

THE FRANKS AND CHARLEMAGNE

Extended bibliography in

Cambridge Medieval History, I, 657, II, 728–32, 801–13; LAVISSE, *Histoire de France*, II, pt. i, 42, 94, 117, 170, 216, 257, and espec. 305, 331.

Classified bibliography of literature in English in

THOMPSON, JAMES WESTFALL, *Reference Studies in Medieval History*, pt. i, 39–41, 61–66.

Nature of Frankish expansion and occupation:

* DILL, S., *Roman Society in Gaul in the Merovingian Age*, bk. i; LAMPRECHT, K., *Frankische Wanderungen und Ansiedelungen*, 1882; *Schröder*, R., "Die Ausbreitung der salischen Franken," *Forschungen zur deutschen Geschichte*, XIX (1879); FUSTEL DE COULANGES, *L'Invasion gérmanique et la fin de l'Empire Romain;* SCHUMACHER, K., *Siedelung und Kulturgeshichte des Rheinlands von der Urzeit bis in das Mittelalter*, 2 vols., (1921, 1925).

Merovingian Gaul and Germany:

LAVISSE, *Histoire de France*, II, pt. i, 42 ff., 117 ff., 170 ff., 216 ff.; DAHN, F., *Die Könige der Germanen*, vii; WAITZ, G., *Deutscheverfassungsgeschichte;* II–III; INAMA STERNEGG, *Deutschewirtschaftsgeschichite*, 1; FUSTEL DE COULANGES, *La Monarchie franque;* TARDIF, J., *Étude sur les institutions . . . de la France: Période mérovingienne.*

The nature of the civilization is especially treated in

* DILL, S., *Roman Society in Gaul in the Merovingian Age*, bk. ii; DALTON, O. M., *Gregory of Tours, History of the Franks*, Vol. I; * MARIGNAN, A., *La Société mérovingienne: Le Culte des saints sous les Mérovingiens;* * FUSTEL DE COULANGES, *L'Alleu et le domaine rural; Les Origines du systeme féodal;* * LOEBELL, J. W., *Gregor von Tours und seine Zeit;* LAVISSE, *Histoire de France*, II, pt. ii, 170–256; VACANDARD, E., *Vie de St. Ouen;* MARTIN, E., *St. Columban;* PLATH, K., *Die Königspfalzen der Merowinger und Karolinger;* ROTH, P., *Geschichte des Beneficialwesens; Feudalität und Untertanenverband;* LESNE, E., *La Propriété écclesiastique en France aux époques romaine et mérovingienne;* GUILHIERMOZ, P., *Essai sur l'origine de la noblesse en France;* DELOCHE, M., *L'Antrustionat royal sous les deux premières races;* BREHIER, L., "Les Colonies d'Orientaux en Occident au commencement du moyen-âge," *Byzantinische Zeitschrift*, XII (1903); Scheffer-Boichorst, P., "Zur Geschichte der Syrer im Abendlande," *Mitteil. f. Oesterr. Gesch.*, IV (1885), 520–50; MUNRO AND SELLERY, *Medieval Civilization*, 60–87. On Frankish registers see TAYLOR, C. H., "Note on the Origin of the Polyptychs" (and literature there cited), *Mélanges d'histoire . . . à Henri Pirenne* (1926), 475–81.

Charlemagne:

The two outstanding works in recent years are:

* DOPSCH, A., *Die Wirtschaftsententwicklung der Karolingerzeit*, 2 vols., (1912), * HALPHEN, L., *Études critiques sur le règne de Charlemagne* (1918). The former author's somewhat radical views have excited wide attention. For criticisms see:
Historische Zeitschrift, CXII; *Vierteljahrschrift f. Sozial- und Wirt-*

schaftsgeschichte, X, 546; *Göttingische Anzeigen*, Apr., 1913; *Revue Historique*, CX, 332, CXV, 222, CXVI, 91; *Moyen Age*, 1922, p. 180; 1923, p. 40; *English Historical Review*, XXIX, 134; *American Historical Review*, XXVII, 102; *Economic Journal*, XXVIII, 428. Dopsch has replied to his critics in *Vierteljahrschrift f. Sozial- und Wirtschaftsgeschichte*, XVII, 41 *ff*.

M. Pirenne's thesis that the rise of Mohammedan sea-power in the western Mediterranean was the decisive factor in destroying western commerce and throwing western Europe into a protracted condition of natural economy, is developed in * "Un contraste économique: Mérovingiens et Carolingiens," *Revue belge de philolôgie et d'histoire*, II (1923), 223 *ff.*, and more popularly in his *Medieval Cities*. See also L. HALPHEN, "La Conquête de la mediterranée par les Europeens an xi ᵉ et xii ᵉ siècle," *Mélanges d'histoire . . . à Henri Pirenne*, 175.

Commerce and trade, social structure, economic conditions:

* DOPSCH, *Wirtschaftsgeschichte der Karolingerzeit*, II; * LOISEL, *Essai sur la legislation économique des Carolingiens;* * IMBART DE LA TOUR, "Les Immunités commerciales," in *Etudes Monod;* INAMA STERNEGG, *Deutsche Wirtschaftsgeschichte*, new ed., 1909, I, ch. v. (severely criticized by Dopsch); WAITZ, G., *Deutscheverfassungsgeschichte*, II, III; KAEMPFER, *Karl der Grosse*, 1910 (excels in economic treatment); LAVISSE, *Histoire de France*, II, pt. ii, 331–56; FAGNIEZ, G., *Documents relatifs à l'histoire du commerce de la France*, I, introduction, pp. xxv–xxxi; LEVASSEUR, E., *Histoire du commerce de la France*, I, 27–44; HUVELIN, *Histoire du droit des foires et des marchés*, ch. vi.; PROU, M., *Les Monnaies carolingiennes*, 1896; SCHULTE, A., *Geschichte des mittelalterlichen Handels und Verkehrs zwischen Westdeutschland und Italien*, 1900; KLEINCLAUSZ, A., *L'Empire Carolingien, ses origines et ses transformations;* FUSTEL DE COULANGES, *Les Transformations de la royauté pendant l'époque carolingienne;* SEELIGER, *Die soziale und oekonomische Bedeutung der Grundherrschaften im früheren Mittelalter;* INAMA STERNEGG, *Die Grossgrundherrschaften.*

For Frisia's unique commerce:

POELMANN, *Geschiednis von den Handel van Noord Nederland, gedurende het Merovingische en Karolingische tijdperk*, The Hague, 1910; KLUMKER, J., *Der friesische Tuchhandel zur Zeit Karls des Grosse*, 1899; PIRENNE, H., "Draps de Frise ou draps de Flandre?" *Revue belge de philologie et d'histoire*, III, 155.

Colonization of Spanish March:

IMBART DE LA TOURS, "Les colonies agricoles en Espagne et l'occupation des terres desertes," in *Mélanges Paul Fabre;* KOVALEVSKY, M., *Die ökonomische Entwicklung Europas*, III, ch. ix (1905).

Crown lands and the *Capitulare de villis*:

* DOPSCH, *Wirtschaftsgeschichte der Karolingerzeit*, I, 107–180, and criti-

cal literature upon Dopsch cited above; * GAREIS, *Die• Landgüterordnung Kaiser Karls des Grossen* (text and German transl., Berlin, 1895); * STEIN-ITZ, B., *Vierteljahrschrift f. Sozial- und Wirtschaftsgeschichte*, IX (1911), 317–72, 481–560; * SCHILL-KRAMER, E., "Organisation und Gross-verhältnisse des ländlichen Grundbesitzes in der Karolingerzeit," *Vierteljahrschrift f. Sozial- und Wirtschaftsgeschichte*, XVII, 247–93; * LOT, F., "La grandeur des fiscs à l'époque carolingienne," *Revue belge de philologie et d'histoire*, III, 57; * SÉE, HENRI, *Les Classes rurales et le régime domanial en France au moyen-âge*, bk. i, chs. i–iii; PLATH, K., *Die Königspfalzen der Merovinger und Karolinger;* GUERARD, B., "Le Capitulare de villis," *Bibliothèque de l'École des Chartes*, ser. iii, vol. IV (French translation); LAM-PRECHT, K., *Deutsche Wirtschaftsleben*, I, 719 ff., 804 ff.; *Deutsche Geschichte*, II, 40 ff.; FLEISCHMANN, W., *Capitulare de villis vel curtis imperii Caroli Magni*, Berlin, 1919; KUMMEL, A., "Die Landgüterordnung Kaiser Karls des Grossen," *Ztschft. d. berg. Geschichtver.*, LI. (German transl. and text); TAYLOR, C. H., "The Unity of the Capitulary de Villis," *Revue belge de philologie et d'histoire*, III (1924), 759.

Church as a landed proprietor:

* SOMMERLAD, T., *Die wirtschaftliche Tätigkeit der Kirche in Deutschland*, II, cii; * GUERARD-LONGNON, *Le Polyptique d'Irminon*, introd.; DOPSCH, *op. cit.*, I, 181–269; HESSELS, J. H., "Irminon's Polyptychum, (811–26); "Polyptychum of the abbey of St. Remi," in *Trans. Philological Society* (London), 1899–1902, 471, 650; DEMANTE, "Des précaires écclesiastiques," *Nouvelle Revue Hist. de Droit*, 1860, p. 45.

Bonifacian Monasteries and East German Colonization:

* SOMMERLAD, T., *op. cit.*, I, 259–348; THOMPSON, JAMES WESTFALL, "East German Colonization," *Annual Report, American Historical Association*, 1915, pp. 125–26; LAMPRECHT, K., *Deutsche Geschichte*, III, 311 ff.; MÜLLER, J., *Frankenkolonisation auf dem Eichfelde*, 1–13; MEITZEN, *Siedelung und Agrarwesen*, II, 401–406; KYLIE, E., "The Condition of the German Provinces as illustrating the methods of St. Boniface," *Cambridge Journal Theol. Stud.*, Oct., 1905; THOMPSON, JAMES WESTFALL, *Feudal Germany*, 387–99.

CHAPTER IX

THE BREAK-UP OF THE FRANKISH EMPIRE

Extensive bibliography in

Cambridge Medieval History, III, 569–72; LAVISSE, *Histoire de France*, II, pt. i, 358, 367, 373, 383, 395–96, 414.
Classified bibliography of literature in English in

THOMPSON, JAMES WESTFALL, *Reference Studies in Medieval History*, part ii, 81–84.

*CALMETTE, J., *La Diplomatie carolingienne du traité de Verdun à la mort de Charles le Chauve (843–77)*; *KLEINCLAUSZ, A., *L'Empire carolingien: ses origines et transformations;* *BOURGEOIS, E., *Le Capitulaire de Kiersey-sur-Oise (877)*; SIMSON, B., *Jahrbücher des deutschen Reiches unter Ludwig dem Frommen*, 2 vols.; DUMMLER, E., *Geschichte des Ostfrankischen Reiches*, 3 vols., 2d ed., 1887–88; LAVISSE, *Histoire de France*, II, pt. i, 358–438; FUSTEL DE COULANGES, *Les Transformations de la royauté pendant l'époque carolingienne*, 1892; HIMLY, A., *Wala et Louis le Débonnaire*, 1849; LOT, F., AND HALPHEN, L., *Le Règne de Charles le Chauve (840–51)*; LESNE, E., *La Hiérarchie épiscopale en Gaule et en Germanie dépuis la réforme de Boniface jusqu'à la mort de Hincmar*, 1905; PARISOT, R., *Le Royaume de Lorraine sous les Carolingiens;* POUPARDIN, R., *Le Royaume de Provence sous les Carolingiens;* NOORDEN, C., *Hincmar, Erzbischof von Rheims*, 1863; WAITZ, G., *Deutscheverfassungsgeschichte*, vol. V. For the land surveys of the church upon which the partitions were based see TAYLOR, C. H., "Note on the Origin of the Polyptychs," *Mélanges . . . à Henri Pirenne*, 475–81, and literature there cited.

The view expressed in this chapter that the partitions of the Carolingian Empire were primarily distributions of the crown lands, from which everything else followed, is my own interpretation. I hope to develop the subject at length in a future work.

CHAPTER X

THE EXPANSION OF THE NORSEMEN

Extended bibliography in

Cambridge Medieval History, IV, 618–24.

Classified bibliography of literature in English in

THOMPSON, JAMES WESTFALL, *Reference Studies in Medieval History* pt. ii, 85–90.

The Norse Fore-World:

The Sagas are the best source of information. An excellent survey of the saga literature may be found in the prolegomena of G. VIGFUSSON's edition of *Sturlinga Saga*, 2 vols. (1878). See also RICHARD CLEASBY's *Icelandic Dictionary, preface* (1874); the introduction to LAING's *Heimskringla;* F. YORK POWELL, *Folklore*, V. (1897), 97. * GJERSET, K., *History of the Norwegian People*, I, secs. 8–26; *WILLIAMS, MARY W., *Social Scandinavia in the Viking Age;* *BUGGE, ALEX., *Norges Historie* (to 1030), (Kristiania, 1910–12); WORSAE, J. J. A., "Danish industrial arts," in *Handbook of South Kensington Museum*, 2 vols., 1882, and *Primeval Antiquities of Denmark* (1882); DU CHAILLU, P. B., *The Viking Age*, 2 vols.; KEYSER, J. R., *Nordmaendenes private liv. i. Oldtiden*, English transl. M. R. Barnard, London, 1863; WEINHOLD, C., *Altnordische Leben*, 1856; NANSEN, F., *In Northern Mists*, 2 vols.

General Works:

* MAWER, A., The Vikings, 1912; * BEAZLEY, C. R., Dawn of Modern Geography, II, 17–111; * BUGGE, A., "Die nordeuropäischen Verkehrswege im früheren Mittelalter," Vierteljahrscrift f. Sozial-und Wirtschafts-geschichte, IV, 227–73; * E. WADSTEIN, Friserna och forntida Landelsvägar i Norden (The Frisians and the Ancient Trade Routes in the North), In Götebargs Kungl. Vetenskaps-och Vitterhetz Samhälles handlingar, Series V. Vol. XXI, 149–228, 274–75, 412–17, 533–38; Gothenburg, 1920 (with map). KEARY, C. F., The Vikings in Western Christendom; HASKINS, C. H., The Normans in Europe; Cambridge Medieval History, III, ch. xiii; RIANT, P., Expeditions et pélerinages des Scandinaves en Terre Sainte au temps des croisades (1865).

England:

LAPPENBERG (Thorpe's transl.), England Under the Anglo-Saxon Kings, II, 18–220; OMAN, C., England before the Norman Conquest, pp. 382–491; HODGKIN, T., Anglo-Saxon England; LARSON, L. M., Canute the Great; GJERSET, K., History of the Norwegian People, I, secs. 11–12, 28–30; BUGGE, A., "Norse Settlements in the British Isles," Trans. Royal Hist. Soc., series IV, vol. IV, 173.

Ireland, Scotland, Western Islands, Iceland and Greenland:

GJERSET, K., History of the Norwegian People, I, secs. 9, 14, 24, 25, 28, 36, 39, 40, 41; ORPEN, G. H., "The Norsemen in Ireland," English Histor-ical Review, July, 1906; April, 1907; HOWORTH, H. H., "The Irish Monks and the Norsemen," Trans. Royal Hist. Soc., VIII, 281; HJALTALIN, J. A., "The Civilization of the First Icelandic Colonists," Proc. Ethnolog. Soc., London, N. S., VI, 176; DASENT, G. W., The Northmen in Iceland; DASENT, The Story of Burnt Njal, or Life in Iceland at the End of the 10th Century (from the Icelandic of the Njals Saga), Edinburgh, 1861, 2 vols.; HOV-GAARD, W., The Voyages of the Norsemen in America, 1914; GIESECKE, C. L., "Norwegian Settlements on the East Coast of Greenland," Proc. Royal Irish Acad., XIV, 47; FISCHER, J., The Discoveries of the Norsemen in America, 1903.

France:

* VOGEL, W., Die Normannen und das frankische Reich (1906); * JORAN-SON, E., The Danegeld in France (University of Chicago dissertation, 1923); THOMPSON, JAMES WESTFALL, "The Commerce of France in the Ninth Century," Jour. Pol. Econ., XXIII (1915), 857–87; LOT, F., "La grande invasion, 856–62," Bibliothèque de l'École des Chartes, LXIX, 1–62 (1908); FAVRE, E., Eudes, roi de France, 207–226.

Russia:

Roos, W., "The Swedish Part in the Viking Expeditions," English His-torical Review, VII, 209–223; THOMSEN, V., The Relations between An-cient Russia and Scandinavia (1877); BURY, J. B., History of the Eastern

Roman Empire, II, ch. xiii; MAVOR, J., *Economic History of Russia*, I, 1–21; MAWER, A., *Vikings*, ch. vii.

CHAPTER XI

SAXON AND SALIAN GERMANY (919–1125)

Extended bibliography in

KÖTZSCHKE, R., *Deutsche Wirtschaftsgeschichte bis zum 17 Jahrhundert*, pp. 48–84 (condensed historical treatment with exhaustive bibliography—valuable); LAMPRECHT, K., *Deutsche Geschichte*, XII, 105–17; GEBHARDT, *Handbuch der deutschen Geschichte*, I, 4th ed. (1909); *Cambridge Medieval History*, III, 604–617.

* NITZSCH, K. W., *Geschichte des deutschen Volkes*, (2d ed., 1892), vol. I; * LAMPRECHT, K., *Deutsche Geschichte*, vols. II–III; * GERDES, H., *Geschichte des deutschen Volkes und seiner Kultur zur Zeit der karolingischen und sächsischen Könige* (1891); * GERDES, H., *Geschichte des deutschen Volkes der sälischen Kaiser und ihrer Zeit* (1898) (the second part of each volume is wholly economic and social history); * THOMPSON, JAMES WEST-FALL, *Feudal Germany*, chs. i–x; *Cambridge Medieval History*, III, chaps. viii–xii. MANITIUS, M., *Deutsche Geschichte unter den sächsischen und sälischen Kaisern* (911–1125) (1889); HAMPE, K., *Deutsche Geschichte im Zeitalter des Salier und Staufer* (2d. ed. 1912); HELLMAN, S., *Das Mittelalter bis zum Ausgange der Kreuzzüge*; WAITZ, G., *Deutscheverfassungsgeschichte*, vols. V, VI, VII; STUTZ, U., *Die Eigenkirche als Element des mittelälterlichgermänischen Kirchenrechts* (1895); FISHER, H. A. L., *The Medieval Empire*, 2 vols. (1898).

CHAPTER XII

FRANCE BEFORE THE CRUSADES (912–1095)

Extended bibliography in

Cambridge Medieval History, III, 587–91; LAVISSE, E., *Histoire de France*, II, pt. ii, 3, 39, 78, 107, 144, 179, 203, 283.

Classified bibliography of literature in English (slight) in

THOMPSON, JAMES WESTFALL, *Reference Studies in Medieval History*, pt. ii, 96–97.

General Works:

* BOISSONADE, P., *Le Travail dans l'Europe chrétienne au moyen âge*, bk. i, chs. vii–ix; * SÉE, HENRI, *Les classes rurales . . . en France au moyen* âge (1901) ; * CALMETTE, J., *La société féodale;* VIDAL DE LA BLANCHE, P., in Lavisse, *Histoire de France,* introduction; LEVASSEUR, *Histoire du commerce de la France;* LAVISSE, *Histoire de France,* II, pt. ii, bk. i; bk. ii, ch. 4; LAMPRECHT, K., *L'Etat economique de la France pendant la première partie du moyen âge,* transl. A. Marignan (1889) ; FLACH, J., *Les Origines de l'ancienne France,* vols. II–III, (1886–1917) ; LOT, F., *Les Derniers Carolingiens* (1891) ; LOT, *Hugues Capet* (1903) ; PFISTER, CH., *Le Règne de Robert le Pieux* (1885) ; TILLEY, A. (editor), *Medieval France,* chs. i, ii (sec. i) ; *Cambridge Medieval History,* III, chs. iv, v.

CHAPTER XIII

ITALY BEFORE THE CRUSADES

Extended bibliography in

Cambridge Medieval History, III, 594–603.

Classified bibliography of literature in English (scanty) in

THOMPSON, JAMES WESTFALL, *Reference Studies in Medieval History,* pt. ii, 95–96.
Many of the works cited in the bibliography upon Italy during the Crusades also deal with this period.
* HARTMANN, L. M., *Zur Wirtschaftsgeschichte Italiens im früheren Mittelalter* (1904) ; * SCHAUBE, A., *Handelsgeschichte der romanischen Völker des Mittelmeergebiets bis zum Ende der Kreuzzüge* (1906) ; * HANDLOIKE, M., *Die lombardischen Städte unter der Herrschaft der Bischofs und die Entstehung der Communen* (1893) ; * SCHUPFER, F., "La Societa milanese all'epoca del risorgimento del commune," *Archivio Giuridico,* III, 115, 252, 460, 732, IV, 309, V, 40 (Bologna, 1869–70) ; * DRESDNER, A., *Kultur-und Sittengeschichate der italienischen Geistlichkeit im 10 und 11 Jahrhundert* (1890) ; * GAY, J., *L'Italie méridionale et l'Empire Byzantin* (867–1071) (1904) ; BRYCE, J., *The Holy Roman Empire* (new ed., 1904), chs. ix, x; VOGEL, A., *Ratherius von Verona und das zehnte Jahrhundert,* 2 vols. 1854; PREVITÉ ORTON, C. W., *History of the House of Savoy;* "Italy and Provence," *English Historical Review,* XXXII, 335; PACH, H., *Die Pataria in Mailand* (1893) ; OVERMANN, A., *Gräfin Mathilde von Tuscanien* (1895) ; MENGOZZI, G., *La Città italiana nell' alto medio evo* (1914), deals with the ninth and tenth centuries.

CHAPTER XIV

THE EASTERN ROMAN EMPIRE (802–1095)

Extended bibliography in

Cambridge Medieval History, IV, 782–850, and espec. 894–98. GIBBON, E., *Decline and Fall of Roman Empire,* ed. J. B. Bury, VI (appendices).

Classified bibliography of literature in English in

THOMPSON, JAMES WESTFALL, *Reference Studies in Medieval History*, pt. ii, 117–20.

General on Byzantine civilization:

* DIEHL, C., *Byzance, grandeur et décadence* (1919); *Études byzantines* (1905); *Histoire de l'Empire Byzantin* (1919), (English transl. published by the Princeton Univ. Press); GELZER, H., *Byzantinische Kulturgeschichte* (1909); BAYNES, N. H., *The Byzantine Empire* (1926); *Cambridge Medieval History*, IV, chs. xxii–xxiii; HESSLING, D. C., *Essai sur la civilization byzantine* (1907); FLEMING, W. B., *History of Tyre*, ch. ix; BOUCHIER, E. S., *History of Antioch*, ch. ix; BRYCE, J., *Holy' Roman Empire*, new ed., ch. xvi; HARRISON, F., "Byzantine History" (the Rede Lecture), in *Among My Books*, ch. xxi; BIKELAS, A., "The Byzantine Empire," *Scottish Review*, XVII–XVIII (1886–87); FREEMAN, E. A., *Historical Essays*, series III, 241; GRENIER, P., *L'Empire Byzantin, son évolution sociale et politique*, 2 vols. (1904).

Historical surveys:

FINLAY, G., *History of Greece* (ed. H. F. Tozer), vols. IV–V, (Oxford, 1877); GIBBON, E., *Decline and Fall of Roman Empire* (ed. J. B. Bury), VI; SCHEVILL, F., *History of the Balkan Peninsula*, chs. viii-ix.

Byzantine commerce before the Crusades:

* HEYD, W., *Histoire du commerce du Levant*, I, 24–74; BURY, J. B., *History of the Eastern Roman Empire from the Fall of Irene to the Accession of Basil* I, chs. x, xiii; BEAZLEY, C. R., *Dawn of Modern Geography*, II, 221–23, 467–514; BRENTANO, L., "*Die byzantinische Volkswirtschaft,*" in Schmoller's *Jahrbuch f. Gesetzgebung*, XLI (1917); NYS, E., *History of Economics*, Chap. I; ASHBURNER, W., *The Rhodian Sea Laws* (1909); BROWN, H. F., *Venice*, pp. 3–4, 16, 22, 29–34, 48–50, 64–68, 80–81, 86–93; *Cambridge Medieval History*, IV, ch. xiii.

Finance, Taxation, and the Land Question:

* ANDREADES, A., "Les Finances byzantines," *Revue des sciences politiques*, II (1911); "Le Montant du budget de l'Empire Byzantin," *Revue des études grecques*, XXXIV (1921); * BURY, J. B., *History of the Eastern Roman Empire from the Fall of Irene to the Accession of Basil*, ch. vii; "The Imperial Administrative System in the Ninth Century," *British Academy, Supplemental Papers*, I (1911); "The Treatise de administratione imperii," *Byzantinische Ztschft.*, XV, 517–77; *Cambridge Medieval History*, IV, chs. xxii–xxiii; GIBBON, *Decline and Fall of Roman Empire* (ed. J. B. Bury), V, 525–33 (land question).

Slavs and Bulgars:

* BURY, J. B., *History of the Eastern Roman Empire from the Fall of Irene to the Accession of Basil*, xi-xii; GIBBON, *Decline and Fall of Roman Empire* (ed. J. B. Bury), V. 543–51; *Cambridge Medieval History*, IV, ch.

vii; Howorth, H. H., *Journal Anthropological Institute*, VII, 329, VIII, 65, IX, 65; Beazley, C. R., *Dawn of Modern Geography*, II, 478–514; Minns, *Scythians and Huns*, p. 543 *ff*.

Russians and Khazars:

* Bury, J. B., *History of the Eastern Roman Empire from the Fall of Irene to the Accession of Basil*, ch. xiii; * Reddaway, W. F., *Introduction to Study of Russian History: Helps for Students of History*, S.P.C.K., London, 1920 (with bibliography); *Cambridge Medieval History*, IV, ch. vii; Howorth, H. H., *Third International Congress of Orientalists, Travaux*, II (1879). On the Khazars see article "Khazars," in *Jewish Encyclopedia*; Bury, J. B., *History of the Eastern Roman Empire*, 394–423. Rostovseff, M., "Les Origines de la Russe kievienne," *Revue des études slaves*, II (1922), 1–18; *Iranians and Greeks in South Russia* (1922), espec. pp. 210–22; *Annual Report American Historical Assoc.* (1920), pp. 165 *ff*.

The conflict with Islam:

* *Cambridge Medieval History*, IV, chs. v. vi; * Bury, J. B., *History of the Eastern Roman Empire from the Fall of Irene to the Accession of Basil*, chs. viii–ix; Bussell, F. W., *The Roman Empire*, 2 vols., 1910 (consult index, espec, on Armenia); Laurent, J., *L'Arménie entre la Byzance et l'Islam* (École Française d'Athènes et de Rome, No. 117, 1919); Anderson, J. G., "The Road System of Eastern Asia Minor," *Journal Hellenic Studies* (1897), p. 22; Le Strange, Guy, *The Lands of the Eastern Caliphate*; Gelzer, H., *Short History of Armenia* (1897); Brooks, E. W., "Byzantines and Arabs in the time of the Abbassids," *English Historical Review*, XVI, 84; Ramsay, W., "The War of Moslem and Christian for Asia Minor," *Contemporary Review*, XC, 1; Oman, C. W., *Art of War in the Middle Ages*, bk. iv, ch. iv; Parker, J. H., "The Origin of the Turks," *English Historical Review*, XI, 431.

CHAPTER XV

THE BAGHDAD KHALIFATE AND THE EXPANSION OF ISLAM

Extended bibliography in

Cambridge Medieval History, IV, 831–36, V, 864–66.

Classified bibliography of literature in English in

Thompson, James Westfall, *Reference Studies in Medieval History*, Pt. i, 55–56.

General Works:

* Heyd, W., *Histoire du commerce du Levant*, I, 24–74; * Kremer, A. Von, *Culturgeschichte des Orients unter den Califen*, 2 vols. (1876–77)

(English transl. S. Khuda Bukhsh, Calcutta, 1920); KREMER, *Culturge-schichte und Streifzüge auf dem Gebiete des Islams* (1873) (English transl. S. Khuda Bukhsh under title *Contributions to the History of Islamic Civilization,* Calcutta, 1905); ARNOLD, T. W., *The Preaching of Islam* (2d. ed. 1913); HUART, C., *Histoire des Arabes,* 2 vols. (1912–13); LE BON, G., *La Civilisation des Arabes* (1884); HELL, JOSEPH, *The Arab Civilization* (transl. S. Khuda Bukhsh, 1926); LE STRANGE, GUY, *The Lands of the Eastern Caliphate;* LE STRANGE, *Baghdad during the Abbassid Caliphate* (1900); MARRAST, A., *La Vie byzantine au vi° siècle,* pp. 305 *ff.* (1881); MUIR, W., *The Caliphate, Its Rise, Decline and Fall* (new ed., 1915); MÜLLER, A., *Der Islam im Morgen und Abendland,* 2 vols. (1885–87); BENJAMIN BEN JONAH OF TUDELA, *Travels* (ed. and trans. by Asher, 1840); FORTESCUE, A., *The Lesser Eastern Churches* (1913); SHEDD, W. A., *Islam and the Oriental Churches* (1904).

CHAPTER XVI

THE CRUSADES

Extended bibliography in

Cambridge Medieval History, V, 867–71; BRÉHIER, L., *L'Eglise et l'Orient au moyen âge: Les Croisades,* chs. i–xiii and separate bib. for each chapter (4th ed., 1911).

Classified bibliography of literature in English in

THOMPSON, JAMES WESTFALL, *Reference Studies in Medieval History,* pt. ii, 121–32.

General histories:

* HENNE AM RHYN, O., *Die Kreuzzüge und die Kultur ihrer Zeit* (1894);
* PRUTZ, H., *Kulturgeschichte der Kreuzzüge* (1883); BREHIER, L., *L'Eglise et l'Orient au moyen âge: Les Croisades,* chs. i–xiii (4th ed., 1911); KUGLER, B., *Geschichte der Kreuzzüge* (2d ed., 1891); HEYCK, E., *Die Kreuzzüge;* ARCHER AND KINGSFORD, *The Crusades;* CONDER, C. R., *The Latin Kingdom of Jerusalem;* STEVENSON, W., *The Crusaders in the East;* NEWHALL, R. A., *The Crusades.*

Pilgrimages:

* BEAZLEY, C. R., *Dawn of Modern Geography,* I, chs. ii–iv, II, chs. iii–iv; HEATH, S., *Pilgrim Life in the Middle Ages;* JONES, G. H., *Celtic Britain and the Pilgrimage Movement* (Society of Y Cymrrhodorion) pp. 90–107, 149–228, 274–75, 412–17, 533–38; LEA, H. C., *Confession and Indulgence,* II, 123–35; *Edinburgh Review,* CXX, 217–49, CIX, 86–120. JUSSERAND, J. J., *Wayfaring Life in the Middle Ages,* pt. iii; *Quarterly Review,* XCIII, 432; CXC, 217; LEA, H. C. *Confession and Indulgence,* II, 123–35; HUGO, T., "Pilgrim Signs," *Archæologia,* XXXVIII (1860), 128.

Causes and motives of First Crusade:

* MUNRO, D. C., *Essays on the Crusades,* ch. i (Burlington, Vermont, 1903); * ARCHER, "The Council of Clermont and the First Crusade," *Scottish Review,* XXVI (1895), 274–95; * MUNRO, D. C., "The Speech of Urban II at Clermont," *American Historical Review,* XI, 231; KREY, A. C., *The First Crusade;* LEES, BEATRICE A., *The Anonymi Gesta Francorum,* introduction; DUNCALF, F., "The Peasants' Crusade," *American Historical Review,* Apr. 1921; HOGARTH, D. G., "The Routes of the Crusaders," *Trans. Royal Geographical Society,* III, pt. ii, 38–78; LEA, H. C., *Confession and Indulgence,* II, 123–35; YEWDALE, *Bohemond; Cambridge Medieval History,* V, ch. vii; WOLFF, T., *Die Bauernkreuzzüge des Jahres 1096* (*Tübingen,* 1891); BRAMHALL, E., "The Privileges of the Crusaders," *American Journal of Theology,* V, 279; MUNRO AND SELLERY, *Medieval Civilization,* 248–56.

The kingdom of Jerusalem and the civilization of the Latin Orient:

* DODU, G., *Histoire des institutions monarchiques du royaume de Jérusalem* (1894); * BREHIER, L., *L'Eglise et l'Orient au moyen âge: Les Croisades,* chs. iv–ix; * REY, E. G., *Les Colonies franques de Syrie au xiiᵉ et xiiiᵉ siècle* (1883); * PRUTZ, H., *Kulturgeschichte der Kreuzzoge* (1883), espec. pp. 1–32, 89–181, 314–54, 396–415; * MUNRO, D. C., *Essays on the Crusades,* ch. i, "Christian and Infidel in the Holy Land" (same article in *International Monthly,* IV, pp. 690 and 726); * STUBBS, W., *Introductions to the Rolls Series,* 325–49; ARCHER AND KINGSFORD, *The Crusades,* chs. xix–xx, and espec. pp. 282–384; CONDER, C. R., *The Latin Kingdom of Jerusalem," Quarterly Review,* CCXCX, iii; MUNRO, D. C., "The Establishment of the Kingdom of Jerusalem, *Sewanee Review* (July, 1924), XVI, 215; CONDER, "Norman Palestine," *Palestine Exploration Fund Society,* XXIX (1890); DAMLAND, F., "The Principality of Antioch during the Crusades," *Archæologia,* XV, 234; *English Historical Review,* XI, 143 (review of Dodu); YEWDALE, *Bohemond;* EISELEN, *History of Sidon,* pt. ii, ch. vi; MUNRO AND SELLERY, *Medieval Civilization,* 257–68; FLEMING, W. B., *History of Tyre,* ch. x.; BOUCHIER, E. S., *Short History of Antioch,* chs. x, xi; NYS, E., *History of Economics,* chs. ix; STEVENSON, W., *The Crusaders in the East;* DE LANESSAN, J. M. A. de, *Principes de Colonisation* (1897); PRESTON, H. G., *Rural Conditions in the Kingdom of Jerusalem* (Univ. of Pa. dissertation, 1903), DUNCALF, F., "The Influence of Environment on the Kingdom of Jerusalem," *Annual Report American Historical Association* (1914), I, 137; MILLER, W., "The Latin Kingdom of Jerusalem," *Quarterly Review,* CCXXX, iii.

Commerce and the Crusades (compare the preceding section and the bibliography on Italy during the Crusades):

* HEYD, W., *Histoire du commerce du Levant,* I, 129–476; * SCHAUBE, A., *Handelsgeschichte der romanischen Völker des Mittelmeergebiets bis zum Ende der Kreuzzüge* (1906); * PRUTZ, *Kulturgeschichte der Kreuzzüge,* espec. 377 ff.; KELLER, A. G., *Colonization,* 60–73; TWISS, SIR TRAVERS, *The Black Book of the Admiralty,* vol. IV, introduction (Rolls Series);

PRUTZ, H., in MUNRO, *Essays on the Crusades*, ch. ii, p. 45 (same article in *International Monthly*, IV [1902], 251).

The Byzantine Emperors and the Crusades:

* CHALANDON, F., *Les Comnènes: Études sur l'Empire Byzantin aux XI*ᵉ *et XII*ᵉ *siècles*, 2 vols. (1900–1913) ; *Cambridge Medieval History*, IV, chs. xi, xii; MUNRO, D. C., *Essays on the Crusades*, ch. iii (same article in *International Monthly*, V [1902]).

Venice and the Fourth Crusade:

* PEARS, E., *The Fourth Crusade; The Latin Kingdom of Constantinople;* * MILLER, W., *The Latins in the Levant*, chs. i–ii; *Cambridge Medieval History* IV, chs. xiv, xv; BREHIER, L., *L'Eglise et l'Orient au moyen âge: Les Croisades*, ch. vii, with bibliography; VILLEHARDOUIN, *Conquest of Constantinople* (Everyman's Library); FOTHERINGHAM, J. K., "Genoa and the Fourth Crusade," *English Historical Review*, XXV, 26; SCHEVILL, F., *History of the Balkan Peninsula*, ch. xi; RODD, R., *The Princes of Achæa;* TOZER, H. F., "The Franks in the Peloponnesus," *Journal Hellenic Studies*, IV, 165; BURY, J. B., "The Lombards and Venetians in Eubœa," *ibid.*, IX, 91; GARDNER, A., *Theodore Lascaris of Nicea*.

Cyprus:

STEWART, B., *Cyprus: the People, Medieval Cities, Castles, Antiquities, and History of the Island* (London, 1908); STUBBS, "The medieval kingdoms of Cyprus and Armenia," *Seventeen Lectures*, ch. viii; COBHAM, C. D. *Excerpta Cypria: Materials for a history of Cyprus* (Cambridge, 1908).

Results of the Crusades:

In the nature of things these were so inextricably interwoven with the transformation of Europe in the twelfth and thirteenth centuries that a bibliography is difficult. See the bibliographies attached to chapters XVII, XVIII, XIX, XXVIII; The following references may be consulted: H. PRUTZ, in Munro, D. C., *Essays on the Crusades*, pp. 45–87. Same art. in *International Monthly*, IV, 251; CUNNINGHAM, W., *Western Civilization, Ancient and Mediaeval*, secs. 103–4; CUNNINGHAM, W., *English Industry and Commerce*, I, 89, 143, 152, 186, 196, 198, 205, 212, 475, and especially sec. 68; CHEYNEY, E. P., *European Background of American History*, chaps. i and ii; BROWN, H. F., *Venice*, pp. 114–15, 116–34, 152, 190–92, 211, 218, 237–38, 251–56, 318, 324–26. For the feud of Venice and Genoa, see pp. 141–48, 158–61, 190–203, 222–34; MUNRO, D. C., and Selery, G. C., *Mediaeval Civilization*, pp. 212–23, 248–68; KELLER, A. G., *Colonization*, pp. 60–73; HUTCHINSON, "Oriental Trade and Rise of Lombard Communes," *Quarterly Journal Economics*, XVI, 413; HELMHOLT, H., *History of the World*, VII, 1–137. NYS, E., *History of Economics*, chap. iv; BLANQUI, J. A., *History of Political Economy*, chap. xiv; BYRNE, E., "Commercial Contracts of the Genoese in the Syrian Trade," *Quarterly Journal Economics*, XXXI, 132; BYRNE, E., "Genoese Trade with Syria in Twelfth Century," *American Historical Review*, XXV, 191; BYRNE, E., "Easterners in Genoa," *Journal American Oriental Society*, XXXVIII, 176; YRIARTE,

C., *Venice*, chap. iii; ADAMS, BROOKS, *The New Empire*, pp. 69–85; DAY, CLIVE, *History of Commerce*, secs. 97–99; MOLMENTI, *History of Venice*. HAZLITT, W. C., *Venetian Republic* I, 141–87, 362–84, 442; HODGSON, F., *Early History of Venice*, chap. vi; HODGSON, F., *Venice in the Thirteenth and Fourteenth Centuries;* PALGRAVE, F., *History of England and Normandy*, IV, 455–68, 522–40; SHAW, W. A., *History of Currency*, pp. 1–6, 9–13; BROWN, RAWDEN, *History of Venice*, pp. 142–46, 158–61; Law, Alice M., "Some Notable Kings Merchants," *Economic Review*, XII, 309; XIII 411; SEDGWICK, H. D., *Italy in the Thirteenth Century*, I, chap. ii; BEAZELEY, C. R., *Dawn of Modern Geography*. II, 394–411; FINLEY, G., *History of Greece*, IV, chap. iii, sec. 1; WIENER, L., "Economic History and Philology," *Quarterly Journal of Economics* (1911), 239; DANVERS, "Persian Gulf Route," *Asiatic Quarterly Review* (April, 1888); YULE, ed., *Travels of Marco Polo* (Hakluyt Society, 1903) Introduction, secs. 9–12 (pp. 41–45).

CHAPTER XVII

ITALY DURING THE CRUSADES

Many of the works pertaining to Germany under the Hohenstaufen also deal with Italy.

Extended and excellent bibliography by Previté Orton in

Cambridge Medieval History, V, 875–77.

Classified bibliography of literature in English in

THOMPSON, JAMES WESTFALL, *Reference Studies in Medieval History*, pt. ii, 114–16, 154–55.

General Works:

* SCHAUBE, A., *Handelsgeschichte der romanischen Völker des Mittelmeergebiets his own Ende der Kreuzzüge* (1906); * HARTMANN, L. M., *Geschichte Italiens im Mittelalter*, III–IV (1915); * YVER, *Le Commerce et les marchands dans l'Italie méridionale au xiii et au xiv⁰ siècle* (1903); * MAS LATRIE, *Traités de paix et de commerce et documents divers contenant les rélations des chretiens avec les Arabes d'Afrique septentrionale au moyen âge*, (1866), supplement, 1872; * *Cambridge Medieval History*, IV, chs. iv, v, xi, xiii; * HEYD, W., *Histoire du commerce du Levant*, I, 129–426; MANFRONI, C., *Storia della marina italiana* (400–1261) (Leghorn, 1899); SEDGWICK, H. D., *Italy in the Thirteenth Century*, 2 vols.; COULTON, G. G., *From St. Francis to Dante* (based on the *Autobiography* of Fra Salimbene); TAYLOR, H. O., *The Medieval Mind*, I, ch. xxi, "The World of Salimbene."

The Lombard Cities:

* HUTCHINSON, "The Oriental Trade and the Rise of the Lombard communes," *Quarterly Journal of Economics*, XVI, 413; * SCHNEIDER, F., *Die Entstehung von Burg und Landgemeinde in Italien* (1924) (remarkable); BUTLER, W. F., *The Lombard Communes;* TESTA, G., *History of the War*

of Frederick I against the Communes of Lombardy (1877); LANZANI, F., *Storia dei communi italiani* (1882); HAULLEVILLE, P. de, *Histoire des communes lombardes dépuis leur origine jusqu' à la fin du XIII° siècle*, (2 vols., 1857); HEGEL, C., *Geschichte der Stadtverfassung von Italien* (2 vols., 1847); HAUSRATH, A., *Arnold von Brescia* (1891); FISHER, H. A. L., *The Medieval Empire*, II, xi; SEDGWICK, H. D., *Italy in the Thirteenth Century*, I, chs. xiii–xv, xviii; HEINEMANN, L., *Zur Entstehung der Stadtverfassung in Italien* (1896); GIANINI, F., *Italieni communi* (1000–1300); VILLARI, P., *Medieval Italy*, bk. ii, chs. iv, ix, x; MENGOZZI, G., *Lacittà italiana nell'alto medio evo* (1914).

Alpine Passes:

HOFFMAN, J. W., "German Alpine Passes in the Middle Ages," *Journal of Political Economy*, XXXI, 826; CLARE, C. L., *The Brenner Pass;* COOLIDGE, W. B., *The Alps in Nature and History;* COOLIDGE, *Alpine Studies* (historical and descriptive essays); UMLAUFT, F., *The Alps: Topography, Geology and History* (1889); PREVITÉ-ORTON, C. W., *History of the House of Savoy* (use index under names of passes); BAEDEKER, K., *Handbook of Switzerland* (eastern Alps, central Alps).

Rome and the papacy:

BALZANI, U., *The Popes and the Hohenstaufen;* GREGOROVIUS, F., *City of Rome in the Middle Ages*, vol. IV; REUMONT, A. von, *Geschichte der Stadt Rom*, 3 vols. (1867–70); HALPHEN, L., *Études sur l'administration de Rome au moyen âge (751–1252)*.

Venice:

* SIMONSFELD, H., *Der Fondaco dei Tedeschi in Venedig und die deutsch-venetianischen Handelsbeziehungen* (2 vols., 1887); * LENEL, W., *Die Entstehung der Vorherrschaft Venedigs an die Adria* (1897); *Cambridge Medieval History*, IV, chs. xiii–xiv; KRETSCHMAYR, H., *Geschichte von Venedig*, vol. I; MOLMENTI, *Venice: the Middle Ages*, II; HAZLITT, W. C., *History of the Venetian Republic;* BROWN, H. F., *Venice;* BROWN, H. F., *Calendar of State Papers, Venetian*, I, introd., pp. li–cxiii, cxxxv–xli; HODGSON, F., *Early History of Venice*.

Genoa:

* BYRNE, E. H., "Genoese Trade with Syria," *American Historical Review*, XXV, 191; * BYRNE, "Commercial Contracts of the Genoese in the Syrian Trade," *Quarterly Journal of Economics*, XXXI, 128; * BYRNE, "Easterners in Genoa," *Journal American Oriental Society*, XXXVIII, 176; BENT, J. T., *Genoa;* CANESTRINI, G., "Il Mar Nero e le colonie degli Italiani nel Medio Evo," *Archivio Storico Italiano*, New Series, IV, pt. i (Florence, 1857); CARO, *Genua und die Mächte am Mittel meer*, 2 vols. (1895–1899); ST ANGELO, C. I. DE, *Caffaro e i suoi tempi* (1894).

Florence, Siena, Pisa:

* DAVIDSON, R., *Geschichte von Florenz*, vol. I (1896) (Italian transl. *Storia de Firenze, Le origini* (1907–1912); CAGGESE, R., *Storia de Firenze*, 3 vols., (1912–21); DA GINO ARIA, *I trattati commerciali della repubblica fiorentina* (1901); SCHNEIDER, F., *Die Reichsverwaltung in Toscana (568–1268)*; SCHEVILL, F., *Siena;* DOUGLAS, LANGDON, *History of Siena;* HEYWOOD, W., *A History of Pisa* (eleventh and twelfth centuries).

Norman Italy and Sicily under (Roger II and Frederick II):

* CURTIS, E., *Roger of Sicily and the Normans in Lower Italy,* (1016–1154); * CHALANDON, F., *Histoire de la domination normande en Italie et en Sicilie* (2 vols., 1907); * HASKINS, C. H., *The Normans in Europe*, chs. vii, viii and bibliography, pp. 248–49; * HASKINS, "England and Sicily in the Twelfth Century," *English Historical Review*, XXVI, 433–47, 641–45; CASPER, E., *Roger II und die Grundung der normannisch-sicilischen Monarchie* (1904); HASKINS AND LOCKWOOD, "The Sicilian Translators of the Twelfth Century," *Harvard Studies in Classical Philology*, XXIII, 155–66, XXV, 87–105; MAWER, A., *Vikings*, chs. xi–xii; NYS, E., *History of Economics*, ch. ii; FREEMAN, E. A., "The Normans at Palermo," *Essays*, series III, 437; FREEMAN, "Frederick the Magnificent," *Essays*, series I, 283; AMARI, M., *Storia dei Musulmani di Sicilia*, 3 vols.

Angevin Italy and Sicily (1268–82):

* JOUBERT, A., *L'Etablissement de la maison d'Anjou dans le royaume de Naples* (1887); * JORDAN, E., *Les Origines de la domination angevine en Italie;* DURRIEU, P., *Les Français dans le royaume de Naples sous le règne de Charles d'Anjou* (1887); MERKEL, C., *La Dominazione de Carlo I d'Angio in Piemonte e in Lombardia* (1891); STERNFELD, R., *Karl von Anjou* (1888); SWIFT, F. DARWIN, *James I of Aragon*, chs. ix–xii.

CHAPTER XVIII

FRANCE DURING THE CRUSADES (1095–1285)

Extended biography in

Cambridge Medieval History, V, 901–902 (to 1280 only); LAVISSE, *Histoire de France*, II, ch. ii, 203, 227, 283, 311, 334; III, ch. i, 1, 28, 83, 122, 203, 297, 364, 390; RAMBAUD, A., *Histoire de la civilisation française*, 117, 135, 150, 160, 177, 206, 239.

Classified bibliography of literature in English in

THOMPSON, JAMES WESTFALL, *Reference Studies in Medieval History*, pt. ii, 97–100.

General Works:

* LUCHAIRE, A., *Histoire des institutions politiques de la France sous les premiers Capétiens*, 2 vols. (2d. ed., 1891); LUCHAIRE, A., *Manuel des in-*

stitutions françaises (1892) ; * LUCHAIRE, A., *La Société française au temps de Philippe Auguste* (2d ed., 1909; English transl. by Krehbiel, *Social France at the Time of Philip Augustus,* 1912) ; * BOISSONADE, P., *Le Travail dans l'Europe chrétienne au moyen âge,* bk. i, chs. vii, viii, ix, x; bk. ii (entire) ; * GARREAU, L., *L'Etat social de la France au temps des croisades;* * SÉE, H., *Les Classes rurales . . . en France au moyen âge;* LAVISSE, *Histoire de France,* II, pt. ii, bk. 2; III, pt. i (entire volume) ; *Cambridge Medieval History,* V, chs. xvii, xix (to 1200 only) ; TILLEY, A. (editor), *Medieval France,* pp. 48–78, 179–92, 201–206; RAMBAUD, A., *Histoire de la civilisation française,* I, chs. viii–xiii; LEVASSEUR, E., *Histoire du commerce de la France;* LEVASSEUR, *Histoire des classes ouvrières en France,* vol. I; LECOY DE LA MARCHE, *La France sous St. Louis;* BEUGNOT, A., *Les Institutions de St. Louis;* DELISLE, L., *Études sur la condition de la classe agricole et l'état d'agriculture en Normandie au moyen âge* (2d. ed., 1903) ; BERGER, E., *Histoire de Blanche de Castille;* GUILHIERMOZ, P., *L'Origine de la noblesse en France au moyen âge;* LANGLOIS, CH. V., *Le Règne de Philippe le Hardi;* LESPINASSE, R. de, *Le Livre des métiers de Etienne Boileau;* PICARDA, E., *Les Marchands de l'eau* (1901) ; FUNCK-BRENTANO, F., *Medieval France,* chs. ii–xiv.

CHAPTER XIX

HOHENSTAUFEN GERMANY: THE LOW COUNTRIES (1125–1250)

Excellent but brief interpretation, with full bibliography, in

KÖTZSCHKE, *Deutsche Wirtschaftsgeschichte,* pp. 84–92; GEBHARDT, *Handbuch der deutschen Geschichte,* I, (4th ed., 1909).

Bibliographies in

LAMPRECHT, K., *Deutsche Geschichte,* XII, 117–25; *Cambridge Medieval History,* V, 850–54, 872–74, 878–84.

Classified bibliography of literature in English (unsatisfactory) in

THOMPSON, JAMES WESTFALL, *Reference Studies in Medieval History,* pt. ii, 114–16, 154–55.
Many of the works previously cited for Chapter XI pertain also to the Hohenstaufen epoch. But add:
* GERDES, H., *Geschichte der Hohenstaufen und ihrer Zeit,* 1908; * INAMA STERNEGG, *Deutsche Wirtschaftsgeschichte,* vol. II, 1891 ; * BACHTOLD, H., *Der Norrdeutsche Handel im 12 und beginnenden 13 Jahrhundert,* 1910; PRUTZ, H., *Kaiser Friedrich I,* 3 vols., 1871–74; BELOW, G. von, *Der deutsche Staat des Mittelalters,* vol. I; LAMPRECHT, *Deutsches Wirtschaftleben im Mittelalter;* NITZSCH, K. W., *Ministerialität und Burghertum,* 1859; SCHULTE, A., *Der Adel und die deutsche Kirche im Mittelalter,* 1910; STUTZ, U., *Die Eigenkirche als Element des mittelalterlichgerman-*

ischen Kirchenrechts, 1895; PHILLIPSON, M., *Heinrich der Löwe,* 1918; POOLE, A. L., *Henry the Lion;* RAUMER, F. VON, *Geschichte der Hohenstaufen,* 6 vols. (5th ed., 1878); KRETSCHMER, K., *Historische Geographie von Mittel-Europa,* chs. v and vii; MICHAEL, E., *Culturzustände des deutscher Volkes während des XIII Jahrhundert,* I, 1–85, 129–204 (1897); WAITZ, G., *Deutsche Verfassungsgeschichte,* V, 185–442 ("Das Volk und seine Stände"); THOMPSON, JAMES WESTFALL, *Feudal Germany,* chs. viii–xi; GASNER, E. *Zum deutschen Strassenwesen* (1889).

CHAPTER XX

EAST COLONIZATION, GERMAN AND SLAV

Bibliography in

KÖTZSCHKE, *Deutschewirtschaftsgeschichte,* 85; LAMPRECHT, K., *Deutsche Geschichte,* XII, 126–28 (1st and 2d ed.); PAETOW, *Guide to Study of Medieval History,* p. 220.

*LAMPRECHT, K., *Deutsche Geschichte,* III, bk. x, ch. ii, pp. 343–88 (3d. ed., 1906); *SCHULTZE, E. O., *Die Kolonisierung und Germanisierung der Gebiete zwischen Saale und Elbe,* 1896; THOMPSON, JAMES WESTFALL, *Feudal Germany,* chs. xi, xiii–xvii; TUTTLE, H., *History of Prussia,* I, chs. i–ii; KÖTZSCHKE, R., *Quellen zur Geschichte der Ostdeutschen Kolonisation* (1912); GERDES, H., *Geschichte der Hohenstaufen und ihrer Zeit,* pp. 428–40; LAVISSE, E., *La Marche de Brandenbourg sous les Ascaniens* (Paris, 1875); INAMA STERNEGG, *Deutsche Wirtschaftsgeschichte,* III, 1.

CHAPTER XXI

THE SCANDINAVIAN COUNTRIES

Denmark:

*BEAZELEY, *Dawn of Modern Geography,* II, 514–48; LEACH, H. G., *Angevin Britain and Scandinavia, Cambridge Medieval History,* III, 309 ff.; ROBINSON, C. H., *Conversion of Europe,* ch. xvi; ALLEN, C. F., *Histoire de Danemarck,* 2 vols., Copenhagen, 1878; DAHLMANN, F. S., *Geschichte von Danemarck,* vols. I–III (1840–   ); NIELSEN, O., *Kiobenhavns Histoire og Besknivelse* (Copenhagen, 1877).

Norway:

Gjerset, *History of the Norwegian People,* I, 174–483; WILLSON, T. B., *Church and State in Norway;* ROBINSON, C. H., *Conversion of Europe,* ch. xvii.

Sweden:

* GEIJER, E. J., *Geschichte Schwedens*, vols. I–III (French trans. by Lundblad, 1840); MONTELIUS, O., *Sveriges historia froan äldsta tid vara dagar*, vols. I–II (Stockholm, 1877–81).

CHAPTER XXII

MOHAMMEDAN AND CHRISTIAN SPAIN

Bibliography in:

BOISSONADE, P., *Études relatives à l'histoire économiques de l'Espagne*, *Revue de Synthèse hist.*, XXIII (1911), 75–97; CAROLIN, *Vierteljahrischrift f. Soz.-und Wirtschafts gesch.* 1913, no. 2; ALTAMIRA, R., *Historia de España*, IV, 587–672 (1914); LAVISSE AND RAMBAUD, *Histoire générale*, II, 719; CHAPMAN, C. E., *A History of Spain*, 527–40; PAETOW, L. J., *Guide*, 149 (*Mohammedan*), 317–20 (Christian); THOMPSON, JAMES WESTFALL, *Reference Studies in Medieval History*, pt. ii, 135–38. Only works in English are cited below.

Mohammedan Spain:

DOZY, R., *Spanish Islam*, transl. F. G., Stokes, 1913; CHAPMAN, C. F., *A History of Spain*, chs. v, vi, viii, ix; BURKE, U., *History of Spain*, I, chs. xi, xvi, xix, xxxvi; WHISHAW, E. M., *Arabic Spain* (1912); ARNOLD, T. W., *Preaching of Islam*, ch. v; LANE-POOLE, S., *Moors in Spain;* PERKINS, C., *Builders of Spain*, I, chs. i–iii; RIANO, *Industrial Arts of Spain;* COPPÉE, F., *Conquest of Spain by the Arab Moors*, II, bk. x (civilization); *Quarterly Review*, CLXXXIX (review of Lane-Poole); Ameer Ali, "Spain Under the Saracen," *Nineteenth Century*, XXXIV, 498; MUNRO and SELLERY, *Medieval Civilization*, 224–39.

Christian Spain:

* MERRIMAN, R. B., *Rise of the Spanish Empire*, I, chs. i–vii; BURKE, U., *History of Spain*, I, chs. xiii, xvii, xviii, xx, xxi, xxiv, xxv; SWIFT, F. DARWIN, *James I of Aragon;* BEAZLEY, C. R., *James I of Aragon;* KLEIN, J., "The Mesta," *Harvard Economic Studies*, No. XXI.

CHAPTER XXIII

MERCHANT TRAVEL IN THE MIDDLE AGES. MARKETS. THE CHAMPAGNE FAIRS. THE CONDUCT OF TRADE

Compare the references on "Italy during the Crusades," and "The Crusades," chapters XVI and XVII.

NEWTON, A. P., and OTHERS, *Travel and Travellers of the Middle Ages* (a series of essays); the contributions include; "Conception of the World in Middle Ages," by the Editor; "Decay of Geographical Knowledge," by Prof. M. L. W., Laistner; "Christian Pilgrimages," by Prof. Claude Jenkins; "The Viking Age," by Prof. Alan Mawer; "Arab Travellers and Merchants," by Prof. Sir T. W. Arnold; "Trade in Eastern Europe," by Baron A. F. Meyendorff; "Land Routes to Cathay," by Eileen Power, "Travellers' Tales," by the Editor; "Prester John," by Sir E. Denison Ross; "Sea-Route to India," by Prof. E. Prestage.

* BEAZLEY, C. R., *Dawn of Modern Geography*, 3 vols.; * BOURQUELOT, F., *Études sur les Foires de Champagne*, 2 vols. (Mém. de l'Acad. d. Inscrip. (1865); * PIRENNE, H., "Villes et marchés," *Revue Historique*, 1898; GUILFOLD, E. L., *Travellers and Travelling in the Middle Ages;* HUVELIN, *Histoire du droit des foires et des marchés;* WALFORD, O., *Fairs, Past and Present.*

CHAPTER XXIV

NEW MONASTIC ORDERS

Extended bibliography in

Cambridge Medieval History, V, 909–920.

Classified bibliography of reading in English in

THOMPSON, JAMES WESTFALL, *Reference Studies in Medieval History*, pt. ii, 110–13, 166–69 (Franciscans and Dominicans).

General:

Cambridge Medieval History, V, ch. xx. * LUCHAIRE, A., *Social France at the Time of Philip Augustus*, ch. vii; * LUCHAIRE, A., *Manuel des institutions françaises*, bk. i (bibliography); GARREAU, L., *L'Etat social de la France au temps des croisades*, 427–62; DOM BERLIÈRE, *L'Ordre monastique des origines au xii*ᵉ *siècle*, 2 vols. (1924); GENESTAL, R., *Rôle des monastères comme établissement de crédit* (1901).

Religious revivalism of the eleventh and twelfth centuries:

* ADAMS, HENRY, *Mont Saint Michel and Chartres* (remarkable); TAYLOR, H. O., *The Medieval Mind*, I, bk. iii; PRIOR, E. S., *History of Gothic Architecture;* LEA, H. C., *Sacerdotal Celibacy.*

Cluny:

* SACKUR, *Die Cluniacenser*, 2 vols. (for reviews see *English Historical Review*, X, 293, XXIII, 762, XXIV, 123); *Catholic Encyclopædia;* MUNRO AND SELLERY, *Medieval Civilization*, 137–52; GRAHAM, ROSE, "Life at Cluny in the Eleventh Century," *Journal of Theological Studies*, XVI (1916); GRAHAM, R., "The Relations of Cluny to Other Monastic Movements," *ibid.*, XV (1915); THOMPSON, JAMES WESTFALL, *Feudal Germany*, chaps. ii–iii.

Cistercians:

* Arbois de Jubainville, *Les Abbayes Cisterciennes* (1868); * Hoffman, E., "Die Entwickelung der Wirtschaftsprinzipien im Zisterzienser-Orden, *Hist. Jahrbuch. d. Görres-Gesellschaft*, xxxi (1910); Dolberg, "Zisterzienser-Mönche und Konversen als Landwirte und Arbeiter," *Studien und Mittheil. aus d. Bened. und Zisterz. Orden.*, xiii (1892); *Catholic Encyclopedia;* Mason, W. A. P., "The Beginnings of the Cistercian Order," *Trans. Royal Hist. Society,* new series, XIX, 169; Graham, Rose, *An Abbot of Vézelay;* Winter, F., *Die Cistercienser des nordöstlich Deutschlands*, 2 vols.

Women under Monasticism:

* Eckenstein, L., *Women under Monasticism;* Wright, T., *Womankind,* ch. v.; Putnam, E. J., *The Lady* (the lady abbess).

Forerunners of St. Francis:

Davidson, E. S., *Some Forerunners of St. Francis* (1927); Sedgwick, H. D., *Italy in the Thirteenth Century,* I, chs. iv, vii.

Franciscans:

* Sedgwick, H. D., *Italy in the Thirteenth Century,* I, chs. vii, xxv; II, vii; * Coulton, G. G., *From St. Francis to Dante;* * Jorgensen, J., *Life of St. Francis of Assisi* (1912); * Brewer, J. S., *Monumenta Franciscana,* II, introd. and chs. vii–ix; Taylor, H. O., *The Medieval Mind,* I, chs. xviii, xxi; Harnack, A., *History of Dogma,* VI, 84–117; Emerton, E., "Fra Salimbene and the Franciscan Ideal," *Harvard Theol. Rev.* (1915); Coulton, G. G., "The Failure of the Friars," *Hibbert Journal* (Jan., 1907); Coulton, G. G., "Sidelights on the Franciscans," *Medieval Studies,* No. III; Jessopp, A., *The Coming of the Friars;* Dubois, L. L., *St. Francis, Social Reformer* (Washington, D. C., 1904); Hewlett, M., "A Medieval Popular Preacher," *Nineteenth Century,* XXVIII, 171; Hewlett, "Autobiography of a Wandering Friar" (Salimbene), *Nineteenth Century* (1905), 1009; Little, A. G., "The Friars of the Sack," *English Historical Review,* IX, 121; Lavisse, *Histoire de France,* III, pt. i, 246–63.

Dominicans:

Galbraith, G. R., *Constitution of the Dominican Order;* Barker, E., *The Dominican Order and Convocation.*

CHAPTER XXV

THE CHURCH AND FEUDAL SOCIETY

The nature of this subject is so complex that it is almost impossible to give a bibliography. Only a few works are here cited of the vast literature.

Extended bibliography in

Cambridge Medieval History, III, 636–38, V, 846–54.

Classified bibliography of literature in English in

THOMPSON, JAMES WESTFALL, *Reference Studies in Medieval History*, pt. ii, 102, 142–50.

Peace of God:

HUBERTI, *Studien zur Rechtsgeschichte der Gottesfrieden und Land-frieden* (1892);; MAITLAND, F. W., *Collected Papers*, II, 290–97; POWICKE, F. W., *Loss of Normandy*, pp. 93–98.

Feudalization of the Church:

* LUCHAIRE, A., *Manuel des institutions françaises*, bk. i; * GERDES, H., *Geschichte des deutschen Volkes zur Zeit der sächsischen Könige*, 651–709; * GERDES, *Geschichte der salischen Kaiser und ihrer Zeit*, 449–564; * GERDES, *Geschichte der Hohenstaufen und ihrer Zeit* 567–643; * STUTZ, U., *Die Eigenkirche als Element des mittelalterlich-germanischen Kirchen-rechts* (1895); *THOMPSON, JAMES WESTFALL, *Feudal Germany* chaps. I–III; * LUCHAIRE, A., *Social France at the Time of Philip Augustus*, chs. i, ii, iv, v, vi, vii; MUNRO AND SELLERY, *Medieval Civilization*, 188–201; WAITZ, G., *Deutscheverfassungsgeschichte*, VII, 183–301; GARREAU, L., *L'Etat social de la France au temps des croisades*, 365–426; IMBART DE LA TOUR, *Les Paroisses rurales dans l'ancienne France* (1900); IMBART DE LA TOUR, *Les Elections épiscopales dans l'église de France* (1890); KOENIGER, M., *Burchard von Worms und die deutsche Kirche seiner Zeit* (1905); HAUCK, A., *Kirchengeschichte Deutschlands*, III; STUTZ, U., *Geschichte des kirchlichen Beneficialwesens von seinen Anfängen bis auf die Zeit Alex-anders III*, I, pt. i (1905); THOMAS, P., *Le Droit de propriété des laïques sur les églises et le patronage laïque au moyen âge* (1906); SCHREIBER, G., *Kurie und Kloster im 12 Jahrhundert*, 2 vols. (1910); LEA, H. C., *Supersti-tion and Force;* LEA, H. C., *Studies in Church History*, 346–391, 524–74; BLATCHFORD, A. N., *Church Councils and their Decrees* (1909); SMITH, A. L., *Church and State in the Middle Ages;* VIOLLET, P., *Institutions poli-tiques de la France*, II, ch. ii (valuable bibliography); PACKARD, S. R., *Europe and the Church under Innocent III.*

The Church as a landlord:

Many of the above works. Compare the bibliography to ch. xxvii.
* KÖTZSCHKE, R., *Studien zur Verwaltungsgeschichte der Gross-grund-herrschaft Werden an der Ruhr* (1901); * COOPLAND, G. W., "The Abbey of St. Bertin," in *Oxford Studies in Social and Legal History*, IV; * NELSON, N., *The Economic Conditions of Ramsey Abbey* (1898); ADY, S. O., *Church and Manor;* LODGE, E., "The Estates of the Archbishop and Chapter of St. André of Bordeaux," *Oxford Studies in Social and Legal History*, III; HALE, W. H., *The Domesday of St. Paul's*, introd. (Camden Society, 1858); JESSOPP, A., *Studies of a Recluse*, 143 ("The Land and

its Owners in Past Time"); STEVENSON, J. S., *Chronicon de Monasterio de Abingdon* (Rolls Series, No. 2), introd., secs. 78–88; *Chronicle of Joceland of Brokeland* (King's Classics); RILEY, H. T., *Registers of the Monastery of St. Albans* (Rolls Series, No. 28), vol. III, introd., pp. xxix, xxxvii; REICHEL, O. J., "Churches and Church Endowments in the Eleventh Century," *Trans. Devonshire Assoc., 1907, 360–63.*

Priests and people:

*TAYLOR, H. O., *The Medieval Mind*, I, ch. xx; *SMITH, TOULMIN LUCY, "Popular Preaching in the Middle Ages," *English Historical Review*, VII, 25; *HASKINS, C. H., "University of Paris Sermons in the Thirteenth Century," *American Historical Review*, X, p. 1; MYRIC, JOHN, *Instructions for Parish Priests* (Early English Text Society, ed. Peacock, 1902); CUTTS, E. L., *Parish Priests and Their People;* HARNACK, A., *History of Dogma*, VI, 108–115; GASQUET, CARDINAL F. A., *Parish Life in Medieval England;* RICHARDSON, H. G., "The Parish Clergy of the Thirteenth and Fourteenth Centuries," *Trans. Royal Historical Society*, series III, vi, 89–128; JESSOPP, A., "Parish Priests in England before the Reformation," *Nineteenth Century*, XXXVI, 46–88 (also in his *Studies of a Recluse*); COULTON, G. G., "Priests and People Before the Reformation," *Contemporary Review*, XCI, 795, XCII, 71; HEWLETT, M., "A Popular Preacher in the Middle Ages," *Nineteenth Century*, XXVIII, 471; SMITH, TOULMIN LUCY, "French Preachers of the Thirteenth Century," *Edinburgh Review*, CLXXIX, 537; SMITH, "Clerical Life in the Thirteenth Century," *Dublin Review*, ser. IV, vii, i; COULTON, G. G., "A Revivalist of Six Hundred Years Ago" (Berthold of Regensburg), *Medieval Studies*, ser. I, no. 2; SYMONDS, J. A., *The Age of the Despots*, appendix iv; LECOY DE LA MARCHE, A., *La Chaire française au moyen âge;* ROSIÈRES, R., *Recherches critiques sur l'histoire religieuse de la France;* WALL, J. C., *An Old English Parish.*

On the preaching of Crusades, see:

*LECOY DE LA MARCHE, A., "La prédication de la croisade au XIII° siècle," *Revue des questions historiques*, XLVIII (1890), 5–28; *ROEHRICHT, R., "Die Kreuzpredigten gegen den Islam," *Zeitschrift für Kirchengeschichte*, VI (1884), 550–72.

The Church and poor relief; hospitals:

Catholic Encyclopædia, III, 594; *Journal of Military Service Institutions*, XII, 734 (on hospitals); *Quarterly Review*, CXCVII, 384–94; MACKAY, D. L., *Les Hôpitaux et la charité à Paris au XIII° siècle* (1923); CLAY, R. M., *The Medieval Hospitals of Old England;* SPEAKMAN, "Medieval Hospitals," *Dublin Review*, N. S. XL (1903), 8; LAMBERT, "Leprosy in the Middle Ages," *Nineteenth Century*, XVI, 467–89; COSGROVE, J. J., *History of Sanitation;* LE GRAND, L., *Statuts d'Hôtels-Dieu et de leproseries* (1901).

Church corruption:

* TAYLOR, H. O., *The Medieval Mind*, I, ch. xx; * LUCHAIRE, A., *Social France at the Time of Philip Augustus*, chs. ii, iv, vii; * LEA, H. C., *Confession and Indulgence*, I, 240–49 and passim; * LEA, H. C., *History of the Inquisition*, passim; * LEA, *History of the Auricular Confession*, passim; * LEA, *History of Sacerdotal Celibacy*, passim (and see review in *Quarterly Review*, CXVII, 514) ; SEDGWICK, H. D., *Italy in the Thirteenth Century*, I, vii; BREWER, J. S., *Opera Giraldi Cambrensis*, II, introd. liv f. (Rolls Series) ; COULTON, G. G., "The Failure of the Friars," *Hibbert Journal*, (1907).

The heresies as expressions of social and economic unrest. There is no monograph upon this subject. The matter will have to be found in the general reading.

General references:

MUNRO, D. C., *The Middle Ages*, chap. xxx; ACTON, LORD, *English Historical Review*, III, 773 (a review of Lea's *Inquisition*) ; LEA, H. C., *Sacerdotal Celibacy*, ch. xxiii; LEA, H. C., *History of the Inquisition*, I, ch. ii; LEA, H. C., "Confiscation for Heresy," *English Historical Review*, II, 235; TURBERVILLE, *Medieval Heresy and the Inquisition;* LUCHAIRE, A., *Innocent III*, vol. II (2d ed. 1906) ; VACANDARD, E., *L'Inquisition* (Paris, 1909) (English transl. P. L. Conway, from first edition (New York, 1908) ; DOELLINGER, J. J. I. von, *Beiträge zur Sektengeschichte des Mittelalters*, 2 vols. (1890) ; BURY, J. B., *History of Freedom of Thought;* TRENCH, R. C., *Lectures in Church History*, ch. xv; NEWMAN, A. H., "Recent Researches Concerning Medieval Sects," *Proc. American Society Church History*, IV, 167 (1892) ; EALES, S. J., *Works of St. Bernard*, I, introd. secs. 51–82; VACANDARD, E., *Vie de St. Bernard; Catholic Encyclopedia* under "Heresy," "Arnoldists," "Waldensians," "Cathari," etc.

The Catharists or Albigensians:

* MOLINIER, A., L'Eglise et la société cathare," *Revue Historique*, XCIV, 225–48, XCV, 1–22, 263–91; * DOUAIS, C., *Les Albigeois* (Paris, 1879) ; * LEA, H. C., *History of the Inquisition*, I, chs. iii–iv, vii–xiv, II, ch. i; * LUCHAIRE, A., *Innocent III, la croisade des Albigeois* (1905) ; LUCHAIRE, A., *Social France at the Time of Philip Augustus* (consult index under "Heresy" and "Albigenses") ; DE CAUZONS, T., *Les Albigeois et l'inquisition* (2d ed., Paris, 1908) ; DOUAIS, C., *L'Albigisme et les Frères Precheurs à Narbonne au XIII° siècle* (Paris, 1894) ; PEYRAT, N., *Histoire des Albigeois*, 3 vols. (Paris, 1870–72) ; MUNRO AND SELLERY, *Medieval Civilization*, 432–57 (from Luchaire) ; HARNACK, A., *History of Dogma*, III, 316–36; VACANDARD, E., *The Inquisition*, iii–v; SCHMIDT, C., *Histoire et doctrine de la secte des Cathares*, 2 vols. (1849).

The Waldensians, or Poor Men of Lyons:

* DE CAUZONS, T., *Les Vaudois et l'Inquisition*, 3d ed. (Paris, 1908) ;

* MÜLLER, K., *Die Waldenser und ihre einzelnen Gruppen bis zum Anfang des 14 Jahrhunderts,* Gotha (1886) ; * PREGER, W., "Beiträge zur Geschichte der Waldesier im Mittelalter," in *Königliche Bay. Akad. der Wiss., phil.-hist. Classe,* XIII (1877), 181–250; see also his "Ueber die Verfassung der französischen Waldesier in der aeltesten Zeit," *ibid.,* XIX (1891), 639–711; DIECKHOFF, A., *Die Waldenser im Mittelalter* (Göttingen, 1851) ; COMBA, E., *History of the Waldensians;* SCHMIDT, C., *Histoire et doctrine de la secte des cathares,* 2 vols. (1849), xcv, 1–22, 263–91; VEDDER, H. C., *American Journal of Theology,* IV, 465; LEA, H. C., *History of the Inquisition* (use index) ; MAITLAND, S. R., *Facts and Documents Illustrative of the History of the Albigenses and Waldensians* (1832) ; MELIA, O., *Origin, Persecutions and Doctrines of the Waldensians* (1870).

Church and papal finance:

* LEA, H. C., *Confession and Indulgence,* I, 275 *ff.*, 404–411, IV, ch. iv; * LUNT, W. E., "The Financial System of the Medieval Papacy," *Quarterly Journal of Economics,* xxiii, 313; * VIARD, P., *Histoire de la dîme ecclésiastique dans le royaume de France au XIIe et XIIIe siècle* (2 vols., 1909, 1912) ; LUNT, W. E., "First Levy of Papal Annates," *American Historical Review,* xviii, 48; LUNT, "Early Assessments for Papal Taxation," *Annual Report American Historical Assoc.* (1917), 265; LUNT, "Papal Taxation in the Reign of Edward I," *English Historical Review,* XXX, 398; LUNT, "The Account of a Papal Collector of Revenue in England in 1304," *English Historical Review,* XXVIII, 313; GRAHAM, "The Taxation of Nicholas IV," *ibid.,* XXIII, 434; GRAHAM, "The Finances of Walton Priory," *Trans. Royal Historical Society,* N. S., XVIII; JENSEN, "The Denarius Sancti Petri," *ibid.,* N. S. XVIII; NYS, E., *Researches in the History of Economics,* ch. ix; SMITH, A. L., *Church and State in the Middle Ages* (on Innocent IV) ; DELISLE, L., *Les Operations financières des Templiers* (Mem. de l'Acad. d. Inscrip. tome XXXIII).

CHAPTER XXVI

FEUDAL SOCIETY

It is impossible to pretend to give a bibliography upon this subject, for it touches every angle of medieval economic and social history. Much of the literature cited upon Germany, France, Italy, the Church, Monasticism, the Manor, the Towns, is pertinent to this chapter also. Without repeating the matter in them, a short list of references is here given. LUCHAIRE'S *Manuel des institutions françaises,* pt. ii, is the best work upon the subject. It has copious bibliographies.

* Dow, E. W., and SEIGNOBOS, C., *The Feudal Régime,* New York, 1902; * VINOGRADOFF, P., *English Society in the Eleventh Century;* * VIOLLET, P., *Institutions politiques de la France,* I, 237; * LUCHAIRE, A., *Social France at the Time of Philip Augustus,* chs. viii, ix, x, xi; ADAMS, G. B.,

Civilization during the Middle Ages, ch. ix; MUNRO and SELLERY, *Medieval Civilization*, 159–211 (realities of feudalism), 240–47 (chivalry); BRISSAUD, J., *French Public Law*; ESMEIN, A., *Cours élémentaire d'histoire du droit français* (6th ed., 1905); HASKINS, C. H., "Knight Service in Normandy," *English Historical Review*, XXII, 636; ESMEIN, A., *History of Continental Criminal Procedure*; LEA, H. C., *Superstition and Force*; ADAMS, HENRY, "Medieval German Law," *North American Review*, CXIII, 198; UPCOTT, *Collection of Papers Illustrating the Manners of the Eleventh and Twelfth Centuries* (there is a review of this remarkable work in the *Quarterly Review*, LVIII, 414–54); HALL, H., *Court Life under the Plantagenets*; BATESON, MARY, *Medieval England*, espec. chs. ii and viii; MACNEAL, E. H., "The Feudal Noble and the Church," *Annual Report American Historical Assoc., 1914*, I, 149; *Cambridge Medieval History*, III, ch. xviii; EVANS, JOAN, *Medieval France*; DAVIS, W. S., *Life on a Medieval Barony*; BALLARD, A., "Castle Guard and Barons' Houses," *English Historical Review*, Oct., 1910; CLARK, G. T., *Medieval Military Architecture*; VIOLLET LE DUC, *Annals of a Fortress* (1876); VIOLLET LE DUC, *The Story of a House* (1874); OMAN, C. W., *The Art of War in the Middle Ages*, espec. bk. vi.; TAYLOR, H. O., *The Medieval Mind*, I, 521–613; COULTON, G. G., *Social Life in Britain from the Norman Conquest to the Reformation*; LAVISSE, *Histoire de France*, III, 1, 364–89; RAMBAUD, A., *Histoire de la civilisation française*, I, bk. ii, 117–238.

The Jews in the Middle Ages.

1. General references:

NEUBAUER AND STERN, "Medieval Jewish Chronicles," 4 vols. (*cf. English Historical Review*, XI, 558); ABRAHAMS, I., *Jewish Life in Middle Ages* (1896); PHILIPSON, D., *Old European Jewries* (1894); GRAETZ, H., *History of the Jews*, III; LEA, H. C., *Confession and Indulgence*, II, 123 ff.; NYS, E., *History of Economics*, chap. vii; PALGRAVE, R. H. I., *Dictionary of Political Economy*, "Jews"; HARRIS, M., *History of the Medieval Jews (711–1492)*; *Jewish Encyclopedia*, Articles on "England," "France," "Germany," "Italy," "Spain"; BEAZELEY, C. R., *Dawn of Modern Geography*, II, chap. xv; SCHAFF, P., *Church History*, V, sec. 77; BLANQUI, *History of Political Economy*, chap. xv; DÖLLINGER, J. von, *Studies in European History*, "The Jews in Europe"; SPIERS, "Disputations between Jews and Christians in the Middle Ages," *Jewish Quarterly Review*, III, 1912–13, 512–37; KAUFMAN, "Jewish Informers in the Middle Ages," *Jewish Quarterly Review*, VIII, 217 ff., 572 ff., 709 ff.; CONDER, C. R., "Oriental Jews," *Scottish Review*, No. 35; SCHAFF, "The Jews in the Middle Ages," *Bibliotheca Sacra*, LX, 547; *English Historical Review*, VII, 543 (a review).

2. The Jews of England:

GRAETZ, *History of the Jews*, III, chaps. xii, xiv, xvi–xvii; MILMAN, H. H., *History of the Jews*, III, Book 25; RIGG, J. M., "The Jews of England in the Thirteenth Century," *Jewish Quarterly Review* (October, 1903; *cf. English Historical Review*, XVIII, 206); RIGG, J. M., "The Expulsion of the Jews from England," *Jewish Quarterly Review*, VII (1894–95), 75–100,

235-58, 428-58, VIII, 360; RIGG, J. M., "Select Pleas and Other Records from the Rolls of the Exchequer of the Jews" (1220-84), *Selden Society* (*cf. Athenæum*, March 22, 1902, p. 364); JACOBS, J., *The Jews of Angevin England;* LEONARD, "The Expulsion of the Jews by Edward I in 1290," *Transactions Royal Historical Society*, N.S., V, 103; Coccos, "Extracts Relating to the Jews from the Close Rolls, 1290," *Transactions of the Jewish Society*, IV (1903); *English Historical Review*, II, 161, 363-65; VIII, 543-44; X, 788, 789; XVII, 551-54; XVIII, 206; XXI, 369; XXV, 322; XXVI, 380-83; HYAMSON, "History of the Jews in England" (*cf. Athenæum*, I, 1908, 228, 442); MAITLAND, F. W., "The Deacon and the Jewess: or Apostasy at Common Law." *Law Quarterly Review*, II, 153-65; GOLDSCHMIDT, *English Jews;* GROSS, C., *Exchequer of the Jews of England in the Middle Ages*, 2 vols.; NEUBAUER, "Notes on the Jews in Oxford," *Oxford Historical Society*, II, 1890; CUNNINGHAM, W., *English Industry and Commerce*, I, sec. 93; POWICKE, F. L., *Loss of Normandy*, pp. 354-56; ABRAHAMS, B., *Transactions of Jewish Historical Society*, II, 1894-95, 76-105; ABRAHAMS, B., "Expulsion of Jews in 1290," *Jewish Quarterly Review*, VII, 1894, 75-100, 428-58; JACOBS, J., Notes on Jews of England under Angevin Kings," *Translations of Jewish Historical Society*, III, 1896-98, 126-43.

3. The Jews of France:

GRAETZ, *History of the Jews*, III, chaps. xi-xvii, IV, chaps. i-v; DARMESTETER, "The Jews of France in the Fourteenth Century," *Fortnightly Review*, March, 1892; *English Historical Review*, VIII, 543.

4. The Jews of Spain:

GRAETZ, *History of the Jews*, III, chaps. vii-xi, xiv-xvii; IV, chaps. ii-xi; ADLER, "The *auto da fe* and the Jew" (*cf. English Historical Review*, XXIV, 345); VILLAMIL, "Jews in Early Spanish History," *Catholic World*, LIV, 86, 360, LV, 649; VILLAMIL, "The Expulsion of the Jews from Spain," *Catholic World*, LVIII, 49; SWIFT, F. DARWIN, *James I of Aragon*, pp. 115, 170-77, 221-24, 233, 245-52; BURKE, U., *History of Spain*, II, 68, 119-28; LINDO, *History of the Jews in Spain and Portugal;* SCOTT, S., *Moorish Empire in Europe*, III, chap. xxiv; ADLER, "Spanish Aides at Constantinople," *Jewish Quarterly Review*, XI, 1899, 526-29; JACOBS, "Spanish Jewish History," *Jewish Quarterly Review*, VIII, 1896; JACOBS, "Sources of History of Jewish Spain," *Jewish Quarterly Review*, VI, 1894, 597-632.

5. The Jews of Italy:

GRAETZ, *History of the Jews*, III, chaps. xiv, xvi, IV, chaps. ii, iv, vi, viii, x; "The Early Settlement of the Jews in South Italy," *Jewish Quarterly Review*, July and October, 1892; *Jewish Quarterly Review*, II, April, 1890; MOLMENTI, *Venice: The Middle Ages*, I, chap. vii; *Jewish Encyclopedia*, VII, 1-10.

6. The Jews of Germany:

NEUBAUER AND STERN, *Original Hebrew and German Translations of Five*

Jewish Chronicles; Jewish Encyclopedia, s.v. "Germany"; GRAETZ, *History of the Jews*, III, chaps. viii–ix, xvi–xvii, IV, chaps. iii–v, vii–ix; HUEBNER, *History of German Private Law*, pp. 83–86.

CHAPTER XXVII

THE MEDIEVAL MANOR: LIFE OF THE PEASANTRY IN THE MIDDLE AGES

The literature upon the Manor is enormous, and much of it is controversial and technical. Unfortunately a large part of the literature in English deals with England, where conditions often widely differed from those on the Continent. A long bibliography may be found in MOORE, M. F., *Two Select Bibliographies of Medieval Historical Study*, 71–167 (1912). The beginning of understanding of the subject is to be found in:
* LAPSLEY, G. T., "The Origin of Property in Land," *American Historical Review*, VIII; ELTON, "Early Forms of Landholding," *English Historical Review*, I, 427; * FUSTEL DE COULANGES, *The Origin of Property in Land*, transl. Mrs. Ashley (2d ed., 1892) ; * MEITZEN, *Siedelung und Agrarwesen*, 3 vols. (with many maps, 1895) ; * KOVALEVSKY, M., *Die ökonomische Entwickelung Europas* (6 vols., Berlin, 1901), vols. I–IV; * VINOGRADOFF, P., *Origin of the Manor;* * VINOGRADOFF, *Villeinage in England;* * GRAS, N. S. B., *History of Agriculture*, ch. iv; * GRAS, *Introduction to Economic History*, ch. iii; * ASHLEY, W. J., *English Economic History*, I, chs. i, v, vi; ASHLEY (in) *Economic Journal*, June, 1913; ASHLEY, W. J., "Villein Tenure." *Annals of American Acad. of Soc. and Polit. Sci.*, I, 412–25; ASHLEY, W. J., *Surveys, historic and economic:* * MAITLAND, F. W., *Domesday and Beyond*, espec. ch. ii; "The Survival of Archaic Communities," *Law Quarterly Review*, IX, 36, 211; "The Continuity of the Open Field System," *Quarterly Journal of Economics*, XX, 62; "Agricultural Services," *Economic Journal*, X, 308; *Encyclopædia Britannica* (11th ed,), article "Domesday Book," by J. H. ROUND; SEEBOHM, F., *The English Village Community* (4th ed., 1890) ; SEEBOHM, *Customary Acres;* LIPSON, I. E., *Introduction to Economic History of England*, I, chs. i–iii; CHEYNEY, E. P., "The Medieval Manor," *Annals of American Acad. Soc. and Polit. Sci.*, No. 101 ; GRAY, H. L., *English Field Systems;* CUNNINGHAM, W., *History of English Industry and Commerce*, I, secs. 79–82.

Medieval farming and the life of the peasantry:

* LUCHAIRE, A., *Social France at the Time of Philip Augustus*, ch. xiii; SIMKHOVITCH, "Hay and History," *Political Science Quarterly*, XXVIII, 385; * CURSCHMANN, F., *Hungersnöte im Mittelalter* (1900) ; HONE, N. J., *The Manor and Manorial Records* (1906) ; USHER, A. P., "Soil Fertility and Soil Exhaustion and their Historical Significance," *Quarterly Journal of Economics*, XXVII (1923), 385–411 ; DAVENPORT, F. G., *The Economic Development of a Norfolk Manor;* CLARK, "Serfdom on an Essex Manor," *English Historical Review*, XX, 479; DELISLE, L., *Études sur la condition ue*

la classe agricole . . . pendant le moyen âge; AVENEL, *Paysans et ouvriers depuis sept cents ans* (1899); LAMPRECHT, K., *L'Etat economique de la France au XI* siècle* (transl. *Marignan*); * Walter of Henley's *Husbandry,* ed. E. Lamond (1890); * CUNNINGHAM, W., "Walter of Henley's Book of Husbandry," *Trans. Royal Historical Society,* new ser. IX; * HANSSEN, G., *Agrarhistorische Abhandlungen,* II, espec. 179–329; * SEE-BOHM, F., *English Village Community,* chs. i, iv, x (valuable maps); * LAMPRECHT, K., *Deutsche Wirtschaftsleben im Mittelalter,* I, pt. i, 331–85; 532–84; * VINOGRADOFF, P., *English Society in the Eleventh Century,* 279–304; COOPLAND, G. W., The Abbey of St. Bertin," in *Oxford Studies in Social and Legal History,* IV, ch. viii; SMITH, L. T., "Medieval English Agriculture," *Quarterly Review,* CLIX, 323; SMITH, L. T., The English Manor," *Quarterly Review,* CCVII, 129; FOWLER, "A Typical Medieval Village," *Quarterly Journal of Economics,* IX, 151; HASBACH, W., *History of the English Agricultural Laborer* (1908); LEADAM, I. S., "Villeinage in England," *Political Science Quarterly,* VIII, 653; JESSOPP, A., "The Land and Its Owners in Past Time," *Studies of a Recluse,* 143–83; JESSOPP, *The Coming of the Friars,* ch. ii; SNELL, F. J., *Customs of Old England,* ch. xviii; ROGERS, J. E. T., *History of Agriculture and Prices,* I, i–ii; ROGERS, *Work and Wages,* ch. ii; CARVER, T. N. *Readings in Rural Economics,* 151–62; JEUDWINE, J. W., *The Foundations of Society and the Land* (1918); CURTLER, W. H. R., *Short History of English Agriculture* (1909); GARNIER, R., *History of the English Landed Interest.* COULTON, G. G., *The Medieval Village* (1926).

Slavery in the Middle Ages:

* PIJPER, *American Historical Review,* XIV, 675; * WERGELAND, A. M., "Slavery in German Society in the Middle Ages," *Journal of Political Economy,* IX, 98 and 398; LEA, H. C., *Studies in Church History,* 524–74, same article in *North American Review,* C, 21; WASHBURN, *North American Review,* XLI, 174; INGRAM, J. K., *History of Slavery;* NIEBOER, H. J., *Slavery as an Industrial System,* ch. iv; CUNNINGHAM, W., *History of English Industry and Commerce,* I (use index); *Cambridge Medieval History,* II, 62–66, 149–50.

Prices and Wages:

GRAS, N. S. B., *Evolution of the English Corn Market,* 11–17, 261–70; ROGERS, J. E. T., *History of Agriculture and Prices,* I–IV; AVENEL, *Histoire économique de la propriété, des salaires, des denrées, et de tous les prix en général,* II–IV.

CHAPTER XXVIII

TOWNS AND GILDS

The general movement:
* ASHLEY, W. J., "The Beginnings of Town Life in the Middle Ages," *Quarterly Journal of Economics,* X, 359; * PIRENNE, H., *Medieval Cities,*

their Origins and the Revival of Trade; * Keutgen, F. W., "The Medieval Commune," *Encyclopædia Brittannica,* 11th ed., VI; 784; * Espinas, G., *La Vie urbaine de Douai au moyen âge* (4 vols., 1913) (remarkable); * *Cambridge Medieval History,* V, ch. xix; Giry and Reville, *The Emancipation of the Towns* (English transl. E. W. Dow); Munro, D. C., *The Middle Ages,* ch. xxix; Adams, G. B., *Civilization during the Middle Ages,* ch. xii; Taylor, H. O., *The Medieval Mind,* 2d ed., supplementary chapter; Cunningham, W., *Western Civilization: Medieval and Modern,* secs. 86–88, 94; Hearnshaw, F. J. C., *Medieval Contributions to Modern Civilization,* chs. viii, ix; Ingram, J. K., *History of Slavery,* chs. iv–v; Nys, E., *Researches in the History of Economics,* ch. iii; Lavisse and Rambaud, *Histoire genérale,* II, 44–76; Schmoller, G., *Mercantile System,* 6–13 (1884); Bucher, K., *Industrial Evolution* (transl. Wickett), 114–33; Below, W. Von, *Probleme der Wirtschaftsgeschichte* 202–257 (1920). Stephenson, C., "The Origin of the Taille," *Revue Belge de Philologie et d'Histoire,* V, 801–70.

Theories of origin:

* Pirenne, H., "Les Constitutions urbaines au moyen âge," *Revue Historique,* LIII (1893), 52–83 ,LVII (1895), 57–98, 293–327; * Bourgin, G., "Origines urbaines," *Revue de synthèse historique,* VII (1903); * Ashley, W. J., *Surveys, Historic and Economic,* 167–226; Hegel, C., *Städte und Gilden der germanischen Völker im Mittelalter* (2 vols., 1891) (against theory of gild origin of towns; compare Keutgen's review in *English Historical Review,* VIII, 120 ff., and *Economic Review,* III, 784); Hegel, C., *Die Entstehung des deutschen Stadtwesens* (1898); Varges, W., "Zur Entstehung der deutschen Stadtverfassung," *Jahrbücher fur National-ökonomie und Statistik,* LXI (1893), 195 ff.; Stephenson, Carl, "The Origin of the English Towns," *American Historical Review,* XXXII, 10.

Italy (See the references to "Italy during the Crusades," ch. XVII.)

France:

Bibliography in *Cambridge Medieval History,* V, 906–908; * Bateson, Mary, "The Laws of Breteuil," *English Historical Review,* XV, 73–78, 302–18, 496–523, 754–57, XVI, 92–110, 332–45; Luchaire, A., *Les Communes françaises* (2d ed., Halphen, 1911); Dow, E., "Some French Communes," *American Historical Review,* VIII (1903), 641–56; Flach, J., *Les Origines de l'ancienne France,* II; Flach, J., *L'Origine de l'habitation en France* (1899) (on rural communes); Viollet, P., *Les Communes françaises* (1900); Giry, A., *Les Établissements de Rouen,* 2 vols. (1883); Giry, A., *Institutions municipales de St. Omer;* Le Franc, A., *Histoire de la ville de Noyon.*

Flanders:

Pirenne, H., *Belgian Democracy* (English transl. J. V. Saunders, Manchester, 1915); Pirenne, H., *Histoire de Belgique,* I; Cunningham, W., *Alien Immigrants;* Ashley, W. J., *Surveys, Historic and Economic,*

240 ff.; BLOK, P., *History of the People of the Netherlands*, I, chs. vii, xiv–xv; VANDER LINDEN, ·H., *Histoire de la constitution de la ville de Louvain*, (1892); REINECKE, W., *Geschichte der Stadt Cambrai* (1896); HAPKE, R., *Brugges Entwicklung zum mittelalterlichen Weltmarkt* (1908), SCHAUBE, A., "Die Wollausfuhr Englands vom Jahre 1273," *Vierteljahrschrift für Sozial- und Wirthschaftsgeschichte*, 1908.

Germany:

* HEGEL, C., *Städte und Gilden der germanischen Völker*, 2 vols. (1891); * HEGEL, C., *Die Entstehung des deutschen Städtewesens* (1898); * LAMPRECHT, K., *Deutsche Geschichte*, IV, 211–52 (transl. in part in MUNRO and SELLERY, *Medieval Civilization*, 358–65); * SCHMOLLER, G., *Strassburgs Blüte* (1875); * PHILLIPPI, *Zur Verfassungsgeschichte der westfälischen Bischofstädte* (1894); BELOW, G. VON, *Das älteste deutsche Städtewesens* (1898); BELOW, G. VON, *Der Ursprung der deutschen Stadtverfassung* (1892); SOHM, R., *Die Entstehung des deutscher Städtewesens* (1890); VINCENT, J. W., "Town Life in the Twelfth Century," *Annual Report American Historical Association* (1898), 415.

Gilds and Industry:

* EBERSTADT, R., *Der Ursprung des Zunftwesens und die älteren Handwerkerbände des Mittelalters* (1900); * KEUTGEN, F., *Aemter und Zünfte;* * DOREN, A., *Untersuchungen zur Geschichte der Kaufmannsgilden im Mittelalter* (1893); * BOISSONADE, P., *Le Travail dans l'Europe chrétienne au moyen âge*, bks. ii, iii; * EVANS, A. P., "The Problem of Control in Medieval Industry," *Political Science Quarterly* (1921); CUNNINGHAM, W., *History of English Industry and Commerce*, vol. I (use index); SAINT-LÈON, M., *Histoire des corporations des métiers* (2d ed., 1909); LEVASSEUR, E., *Histoire des classes ouvrières*, vol. I; WAUTERS, A., *Les Gildes communales* (1874); GIRY, A., *Institutions municipales de Saint-Omer* (1877); GROSS, C., *The Gild Merchant* (2 vols., 1890); SALZMANN, L., *English Industries in the Middle Ages* (2d ed., 1923); RENARD, GEORGES, *Gilds in the Middle Ages;* MILLETT, F. B., "Craft Gilds of the Thirteenth Century in Paris," *Bulletin Hist., Polit. Econ.*, Queen's University, no. XVII (1915); DIXON, E., "Craftswomen in the Livre des Métiers," *Economic Journal*, V (1895).

INDEX

INDEX

A

Aachen: advantageous location of, 223; council of (816), 650; development of, 297-98; fair established at, in 1173, 505; favorite residence of Charlemagne, 222; market in Carolingian era, 221

Abbey, abbeys (*See also* Monastery, monasteries): agrarian economy of, in North Italy, 322; commercial activity of, 264, 308; consolidation of, 604; destruction of, by Norsemen, 305; distribution of, in treaty of Verdun, 247; established by Boniface in Hesse, 215; feudalization of, in 9th century, 244; fishery interests of Norman, 308; fortification of German abbeys, 286; in Paris in 9th century, 263; increase of lands of, 238; land surveys of, 247; military activity of, 305; number of, in France, 603; of Lower Austrasia in 7th century, 223; organization and personnel of, 628; regulation under Benedictine Rule, 143-44; right of advowson over, 243; secularization of lands of, by Charles Martel, 215-16; suppression of, by Philip Augustus, 642

Abbot, abbots: abuse of immunities by Frankish, 204; as French feudatories, 474; as landholders, 131; as vassals, 658; deposition of, 641; despoiled by brigands, 254; duties of, 628; feud with feudality, 251; feudal status of, in Frankish Empire, 216; Frankish as landed proprietors, 200; German oppose reforms of Henry IV, 301; gifts to, from imperial fisc by Louis the Pious, 243; imitated Carolingian proprietary system, 226; in Byzantine monasteries, 173; intimidation of small proprietors by, in 9th century, 233; nullify rulings of council of Chalcedon, 141; opposition of Byzantine to reforms of Leo III, 180; powers of, in Benedictine monasticism, 143-44; strife with bishops for lands, 249; used as officials by Charlemagne, 238

Abd-er-Rahma III: builds aqueduct, 548; government of, 547; Spanish khalif, 339

Abyssinia: Arab penetration into, 192; Justinian's alliance with, 166; Roman relations with, 21

Accolæ, obscure class of freemen, 752

Accounting: development of, 431

Acre: attacked by Bibars of Egypt, 426; capture of, in 1291, 427; conflict between Genoa and Venice and Pisa at, 411, 421; in 13th century, 424; Italian *fondachi* in, 404; merchants of Marseilles and Montpellier at, 484; recovery of, in third crusade, 412

Acre (land unit): origin of term, 736

ACTON, LORD: on influence of property in feudal age, 703

Adalberon, Bishop of Laon: his conception of society, 707

ADAM OF BREMEN, German historian: on Denmark, 540; on Sweden, 545

Aden: Arabic naval base, 371; commercial importance of, 355

Adolph, count of Holstein: colonies of settlers founded by, 302, 511; recovery of "lost provinces," 520

Adprisio, type of land tenure in Spanish Mark, 236

Adriatic: factor in Venetian development, 318; origin of names of ports on, 17; Venetian jurisdiction over, 584

Adversaria, day-book in Roman banks, 44

Advocate (*advocatus, avoué, vogt*): secular official of church, 233, 655

Advowson: Charlemagne's possession of, 243; importance of, in rural localities under early church, 83; in feudal age, 652; right of, enforced by Frankish nobles, 217

Ædificium, a form of Roman proprietorship, 36

Ægean archipelago: control of commerce of, by Constantinople, 157

Ægean Sea: Charles of Anjou's designs in, 458; Vandal pirates in, 117

Aelfric: his social theory, 707

Afforage, see Forage

Africa: acquisitions of Norman Kingdom in, 452; Arab conquest of, 191-92; Arabic penetration into interior, 368-71; benefits from Roman rule, 6; Berber invasions from, into Spain (in 1087, 1146), 551; bound to Europe by Mediterranean, 3; Byzantine administration of, 129; Carthage as a literary centre, 11; commerce, industry, agriculture of Roman, 8-12, 22; commerce of Spain with, 550; commerce of Vandal Africa, 112, 116-17; decline of, 11-12; Donatist heresy in, 81; 114-16; essentially Punic nature of, 114; export of olives, 10; export of wheat from, to Rome, 4; Fatimite conquest of, 366; Genoese trade in, 449; gilds in, 10; grievances against Roman Empire, 114; hatred of Byzantine rule in, 190; imperial fisc in, appropriated by Vandal kings, 105; importance of Tunis in, 562; influence of, on Vandals, 113; influence on Roman politics, 10; Justinian's conquest of, 112; land monopoly in, 32-33, 36; merchants from, at fair of St. Giles, 484; monasticism in, 142; Moorish raids on, 11; persistence of Punic speech in, 11; Pisan trade in, 450; poor harbors on coast of, 3; prosperity of, restored by Constantine, 11; prosperity of, under Mohammedan rule, 195; racial ingredients in, 10-11; relations of Aragon with, 562; remission of taxes by Honorius, 43; rival of Egypt as granary of Rome, 9; Romanization of, 9; ship-building in, 10; slavery in, 10; social condition in, 10; Spanish Arabs' relations with, 547; spread of Christianity in, 57; Syrian influence in, 156; trade relations with Arabia, 184; Vandal invasion of, 34; Vandal land settlement in, 104

Agobard, Bishop of Lyons: anti-Semitism of, 258; hostility to Bernhard of Septimania, 260; on "poor priests," 655

Agrarian (*See also* Agriculture): *Agrarian Code* of Leo III, 179; influence of heresies on agrarian revolution, 82, 114-16

Date Due		
For Western		
Civilization		
Students only		

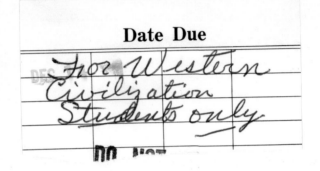